ARISTOTLE'S THEORY OF
PRACTICAL COGNITION

BY

TAKATURA ANDO

*Litt. D. Professor of Philosophy
at Ritumekan University, Kyoto*

SECOND EDITION

THE HAGUE
MARTINUS NIJHOFF
1965

Copyright 1965 by Martinus Nijhoff, The Hague, Netherlands
All rights reserved, including the right to translate or to reproduce this book or parts thereof in any form

Department of Psychiatry Library
The New York Hospital
Cornell Medical Center

FIRST EDITION 1958
SECOND EDITION 1965

PREFACE

I have much pleasure in writing a preface to Mr. Takatura Ando's book on Aristotle. Apart from his intrinsic importance, as one of the three or four greatest of all philosophers, Aristotle is important on having given for many centuries the greatest influence in moulding the thought of European countries. The language difficulty has no doubt prevented him from exercising very much influence on Japanese thought, and I welcome very warmly to hear that Mr. Ando is about to have his book printed in Japan. I hope it will be widely circulated, as it must certainly deserve that.

W. D. ROSS

AUTHOR'S FOREWORD

In publishing this book, I cannot prohibit myself of reminding the days and nights when it was written. In that era of world-wide madness, Aristotle's philosophy was the only refuge wherein my depressed mind could come to life. It was written bit by bit under all desperate circumstances throughout the war time. My heart was set on the completion of this work while the fate allowed me to live. It was nearly carried out by the end of the war. Having no hope of survival, I buried my manuscript in the earth, without however any expectance of a better lot for it.

The situation grew worse and worse. Towns and cities were burnt and perished day by day. There remained only few of them. In a summer night of 1945, an inauspicious siren blew as if pronouncing our end. I let my wife take refuge with the child, and lied alone on the ground beside the hole in which my manuscript was stored. The blue sky was scattered with twinkling stars, and the buzzying of air corps came far over from the depth of serene night. I was gazing the stars with resignation and despise to human nature, but the corps passed over my head without making any attack. Few minutes later, the sky grew red near the horizon, and I found that the victim of that night was the unfortunate neibourghing city. After few days the citizens of Hirosima and Nagasaki met the atmost misery in the history. The war was over, and I survived with my manuscript.

Since that time I tried to publish this manuscript only in vain. At last, I came to the idea to translate it in English and show it to Sir W.D. Ross. When this idea was realized, to my great joy, he gave me a letter full of favour. He acknowledged that he was in the same opinion with regard to many of my arguments, and guaranteed that my treatise would be able to contribute to modern study of Aristotle.

Being much encouraged by this letter and following his advice, I engaged in revising my English by the aid of Dr. S. Nivison of

Stanford University. Now, I am firmly convinced of myself being the most fortunate fellow who lived under that starly heaven, not only to enjoy again the Lipton tea, of which I sadly dreamed in that dreary nights, but also to get the favour of an eminent British scholar, not only to taste again Californian raisins that I vainly desired in that weary days, but also to receive kindness of an excellent American scholar.

I debt my English also to my previous colleague Mr. Tyuzo Utidate, who read through my manuscript and gave many advices. My special thanks are due to Prof. John D. Goheen of Stanford University, who paid warm attention to my work and gave me some help. I am grateful to Miss Nobuko Iwai for her assistance. As regards English rendering of the text, I owe much to Oxford translations and Hicks's De Anima.

1958   T.A.

PREFACE TO THE SECOND EDITION

The correction of this new editon was restricted to numerous misprints and some grammatical errors, not because the author found little demand for change but because he found that most of the faults could not be improved unless they were rewritten. It is doubtful whether this book in such a defective form is still worthy of circulation; the author humbly begs tolerance of readers for his negligence of thoroughgoing revision.

1965   T.A.

CONTENTS

INTRODUCTION GENERAL REMARK ON THE SUBJECT OF INQUIRY . . . 1

CHAPTER I THE STRUCTURE OF THE SOUL
§ 1. Soul and Body 5
§ 2. The Problem of νοῦς ποιητικός 17
§ 3. Against Brentano's Interpretation 33
§ 4. Solution of the Problem 55
§ 5. Comparison with Plato's Thought 75
§ 6. Parts of the Soul 85

CHAPTER II THE FUNCTIONS OF THE SOUL
§ 1. The Development of Functions 98
§ 2. The Reference of Functions 114
§ 3. Desire and Pleasure 136
§ 4. Voluntary Act 145

CHAPTER III PRACTICE AND PRODUCTION
§ 1. Practice and Production 175
§ 2. Comparison with Kant's Theory 190
§ 3. The Relation between Practice and Production 200

CHAPTER IV THE STRUCTURE OF INTELLECT
§ 1. The Classification of Intellect 208
§ 2. δόξα and δοξαστικόν Part 217
§ 3. Practical and Theoretical Cognitions . . . 227
§ 4. Practical Reason 236
§ 5. Prudence 256

CHAPTER V THE PRACTICAL SYLLOGISM

§ 1. Deliberation 266
§ 2. Practical and Productive Syllogisms . . . 274
§ 3. Practical Cognition of Ends 284
§ 4. Continence and Temperance 300
§ 5. The Relation of Practical and Productive Syllogisms 310
§ 6. Comparison with Kant 316

INDEXES 323

INTRODUCTION

ALL sciences start with Aristotle, as all roads lead to Rome. The dominance of Aristotelianism in the mediaeval period was not conducive to the scientific spirit, to be sure, but that despotic authority which did not tolerate any criticism was the result of scholastic dogmatism rather than the fault of Aristotle's philosophy. The anti-Aristotelianism of the Renaissance actually had the effect of restoring Aristotle from the darkness of monasteries into the daylight of Hellas. The modern age has started with depreciating Aristotle in contrast to Plato, but as this reaction calmed down, men turned towards the re-estimation of Aristotle. In truth, Platonism in the Renaissance was no more than an artistic enthusiasm, and from the scientific point of view, Plato was no match for Aristotle.

Of course we are now aware of the old mistake of interpreting Aristotle as the opponent of Plato. Aristotle was the greatest successor of Plato, and to suspect him of ingratitude is only to betray the mean disposition of a petty-minded person. The influence of the teacher's theory on him is particularly remarkable in practical philosophy. It is not too much to say that Aristotle's practical philosophy owes the greater part of its content to Plato. But it is not the main subject of our study to follow the development of theory between this great master and his great disciple. We are rather interested in the scientific formulations and the positive foundations which the latter gave to the material inherited from the former.

Now to be rational means to be "mediated" — in Hegelian terminology — and systematic, and to be positive means to give empirical grounds to ideas. Aristotle surely was lacking in the genius of brilliant phantasy, but it was his remarkable merit that he formulated the ideas which were so to speak floating, both in the prophetic character of Socrates and in the poetic disposition of Plato, into a strictly conceptual system. His rational and positive foundation for practical philosophy was achieved in the region of politics, through his exhaustive study of constitutions, of which we have a glimpse in the *Atheniensium Respublica;* the equivalent of this, in the region of ethics, is the abundant knowledge contained in his psychological and biological works. Aristotle's practical philosophy was neither a poetical phantasy nor a system deduced from metaphysical principles. It has been a modern prejudice since Bacon and Descartes to condemn this philosopher as a dogmatic metaphysician. Ironical as it is, one betrays his own dogmatism if one accuses Aristotle of being a dogmatist.

Indeed, how much knowledge do we require to understand the thoughts of a person ! As far as man is a historical and social being, we are unable to understand him apart from his historical situation and social circumstances. We ought to survey the whole work of a thinker, and combine this survey with the comprehensive study of his circumstances—especially in approaching such a great philosopher as Aristotle.

It is not sufficient to investigate only the three Ethics and the Politics, in order to comprehend his moral thought. It is the main subject of this study to inquire how the ethical theory is founded in and correlated with his psychological, physiological, biological and other works.

Needless to say, conduct or morality comprises not only private acts, but also social and political ones. Hence, in Aristotle's system, Ethics and Politics are connected with each other so closely that the one is in a sense part of the other. In order to explain conduct completely, we must investigate both Ethics and Politics. But our study at present, being confined to the fundamental structure of conduct, will turn to its psychological and physiological foundations, rather than to its social and political context. Of course, this is a limitation for the sake of convenience, and nothing more. Our problems, and order of investigation then, will be as follows:

In the first place, conduct consists of the voluntary acts of mankind, which are not only bodily actions, but also are mental. Since, however, the soul depends somehow upon the body, and its functions are multitudinous, we should inquire about the relation between soul and body as well as the correlations among the functions of the soul. Further, while conduct is not pure contemplation, it can none the more dispense with intellect; it is in a sense rational and in another sense irrational. What then, are the essences of and the relation between the rational and the irrational functions of the soul ? Especially, since conduct, as a rational and irrational act, is either an technical production or a moral practice, how are these acts to be distinguished and related to each other ? Next, how is the intellect which dominates conduct constructed ? What difference is there when it acts theoretically and when it acts practically ? After having clarified these points, we shall proceed to ask in what way intellect dominates practice, and particularly, what different forms this intellect takes in the case of production on the one hand and in that of practice on the other. To inquire into these problems as comprehensively as possible through Aristotle's own statements, and to grasp his thought as systematically as possible—these are the ends of our present study. Thus considered, we shall begin by inquiring into the structure of the soul, secondly study the functions of it, thirdly divide conduct into practice and production, fourthly inquire about the intellect which dominates them, and conclude with the inquiry into the practical syllogism.

NOTE

In view of some criticism, it seems to be necessary to make some explanation as to the meaning of my special terminology. I admit that the words "mediation" and "moment" are alien to Anglo-American readers, and that it is not without reason that they became the objects of complaints. In fact, these words are due to Hegel, and should be understood as the translations of "Vermittlung" and "Moment". Mediation of course contains the ordinary meaning of "intermidiary" which combines opposite terms that cannot interact directly. But when the opposite terms A and B are thus combined and there happens a synthesis D, not only the original middle term C, which combined A and B, but also both terms A and B acquire the function of medium from the point-view of the newly developed stage D. We may then say that "A is mediated by B, and B is mediated by A". In this "dialectical synthesis" A and B are called the "moments" (of D), i.e., the dynamic elements of dialectical development or dialectical synthesis. Though A and B have changed into D, they are *mutatis mutandi* held in D as its constituents. There might be objection as to the special terminology and further as to whether it is really up to the Hegelian usage of the words. I cannot for the moment discuss this point in detail. Anyhow, this is just what I implied by these words when I wrote this book under the strong influence of Hegelianism which was prevalent in Japanese philosophical circle. I would have avoided such ambiguous expressions together with other inappropriate terms, if I could rewrite the book. For the time being, however, I must content myself with this short appological comment. 1965.

CHAPTER I

THE STRUCTURE OF THE SOUL

§ 1. SOUL AND BODY

IN considering an object, Aristotle always attempted to reduce it to one of his categories. But when he says that the soul is substance, he does not only reduce it to the category of substance, but also in a sense makes it the substance itself.[1]

Now substance has many meanings. It means in one case matter, in another form, or an individual composed of matter and form. Dealing with the soul, Aristotle at first points out the three meanings of substance,[2] and argues that substance in the proper sense is the body composed of form and matter, especially a natural body or the body which is organized by φύσις or nature. Of these natural bodies, some have life, and some do not. Hence, a natural body possessed of life must also be a substance composed of matter and form. Whereas the living being consists of life and body, the principle of life being the soul, the material element which is common to living entities and lifeless must be the body. The body is surely not a predicative attribute, but the substratum, to which predicates belong. It is the matter which is determined by attributes. The formal principle of a living being must be the soul, which, therefore, is said to be substance in the sense of form. It is substance, not in the sense of a corporeal object, but a formal

---

[1] Strictly speaking, to ask what is the substance, i.e. the essence or definition, of the soul is one thing, to reduce it to the category of substance is another, and to make it the substance of the body is yet another. De An. I. 1. 402 a 7: ἐπιζητοῦμεν δὲ θεωρῆσαι καὶ γνῶναι τήν τε φύσιν αὐτῆς καὶ τὴν οὐσίαν, is the first case; ibid. 402 a 23: πρῶτον δ' ἴσως ἀναγκαῖον ἐν τίνι τῶν γενῶν καὶ τί ἐστι, λέγω δὲ πότερον τόδε τι καὶ οὐσία ἢ ποιὸν ἢ ποσὸν ἢ καί τις ἄλλη τῶν διαιρεθεισῶν κατηγοριῶν, is the second; and ibid. II. 1. 412 a 19: ἀναγκαῖον ἄρα τὴν ψυχὴν οὐσίαν εἶναι ὡς εἶδος σώματος φυσικοῦ δυνάμει ζωὴν ἔχοντος, must be the third. Concerning the difference between the expressions εἶδός τι and εἶδός τινος, which holds also for the case of οὐσία τις and οὐσία τινος, cf. Jaeger, Aristoteles, 44, and Nuyens, L'evolution de la psychologie d'Aristote, 85.

[2] De An. II. 1. 412 a 6; 2. 414 a 15; cf. Met. VII. 10. 1035a 2; 15. 1039 b 21; VIII. 2. 1043 a 19; X. 3. 1054 b 4; XII. 3. 1070 a 9, 12; 4. 1070 b 13.

principle, which gives life to a material body, or rather it is the life itself.[1]

Seeing that the animal is a natural being endowed with life, and the principle of life in a living being is the soul, which is the formal element of it, should we then define the soul as the form of a natural being possessed of life? But this is not strict enough. The expression "a natural being possessed of life" involves the idea of form, because life is nothing but the formal principle. Therefore, the definition "the form of a natural being possessed of life" would involve the idea of form twice. The substratum, to which form belongs, should be, strictly speaking, "a natural being potentially possessed of life". Thus we come to Aristotle's definition of the soul: "substance, in the sense of the form of a natural being, potentially possessed of life".[2]

On the other hand, form is said to be the actuality of matter, matter the potentiality of form.[3] It follows then, that substance in the sense of form is actuality, and the soul is the actuality of the body.[4] But ἐντελέχεια or actuality has two meanings. It may be explained by the analogy of ἐπιστήμη and θεωρία, i.e. knowledge and contemplation.[5] Compared with ignorance, knowledge has already a form, which however is not completely actual, but remains in a sense potential; while the complete reality of it is in the act of contemplation. The potentiality of contemplation in a layman is absolutely passive; it requires studying before it can develop; but the potentiality of an educated man is an actual potency, which is able to develop by itself into contemplation, and may educate an ignorant man.

δύναμις i.e. potentiality or possibility, has also many meanings: most often it is used in a limited sense of passivity. As we have explained elsewhere,[6] when the term δύναμις is used exclusively of the passive potentiality of an ignorant person, the actual potency

---

[1] De An. II. 2. 414 a 18; De Juvent. I. 467 b 14.
[2] De An. II. 1. 412 a 19.
[3] Met. IX. 8. 1050 b 2; a 16; De An. II.1. 412 a 10; 2. 414 a 17; cf. Met. VIII. 2. 1043 a 20; 3. 1043 a 33; b 1; XII. 5. 1071 a 9.
[4] De An. II. 1. 412 a 21.
[5] De An. II. 1. 412 a 9; Met. X. 6. 1048 a 34; Phys. VIII. 4. 255 a 33; De Sensu 4. 441 b 22; Gen. An. II. 1. 735 a 9; Trendelenburg, De An. 314 f.; Bonitz, Met. II. 394.
[6] De An. II. 5. 417 a 21-b 15; cf. Ando, Aristotles no Sonzairon 1958, p. 197 ff. The summary of this inquiry is as follows:—Aristotle admitted two kinds of poten-

of an educated man is expressed by the term ἕξις or *habitus*. Compared with the material and passive potentiality, it is in a sense a formal principle and actuality, yet falling short of the complete actuality and remaining in a sense potential. In what sense, then, is the soul said to be actuality ? It exists continuously, whether man is awake or asleep. Otherwise it would cease to exist when we are asleep and exist again when we are awake. So that, it would by no means be the unity of a person or the living principle of an animal. Now sleeping is related to waking just as knowledge is related to contemplation. So, the soul is the actuality of the body; but its actuality is not like that of contemplation, but like

tiality: the principle of motion or change in another thing or in the thing itself *qua* other, and the principle of being moved or changed by another thing or by the thing itself *qua* other. The one may be called active potentiality or potency, and the other passive potentiality. According to this definition, potentiality is assumed to be possessed by an actual thing. On account of this actual basis, this kind of potentiality essentially tends to take a single direction, though this appears to be inconsistent with Aristotle's own statement that every potentiality is "the potentiality of opposites". Potentiality involves in itself opposite moments of motion and rest, or more generally, of being and not-being, yet none the less it tends to go in one direction of motion or being. Being potential, it is essentially two-sided, but being the principle of motion or being, it must tends in only one direction. It may become actual or may not become actual, but in either case it is the cause of motion or being, and not the cause of rest or not-being. This fundamental character of potentiality remains the same even in the case of rational potency, which is considered by Aristotle to be referring to contrary ends. It is also to be seen in passive potentiality, which might appear at first glance to be quite indefinite and neutral. As far as it is the principle of motion and reality, even passive potentiality must have some particular quality. The matter of a particular thing is limited to a particular kind, as Aristotle says in De An. II. 8. 419 b 14: "It is not concussion of any two things taken at random which constitutes sound." Seeing that even passive potentiality tends in one direction, we must conclude from this that potentiality as the principle of motion or reality cannot be purely passive and of neutral character.

On the other hand, passive potentiality is assumed by Aristotle to be essential to matter. The pair concept of matter and form is earlier in his thought than that of potentiality and actuality. Aristotle constituted his metaphysical theory by ellaborating the concepts of matter and form into those of potentiality and actuality. This ellaboration was made with the utmost completeness, yet the heterogeneity of the two pairs of concepts could not be eradicated. Form corresponds to reality, and matter to potentiality. Yet neither is form identical with reality, nor matter with potentiality. Matter is identical only with passive potentiality. We may rather say that passive potentiality is the form considered in matter, or so to say, an accidental mode of matter. The concept of matter surely refers to that of form, but unlike potentiality which developes to actuality,

that of knowledge. In other words, the soul is the first actuality of a natural body, potentially possessed of life.¹ Since such a natural body is called an organism, the soul is also said to be the first actuality of an organic body.² Of course, this "first" means, not "excellent", but on the contrary, incomplete and rudimentary: we might as well say that the soul is the "second potentiality" of the body, or its ἕξις.

Soul is the substance, in the sense of form, or it may be said to be the substance of an organic natural being. It may also be said to be the λόγος, the concept, or the essence of such a natural being.³ For example, if an axe were a natural being, to be an axe would be its essence or soul. But, since in fact, the axe is not a natural being, but an artificial tool, to speak of the "soul" of the axe is no more than a metaphor. At any rate, the cutting function of the axe, seeing of the eye, and the waking state of the soul, are complete actuality, i.e. actuality in the second sense.

The soul itself is the first or incomplete actuality, just like the cutting faculty of the axe or the seeing faculty of the eye. The body, which is the substratum of the soul, is lower than that. It is no more than a potential being to the latter, just as iron is

matter subsists as an immanent constituent of being. Therefore, the concept of passive potentiality is, in truth, a kind of *contradictio in adjecto*.

At any rate, active potentiality especially tends in a single direction on account of the actual reality of its substratum. In this point the concept of potentiality passes over into that of ἕξις. Similar to active potentiality, ἕξις also tends in one direction, and has an actual substratum. The only difference between the two is that the latter presupposes an actual form of the same genus. But this last mark of ἕξις is after all the development of the essence of active potentiality, for Aristotle admits that actuality is prior to potentiality both in nature and in art. On the other hand, passive potentiality passes over into the concept of ἐνδεχόμενον. This term means the possibility of being thus as well as of not being thus. Such a kind of potentiality, in which the opposite moments are completely neutralized, is in truth, merely ideal possibility. It is possible only "with respect to knowledge", or "the being of which the contrary is not necessary". It is nothing more than logical consistency. In this kind of potentiality, there can hardly be found any actual substratum. This substratum of minimum actuality is the so-called primary matter. Cf. also Hicks's note on 412 a 27.

[1] De An. II. 1. 412 a 27.   [2] De An. II. 1. 412 b 5.
[3] De An. II. 1. 412 a 19; b 16; Met. VII. 10. 1035 b 14; 11. 1037 a 15; Gen. An. II. 4. 738 b 27;   Met. VIII. 3. 1043 b 34. λόγος would be the expression of εἶδος, and τὸ τί ἦν εἶναι is the most specialized form which determines the being completely.

to the axe, and the pupil is to the eye. As the axe is an iron possessed of cutting ability, the eye a pupil possessed of sight, so the living being is a body possessed of soul, or in other words it is constituted of soul and body.[1] As is evident from the above analogy, this constitution is not a mechanical composition of independent elements, but an organic and fundamental unity. Hence it is said that there is no need to inquire whether soul and body are one, any more than whether the wax and the imprint are one.[2] It is not that soul and body, existing independently, compose a living being mechanically, but that soul is the active power in body, while body is the ὄργανα or tool whereby soul presents itself.[3] As far as the soul is the actuality of the body, it is necessary that both are really inseparable. The only possible distinction would be conceptual. Aristotle's theory is anything but a mechanical dualism which presupposes independent elements or principles, and then composes the reality from them, or a monism which deduces the one from the other. It seems more harmonious with our present view of the soul, than are modern metaphysical theories which are more or less one-sided and abstract.[4]

Aristotle, however, does not remain a positivist. His philosophical interest tends towards metaphysics, and towards religious and practical problems. As aforesaid, soul and body are different only in concept, but identical in reality. Yet there is a further question. The soul, in so far as it is the actuality of the body, is really inseparable from it, to be sure, but if there should be another soul which is not directly the actuality of the body, such a soul would not of necessity be inseparable from the body in reality.[5] Even though the principle of life in a living being be the soul, not all souls would of necessity be the principle of a living being. Is there, indeed, such a transcendent soul, which is quite independent of the body?

In order that such a question might be possible, there must be some specific difference among souls. Now, the fact that there

[1] De An. II. 1. 412 b 19-413 a 3; Met. VII. 11. 1037 a 5.
[2] De An. II. 1. 412 b 6.
[3] De An. II. 4. 415 b 18; cf. Zeller, Ph. d. Gr. II. 2. 486; Baeumker, Das Problem der Materie in der griechischen Philosophie, 262.
[4] Scheler, Die Stellung des Menschen im Kosmos, V. 1; cf. Nuyens, op. cit. 73-78.
[5] De An. II. 1. 413 a 4-8; Gen. An. II. 3. 736 b 21; Part. An. I. 1. 641 b 9 f.

is a difference of degree among living beings, though all have souls, suggests a difference of species in the souls themselves.[1] This difference as to souls among living beings is due not only to bodily difference, but also corresponds to a difference among the souls themselves. Rejecting the transmigration theory, which only admits differences as to souls and neglects bodily differences, Aristotle says such an opinion is as absurd as the supposition that the art of building could embody itself in a flute.[2] In the same way, we might say that it is just as absurd to admit only bodily difference without admitting difference of souls. His not mentioning this side of the matter could hardly have been due to carelessness. We must rather suppose he did not because this was too evident to be worth mentioning.

Of course, in so far as the differentia of the soul are completely parallel to those of the body, and in so far as there is no element of the soul which is independent of the body, we can never admit a transcendent soul. Once the soul is defined as the form of the body, it is by no means independent of the body. But is it so evident that the soul is nothing but the form of the body? It is rather something, which thinks, perceives, moves, and takes nourishment. It would seem to be the unity of these functions, or the "subject" underlying them. The form of the body should be something our idea of which is arrived at empirically by induction from these functions. If we define the soul *a priori* as simply the form of the body, and thereby deny the existence of a soul which is independent of the body, without doubt this will be nothing but a *petitio principii*.

A true positivist will at first observe and compare various forms of soul, and afterwards decide whether there is a transcendent soul or not. This was the way which Aristotle really followed. That the soul is the form of the body, is not, at the moment, an ultimate difinition; rather, it ought at first to be taken as a mere hypothesis.[3]

It was not, however, original with Aristotle to divide the soul into parts or admit a transcendent soul. Such a view of the soul is

---

[1] Cf. Brentano, Die Psychologie des Aristoteles, 53.
[2] De An. II. 2. 414-28; I.3. 407 b 13 ff.
[3] De An. II. 2. 413 a 11 ff.; 3. 414 b 20 ff.; 415 a 12. According to Nuyens, this is the final stage of thought which Aristotle attained in his last period. But even Nuyens could not deny that Aristotle preserved to the last the transcendent reason which is independent of the body; cf. op. cit. 311 ff.

a metaphysical heritage from Plato and his predecessors. Further, even the idea of the soul as the form of the body, is not entirely original.[1] If one admit that the soul is the form of the body, the former is certainly not separable from the latter. This is not Plato's thought, to be sure, but when Plato says that the soul is the principle of life, whereby one can act as a living body, the distance of the two theories is not so great. The only difference is in whether the separability of the soul be admitted. As we shall see later on, Aristotle in fact limited the separability of the soul, yet never denied it. It would be an unhistorical and abstract view, to explain away Aristotle as a mere oponent of Plato. We should never forget that Aristotle was a successor to, no less than an opponent of, his master. This is not a paradox; on the contrary, he could not but be an opponent in order that he might be a true successor — for surely this is the destined course of all great disciples.

No doubt, to make the soul the form of the body is a most suitable view for Aristotle as a biologist. But the fact that he could not stop there, proves that he was very much a metaphysician in the tradition of Platonism. To speak more fundamentally, the religious and practical impulses of the Greek spirit were beating in his mind. Aristotle was not a mere biologist, but far better a moralist and a metaphysician.[2]

It is well known that Plato divided the soul into three parts,

[1] Plato, Phaedo, 105 C: 'Ἀποκρίνου δή, ἦν δ' ὅς, ᾧ ἂν τί ἐγγένηται σώματι ζῶν ἔσται; Ὧι ἂν ψυχή, ἔφη. Crat. 399 D. Ὡς μὲν τοίνυν ἐκ τοῦ παραχρῆμα λέγειν, οἶμαί τι τοιοῦτον νοεῖν τοὺς τὴν ψυχὴν ὀνομάσαντας, ὡς τοῦτο ἄρα, ὅταν παρῇ τῷ σώματι, αἴτιόν ἐστι τοῦ ζῆν αὐτῷ, τὴν τοῦ ἀναπνεῖν δύναμιν παρέχον καὶ ἀναψῦχον, ἅμα δὲ ἐκλείποντος τοῦ ἀναψύχοντος τὸ σῶμα ἀπόλλυταί τε καὶ τελευτᾷ· ὅθεν δή μοι δοκοῦσιν αὐτὸ "ψυχὴν" καλέσαι.

Corresponding to these passages, we find in Aristotle, De An. I. 1. 402 a 6: ἔστι γὰρ οἷον ἀρχὴ τῶν ζῴων.; ibid. II. 4. 415 b 8: ἔστι δὲ ἡ ψυχὴ τοῦ ζῶντος σώματος αἰτία καὶ ἀρχή.; ibid. II. 2. 414 a 12: ἡ ψυχὴ δὲ τοῦτο ᾧ ζῶμεν καὶ αἰσθανόμεθα καὶ διανοούμεθα πρώτως·; Part. An. I. 1. 641 a 18-21: ἀπελθούσης γοῦν οὐκέτι ζῷόν ἐστιν, οὐδὲ τῶν μορίων οὐδὲν τὸ αὐτὸ λείπεται, πλὴν τῷ σχήματι μόνον, καθάπερ τὰ μυθευόμεθα λιθοῦσθαι,

[2] Hence I cannot easily yield to Nuyens's hypothesis, which admits three stages of development in Aristotle's concept of the soul, viz. the earliest view of mechanism, and the transitional view of instrumentalism, and the final view of hylemorphism. These three kinds of view are rather juxtaposed with one another and none is entirely abondoned. That Aristotle remained a metaphysician till the last period, Nuyens none the less confirms; cf. op. cit. 54.

the λογιστικόν or the reasoning part, the θυμικόν or the passionate, and the ἐπιθυμητικόν or the appetitive.¹ A pseudo-Aristotelian script, the *Magna Moralia*, also ascribes to Plato the duopartite theory, which divides it into the λόγον ἔχον or the rational, and the ἄλογον or the irrational.² But though Plato himself mentions the duopartite theory, he does not maintain it as his own. Aristotle also treats the two theories distinctively in his *De Anima*.³ Since the tripartite theory is proper to Plato, the other must be ascribed to some one else.

Presumably, it may be, as Hicks conjectured, a vulgar opinion before Plato, which provided a basis for his tripartite theory. In his early work, the *Topica*, Aristotle still follows, in the main, Plato's tripartite theory.⁴ According to Arnim, this is not a division of the faculties, but of the substantial parts of the soul itself.⁵ Merely functional parts would have to stand parallel to each other, without mutual interference. If such a part as the reasoning part or the appetitive part were regarded as a faculty, there would be no such conflict as Plato posits between βούλησις or wish and ἐπιθυμία or appetite, the former operating in the reasoning part, the latter in the appetitive. But according to the tripartite theory, each part has a special power of reasoning or desiring, and struggles with the others. Nor is such a division of the soul a matter of a mere difference of viewpoints, as a sphere appears convex from outside and concave from inside. Parts thus divided by viewpoints would never conflict with each other. Therefore, a substantial and real division must be indicated. So argues Arnim.

We cannot deny that Plato's tripartite theory is in the main a substantial division. Aristotle also may have been under the yoke of his master's theory in his early period of the *Topica*. But in the middle or later period, as we see his thought in the *De Anima*

[1] Plato, Rep. 4. 435-442; 6. 504 A. 8. 550 A. 9. 571; 580 E; 581; Tim. 69 E-72; 89 E; Leg. 9. 863.   [2] Mag. Mor. I. 1. 1182 a 23.

[3] De An. III. 9. 432 a 25.   [4] Hicks's note on 432 a 26, 411 b 25. Régis assigns this division to Pythagoreans; cf. L'opinion selon Aristote, 58.

[5] Arnim, Das Ethische im Aristotelischen Topik, 6-12; Strümpel, Die Geschichte der theoretischen Philosophie, 324 ff.; cf. also Brandis, Handbuch der griechisch-römischen Philosophie, II. b. 1168 f.; Zeller, Ph. d. Gr. II. 2. 499 n. 5. The following proposition seems to prove Arnim's opinion: De An. III. 9. 432 b 3-7; πρὸς δὲ τούτοις τὸ ὀρεκτικόν, ὃ καὶ λόγῳ καὶ δυνάμει ἕτερον ἂν δόξειεν εἶναι πάντων. καὶ ἄτοπον δὴ τοῦτο διασπᾶν· ἔν τε τῷ λογιστικῷ γὰρ ἡ βούλησις γίνεται, καὶ ἐν τῷ ἀλόγῳ ἡ ἐπιθυμία καὶ ὁ θυμός· εἰ δὲ τρία ἡ ψυχή, ἐν ἑκάστῳ ἔσται ὄρεξις.

or the *Ethica Nicomachea*, the tripartite theory is criticized and given up, and there appears a reflection upon the principle of division; thus, Aristotle asks whether there are various kinds of soul, or one soul with several parts, and if the latter is the case, are these parts divided conceptually or are they separable τόπῳ i.e. by place ?[1] The expression τόπῳ is somewhat ambigous, and is rendered elsewhere by such words as ἀριθμῷ "numerically", κατὰ μέγεθος "by magnitude", or πεφυκότα "naturally". Aristotle here seems to be at a loss to find a suitable expression. We may probably understand his notion as that of a substantial or real separability which is more than a mere difference of concept.[2]

There is no doubt, in the first place, that the soul is divisible conceptually.[3] The division of the soul into the vegetable, the animal, and the human, or into the nourishing, the sensible, and the reasoning, might be assumed to be a conceptual division, the principle of which being the functional differences of the soul.[4] But not all divisions are conceptual, or depend upon functional differences. According to Brentano, on the contrary, Aristotle rather intended to establish a substantial division, and attributed to each part several functions — the principle of this division being a biological classification.[5] Though this be admitted, still the basis of the biological classification is nothing but the functional differences of living activities, so that the functional division must none the less be the most fundamental. At any rate, Brentano thinks, that since there are some genera of animals which exhibit some of these functions together, the soul might be divided into substantial parts which support those groups of functions. On this point, we shall make inquiry later on. At present, we must inquire first of all in what sense these parts of the soul which were divided functionally hold their independence against one another, and whether they are merely conceptual-functional parts, or have a real independence. This inquiry is connected with the question whether some function may act apart from the body.[6] If there is such a function, the part which has it would be really separable

[1] De An. I. 1. 402 b 1; II. 2. 413 b 13; III. 4. 429 a 10; Eth. Nic. I. 13. 1102 a 28.
[2] Aristotle might have avoided the word οὐσία, because it has many meanings, "concept" being only one of these meanings.
[3] De An. II. 2. 413 b 29-32.   [4] De An. II. 3. 414 b 20.
[5] Brentano, Psych. d. Arist. 57 ff.; cf. De An. II. 2. 413 b 32-414 a 1.
[6] De An. I. 1. 403 a 10. II. 1. 413 a 3.

from other parts. Whether soul and body are really inseparable, or absolutely separable, it would still be doubtful whether their parts are really separable from each other. But if some parts are separable from the body and the others not, the former would be separable from the latter. Now, without doubt, some part of the soul, e.g. the sensible, is inseparable from the body.[1] So the key to the question whether the parts of the soul are really separable, will be whether another part, e.g. the reasoning part, might act apart from the body. Is there then, as a matter of fact, such a special part in the soul?

We find this key in the beginning of the *De Anima*. Here Aristotle asks whether the πάθη of the soul be peculiar to the soul, i.e. whether they be separate from the body, the author answers as follows: "It seems that in most cases it (the soul) neither acts nor is acted upon apart from the body: as, e.g. in anger, courage, desire, and sensation in general. Thinking would, most of all, seem to be peculiar to the soul. Yet if thinking is also a part of imagination, or not independent of imagination, it will follow that even thinking cannot be independent of the body. If, then, there be any of the actions or affections of the soul which are peculiar to it alone, it will be possible for it to be separated from the body: if, on the other hand, there is nothing of the sort peculiar to it, it will not be separable. It will be like what is straight which has many properties—for instance, it touches the brazen sphere at a point—yet the straightness will by no means so touch it if separated [from other concomitants]. In fact it is inseparable, since it is always conjoined with body of some sort. So, too, the πάθη of the soul appear to be all conjoined with body: so it is with anger, fear, pity, courage, and also with joy, love and hate; for the body is somehow affected simultaneously with them."[2]

In the foregoing passage, we must first of all explain the meaning of the term πάθη. The word derives from πάσχειν, "to suffer," and means a passive state, or passivity. More concretely, it means in a narrower sense certain mental experiences such as sensation and feeling, in a wider sense the modes of being in general. If we take it in the wider sense, and mean by it the modes or functions of the soul in general, we should conclude that the soul is quite inseparable from the body, seeing that the πάθη of the soul cannot exist apart from the body. But if we may take it in the narrower

---

[1] De An. III. 4. 429 b 5.   [2] De An. I. 1. 403 a 3 ff.

sense, it by no means follows that the soul is inseparable from the body.

Now, the examples of πάθη here mentioned, are anger, courage, desire, and so on, and they appear to be summed up as sensation in general. This "sensation in general", however, may mean sensation in the strict sense, instead of the sum of the above mentioned feelings. Be that as it may, anger, courage, desire, and sensation in general do not exhaust the functions of the soul. The enumeration is also, later in the passage limited to such feelings as "anger" "mildness", "fear", "pity", "courage", etc.[1] In addition to this, we may note that "action", ἔργον, is here distinguished from "affection", πάθημα, while in another place,[2] "affection", as opposed to "action," is illustrated by "thinking", "sensation", and "pleasure". Among these only thinking might be conceived as an ἔργον, while the others would be πάθη. On these grounds, we may conclude that πάθη here should be taken in the narrower sense, and might not necessarily deny the real separability of the soul from the body, even if all πάθη of the soul are combined with the body. How then, shall we treat the sentence, "If thinking is also a part of imagination or not independent of imagination, it will follow that even thinking cannot be independent of the body."? Are we compelled to understand it as asserting that the term πάθη —as it would in the wider sense—includes thinking, and that all functions of the soul without exception are conjoined with the body and inseparable from it? According to Hicks too, πάθη should be taken as modes in general, which are not limited to special passions. It follows therefore that the soul is generally inseparable from the body, and its parts are also really inseparable from each other. Even admitting that the meaning of πάθη be limited to the narrower sense, in so far as thinking presupposes imagination as its *sine qua non*, the possibility of reason being really separable from the body will be threatened. Even if thinking were not an activity, but a passivity, of the soul, since, nevertheless, it cannot exist apart from the body, the soul as a whole will be unable to exist apart from the body; it would then be to no point to argue about the extent of the word πάθη.

One might thereupon propose a suggestion: What is said about thinking in the above quotation—that it is a part of imagination

---

[1] De An. I. 1. 403 a 16; b 17; Eth. Nic. II. 4. 1105 b 20.
[2] De An. I. 5. 409 b 14-17.

or not independent of imagination—is expressed as a hypothetical proposition, not a categorical assertion. It may not be Aristotle's own thought, but a mere presumptive supposition. Such a suggestion might well be defensible if we limit ourselves to this particular text. But on turning to Aristotle's own theory, we shall soon find that this suggestion is unacceptable. Aristotle is not advancing a mere hypothesis, but an indirect assertion of his own belief. He may have preferred such a modest expression, because the sentence is anticipatory and detailed investigation is expected to follow. In fact, what he here merely supposes, he often asserts later on. We meet everywhere such an affirmation as "The soul does not think without imagination",[1] or "At the very time when he is thinking, he must have an image before him",[2] or "The reason does not think of outer objects except being combined with sensation"[3] and the like.

If thinking presupposes imagination and imagination presupposes the body, reason as a thinking faculty would be inseparable from the body. If thinking and reason, which are most likely to be separate from the body, should not be so, much less then will the other parts of the soul be so. Should we then take the $\pi\acute{a}\theta\eta$ of the soul for modes in general, including not only feelings but also all the functions of soul? Indeed the ground of the argument upon which we have tried to determine the meaning of the term $\pi\acute{a}\theta\eta$ was, strictly speaking, probable but not necessary. In this way, however, we can by no means solve all difficulties, for we continue to encounter in Aristotle views which contradict this interpretation. Aristotle, while admitting on the one hand, that the various parts or functions of the soul are inseparable from the body, on the other hand says: "Only reason would seem to be a distinct species of soul, and it alone is capable of separation from the body",[4] or "The reason is doubtless a thing more divine and is impassive",[5] or "Only the reason comes from outside and is alone divine, for the activities of body do not communicate with it",[6] etc. The cause of reason's being free from such hindrances as beset the sensitive faculty, which cannot feel after too strong a sensation, is that, "The sensitive faculty cannot exist apart from the body, while the reason

---

[1] De An. III. 7. 431 a 16;   De Mem. 1. 449 b 31.
[2] De An. III. 8. 432 a 8;   a 13.   [3] De Sensu. 6. 445 b 16.
[4] De An. II. 2. 413 b 24.   [5] De An. I. 4. 408 b 29;   cf. b 24.
[6] Gen. An. II. 3. 736 b 27.

is separable". The reason is distinguished from other parts of the soul, in that the former is separable, while the latter are really inseparable and only distinguished conceptually from the body.[1] Would not these and other similar propositions contradict the previous view, that reason being a kind of imagination or at least requiring it, forms a unity with and is inseparable from the body ? We have now encountered a serious difficulty. How should this ἀπορία be solved ?

§ 2. THE PROBLEM OF *ΝΟΥΣ ΠΟΙΗΤΙΚΟΣ*

The reason is considered on the one hand to be really inseparable from the body and from other parts of the soul, while on the other hand it is said to be incapable of thinking without being mediated by the body. Since such a part is functionally inseparable from the body, it cannot really exist independently either. Confronting this difficulty, one might immediately conjecture whether it be not due to the fact that the books of *De Amnia* might have been written in different periods. For splendid indeed have been the contributions of such a philological approach to the study of the systems of Plato and Aristotle. And in fact Jaeger himself refers, though only occasionally, to this point in his notable work upon the development of Aristotle's thought. But he does not go beyond indicating that the third book of the *De Anima*, which involves the problem of reason, is one of the oldest and most durable elements of Aristotle's philosophy, being quite Platonic and not scientific, and that it in this respect forms a contrast with the arguments about soul and sensation in the first two books, together with the *Parva Naturalia*, whose subject and method are consistently biological and psychological.[2] But unhappily, we reach no conclusion from these facts alone as to the different periods of the formation of these books, as they are too insufficient for any proof. Further, though Jaeger contrasts the whole third book with the other two, seeing that it contains the Platonic view of reason, we must point out that the idea of the separability and

---

[1] De An. III. 4. 429 b 3.

[2] Jaeger, Aritsoteles, 355 ff. Perhaps he considered the theory of reason in De An. II. to be Platonic because of its resemblance to the statements in Met. XII. 9.

immortality of reason is not confined to the third book,[1] and moreover the first three chapters of the third book, in treating sensation and imagination, continue the arguments of the preceding book, while the reason-theory in question appears only in the fourth chapter. The arguments in this fourth chapter differ seriously from those of the following fifth, the latter being by no means Platonic. Moreover, as we have seen above, the Platonic tripartite theory as well as the duopartite theory is criticized in the ninth chapter, and various additional parts are enumerated, such as nutritive, sensitive, imaginative, and desiring; Jaeger himself admits this last to be the true theory of Aristotle in his last period. Thus, if we should distinguish differences of period in the books of *De Anima*, the question would be not about the difference between the third and the other two, but about the relation between the different parts within the third book itself. Namely, it would be only the fourth chapter of the third book, that might be conjectured to be earlier. Nevertheless, there is no proof of the early formation of the fourth chapter, except the aforesaid difference from the fifth. As we have not yet had a decisive philological study on the formation of the *De Anima*,[2] we must content ourselves with deeming it a comparatively late work. Even if the theory of the separable reason seems to belong, in its content, to Aristotle's early thought, we should not shun a philosophical solution of this *aporia* by resorting to the hypothesis of development. I by no means intend to restrict myself to speculation, paying no regard to philological method. Yet I cannot but warn against the danger in the attempt to solve all difficulties of thought through a philological interpretation, out of excessive admiration for the splendid results that the studies of Jaeger and his followers have accomplished. We ought all the more to bear this in mind, lest we should lose sight of the marvellously realistic spirit of Aristotle, who was so ready to sacrifice a systematic coherence in order that he might take a whole view.

[1] De An. I. 4. 408 b 18, 29; II. 2. 413 b 24.
[2] Nuyens's excellent study, Ontwickelings momenten in de zielkunde van Aristoteles, was published in 1939, its translation in French in 1948. I did not know this work when I wrote this passage, but even this excellent study does not compel me to change the opinion fundamentally. At any rate, Nuyens's criticism against Jaeger concerning the chronology of De Anima, especially III.4 is very instructive.

Now that the philological method fails to give us a satisfactory solution, we must naturally try for ourselves to solve the problem by a speculative method. Such an attempt might also contribute something, at least indirectly, to the study of the formation of this work. Even if not, our chief interest does not lie so much in the historical facts as in the logical connections of thought that we may discover in the works left to us. For this purpose, I would propose a new hypothesis:—May not the problem concerning the separability of reason be solved by distinguishing within reason what is combined with body through the medium of imagination, and what is not? It would seem to be a point in favour of our hypothesis, that Aristotle distinguishes active and passive reasons in the fifth chapter, immediately following the fourth chapter in which he maintains the separability of reason. We are now confronted with the famous problem of νοῦς ποιητικός which has caused endless discussions in the history of philosophy.

The only source for Aristotle's thought on the point in question is the following short section. De An. III. 5. 430 a 10 ff.:
ἐπεὶ δ' ὥσπερ ἐν ἁπάσῃ τῇ φύσει ἐστί τι τὸ μὲν ὕλη ἑκάστῳ γένει (τοῦτο δὲ ὃ πάντα δυνάμει ἐκεῖνα), ἕτερον δὲ τὸ αἴτιον καὶ ποιητικόν, τῷ ποιεῖν πάντα, οἷον ἡ τέχνη πρὸς τὴν ὕλην πέπονθεν, ἀνάγκη καὶ ἐν τῇ ψυχῇ ὑπάρχειν ταύτας τὰς διαφοράς. καὶ ἔστιν ὁ μὲν τοιοῦτος νοῦς τῷ πάντα γίνεσθαι, ὁ δὲ τῷ πάντα ποιεῖν, ὡς ἕξις τις οἷον τὸ φῶς· τρόπον γάρ τινα καὶ τὸ φῶς ποιεῖ τὰ δυνάμει ὄντα χρώματα ἐνεργείᾳ χρώματα. καὶ οὗτος ὁ νοῦς χωριστὸς καὶ ἀπαθὴς καὶ ἀμιγής, τῇ οὐσίᾳ ὢν ἐνέργεια. ἀεὶ γὰρ τιμιώτερον τὸ ποιοῦν τοῦ πάσχοντος καὶ ἡ ἀρχὴ τῆς ὕλης. τὸ δ' αὐτό ἐστιν ἡ κατ' ἐνέργειαν ἐπιστήμη τῷ πράγματι· ἡ δὲ κατὰ δύναμιν χρόνῳ προτέρα ἐν τῷ ἑνί, ὅλως δὲ οὐ χρόνῳ· ἀλλ' οὐχ ὁτὲ μὲν νοεῖ ὁτὲ δ' οὐ νοεῖ. χωρισθεὶς δ' ἐστὶ μόνον τοῦθ' ὅπερ ἐστί, καὶ τοῦτο μόνον ἀθάνατον καὶ ἀΐδιον. οὐ μνημονεύομεν δέ, ὅτι τοῦτο μὲν ἀπαθές, ὁ δὲ παθητικὸς νοῦς φθαρτός, καὶ ἄνευ τούτου οὐθὲν νοεῖ.

"But, as in the whole of nature, there is on the one hand something which serves as matter for each kind (and this matter is potentially all the members of the kinds), while on the other there is something which serves as the cause or agent because it makes them all, as e.g. the art is related to the matter that has been affected. These differences must exist, therefore, of necessity also in the soul. And so while such a reason exists because it becomes all things, the other does because it makes them all, like a certain kind of *habitus* such as light. For light also in a certain way makes what are potentially colours into actual colours. And this reason is separable, impassive and unmixed, being in its substance actual. For that which acts is always superior to that which is acted upon, as principle is to matter. Now actual knowledge is identical with the object of knowing, but potential knowledge is prior in time in the individual case, though considered as a whole it is not prior in time. But it is not at one time thinking and at another not. It is only when separated that it is just what it is, and this alone is immortal and eternal. But we do not remember, because it is impassive, while the passive reason is mortal, and one does not think without this."

Anticipating the result of our inquiry, let us paraphrase this passage as follows: Since all natural beings consist of matter and form, the soul, being a kind of natural being, should have matter and form; and so also with the reason as a part of the soul. In the reason, the material part is potential and passive, but the formal part is actual and active. The former is mortal, while the latter is immortal. It is the latter that can continue to exist apart from the body, or rather hold its proper being in such a separate condition. It is an eternal action, but has no memory which is the mark of human or animal consciousness. Nevertheless, our thinking is possible only through the cooperation of active and passive reasons.

According to our interpretation, Aristotle admitted both separable and inseparable reasons, and there is no real contradiction in this. But to maintain this apparently simple interpretation, we must solve many difficulties, for the history of arguments about this problem could form a volume in itself. We shall content ourselves with a short summary, following Brentano.[1]

To begin with, Aristotle's own disciple, Theophrastus,[2] seems to have taken not only the active reason but also the passive as immaterial, and to have made both of them the faculties of a subject which is an essential constituent of man.[3]

Alexander of Aphrodisias, on the contrary, made the active reason separate from human nature. It was for him a purely spiritual or rational substance, the first ground of things, and the

[1] Brentano, Psych. d. Arist. 5-36. [2] Themistius, Paraph. d. anim. f. 91.
[3] Brentano contrasted Eudemus to Theophrastus, but since the Eth. Eud. is proved by Jaeger to be an early work of Aristotle's, we must naturally omit him.

divine intelligence itself.¹ While the passive faculty which he called νοῦς ὑλικός² was thought to depend upon a certain mixture of the elements in the human body, man's soul was deemed to depend, on the whole, upon the body, both in respect to thinking and to being; it was perishable with the body.³ There were also some who took the νοῦς ποιητικός for God,⁴ while others identified it with directly recognized propositions and their consequences.⁵

These two theories of antiquity continued throughout the mediaeval and modern ages as the two preeminent opposing points of view. Firstly, Avicenna, an Arabian philosopher, being without doubt under the influence of Alexander, assumed only "the reason that becomes all things" to be a human faculty, while "the reason that makes all things" he held to be superhuman. The former, i.e. the *intellectus materialis*⁶ or νοῦς δυνάμει is the cognitive faculty of man, through which he grasps the rational forms. Its subject is not a bodily organ, but the soul. The highest spiritual part of the human soul does not mix with the body,⁷ but is above the death of the body and imperishable.⁸ νοῦς δυνάμει as such a part, recognizes potentially, but in order that the knowledge may become actual, it must be supplied with ideas from a pure, spiritual substance, which is independent of human beings.⁹ Every rational form exists previously within pure spirits, the highest¹⁰ of which moves the next and so on till at last it reaches active reason, i.e. the *intelligentia agens*, which is called by him the giver of forms. Out of the active reason, rational forms stream into our mind. All that the φαντασία can do, is to make the *intellectus materialis* ready for accepting the emanation.¹¹ It is

---

[1] Alex. Aph. De An. I. 139 b; 144 a.

[2] A denomination derived from De An. III. 5. 430a 10, 13, 19, and continued by Arabian philosophers.   [3] Alex. Aph. De An. I. 126, 127.

[4] Themist. Paraph. d. An. 89.

[5] Presumably, their interpretation is founded upon such passages as An. Post. II. 19. 100 b 8; Eth. Nic. VI. 3. 1139 b 17; 1141 a 5.

[6] In the traditional latin version, νοῦς δυνάμει is always translated as *intellectus*, while νοῦς ποιητικός is usually rendered as *intelligentia*. In the writings translated from Arabian, the latter means a bodiless spirit. Cf. Thomas Aquinas, Summ. Th. I. a 79. 10.   [7] Lib. Natur. VI. p. 5. c. 2. princ.

[8] Ibid. p. 5. c. 2. This thesis is applied not only to a universal spirit, but also to individual souls; cf. Brentano's note *ad loc.*

[9] Lib. Natur. VI. p. 5. c. 5. princ.

[10] This is not God, but the first intelligence that moves the highest sphere; cf. Brentano's note *ad loc.*   [11] Lib. Natur. VI. p. 5. c. 5.

none the less a necessary arrangement, in so far as the human soul is bound with the body.¹ The *intellectus materialis* can be illuminated by the *intelligentia agens* and get a universal knowledge only through individual φαντασία. Those ideas are not kept in the *intellectus materialis*.² They must stream into it anew from the *intelligentia agens* whenever we recognize spiritually.³ Learning is nothing but the acquisition of a complete *habitus* enabling oneself to combine with the *intelligentia agens* in order to acquire rational forms.

According to Averroes, another representative of Arabian philosophy, Aristotle made not only the active reason, but also the passive, pure spiritual substances essentially separate from sensible man. Spiritual cognition is not innate to man. A child is said to be spiritual in so far as it has a rational faculty in potentiality.⁴ Man is not specifically different from irrational animals, because the differentia of man is not a spiritual, but a sensitive faculty, which Aristotle calls νοῦς παθητικός,⁵ the *intellectus passibilis*.⁶ It is seated in the central cells of the brain,⁷ and through this faculty, we can distinguish individual images. But the animal has, instead of it, only a certain judgement through natural instinct (*virtus aestimativa naturalis*),⁸ in virtue of which the lamb observes

¹ Cf. Lib. Nat. VI. p. 5. c. 5.
² Sensible forms have their treasury in imagination and memory: imagination being the repository for *sensus communis* or *phantasia*, and memory for estimative or sensible cognition. But there is no treasury of ideas for *intellectus materialis*. For if that were the case, since a spiritual subject actually knows those things that are involved in it, and since to have the forms in itself means the same thing as to recognize them, the treasury of ideas would be a faculty of a bodily organ. But this is impossible, because no form that is involved in a faculty which uses in its operation a bodily organ, is intelligible except potentially. Cf. Brentano, Psych. d. Arist. 12.
³ Ibid. n. 33. Lib. Natur. VI. p. 5. c. 6, where among the four alternatives— viz., that either the treasury of intelligible forms is in a bodily organ, or in the spiritual part, or there is no such treasury, or *inielligentia agens* acts as a medium that combines the forms with the soul—the last is chosen. In spite of Brentano's opposition, this theory of Avicenna's about νοῦς ποιητικός seems to me fairy probable.   ⁴ De An. III. 1. c. 5. Venet. 1550 f. 164 b.
⁵ De An. III. 5. 430 a 24.
⁶ De An. III. 4. c. 20 f. 171 b.   ⁷ De An. III. 5. c. 20 f. 174 b.
⁸ Avicenna called the two faculties *virtus cognitiva* and *virtus aestimativa* or *existimativa* (Lib. Natur. III. p. 1. c. 5). Brentano points out that Averroes, sometimes, e.g. in De An. III. 1. c. 20 f. 171 a, says that the *intellectus passibilis* is the *virtus imaginativa*, but sometimes identifies it with the *virtus*

the wolf as its enemy. Man is different from other animals in so far as he has a disposition towards a spiritual cognition.[1] He gains a habitual knowledge through the activity of *intellectus passibilis*, and through its combination with imagination and memory. The subject of this knowledge is not a spirit, but the *intellectus passibilis*.[2] On the other hand, the actual spiritual cognition is found only in a spiritual faculty, to which man attains through the combination of *intellectus materialis* and *intellectus agens*. *Intellectus materialis*[3] is called material because it stands only in a relation of potentiality to intelligible forms,[4] and *intellectus agens* is called so, because it makes the sensible images in man, which are potentially intelligible, i.e. the *phantasma*, actually intelligible, and thus moves the material intellect.[5] The *intellectus materialis* receives from imagination the intelligible forms, which are received by the *intellectus agens*, while this *intellectus agens* itself does not think them.[6] Each of these two spiritual beings is one substance and is not divided into many by the multiplicity of knowing persons.[7] They alone are the eternal in the man, while those parts of his being that are peculiar to him as an individual perish with the body. Thus at first, the sensitive thinking faculty of the *intellectus passibilis* combined with imagination and memory makes the images ready for the agency of the *intellectus agens*.[8] When the *intellectus agens* makes the images rational,[9] the *intel-*

cognitiva, which is superior to the imaginative faculty. On account of this, Brentano takes the former term as a somewhat indefinite expression for the sensible faculty in general. This seems to be a matter of considerable importance, since it is just Brentano who took the νοῦς παθητικός as identical with the φαντασία. We shall examine this point hereafter.

[1] De An. III. 1. c. 20. 171 b.   [2] Ibid.

[3] The *intellectus materialis* is distinguished from the *intellectus passibilis* in De An. III. c. 20. 171 a etc. Averroes, nevertheless, declares clearly that the *intellectus materialis* is also spiritual: e.g. De An. I. 1. c. 12; III. 1. c. 4. 160 a 4; c. 20. 171 b.   [4] De An. III. 1. c. 5. 160 b.

[5] De An. III. 1. c. 5. 165 a; ibid. 5. c. 30. 178 b.

[6] De An. III. 1. c. 19. 170 a. Not that it thinks nothing, but that its object belongs to another higher world, viz., the world of spirits.

[7] Averroes maintains that the *intellectus materialis* is also indivisible and one in all. De An. III. 1. c. 5. 163 b; ibid. 164 a; 165 a etc. Brentano laughs at this, but in as much as the *intellectus materialis* is a spiritual faculty and is distinguished from the *intellectus passibilis*, this is not so ridiculous as it might at first seem.   [8] De An. III. 1. c. 7. 167 b.

[9] The act of the *intellectus agens* must precede that of the *intellectus materialis*: De An. III. 1. c. 36. 178 b.

lectus materialis receives from them the images, intelligible concepts, or forms of sensible things.[1] Thus the intelligible forms have twofold subjects, viz., images and the *intellectus materialis*.[2] Since these two are united with the same intelligible form, the form of the *intellectus materialis* must also be combined with us through the images. And in as much as each form constitutes a unity with its subject, the *intellectus materialis* itself is also united with us, and we recognize through it as if through an innate faculty of cognition.[3]

As for our union with the *intellectus agens*, it grows gradually with the advance of our knowledge about the corporeal world during our lifetime.[4] The *intellectus materialis* receives the *intellectus agens* together with the truth that was recognized, just as the pupil receives light together with actual colour.[5] Thus, when the knowledge of the whole corporeal world is accomplished, the *intellectus agens* is completely united with us, and the whole area of spirit will be revealed, since the *intellectus agens* has at this moment a complete knowledge about all spiritual substances of nature.[6] He who has received the *intellectus agens* most completely in his *intellectus materialis*, recognizes[7] what the *intellectus agens* recognizes. This is the highest happiness.[8]

Averroes' theory gained a remarkable acceptance not only in the Islamic world but also in Christian Europe, in spite of the queer mysticism and sophistical expressions he exhibits. As a result, the great scholastics, especially Thomas Aquinas, found it necessary to fight against his philosophy with all their strength, condemning the great Arabian as a depraver of Aristotelian philosophy.[9]

The explanation of St. Thomas agrees in the main with the fragments of Theophrastus which are kept in the *paraphrasis* of Themis-

---

[1] De An. III. 3. c. 18. 169 b.   [2] De An. III. 1. c. 5. 163 b.
[3] De An. III. 1. c. 5. 164 b. Though everyone recognizes through one and the same *intellectus materialis*, it dose not follow of necessity that we recognize one and the same thing, because we receive the forms from phantasmata. These phantasmata are not confined to our own, but are derived from all living men of the world, so that, we shall never be in need of them in order to think. Knowledge develops or passes away only *per accidens*, i.e. in so far as it is combined with the individual Socrates or Plato. Cf. Brentano, Psych. d. Arist. 19, n. 53, 54, 55.
[4] We cannot expect the survival of pure spirit or the highest happiness in another life, because our individual personalities cease to exist with death.
[5] De An. III. 5. c. 36. 179 b.   [6] Ibid.
[7] De An. III. 5. c. 36. 180 a.   [8] De An. Beatitud. c. 4. and 5.
[9] Opuscul. XV. De unitate intellectus contra Averroistas.

tius. According to him, not only the *intellectus agens*, but also what he terms the *intellectus possibilis*[1] is something immaterial, and the latter as well as the former belongs to human nature. They are not pure spiritual substances as Averroes says, but faculties of the human soul. When Aristotle says that they are separated from the body,[2] he only means by this that they have no organs like vegetable and sensitive faculties, but find their subject in the soul. The human soul has its own faculty, superior to material powers. Both reasons are in their being and function incorporeal and not mixed with matter.[3] The *intellectus possibilis* is the cognitive faculty proper to the spiritual part. All our ideas are found in it, though not actually from the beginning. The *intellectus possibilis* is itself at first merely like a *tabula rasa*. It gains intelligible forms through a kind of passivity. Hence Aristotle[4] says that thinking is a passivity.[5]

Now passivity presupposes an agent; therefore Aristotle says that our knowledge comes from sensation.[6] This agrees with the statement that the soul does not think without images.[7] But as no corporeal thing can give an impression upon an incorporeal thing, a mere faculty of a sensible body is not sufficient to account for our thought; rather, a superior faculty is required—"The agent is superior to that which is acted upon."[8] This superior agent is the so-called *intellectus agens*. The images which have matter are rational only potentially, but the *intellectus agens* abstracts the forms from these images and makes them actually rational. Therefore the *intellectus agens* is the real agent of spiritual cognition, while the images are only the secondary cause, or so to say, the "matter" of the cause.[9] The *intellectus agens* illuminates the images which relate to reason as colour to sight, and it abstracts from them intelligible forms. Through this illumination and abstraction, we receive in our *intellectus possibilis* the copy of the universal essence of a thing without its individual determinations.[10]

[1] St. Thomas called the reason that is every thing in potentiality *intellectus possibilis*, instead of *intellectus passibilis* like the Arabians, according to De An. III. 4. 429 a 21. [2] De An. III. 4. 429 b 5; ibid. 5. 430 a 17.
[3] Comment. de An. III. lect. 7. [4] De An. III. 4. 429 a 13.
[5] Summ. Th. 1 a 79, 2 corp. [6] E.g. An. Post. II. 19. 100 a 10.
[7] De An. III. 5. 430 a 18. [8] De An. III. 5. 430 a 18.
[9] Summ. Th. 1 a 84, 6 corp.
[10] Ibid. 85, 1. ad 4.

This interpretation of St. Thomas agrees in the main, as we have noted, with that of Theophrastus, and was greatly esteemed by Brentano. Nevertheless, it has been accused of several difficulties. One of these is that, as Durandus[1] pointed out, though the *intellectus agens* is said to make the images spiritual, through bringing something spiritual into them, it would be, in fact, impossible for a sensitive faculty combined with a sense organ to have any spiritual attribute. So that the function which is assigned to the *intellectus agens* should be impossible. Moreover, if the *intellectus agens* makes the images spiritual, they would no longer remain images. Yet Aristotle says on the other hand that we cannot think without having at the same time in us the corresponding images.[2] Consequently, the images would not have been changed into higher intelligibles even at the moment of cognition. Durandus himself denied the *intellectus agens* altogether.

Hence Suarez[3] also tried to reform the theory of St. Thomas, though he himself did not think that he had departed from Thomas's views. According to Suarez, abstraction is not the act of the *intellectus agens* upon sensible images, but is innate to reason, the presence of sensible images being enough for the act of reason. But sensible images do not act upon reason. It is not that reason brings sensible images into the *intellectus possibilis*, but rather that reason makes in itself a rational image of an object, its act of abstraction giving no change to sensible images.

Brentano criticizes the theory as follows: Suarez admits the image merely as an assistant cause of spiritual thinking; this may be suitable for Plato, who believed the ideas to be innate to the soul, but not for Aristotle who admitted no innate ideas for the spiritual or rational part. Again, it would be just as inappropriate to ascribe to the *intellectus agens* an innate idea or thought. On the other hand, the image, being matter, cannot act upon the spirit, so that there is wanting the active principle which might actualize the potential thought. Even if the *intellectus agens* makes out the idea in the spirit, since the image gives no change to it, the power to engender all ideas must be included in it from the beginning. Why, then is there any reason at all for saying that knowledge is impossible without sensation? Why is actual

---

[1] Sent. 1. dist. 3. q. 5.   [2] De An. III 8. 432 a 8.
[3] De An. 1. IV.

THE PROBLEM OF *ΝΟΥΣ ΠΟΙΗΤΙΚΟΣ*

cognition impossible without individual images even after we have once acquired knowledge?[1] Moreover, the *intellectus agens* makes no effort, and effort which is necessary to all actions.[2] In short, this interpretation of Suarez would not agree with Aristotle's theory. —As to whether Brentano's criticism is right or not, we shall see later.

Turning to modern interpreters, let us take up at first Trendelenburg.[3] According to him, reason sometimes is combined with the other parts of the soul and cannot exist without them; such a reason is called νοῦς παθητικός.[4] But sometimes it lies beyond the other functions of man, and rules them: in this case it is called νοῦς ποιητικός. νοῦς παθητικός is that which puts together all the lower faculties that are necessary for the cognition of a thing. It is called νοῦς παθητικός because on the one hand, it is completed by the νοῦς ποιητικός, and on the other hand, it is acted upon by the object of thought.[5] Its function is to acquire a universal concept through the comparison of individual sensations with each other.[6]

As for the νοῦς ποιητικός, it is not divine reason itself, but belongs to man,[7] and is not a single entity common for all.[8] Aristotle does not explain the essence and function of this reason.[9] What is evident is only that it comprehends the first and the last principles of knowledge. It is the ultimate witness of truth,[10] without which we have no assurance of anythings.[11] Our νοῦς ποιητικός is not the divine reason, yet it is something godlike, and the divine reason itself is also a νοῦς ποιητικός. Aristotle suggests in a certain place the resemblance of human reason and divine, without defining there or elsewhere in what manner human reason participates in the divine reason.[12] In as much as he has taken it to be something holy, he is led to assume that it does

---

[1] De An. III. 8. 432 a 8.   [2] Cf. Brentano, Psych. d. Arist. 28.
[3] Trendelenburg, Comm. in Arist. d. An.   [4] Ibid. 168.
[5] Ibid. 493.   [6] Ibid. 173.   [7] Ibid. 492.   [8] Ibid. 493.
[9] Ibid. 496.   [10] Ibid. 494, 495, 173.

[11] There is no science of principles: they are rather impossible of proof—even the νοῦς παθητικός cannot be the proof of them, for it depends upon the comparison of sensations, and we would have fallen into a vicious circle if we employed it. Therefore, there remains only the νοῦς ποιητικός, which apprehends the first principles by its own faculty.—So infered Trendelenburg, Comm. in Ar. d. An. 173.

[12] Met. XII. 7. 1072 b 18-30.

not develop from matter, but comes from without, i.e. is derived from God.[1] Trendelenburg is confident of the conformity of this thought with Aristotle's whole theory of the soul.[2]

Against this interpretation, Brentano at present points out one difficulty. In *De An.* III. 4, where Aristotle speaks only about the reason which becomes all things, he makes it belong to the ψύχη νοητική, unmixed with the body, separated from it, pure, and without matter. It is only in the beginning of the fifth chapter, that the νοῦς ποιητικός is introduced.[3]

Brandis also takes the νοῦς ποιητικός as belonging to the individual. It is the cognition of *per se* true and certain principles,[4] while the νοῦς παθητικός is a mediated thought.[5] Human reason is free from matter, but in so far as it derives the material for mediated thinking from sensation, i.e. in so far as it needs images for such thinking, it is called νοῦς παθητικός. It is neither simple nor eternal. Reason in the strict sense, i.e. the theoretical and actual reason, has its true being only when it is separated from the body. Man's proper self is founded upon it. That it acts upon us, means not that it is a manifestation in us of the universal world-spirit, but that it is independent of our body.[6]

Brentano prefers Brandis to Trendelenburg in admitting the reason which becomes all things to be human. But, on the other hand, he points out the difficulty in explaining why that reason that belongs to the rational part of the human soul should perish with the body, and why actual reason should not be a faculty of thinking, if it be not the divine reason but proper to individual souls; for to admit that such a reason always thinks would be contrary to experience, nor would it agree with Aristotle's theory.[7] Yet it cannot receive a thought anew, for such an act will belong rather to the reason that is in potentiality, of which it is said not that it becomes a mediated thought but that it becomes all things,[8] i.e. all the intelligibles, as Aristotle explained in the eighth chapter.[9]

---

[1] Comm. in Ar. de An. 492 f. [2] Ibid. 175.
[3] Ibid. 496. [4] Cf. Brentano, Psych. d. Arist. 31. n. 100.
[5] Brandis, Handbuch. II. 2. 2. 1177. [6] Ibid. 1178.
[7] Brandis, Die Entwicklung der griechischen Philosophie, 518.
[8] De An. III. 4. 430 a 5; An. Post. II. 19. 99 b 26.
[9] De An. III. 5. 430 a 14.

While these two interpretations approach that of Theophrastus in so far as they reduce the νοῦς ποιητικός to the individual, there is in the modern age another theory which resembles Alexander and Arabian philosophers. According to Ravaisson,[1] man has only passive reason. This is the universal potentiality in the world of ideas, just as the first matter is in the world of reality. On the contrary, the νοῦς ποιητικός is the absolute intelligence, or the creative act which actualizes all potential forms and brings forth all thoughts. This reminds us of Avicenna, except that he made all thoughts flow out directly from the *intelligentia agens*, while according to Ravaisson, Aristotle admits that one thought, as a secondary principle, arouses another thought in us, so that occasionally a higher substance should be thought of as the first mover. This, God himself, gives the principles directly, and from these principles all knowledge and all speculative thinking flow out. The divine wisdom gives also initial light to the distinction of good and bad, and gives to will the first impulse, so that virtue appears merely as an implement of absolute thought. In the further determination of the νοῦς, which is all things in potentiality, Ravaisson agrees almost completely with Alexander. The sensible principle is, at bottom, identical with the intellectual and intelligible principles. Hence reason also compares and distinguishes the abstract form, which is its proper object, with and from the sensible form. Thus the difference between sensation and reason is reduced to a distinction between the two sides of one being. Consequently reason is bound with the body in its existence, and nothing that is proper to man is immortal.

Brentano's criticism is as follows: Firstly, as aforesaid, the reason which becomes all things, i.e. the *intellectus possibilis*, would in this theory have to be the faculty of a bodily organ, and this is not compatible with Aristotle's own statements. If such a reason had been found in an organ, the power of the first mover would have reached this as well as it does sense. But it can bring nothing spiritual into a power which is mixed with matter. Further, if reason should be identical with sense, differing only in state, it would by no means be a power without actuality. Because when it seizes the first universal presentation, it would have to be preceded by sensation. If that were the case, Aristotle would assume the direct interference of God for the production of the first

[1] Ibid. 8. 431 b 22; cf. 4. 429 a 17; 429 b 30.

sensation rather than for the awaking of the first universal thought.

Among those who also take the νοῦς ποιητικός as the spirit which is separate from human nature, Renan found this theory to have a considerable resemblance to the view of Malebranche.[1] He could not find the theory compatible with the general spirit of the Peripatetic philosophy, and was compelled to assign it to another thinker. Aristotle might, he thought, have borrowed it from Anaxagoras, taking, however, little care about the contradiction that might result between this theory and the *Analytica* or even the *De Anima*.

Indeed, there would scarcely be any need for criticism of this interpretation, as Brentano observes. A primitive philosopher or an eclectic might have expressed such a fragmental idea, but we can by no means conceive that Aristotle, who was a most clear-minded and systematic philosopher, would have overlooked such an evident contradiction. It is, nevertheless, quite another problem to inquire about the origin of the idea of separate reason, or the νοῦς ποιητικός.

Zeller also takes the νοῦς ποιητικός as the universal spirit, or the absolute thingking of God. In this respect and herein alone, he might belong to the tradition of Averroism, as Brentano says. But it is doubtful whether he is any the more free from the same difficulties. According to Zeller,[2] the νοῦς ποιητικός is the universal spirit and the absolute thought of God. It is quite unique and thinks only itself. The thought of man, in so far as it has not developed from experience, is one and the same with this. Zeller points out, on the other hand, that Aristotle seems to have admitted that the νοῦς ποιητικός belongs also to individual souls;[3] but Brentano asks, implicitly, how is it possible that such a unique and indifferent reason should be the principle of human thinking. According to Brentano, Zeller has no means of explaining the reason that becomes all things, or the combination of it with the νοῦς ποιητικός, so that he finds himself compelled to attribute it to the bodily part like a sense;[4] yet on the other hand he is unable to deem it something material, and so censures Trendelenburg charging that he altered in this respect the theory of Aristotle.[5] Thus Brentano criticizes Zeller so severely as to

---

[1] Ravaisson, Essai s. l. metaph. d'Arist. I. 586 f.; cf. II. 17, 19.
[2] Renan, Averroès et l'Averroisme, 96.   [3] Zeller, Ph. d. Gr. II. 2. 567 ff.
[4] Ibid. 441 n. 3.   [5] Ibid. 443 n. 4.

judge his interpretation a queer misunderstanding without any merit. But the criticism seems to me somewhat party-spirited and even suspicious of ill feeling. That it is quite unreasonable, I shall endevour to show hereafter, examining the difficulties point by point.

§ 3. AGAINST BRENTANO'S INTERPRETATION

To begin with, we shall first take up Brentano's theory, which is a continuation and a development of St. Thomas' theory, as a position in radical opposition to our interpretation. Brentano admits, in Aristotle's passage, three concepts of reason instead of two; — νοῦς ποιητικός, νοῦς δυνάμει, and νοῦς παθητικός.[1] This does not mean, however, that there are three kinds of reason, reason in the proper sense, to which the human thinking faculty is to be attributed, should be confined to the potential or receptive reason. It is nothing more than a faculty which realizes itself in receiving forms.[3] The other two are reason only in an accidental sense.[2] Active reason is the active principle of human thinking, and belongs to the human soul, especially to the rational part of it. Hence it is called reason in an accidental sense.[4] It is identical with receptive reason *dem Subjekte nach*, but different *dem Sein nach*.[5] The receptive reason is potential, while the active reason is actual.[6] The former thinks, while the latter makes the other think.[7] The active reason acts at first upon the sensible part without consciousness, and making actual the rational forms which are involved in it potentially as φαντάσμα or images, gives them to the receptive reason. Thus the receptive reason realizes in itself an actual thought.[8] In short, the active reason acts directly upon the sensible part, and only indirectly upon the receptive reason. It follows that not only inseparability, impassiveness, and unmixedness, but also eternity and immortality, which we have considered to be the marks of active reason, are not limited to it, but common to human reason as well, and would be attributed primarily to receptive reason.[9]

---

[1] Ibid. 442 n. 1.   [2] Brentano, Psych. d. Arist. 143 ff.
[3] Ibid. 167, 175.   [4] Ibid. 170 ff.   [5] Ibid. 167.
[6] Ibid. 167, 178.   [7] Ibid. 204.   [8] Ibid. 147, 173.
[9] Ibid. 175 ff.

What, then, does the term "passive reason" mean? It is not the same as the receptive and potential reason, but is rather the φαντασία or imagination,[1] which acts as a medium when this reason thinks something. The passage "this is perishable", implies only the transiency of imagination, rather than the mortality of the rational part. Further, according to Brentano, besides the active reason, which is immanent in our mind, there is a divine reason, which thinks throughout eternity,[2] and not "sometimes thinks and sometimes does not". Active reason may be combined with the sensitive part only through this divine reason.[3]

We never mean to grudge due praise to the profound scholarship of Brentano, to say nothing of his great predecessor. Nor can we but admire their comprehensive demonstrations. It would seem to be their Christian prejudice that has led them to this scholastic misinterpretation, in spite of all their erudition and vigorous thinking. But this theory is so far-fetched as to be beyond any defence. We might sum up the differences between his interpretation and ours as follows. 1) We take reason throughout in the proper sense, while Brentano assumes both active reason and passive to be reason in an accidental sense, so that, strictly speaking, there would in his theory be no idea in Aristotle of the division of human reason. 2) We admit only active reason and passive reason and nothing more, at least in the passage in Aristotle under discussion. Potential reason is one and the same with passive reason, and active reason is divine as well as human, whereas Brentano treats active reason, potential reason, receptive reason and divine reason as quite different from each other. 3) We assign eternity, immortality, and unmixedness to active reason exclusively, taking these attributes as tantamount to the separability of the reason from the body. But Brentano considers them to be the attributes of human reason in general, especially that of receptive reason and potential reason. To us, what is immortal is only active reason, but to Brentano, each individual person is immortal.

"But, as in the whole of nature, there is on the one hand something which serves as matter for each kind (and this matter is potentially all the members of the kinds), while on the other there is something which serves as the cause or agent because it makes

---

[1] Ibid. 208. [2] Ibid. 182. [3] Ibid. 188.

them all, as e.g. the art is related to the matter which has been affected." In this sentence, in the first place, matter and potentiality, cause and agent, being identified with each other, the former two concepts are opposed to the latter two, while cause and agent might be taken, in the main, to be the same as form and actuality.[1] In the second place, this opposition is stated to be common to the whole of nature. We shall at once expect from this, that a given natural being will be divided into two moments, form and matter. That is to say, in the next proposition, one should have had to state that the natural organism is divided into matter and form (or "soul") before speaking of the opposite moments in the soul itself, considered as the "form of a natural being". Much less is it to be expected that Aristotle would so on at once to talk about this opposition in the reason as the formal moment of the soul. Whereas we find in the text, "These differences must exist, therefore, of necessity also in the soul", which demands at a stroke the difference of matter and form in the inner constitution of the soul. Then, immediately following this, it is said: "And so, while such a reason exists because it becomes all things, the other does because it makes them all, like a certain kind of *habitus* such as light." Here we seem to have yet another leap of argument, in which Aristotle applies this opposition even to the constitution of reason itself as a part of the soul, for in this last proposition, the reason which becomes all things is, no doubt, different from the reason that makes all things;—the former being material and potential, the latter corresponding of necessity to cause or agent.

It is not, however, difficult to resolve our doubts about such a double leap. One may indeed call it a leap, if one please, but the entire argument presupposes the fundamental uniformity of nature. The opposition of matter and form in nature is not absolute and discrete, but relative and continuous. What is form to one thing is matter to something else. The opposition is universal to all stages and areas of nature, and makes a continuous scale. In so far as such a universal principle is admitted in the first proposition, the leap is no more than an appearance. If one demand a formal completeness, the argument may be stated thus: since in the

[1] Form and matter are static concepts, while potentiality and actuality are dynamic, so they do not coincide with each other; form is not always actual, nor is matter always potential. Cf. p. 6, n. 6.

whole of nature there is the difference of matter and form, in living beings, body must be matter and soul form, and in soul, irrational parts are matter and reason is form; and so in the same way reason may be divided into the material and the formal.

We may note, incidentally, that, "such a reason", which becomes all things, refers, no doubt, to the reason which was discussed in the previous chapter, viz., that reason which receives forms. Hitherto, Brentano's theory has not conflicted with ours. But, thus considered, Aristotle is surely dividing the reason in the proper sense into two, and Brentano's theory must be condemned as constrained in taking the active reason to be reason in an accidental sense. He insists that active reason is not the reason in the proper sense, because it is the principle that makes others think, not the subject that thinks: it is called reason only because it is involved in the rational part of the human soul. But action is the actuality of the agent, no less than that of the patient, and thought is the actuality of that which makes one think, no less than that of the thinking subject.[1] Wherefore, admitting that the active principle of thought exists in the human soul, especially in the rational part of it, what, may we ask, is the active reason other than a kind of reason itself, or the essential moment of it? We can by no means understand that there should exist in the rational part something other than reason in the proper sense.

In our acquired knowledge, then, there are both the reason which receives forms and becomes all things, and the reason which makes all things. The one is matter and potential, while the other is cause and agent. The activity and actuality of the former reason is explained more clearly through the metaphor of light. "For light also in a certain way makes what are potential colours into actual colours."[2] Such being the case, there cannot be any

---

[1] Phys. III. 3. 202 a 13; De An. II. 2. 414 a 8, 25; III. 2. 426 a 16; 7. 431 a 1; 431 b 16.

[2] "What are potentially colours" means the sense, rather than a coloured body in darkness. It is true that a body has an actual colour through being seen, and that light is the principle that makes a body visible. Hence it seems as if we might as well say that it makes a body have an actual colour. But this is not correct. We must investigate the matter more carefully, examining Aristotle's own theory of vision.

De An. II. 7. 418 a 26-28: οὗ μὲν οὖν ἐστὶν ἡ ὄψις, τοῦτ' ἐστὶν ὁρατόν. ὁρατὸν δ' ἐστὶ χρῶμα μέν, καὶ δ λόγῳ μὲν ἔστιν εἰπεῖν, ἀνωνυμόν δὲ τυγχάνει ὄν· The secondary object which is said to have no name, means in reality the phosphores-

doubt what is meant by "this reason" in the following sentence: —"And *this reason* is separable, impassive, and unmixed, being in its substance actual." In contrast to the phrase "such a reason",

cent; cf. 419 a 3. But the primary object of sight is colour; 418 a 31-b 3: πᾶν δὲ χρῶμα κινητικόν ἐστι τοῦ κατ' ἐνέργειαν διαφανοῦς, καὶ τοῦτ' ἔστιν αὐτοῦ ἡ φύσις. διόπερ οὐχ ὁρατὸν ἄνευ φωτός, ἀλλὰ πᾶν τὸ ἑκάστου χρῶμα ἐν φωτὶ ὁρᾶται. Cf. also ibid. 419 a 9-11; 418 b 4-10. Though colour is seen through light, it is not light but colour that is active. It is not that colour is illuminated by light (i.e. is passive), and reflects on the eye (i. e. is active), but that colour acts immediately upon a transparent medium, light being its actuality, and through this acts upon the eys. The sequence of the visional sensation is colour—a transparent medium, i.e. light—eye.

Why, then, does it need a transparent medium or light ? Aristotle answers: ibid. 419 a 12-21: ἐὰν γάρ τις θῇ τὸ ἔχον χρῶμα ἐπ' αὐτὴν τὴν ὄψιν, οὐκ ὄψεται· ἀλλὰ τὸ μὲν χρῶμα κινεῖ τὸ διαφανές, οἷον τὸν ἀέρα, ὑπὸ τούτου δὲ συνεχοῦς ὄντος κινεῖται τὸ αἰσθητήριον. οὐ γὰρ καλῶς τοῦτο λέγει Δημόκριτος οἰόμενος, εἰ γένοιτο κενὸν τὸ μεταξύ, ὁρᾶσθαι ἂν ἀκριβῶς, καὶ εἰ μύρμηξ ἐν οὐρανῷ εἴη· τοῦτο γὰρ ἀδύνατόν ἐστιν. πάσχοντος γάρ τι τοῦ αἰσθητικοῦ γίνεται τὸ ὁρᾶν· ὑπ' αὐτοῦ μὲν οὖν τοῦ ὁρωμένου χρώματος ἀδύνατον· λείπεται δὴ ὑπὸ τοῦ μεταξύ, ὥστ' ἀναγκαῖόν τι εἶναι μεταξύ· κενοῦ δὲ γενομένου οὐχ ὅτι ἀκριβῶς ἀλλ' ὅλως οὐθὲν ὀφθήσεται.

Colour cannot oct directly upon the eye; it acts only indirectly through giving colour to a transparent medium. It is true also with smelling, hearing, and all other sensations whatsoever. Cf. ibid.419 a 25-30; 421 b 17 ff.; 418 b 26-419 a 1. The transparent can mediate between colour and the eye, only when it is actualized into light. Light is the actuality of the substance which is involved in the heavenly bodies or in the air, the water, etc., i.e. the actuality of αἰθήρ; cf. De An. II. 7. 418 b 9-13; De Sensu 3. 439 a 16 ff. It is the colour itself, that acts upon the transparent and makes light in a certain sense colour, but that which makes the transparent actually what it is, is not light but fire. Light is the actuality of the transparent which is actualized by fire. So colour is seen only in light. But, ibid. 419 a 23-25: πῦρ δὲ ἐν ἀμφοῖν ὁρᾶται, καὶ ἐν σκότει καὶ ἐν φωτί, καὶ τοῦτο ἐξ ἀνάγκης· τὸ γὰρ διαφανὲς ὑπὸ τούτου γίνεται διαφανές.

Such was Aristotle's concept of light, to which the active reason was compared. Active reason was said to "make all things, like a ἕξις such as light". Now ἕξις is an active power which is founded upon an actual thing; cf. p. 6, n. 6. As regards light, it is the function of a transparent medium. This medium is acted on by fire and colour, and acts upon the eye. Therefore, the active reason which is compared to light, would act upon the passive reason rather than upon the object. Brentano does not lose sight of this essential idea, we must admit. But in order to maintain his interpretation that the active reason acts upon image (φάντασμα) and actualizes the rational forms which are potentially included in it, he emphasizes the word τρόπον τινα, and diminishes the actuality of active reason. This is after all a distortion: cf. Brentano, op. cit. 173.

which occurs previously, this refers to the active reason exclusively, which acts as an active principle like light. But it is otherwise with Brentano. Even St. Thomas and Brentano do not deny that "this reason" indicates the active reason, but they read it somewhat arbitrarily as "even this reason", and, pointing out that separability, impassiveness, and unmixedness are attributed to the potential reason no less than to the active,[1] restrict the proper attribute of the latter only to actuality. Indeed in the fourth chapter and elsewhere, these three characteristics are attributed to reason in general, and reason is mainly defined as the faculty of receiving forms. Still we must remind ourselves that Aristotle divides the reason into the active and the potential only in this one place. From the fact that these characters are attributed in other places to mere reason, we can by no means conclude that they are common both to the active reason and the passive. The attributes which were assigned vaguely to reason in general, when it is taken as a simple entity, might be limited to the active reason, when it is divided into parts.[2] And this would be the conclusion we would expect in Aristotle, who following Plato, at first admitted these attributes and immortality, to soul in general; then limited them to reason alone, and yet recognized that the action of reason refers to body through imagination; such a conclusion is the one he should naturally have arrived at in order to avoid contradiction. It seems to support our interpretation, that the passage in question has such a definite expression as "this reason"; and the actuality of this reason seems to be stated rather as the ground of the other attributes, than as a mere coordinate member.[3] Strictly speaking, what is separable, impassive, and unmixed is confined to the actual or active reason. It seems to us that there is a remarkable discrepancy between the fourth and fifth chapters of the *De Anima*, and it is impossible for us to understand them coherently as expressing the same thought. On account of such an unfortunate attempt, Brentano was led to mistake the real meaning of the fifth chapter. We should like to take this chapter as the last attempt by Aristotle to resolve the difficulties in the notion of reason which are not reconciled in the fourth chapter and elsewhere.

---

[1] Brentano, op. cit. 175; De An. III. 4. 429 b 5; a 5, 15, 29, 18, 24. Brentano reads this sentence "*Auch dieser Verstand ist frei vom Körper usw.*"; but in this case the text should be καὶ οὗτος δὲ ὁ νοῦς χωριστὸς κτλ.; cf. Zeller, op. cit. 571. n. 2.   [2] Zeller, op. cit. 577 n. 2.   [3] Cf. Hicks's note *ad loc.*

But suppose we grant his contention that separability, impassiveness, and unmixedness are the attributes of reason in general. Presumably, this case, separability means, as it is usually understood to mean, real separability from the body, impassiveness, not being affected by the body; and unmixedness, not coexisting with the body; so interpreted, Brentano's contention would contradict with the fact that the action of reason for Aristotle relates to the body through the medium of imagination, as it is passive through receiving the forms of objects, and consequently coexists with the body. In order to be rid of this difficulty, Brentano is obliged to take the meaning of these attributes quite in a different way. Namely, according to him, χωριστός means here not separability from the body, but real separateness, and indicates the fact that the action of reason is not founded upon the body. And ἀπαθές means not that the active reason is impassive, but that it is unchangeable and does not lose its essence. Also, ἀμιγής means not that it does not coexist with the body, but has either the same meaning as the "separateness" (χωριστός), or means that active reason, being pure actuality, does not mix with potential beings, while receptive reason, being pure potentiality, does not mix with actual beings. However ingenious this interpretation might be, its unnaturalness is indefensible.[1] Taking χωριστός as actual separateness, it would indeed be difficult to attribute it to reason,[2] but in fact it is separability rather than separateness. Whenever Aristotle merely uses the term χωριστός with reference to reason, he means thereby almost without exception real separability from the body. Even if we allow Brentano to interpret this term as meaning that the function of reason is not founded upon the body, still, since it is a fundamental supposition of Aristotle that

[1] Brentano, op. cit. 177 f.
[2] Since Brentano takes it as actual separation, he feels difficulty in the sentence: χωρισθεὶς δ' ἐστὶ μόνον ὅπερ ἐστί κτλ. If it were read as separation, it would be incomprehensible that here again the expression "when separated" should appear in a discussion of the active reason. In so far as one takes the word χωριστός as "being in its activity independent of the body," one would avoid the difficulty. For what is χωριστός in this special meaning, may be separated from the body after death. But if such were the real meaning of χωριστός, it would be nonsense, if not a paradox, to say that reason is separated after death. We should rather take the word χωριστός as "separable", i.e. potentially separate. This is confirmed by De An. III. 7. 431 b 17: ἆρα δ' ἐνδέχεται τῶν κεχωρισμένων τι νοεῖν ὄντα αὐτὸν μὴ κεχωρισμένον μεγέθους, ἢ οὔ, κτλ. Here, reason is no doubt not separated actually from the body.

the soul is separable from the body if there be any function of the soul which is independent of the body, it follows that Brentano could not but arrive at the conclusion that reason is really separable from the body.[1] Furthermore, as far as reason presupposes of necessity imagination, Brentano's interpretation that the function of reason is not founded upon the body is inadmissible from the beginning. If we restrict ἀπαθές to the sense of signifying that a thing does not lose its essence through passivity, such an "apathy" will cease to be a property exclusively of reason, and will be predicable even of the sensible faculties.[2] Last of all, the concept ἀμιγής is primarily borrowed from Anaxagoras, and Aristotle almost always mentions Anaxagoras when he uses this word; we should therefore understand it in the original sense it has in Anaxagoras. In this sense, however, it means the unmixedness of reason with the body and its pure separability from the body.[3] Finally, we must emphasize the following results: If we can get rid of the contradiction above mentioned by interpreting, as Brentano does, these attributes in the negative sense, then reason as a whole, comprising the active and the passive,

[1] De An. I. 1. 403 a 10 f.: εἰ μὲν οὖν ἐστί τι τῶν τῆς ψυχῆς ἔργων ἢ παθημάτων ἴδιον ἐνδέχοιτ' ἂν αὐτὴν χωρίζεσθαι·—Of course, χωρίζεσθαι ἐνδέχεται is potential separation.

[2] De An. III. 7. 431 a 4 f.: φαίνεαι δὲ τὸ μὲν αἰσθητὸν ἐκ δυνάμει ὄντος τοῦ αἰσθητικοῦ ἐνεργείᾳ ποιοῦν· οὐ γὰρ πάσχει οὐδ' ἀλλοιοῦται. Thus, Brentano's attempt to distinguish ἀπαθές and οὐ πάσχει, and to admit only the latter to reason, is not successful. Further, ibid. III. 4. 429 a 29 f.: ὅτι δ' οὐχ ὁμοία ἡ ἀπάθεια τοῦ αἰσθητικοῦ καὶ τοῦ νοητικοῦ, κτλ. Here the impassivity of sense is surely distinguished from that of intellect; sense is impassive, none the less. But this distinction is not the same as the following one. Ibid. II. 5. 417 b 2-5: οὐκ ἔστι δ' ἁπλοῦν οὐδὲ τὸ πάσχειν, ἀλλὰ τὸ μὲν φθορά τις ὑπὸ τοῦ ἐναντίου, τὸ δὲ σωτηρία μᾶλλον τοῦ δυνάμει ὄντος ὑπὸ τοῦ ἐντελεχείᾳ ὄντος καὶ ὁμοίου οὕτως ὡς δύναμις ἔχει πρός ἐντελέχειαν. Both sense and intellect are ἀπαθές in the former sense, as is evident from the statement in 431 a 4, and yet passive in the latter sense. The difference, in truth, consists in that the intellect is separable from the body: ibid. III. 4. 429 b 3-5. Consequently, intellect is particularly impassive, because it does not differ from the body, and such an intellect must be, strictly speaking, the active reason. Hence Zeller assumes this to be, in reality, a remark about the active reason. Cf. Zeller, op. cit. 571. n. 2.

[3] Anaxagoras, Fr. 12; cf. Met. I. 8. 989 b 15; Phys. VIII. 5. 256 b 25; De An. I. 2. 405 a 17. None of the proofs that Nuyens presents against this view, is persuasive (op. cit. 285). Cf. also Gen. An. II. 3. 736 b 28: οὐθέν γὰρ αὐτοῦ τῇ ἐνεργείᾳ κοινωνεῖ σωματικὴ ἐνέργεια, which undoubtedly implies that νοῦς is not mixed with the body.

would be really inseparable from the body, and we should arrive at the ironical result that there cannot be any real separability among the parts of the soul. For, he insists that these are all attributes of reason in general, and that none of them signifies real separability from the body. Instead of overcoming the difficulties, this will only lead to the absolute denial of the desired conclusion as to separability of reason and the real separability of a part of the soul. Yet this very conclusion was absolutely necessary for St. Thomas and Brentano. Hence it is not only necessary for us to keep the unique status of active reason, but it was also necessary for St. Thomas and Brentano to give up their interpretation if they were to reach the conclusion they must reach.

The above discussion would be enough to prove that "this reason", which "is separable, impassive, and unmixed being in its substance actual", should be the active reason, and this only. This is confirmed also by the succeeding proposition in the text: "For that which acts is always superior to that which is acted upon, as principle is to matter." We cannot explain why he asserts here the superiority of the agent to the patient, unless we take the subject of the above mentioned attributes to be active reason and make these words explain the unique status of this reason as against the potential and material reason.[1] We should also notice that the correlative concepts of "patient" and "matter" stand in the same contrast to "agent" and "principle", as do those of "matter" and "potentiality" to "cause" and "agent". So far, on the other hand, our investigation has concerned opposition between the reason which becomes all things and the reason which makes all things. From the above data, we must conclude as follows:

[1] According to Brentano, to talk about the primacy of active reason is meaningful only if one presupposes the immortality of reason in general; viz., since reason is, as a whole, immortal, it is meaningful to add, "so much the more is the active reason immortal". If, on the contrary, we should interpret this as meaning that the passive reason is mortal, but as the active principle is superior to the passive principle, the active reason is thus also immortal, it would then appear as if there were no difference as to immortality between them; cf. Brentano, Aristoteles Lehre vom Ursprung des menschlichen Geistes, 6, n. But, this does not of necessity lead to such a conclusion. Whether there is difference of degree as to immortality or not, it matters nothing. What is necessary is to admit that immortality is a suitable attribute of the superior being. Superiority is a *conditio sine qua non* of immortality, though not its sufficient condition. Aristotle neither admits superiority to be the sufficient condition, nor is it his duty to mention it.

potential reason is the matter, the patient, and the reason which becomes all things, while active reason is the principle, the cause, the agent, and the reason which makes all things. This conclusion will be relevant, when we argue as to the identity of the passive reason and the potential reason.

We must suspend awhile the above line of reasoning, for the next proposition which we find in the text seems to be in all respects an interpolation. In so far as we take the above arguments to have been made about the opposition of the active and the passive reason, we cannot repress the feeling of suddenness in the sentence: "Now actual knowledge is identical with the object of knowing, but potential knowledge is prior in time in the individual, though considered as a whole, it is not prior in time."[1] This actual knowledge would imply sort of contemplation which was opposed previously to knowledge as habit, and not the habitual knowledge of a scholar as distinguished from the possible knowledge in an ignorant person;[2] whereas the active and the potential reason are the principles of such actual thinking, but not the actual knowledge itself. Why then, should one inquire about actual knowledge in particular? St. Thomas says that Aristotle, changing his argument at this point, takes both active and potential reason together as potential knowledge, and asks then about actual knowledge.[3] If the text is thus understood, the next statement must be applied exclusively to actual knowledge. Not only does actual knowledge have absolute precedence over potential knowledge, but also the determination, "It is not at one time thinking and at another not", should be predicated of actual knowledge rather than of active reason. Nevertheless, it would be, for us, a superfluous expression, if not nonsense, to say that actual knowledge is "not at one time thinking and at another not". This sentence, therefore, should be taken somewhat differently than as a clarification of "actual knowledge". Now we have learnt from Aristotle, that God is that reason which continues thinking, and that in which a human being partakes through contemplation from time to time;[4] and we also know that the ground of this tem-

---

[1] Themistius substituted ἁπλῶς for ὅλως. This reading is surely more natural but sometimes ὅλως is used synonymously with ἁπλῶς; cf. Hicks's note ad loc.
[2] De An. II. 5. 417 a 22-29; cf. Met. XII. 9. 1074 b 38 ff.
[3] St. Thomas, De An. Comm. 740-742.
[4] Met. XII. 7. 1072 b 14-16; ibid. 24-26. 1075 a 7-9: ὥσπερ ὁ ἀνθρώπινος νοῦς ἢ ὅ γε τῶν συνθέτων ἔχει ἔν τινι χρόνῳ οὕτως δ' ἔχει αὐτὴ αὑτῆς ἡ νόησις τὸν ἅπαντα αἰῶνα, οὐ γὰρ ἔχει τὸ εὖ ἐν τῳδὶ ἢ ἐν τῳδί, ἀλλ' ἐν ὅλῳ τινὶ τὸ

porality of human thinking was called in question at the end of the fourth chapter,[1] which precedes immediately to the statement at issue. Consequently, we must take the subject of the sentence, "It is not at one time thinking and at another not " as the being which somehow surpasses the temporality of a human being. This, I dare say, is the active reason. Only thus are we able to understand the connection with the next sentence: "It is only when it is separated that it is just what it is, and this alone is immortal and eternal." But herein again, Brentano's opinion is opposed to ours. He also conceives that which "is not at one time thinking and at another not", to be the divine reason, but he assumes this reason to be actual knowledge[2] rather than the active reason. The latter is not divine, because it exists in the human mind. Accordingly, the paraphrasis of St. Thomas would be neither nonsensical nor superfluous as we have criticized, but the very expression of the eternal thinking of the divine reason.

At this point, both for St. Thomas and Brentano, the statement about divine reason has come to an end. The next sentence: "It is only when it is separated that it is just what it is, and this alone is immortal and eternal", can by no means be admitted by them as a statement about the divine reason. Divine reason was distinguished from active reason in that the former is transcendent, and the latter immanent. But that reason which comes to its proper ἄριστον, ὂν ἄλλο τι. I prefer Ross's reading to Bonitz's; Ross inserts γάρ after ὥσπερ, omits the ἤ after νοῦς, and substitutes δή for δε after οὕτως. But I would transpose the words and posit ὥσπερ...... ὂν ἄλλο τι after οὕτως...,αἰῶνα,—not as an interrogative sentence. This does not, as Bonitz and Schwegler suppose, concern discursive thinking and intuition, but rather as in Ross's interpretation, it has to do with the thinking activities of the divine and human reasons. And according to my transposition, οὐ γάρ...ὂν ἄλλο τι would be the statement about divine thinking. Thus ἐν τινι χρόνῳ corresponds to ἐν τῳδὶ ἢ ἐν τῳδί, and τὸν ἅπαντα αἰῶνα, to ἐν ὅλῳ τινί. Further, οὐ γάρ...ὂν ἄλλο τι would correspond to the sentence in question, viz., De An. III. 5. 430 a 22 f.: ἀλλ' οὐχ ὁτὲ μὲν νοεῖ ὁτὲ δ' οὐ νοεῖ...καὶ τοῦτο μόνον ἀθάνατον καὶ ἀΐδιον. Thus I would translate the above quotation as follows: — "Just as human reason or the reason of a composite being is in a certain period of time, so is the (divine) self-thought throughout eternity, for since this (i.e. divine reason) is different from that (i.e. human reason), it enjoys the good not just in this or in that period, but the best in the whole.

[1] De An. III. 4. 430 a 5.
[2] Brentano, op. cit. 182. De Corte also follows this interpretation: cf. La doctrine de l'intelligence chez Aristote, 65, 69; cf. also Nuyens's criticism on this point. op. cit. 33 f.

being only when it is separated would obviously have to be in the state of combination with the body till then. Needless to say, such a reason cannot be the divine reason, which is absolutely transcendent. Nevertheless St. Thomas and Brentano would not be content to make it merely the active reason, for they have attributed separability, immortality etc., not only to active reason, but also to reason in general. It follows that, for them, the subject of this sentence must be nothing other than human reason in general. Thus, according to their interpretation, this chapter speaks at first about the active and the potential reason (450a 10-19), then turns to the opposition between actual knowledge and potential knowledge or human reason (19-22), and then returns again to the problem of human reason in general. But we can hardly consent that Aristotle might be dealing in such a short statement with such manifold themes, while saying nothing about the subject of these themes. The matter would be somewhat improved, if there were either the idea of divine reason being distinct from active reason, or at least some evidence of such a distinction. But we cannot find any such evidence except certain somewhat incomprehensible references to actual knowledge. Brentano's argument about the distinction between the active and the divine reason is too weak to be examined. For its refutation, it will be enough to point out the fact that to say nothing of active reason, even human reason is said to be divine. Reason, even that of a human being, is essentially divine.[1] Active reason is not deprived of divinity because of its being in the human soul. It is transcendent as well as immanent, human as well as divine.[2] Otherwise, man would be unable to think. Man thinks only through being illuminated by divine reason. Man thinks in God, while God realizes His thought in man. I would neither deny the difference between the divine and the human reason, nor make the active reason directly equal

[1] De An. I. 4. 408 b 29; Eth. Nic. X. 7. 1177 a 15; b 30.
[2] Eth. Nic. X. 7. 1177 a 13-17; 1177 b 26-1178 a 3; Met. XII. 10. 1075 a 11-15. De Corte argues that as the active reason is said to be in the soul, if it were assumed to be the subject of eternal thinking, there must be human thinking which is eternal and continues without interruption (op. cit. 66). I would not align myself with Nuyens in maintaining that Aristotle's statement at issue does not amount to saying that the active reason is in the (human) soul. Rather I would combine these opposite views by assuming that this does not necessarily prevent our supposing the active reason to depart some times from the human soul and exist independently; cf. Nuyens, op. cit. 34.

to the reason of God, but only reject the abstract thought which divides them absolutely. In short, the subject of the propositions in question must be conceived to be the divine active reason, which is immanent as well as transcendent. Consequently, against the scholastic interpretation of St. Thomas and Brentano, we conclude that the clause about actual knowledge is an interpolation.[1]

Then, next in the text, we encounter the sentence: "We do not remember, because it is impassive." Since the verb remember takes the nominative plural form, "reason" cannot be the grammatical subject. Accordingly, former interpreters considered the subject to be ourselves, and argued whether the object should be the eternal action of active reason or its life before birth and after death.[2] Thus understood, the plural subject of the denied remembrance, is either the passive reason or a part of the concrete soul which has body, e.g. imagination. But then, the impassiveness of active reason, which is here deemed to be the object, would not be the ground why the subject of this memory does not remember the action of such a reason. The condition of memory is that its

---

[1] This is not an arbitrary omission. The same sentence is found also in ch. 7. 431 a 1, which is its proper position. It is possible that it appears here out of place, and that ch. 7 is its source. So also Kampfe, Kail, and Susemihl.

[2] Hicks takes this to be that we individuals who are born and will die, do not remember the eternal act of active reason, because active reason is impassive and cannot be the object of memory. But this proves nothing, since what memory requires is the passivity of the subject, rather than that of the object. Further, he does not take account of temporality as a condition of memory, but if memory be taken as a kind of consciousness, to know God and to participate in His eternal thinking would in itself be to remember the active reason.

The following interpretations supplement the first, by taking account of temporality. According to Trendelenburg, man does not now remember the fact that the active reason had thought in the previous state of existence. But as man comes into existence with his birth, it is merely a matter of course that he does not remember the facts when he did not exist. That the active reason is impassive explains nothing about this fact. The third interpretation is one held by many commentators from early times; according to it, man does not remember the fact that the active reason might continue to exist after death. But as far as the subject of memory is a particular man, there cannot be any memory whatsoever after his death, and the impassivity of the active reason gives no more account of absence of memory; memory about future life is a *contradictio in adjecto*. There is a fourth theory that explains this with reference to the decline of memory through old age. Cf. De An. I. 4. 408 b 27. This is held by Plutarchus, and is partly adopted by Brentano, but it is less probable. If this were the real meaning, memory would be absent not because the active reason is impassive, but because the passive reason is mortal. And we sould state not that we do not remember, but that we forget.

subject should be a part of the soul which is conjoined with bodily changes, rather than that its object should be passive. For instance, we remember a poem, because our body reserves the impressions which were affected through the recital, and the soul is acted upon by these reserved impressions. There is no need of this poem itself being somehow passive. Therefore, the real subject of this remembrance would be ourselves as the active reason.[1] This is not impossible, in so far as we do not deny the immanence of active reason. Active reason does not remember, because it is impassive, while memory is possible only when the soul is acted upon through the body. Thus, both what does not remember and what is impassive are the active reason. It is not passive in so far as it is an *active* reason: it is not affected through bodily changes. Consequently, it has neither imagination nor memory. Nothing can be more evident to us, than this. But not so for St. Thomas and Brentano; this, however, is not to be wondered at, for they considered previously that reason in general is eternal and immortal, while the reason which is said to be impassive, must, either from the construction of the sentence or from the context of meaning be the same as this reason. But it seems that Brentano does not identify "ourselves" who do not remember with the reason itself. We may think that reason in general, being impassive, does not remember. But if that is all, it does not matter whether reason itself is immortal or not, since reason is never the subject of memory, in whatever state it may be. We cannot admit any particular need of mentioning here that it does not remember. This somewhat ambiguous interpretation of Brentano's might be expatiated as

[1] We may confirm the conjecture by referring to other descriptions of memory. According to De An. I. 4. 408 b 27, the reason does not remember because it is impassive. Also in De Memor. 1. 450 a 12, memory requires that the subject should have sense, the object being out of the question. It is true that De Memor. 1. 450 a 24 concerns the object, viz., καὶ ἔστι μνημονευτὰ καθ' αὑτὰ μὲν ὅσα ἐστὶ φανταστά, κατὰ συμβεβηκὸς δὲ ὅσα μὴ ἄνευ φαντασίας. But with this condition, not only the active reason, but also the passive reason cannot be the object of memory. For to say that the passive reason does not think without imagination, is not the same as to say that the passive reason itself cannot exist without imagination. That a potential being would have no memory if memory were the function of pure reason, means that the transcendent reason or the so-called active reason is not the subject of memory rather than that the passive reason which is accompanied by the body, cannot make such an independent reason the object of memory. Zeller's opinion, though implicitly, seems to agree with us; cf. op. cit. 572.

follows:[1] —It is not just reason but concrete individuals, that do not remember. Man consists of immortal reason and mortal soul together with the body which is also perishable. Though the reason in us is immortal, its eternal life is by no means remembered by us. Because, on the one hand, this reason itself, being impassive, is not the subject of memory, but on the other hand, the part of the soul which is the subject of memory, is mortal, so that we may enjoy our life as long as we live in this world; the reason before birth and after death neither remembers itself nor can it be the object of memory. This is supported, as we shall state afterwards, through identifying passive reason, which is mortal, with imagination, which was regarded by Aristotle as the subject of memory. This interpretation does not of necessity conflict with Aristotle's theory, if we may allow the supposition that the impassive reason which is immortal and eternal is the receptive reason of man, while the passive reason which is mortal is imagination or the faculty of *sensus communis*, which is quite different from this receptive reason.

The assertion that reason generally does not remember, may sound strange to the ears of those who think consciousness to be the essence of reason, and memory to be the necessary condition of consciousness. Nevertheless, we cannot deny that Brentano's interpretation is, in this respect only, very surely grounded upon Aristotle. According to Aristotle, memory, as well as love, hatred, and reasoning, are not attributes of reason itself, but of the concrete individual, who possesses it.[2] Memory concerns itself not only with the object of sensation,[3] but also with that of reason, and

---

[1] Brentano, op. cit. 207-209.   [2] De An. I. 4. 408 b 25-28.

[3] De Memor. 1. 450 a 12-16. The direct object of memory is not concept, but image. Since, however, the soul does not think without image (De Memor. 1. 449 b 30; De An. III. 7. 431 a 17), the object of thought may be accidentally the object of memory (De Memor. 2. 451 a 28 f.). The object of thought accompanies memory through being accompanied by image. Image is *per se* the object of memory, while concept is so only *per accidens* (De Memor. 1. 450 a 23). Considered from the side of the subject, memory is concerned directly with image, and only indirectly with concepts. Consequently, memory is impossible without image. While concepts are universal and eternal, memory is a habitual state of special experience, and the mere acceptance of concepts might well be thought, but is never memory (De Memor. 1. 451 a 1). One and the same instance of thinking, in so far as it is seen as the recept of an eternal concept, is contemplation; but in so far as it is seen as the recognition of a past experience, it is memory: De Memor. 1. 449 b 24 f.; 450 b 24-27; 451 a 26. The

even in this latter case, it cannot act without imagination.[1] Whereas imagination is a mode of common sensation, memory belongs primarily to the first sensible faculty or *sensus communis*,[2] though sometimes it is attributed accidentally to reason. It follows that memory is not confined to the human being who has opinion and prudence, but also is found in some other animals. If it

subject which accepts eternal concepts being the passive reason, that which has special and temporal facts as its object, is the imaginative faculty. The thinking which appears as the object of such a subject might be said to be one sort of image. What one remembers is that he has experienced, not the contents of thought itself. The contents of thought are remembered only accidentally. De Memor. 1. 449 b 18-23.

[1] De Memor. 1. 450 a 12 f. But strictly speaking, it is not sufficient to prove that memory is the act of the imaginative faculty, in so far as we say that memory is impossible without image. For that statement may be applied to thought as well; and indeed, it actually is so applied: De Memor. 1. 449 a 31, or De An. III. 7. 431 a 17. If we should assign memory to the imaginative faculty, only because it cannot act without image, from the same ground we should assign reason to imaginative faculty. But even in the case of human thinking, which cannot occur without image, reason is by no means merely a function of the imaginative faculty. It ought rather to be the function of the passive reason. Therefore, there must be a differentia. Aristotle does not explicitly mention it. But presumably this is because thinking concerns the universal, while memory has to do with special sensible forms. In other words, thinking is only mediated by image, while memory is directly concerned with image and does not go further (cf. De Memor. 1. 450 a 23). As mentioned above, even if the object of thought be the object of memory, it is not so *per se* but *per accidens*. The object of thought may be, in a sense, image, only because image which acts as the medium is the object of memory.

[2] Cf. ch. II. 2. In short, imagination is a habit (De Somn. 2. 459 a 24), of receiving impressions upon soul and body through sensation or thinking. (De An. III.3. 428 b 10. 30. De Somn. 1. 459 a 17). It is, so to say, a weakened sensation (Rhet. I. 11. 1370 a 28); sensation, however, refers to an actually existent corporeal substance, or to a being which has matter, while imagination is something like the remnant of a sensation, which can exist without object (De Somn. 2. 460 b 7), being itself deprived of matter (De An. III. 8. 432 a 9). When this imagination is referred to a past experience, it becomes the object of memory (p. 45, n. 2, 3). So, imagination presupposes sensation, but is not identical with it. In as much as imagination is not universal like thought, it is similar to sensation (De An. III. 8. 432 a 9), and it is assumed to be a function of the sensitive faculty (De Somn. 1. 459 a 16). But, a special sense feels a special sensation with a special object; it is by no means the faculty of keeping experiences or of comparing and discriminating them. Such an immediate regulative faculty of sensations must be universal, for all its sensible character. This is the so-called *sensus communis*, which is also called the first sense, in indication of its superiority to

belonged to the rational part, most animals would have no memory,[1] whereas in fact, most, if not all, of them do remember. This being Aristotle's own remark, there remains no doubt that memory was considered not to be a function of reason in general, much less of the active reason. In this respect, it might seem more faithful to understand the phrase "οὐ μνημονεύομεν δέ" as Brantano did,

other senses. It is placed in the heart as the central organ of the body, on account of its uniting function (De Juvent. 3. 469 a 5). Aristotle, feeling a difficulty in the orientation of imagination, assigned it to *sensus communis*, with some hesitation.

[1] Cf. De Memor. 1. 450 a 12 ff. We might doubt whether it is right to deny that memory is the essential act of the rational part. In this argument, memory is ranked with love, hatred, and thought, but thought is no doubt an act of reason. Thinking, as well as memory, cannot act without imagination, to be sure. Therefore, if one says, for this reason alone, that memory is not a function of the rational part, he must also admit that thinking likewise is not its function. Such a rational part is hardly a human intellect. We find a statement which perhaps proves this. In succession to the observation that if memory were a function of the rational part, most animals would have no memory, it is said, according to the traditional text, ibid. 450 a 18: ἴσως δ' οὐδενὶ τῶν θνητῶν. If memory were a function of the rational part, how could it be that what is mortal does not have memory at all? Man is mortal, yet it has intellect. An act which a mortal rational being cannot partake in, is certainly not human. Aristotle would have implied herewith that intellectual activity in the proper sense is beyond human intellect, which is accompanied by the body. But human thinking is, of course, the act of human intellect. Consequently, the proper act of intellect would not be human thinking. Such a pure intellect would not be the subject of human thinking. Thus understood, the intellect which cannot be the subject of memory should be a transcendent pure reason. Thus, in so far as this premiss is concerned, we may infer that what does not remember is just this active reason. Now let us remind ourselves that it is only in De An. III. 5 that Aristotle divided reason clearly into the active and the passive. In De Memor., it is taken as a whole to be a divine faculty. It is natural enough that memory, which was thus excluded from reason, should find no refuge except in *sensus communis*. But now, when reason is divided into the active and the passive, the latter being perishable and affected in a manner by the body, it is doubtful whether the memory should be shut out from this passive reason. Passive reason is a mental faculty which is combined with the body through imagination. It was the refuge for Thinking, who had been banished with Memory from Reason, under the same pretext that they had some connection with Imagination. In that case, Memory, once compelled to lodge, in the Imaginative Part, might be accepted in the new home of Passive Reason, who has already become independent of his stern father. Moreover, there is in imagination the intellectual as well as the sensible (De An. III. 10. 433 b 28), and knowledge is considered to be, in a sense, memory (De Memor.

to mean that reason in general does not remember, than to restrict the subject to active reason. But we must at first call attention to the fact, that though active reason does not remember because of its impassivity, it does not follow that passive reason should remember because of its passivity. As the inversion of "All the impassive do not remember", is not "All the passive remember", but rather "Some passive remember", passive reason does not necessarily remember, though it is passive, just as the nutritive part does not remember, though it is none the less passive.

Our opinion at no point contradicts this idea of Aristotle's. One might, however, raise another objection to it: If memory is not the function of reason in general, it would be in all respects unnatural to observe in particular that active reason does not remember because it is impassive. To this objection we answer as follows: Aristotle is not asking here what the subject of memory is, but why, in spite of the immortality and eternity of active reason, its imperishable action is not accompanied by memory. Therefore, there is no difficulty in supposing him to be saying that the active reason does not remember, even though not remembering is not confined to the active reason. Besides, for his purpose, it is by no means necessary to deny every positive and sufficient condition one after another, but enough to mention a negative condition, i.e., that it cannot be the subject of memory.

We will not assert that memory either is or should be, the act of passive reason, but will be content with proving merely that the real subject of οὐ μνημονεύομεν δέ is active reason. I believe we have succeeded through the above arguments in making clear that this is at least as probable a hypothesis as that of Brentano. But hitherto we have only compared our interpretations, while accepting the assumption that, in accordance with Brentano's theory, the immortal, imperishable, and impassive reason is the receptive

---

1. 499 b 18). Then, is it not possible that at least such a rational and intellectual memory is a function of the passive reason? Concerning the passive reason, we have no detailed explanation except the statement in question, where it is contrasted with the active reason. Besides, Biehl replaces θνητῶν in the above quotation, with θηρίον. This revision makes our interpretation impossible. Yet it appears to be quite plausible, so I do not demand for my conjecture any value more than that of a mere hypothesis. Speaking more moderately, passive reason would be different from the imaginative faculty in that its objects are universal concepts, while memory, being the reproduction of imagination, belong to a subject different from passive reason.

reason of man, whereas passive reason means the imagination, which is quite a different thing. Brentano's theory owed its plausibility to this assumption, to which we can by no means consent. According to Brentano, receptive reason means the faculty of accepting the rational form which had been involved in the image and was realized through a power, called active reason, which, however, is not the reason in the proper sense. This receptive reason is itself an indefinite faculty of knowledge, or a passive potentiality of receiving infinite numbers of forms—the intellect as *tabula rasa* which reappears in Locke's philosophy. It acts only in dependence upon imagination, which, on its part, is inseparable from the body. What, then, is meant by such a reason's being immortal and imperishable? That the reason which cannot act without body, not only persists after death, but also just then exists in its real state, would mean that what never acts exists eternally, and that it is just its never acting that is the real state of it. This reason would have to be a complete *tabula rasa* with no form of its own, or a complete potentiality which has no actual form. To say that such a reason exists separately, would mean that what has no actual form exists by itself. What an absurd idea it is to talk about an eternal being without form, and to make it a divine reason that comes from outside to the finite human being! As Aristotle has said, "If it thinks nothing, what is there here of dignity? Such a reason would be just like one who sleeps."[1] What is then the course of thought whereby Brentano takes the passive reason for imagination? To us, who understood the reason which is immortal, impassive, and hence does not remember, to be the active reason, the clause "ὁ δὲ παθητικὸς νοῦς φθαρτός" is nothing but an appropriate opposition to it. Active reason is impassive and immortal, while passive reason is mortal. Whereas according to Brentano, passive reason is immortal no less than active reason. That it is ἀπαθές means not that it suffers no influence from body, but that it does not lose its essence through being acted upon. Thus understood, without doubt, the clause "ὁ δὲ παθητικὸς νοῦς φθαρτός" loses its actual significance utterly; the impassivity of actual reason is diluted, and its rigid opposition to passive reason would not be maintained. Once it is admitted that reason in general is immortal and impassive, this passive reason, being mortal, can no longer be said to be a real reason. Hence St. Thomas distinguishes

---

[1] Met. XII. 9. 1074 b 17.

the passive reason from the material and the potential reason,[1] and assignes the former to the sensible part, while Brentano likewise explains the passive reason as the imagination which mediates the active reason and the receptive-potential reason.[2] Such a sensible part or imagination would be called reason, because it partakes in the reason. Passive reason would be no more than reason in an accidental sense. Consequently, the mortality of passive reason would only mean that imagination perishes with the body, but this mortality would not extend to the receptive and the potential reason of man. Naturally, human reason would be this receptive and potential reason, which is just that reason that was said to be immortal and imperishable. But here we cannot repress the question, how can human reason be immortal, if it is at all, as he says, acted upon and conditioned by imagination? Was it not the theory of Aristotle that human reason must be taken as really inseparable from the body, if it cannot act without imagination? Was this not the proposition from which we have started our investigation? A human reason which is quite inseparable from the body, would of necessity perish with the body, and would be mortal.

Further, if passive reason is identical with imagination, why should it be discussed in this very place? Especially what is the necessity that it should be referred to by the accidental denomination of *passive reason*? According to Brentano, imagination is here mentioned as the condition of memory and thought, in order to explain why memory declines and perishes in spite of the eternity of reason.[3] Human reason being impassive—in the special meaning which has been stated above—it has no memory, but such a reason also does not think without imagination. This is just what the clause "οὐ μνημονεύομεν δέ" really means. Imagination is called passive because it is acted upon by active reason, which is a special faculty of realizing forms. This imagination acquires the name of reason accidentally, since on the one hand it is acted upon by the rational part, and on the other it acts upon the same part. If those two parts of the explanation are taken separately, they contain nothing impossible. But, if, in truth, imagination be introduced into the argument because human reason or the receptive faculty of thinking cannot think without

---

[1] St. Thomas, De An. Comm. 745.   [2] Brentano, Psych. d. Arist. 208.
[3] Brentano, op. cit. 209.

it, how then does this imagination relate to human reason ? Is not imagination active, while reason is receptive ? Was it not said that the receptive reason cannot think unless it suffers and receives forms from imagination ? Now that imagination is considered in such a reference, it ought rather to be active than passive. It was said that imagination is called reason accidentally owing to its necessity for the functioning of human reason. Let us grant this for the moment. Yet, if this alone is why imagination is called "reason", it might be called active reason as well as passive. The term "active reason", on the contrary, is applied already to another faculty, which acts only indirectly upon the receptive reason—this alone being the true reason of man—through acting at first upon human sensibility. Why then should such a faculty be active, while imagination is passive reason ? Isn't reason in the proper sense, from which these faculties get the name of reason, man's receptive reason ? Which of them, then, is more directly active upon this receptive reason ? Is it not imagination directly, and active reason only indirectly ? According to Brentano, imagination is acted upon by active reason. If this be admitted, then active reason is called reason accidentally, only through being related to human reason, but never until then and by itself. Therefore imagination would have no ground of being called passive reason, even though active reason acts upon it. Active reason was attributed in a sense to the rational part of the human soul, to be sure, yet Brentano would never admit it to be a kind of human reason in the proper sense. If imagination is to be called reason accidentally through being related to man's receptive reason, it ought rather to be a kind of active reason, while receptive reason would more likely be called passive reason. Moreover, if imagination ought to be called *passive* reason, since it is the so-called active reason that acts upon imagination, the true *reason* must be just *this* active *reason*. Seeing that imagination is thus active upon the receptive reason, in talking about imagination as the necessary condition of thinking, why on earth should one choose such an ambiguous concept as *passive* reason ? This would be quite comprehensible, if imagination were commonly called passive reason. But in fact, this concept appears only once in all of Aristotle's works. If one makes reason in general impassive and eternal at all, he will commit a *contradictio in adjecto* in calling "reason" what is passive and temporal. Brentano assumes that Aristotle called imagination reason in a certain sense, but, none of the evidence that he cites expresses Aristotle's own theory.[1] Even if we admit a certain degree of probability for his proof, would it not seem at least rather careless, and even unnecessary, to use such a contradictory expression in the same sentence ?

After saying that the reason which is immortal, eternal, and does not remember, is "impassive", Aristotle adds the words, "while passive reason is mortal". With regard to this statement, it is quite unnatural to take the former for reason in general, the latter as a kind of sensibility which is called reason only accidentally or as imagination. Especially, that reason of which Aristotle says "ὁ δὲ παθητικὸς νοῦς φθαρτός," is opposed to the reason of which it was said "τοῦτο μόνον ἀθανάτον καὶ ἀμιγής", i.e., the reason which is referred to by the words, "οὗτος ὁ νοῦς" and which is "χωριστὸς καὶ ἀπαθὴς καὶ ἀμιγής". Thus, both passive reason and οὗτος ὁ νοῦς must be kinds of reason. Now οὗτος ὁ νοῦς being active reason, passive reason as its opposite must be the potential and material reason which was regarded previously as contrary to active reason, the so-called receptive reason of St. Thomas and Brentano.

It is a more constrained interpretation to make both receptive-potential reason and passive reason stand in opposition to active reason. In Aristotelian expression, moreover, the contrary to ποιητικός is παθητικός rather than δυνάμει, while the contrary to δυνάμει should be ἐνεργείᾳ, so that again the contrary to active reason should be passive reason. It might seem then, as if there were potential reason or active reason besides them. But in fact, active reason is just actual and passive reason is just potential. Let us remind ourselves of our provisional conclusion: "Potential reason is the reason which is material and passive, and which becomes all things, while on the contrary, active reason is principle, cause, agent, and that which makes all things." We must here take notice of the fact that though Aristotle also admits in reason the opposition of matter or the potential to cause or agent, yet he never uses the terms "potential reason" or "active reason" while

---

[1] Brentano, ibid. cites Eth. Nic. VI. 12. 1143 b 4, as an example of calling sensation reason; De An. III. 3. 427 b 27, as an example of counting the imaginative faculty in reason; and De An. III. 10. 433 a 9 etc., of calling it reason or a kind of thinking. Cf. Zeller's criticism on these points, op. cit. 576. n. 5.

he does use the term "passive reason".[1] We have used those complex concepts only for convenience' sake or by convention. It may be that he set up in opposition to matter and the potential, not form or the actual, but cause, principle, and agent, because the actuality of reason is the perfection of its activity, and actual reason in the proper sense would coincide with contemplation. The faculty which is the cause of actual reason or contemplation, yet other than and opposed to the material and passive faculty, might be called active reason. It is not a complete actuality of thought, but the active principle of contemplation, the reason as a *habitus* ($ἕξις$) or active potentiality. Thus active reason may sometimes be called actual, but more often explained as a cause or agent. Whereas on the other hand, there is neither ground for distinguishing potential reason from passive reason, nor a real distinction between them. As we have seen above, since the statement preceding the concept of receptive reason has contrasted matter, the potential, and the passive with principle, the actual, and agent, it would be an extraordinary leap of thought, if this receptive reason should not be the potential reason, but a sort of sensibility which is quite different from that.[2] Besides, it is Aristotle's constant belief and often repeated saying that matter as matter is passive. Hence, it is quite inconsistent with Aristotle's system to distinguish passive reason from potential and material reason.

From all of the foregoing considerations, it seems probable that Aristotle, dividing reason into the active and the passive, took the former as eternal, immortal, and separable from the body, and the latter as mortal and inseparable. Receptive reason is mediated by imagination, which, being the function of the sensitive part, is not separate from the body. But active reason is separable from imagination, and so also from the body. Even if it may sometimes exist in the soul, in its essence, it is separate from it and transcendent.

---

[1] The word $ποιητικὸς\ νοῦς$ should have been avoided because it might be mistaken for that productive intellect, which is correlative with $πρακτικὸς\ νοῦς$ and $θεωρητικὸς\ νοῦς$. Cf. Zeller, op. cit. 570 n. 4. $νοῦς\ δυνάμει$ was inconvenient, because not only $νοῦς\ παθητικός$, but also active reason is a kind of $δύναμις$.

[2] Gen. et Corr. I. 7. 324 b 18: $ἡ\ ὕλη\ ᾗ\ ὕλη\ παθητικός$;ibid. I. 4. 320 a 2, 10; 328 b 11; II. 9. 335 b 30; De An. II. 2. 414 a 10; Meteor. I. 2. 339 a 29; IV. 10. 388 a 21; 11. 389 a 30; Met. X. 4. 1055 a 30.

Now at last we come to the incomplete proposition: "καὶ ἄνευ τούτου οὐθὲν νοεῖ." Every possible interpretation has been attempted for this passage. According to Simplicius, for example, it means that active reason never thinks without passive reason. So, whether passive reason be identical with imagination or not, this will lead to the same conclusion, that reason cannot exist without body. Zabarella also explains that active reason does not think without passive reason, but he endeavoured to keep the separation and transcendency of reason by dividing the action of active reason into eternal thinking and human thinking and by saying that without passive reason human thinking will perish, but not thinking in general. In modern ages, Zeller is almost of the same opinion.[1] Whereas to St. Thomas, the passage means that reason does not think without passive reason, and though human reason persists after the death of the body, it no longer thinks in the same manner as it now does.[2] To Brentano, who identifies passive reason with imagination, it means that reason does not think without imagination.

Indeed it was Aristotle's own theory, that human reason does not think without imagination. But we can by no means understand such an idea as that of St. Thomas and Brentano, i.e., that human reason, while being unable to act without the medium of body, does none the less persist after the death of body, and yet neither thinks nor has memory.[3] We would prefer rather to follow another interpretation, that of Trendelenburg and Hicks, and understand the passage to mean that passive reason does not think without active reason.[4] If the passage is thus understood, we can admit without difficulty that active reason is eternal and immortal, so that passive reason can think as far as it comes into contact with it; and that this active reason, when separated from the body and passive reason, no longer thinks with human memory, though it has some sort of reality none the less. What, then, is this active reason or its action? And what kind of thing is this passive reason of man, which receives the act of the active reason?

[1] Cf. Hicks's note *ad loc.*   [2] Thomas Aquinas, op. cit. 745.
[3] Cf. Brentano, op. cit. 18 n. 45. Teichmüller, Studien zur Geschichte der Begriffe, 434 f.
[4] Zeller's objection to this interpretation is that the last sentence which begins with οὐ μνημονεύομεν δέ and ends with ἄνευ τούτου οὐθὲν νοεῖ, should have been mentioned as the reason why we do not remember, so that, if we should take this as meaning that the passive reason does not think without the active reason,

§ 4. SOLUTION OF THE PROBLEM

As we have mentioned above, Aristotle divided reason into the active and the passive only once, in *De Anima* III. 5. We find no more direct discussion about the essence of these reasons. All we can do, then, is to sift out of the words which apply merely to reason, attributes that might differentiate themselves so as to apply uniquely to the active or the passive reason. Taken as a single entity, reason with all its separability from the body and transcendent origin, cannot receive the forms of objects without the medium of the body. These two moments of reason seem to be incompatible with each other. Reason being on the one side divine, is yet on the other hand mundane. It is actual, yet potential; it is immortal, yet mortal. On account of the first moment, reason must be transcendent, but on account of the second, it must be a function conjoined with the body.[1] When these moments of

---

the subject which does not remember would be the passive reason; but it is a matter of course that the passive reason does not remember the time when it did not exist; there is no need of mentioning the reason for this fact. But since the subject which does not remember ought rather to be the active reason, and the reason why it does not remember is that it is impassive, whereas ὁ δὲ παθητικὸς νοῦς φθαρτός etc. makes another sentence, there is therefore no difficulty, as Zeller points out. Unless we revise the text, Zeller's theory, which binds τοῦτο μέν and ὁ δὲ with ὅτι would be gramatically more natural. But, substantially, it seems to be more natural to admit that ὁ δὲ παθητικὸς νοῦς φθαρτός contrasts with τοῦτο μόνον ἀθάνατον καὶ ἀΐδιον. Even if we should admit Zeller's theory, it is certain that the real subject of οὐ μνημονεύομεν must be the immortal active reason.

[1] Referring to Met. XII. 3. 1070 a 21-27, Brentano insists that Aristotle's thought is inconsistent with Zeller's opinion, i.e., that the reason precedes the body (Aristoteles Lehre vom Ursprung des menschlichen Geistes, 16 ff.). The quotation is as follows: τὰ μὲν οὖν κινοῦντα αἴτια ὡς προγεγενημένα ὄντα, τὰ δ' ὡς ὁ λόγος ἅμα. ὅτε γὰρ ὑγιαίνει ὁ ἄνθρωπος, τότε καὶ ἡ ὑγίεια ἔστιν, καὶ τὸ σχῆμα τῆς χαλκῆς σφαίρας ἅμα καὶ ἡ χαλκῆ σφαῖρα εἰ δὲ καὶ ὕστερόν τι ὑπομένει, σκεπτέον· ἐπ' ἐνίων γὰρ οὐδὲν κωλύει, οἷον εἰ ἡ ψυχὴ τοιοῦτον, μὴ πᾶσα ἀλλ' ὁ νοῦς· πᾶσαν γὰρ ἀδύνατον ἴσως. But the reason which coexists with the body is nothing but the human intellect which is passive in its nature. If the whole reason should coexist with the body as its form, then, no doubt, it must perish with the body. If the passive reason be like the health of a body or the figure of a bronze cube, the active reason might be compared to a cubinal figure itself.

reason were divided by Aristotle and distributed into the active and the passive reason, divineness, actuality, and immortality were confined by him to the former. Therefore, passive reason can no longer be a divine being, but must be earthly and potential—a faculty of the mortal soul which is combined with the body.

Aristotle seems to have had no distinct idea of a bodily organ of thought. He only conjectures that it might be sought either in the heart or in the brain, yet does not decide which is more probable. But since prudence as a kind of intellect is assigned to the heart, and the physiological function of the brain is considered to be to cool the blood,[1] and to preserve the whole body,[2] the organ of intellect seems rather to be assigned to the heart. At any rate, it is undeniable that Aristotle has admitted a material and physiological substratum to human thinking.[3]

About passive reason and its physiological basis, we shall inquire afterwards. Our present concern is rather with active reason, which is the active principle of thought and the divine element in us. As aforesaid, the question has been much discussed since ancient times, whether active reason is immanent or transcendent, and how it relates to the human reason and the divine. The point where the interpretations diverge is the problem whether the active reason is immanent in the human soul as its function, or transcendent as the divine reason.[4] But these two theories are not really incompatible. Though the active reason may sometimes be separate from human reason, it is not always separated from it. In so far as it exists apart from human reason, it is truly the divine reason, but in so far as it is combined with the passive reason and realizes the thought of man, it is certainly human. Divinity is not absolutely unhuman, but it is rather the essence

---

[1] Part. An. II. 7. 652 b 20 ff. Plato is more advanced or at least nearer to the modern theory in making the head the seat of reason; cf. Tim. 44 D; 13 C-D.

[2] Part. An. II. 7. 652 b 7.

[3] Cf. De An. III. 4. 429 a 26. *In re* Kampe's attempt to admit a material substratum to reason (Erkennthistheorie des Aristoteles, 12-49), cf. Zeller's criticism in Ph. d. Gr. II. 2. 568 n. 3. Cf. also De An. II. 4. 408 b 5; Met. IX. 10. 1035 b 25.

[4] The trenscendent theory is supported by Alexander, Avicenna, Averroes, Ravaisson, Zeller, etc., while the immanent theory is supported by Theophrastus, Themistius, Thomas Aquinas, Brandis, and Brentano. Trendelenburg, standing in the middle, is most akin to our interpretation. Cf. ch. II.

of man in the ideal sense.¹ Man has connection with God, only through participating in the active reason. And since the active reason is not the same as human reason, man is a being who sometimes thinks, and sometimes does not.² We should understand Aristotle without any Christian prejudice. From the Greek point of view, man is the beloved child of God, who enjoys the fruit of wisdom as a gift of the Father, rather than through the evil temptation of the snake.

If it be admitted that the active reason is neither the transcendent divine reason nor immanent human reason exclusively, but both transcendent and immanent, divine as well as human, what then is the perfect essence and function of this active reason ? What sort of activity has this reason upon the passive one ? Reason was divided into the active and the passive, in accordance with the mode of its involvement in the act. And the act of reason is thinking.³ So that, the active reason is the active, and the passive reason is the passive principle, of thinking. How then does thinking come into activity ? According to Aristotle, human knowledge, thinking as well as sensation, is brought about through the cognitive faculty being acted upon by and receiving the form from the object.⁴ If the cognitive faculty has any actual form of its own, it cannot reflect the object as it is. Therefore, it has no actual form before cognition, yet has all forms potentially.⁵ Sense as a part of the soul has potentially all forms of sensible objects, and reason is potentially the same as the objects of thought.⁶ When a certain sensible object acts upon one of the senses, which has infinite forms in passive potentiality, the special form of this object is actualized in the sense; and this actual form is the sensation of man.⁷ In the same way, when an object of thinking gives an actual form to the reason which has infinite forms in passive potentiality, human thinking occurs.⁸ What makes the potential sensation in sense actual, is the object of sensation; what realizes the potential thought in reason is the object of thought. No doubt,

[1] Eth. Nic. X. 7. 1177 a 13; 1177 b 25.
[2] De An. III. 5. 430 a 22; Met. XII. 7. 1072 a 16; 1075 a 7; De An. III. 4. 430 a 5.   [3] De An. I. 3. 407 a 20.
[4] De An. III. 2. 427 a 9; 4. 429 a 13-18.
[5] De An. III. 4. 429 a 18-24; 429 b 30 f.
[6] De An. III. 8. 431 b 26-432 a 3; cf. ibid. II. 5. 416 b 33; 417 a 6; 418 a 2.
[7] De An. II. 11. 423 b 31-424 a 2; III. 7. 431 a 4 f.; III. 2. 425 b 26.
[8] De An. III. 7. 431 b 16 f.: ὅλως δὲ νοῦς ἐστὶν κατ' ἐνέργειαν τὰ πράγματα (νοῶν).

a concrete object accompanied by matter cannot act upon sense or reason. Though sense and reason may be "the same" as their objects, sensation or thought can by no means be identical with concrete objects. They are the reception of the forms of objects without their matter.[1] The reception of forms together with matter, might well be vegetable nutrition, but never sensation. Such a reception is affection in the proper sense, i.e. affection through which the subject changes its character.[2] Sensation and thinking differ from this in receiving only forms.[3] Sensation receives directly the forms of things, while thinking receives not the forms of things but the form of forms.[4] Now, the thinking of man having such a constitution, its active principle must be the form of forms as its object, while human reason as its subject must be the passive principle which receives the form of forms—Aristotle's "place of forms."[5] But we have previously concluded that the active principle of thinking is the active reason, and that it is of divine essence. Hence it is evident that this divine active reason is nothing but the form of forms as the object of thinking.

What, then, is the form of forms as the active principle of thinking? Admitting that the object of sensation is the form of things, while that of thinking is the form of forms, we might presume herewith, that the object of thought is a higher form which is founded upon sensible objects. And the relation between such a higher form and sensible objects seems to correspond, to the relation of thinking to sensation. Namely, we have seen above, reason does not think without being mediated by imagination,[6] and imagi-

[1] De An. III. 8. 431 b 26; ibid. III. 2. 425 b 23 f.; II. 12. 424 a 17-24; III. 4. 430 a 6-9.

[2] De An. II. 12. 424 a 32-b 3.

[3] De An. II. 5. 417 b 2-7; III. 7. 431 a 4 f.

[4] De An. III. 4. 432 a 2 f; καὶ ὁ νοῦς εἶδος εἰδῶν καὶ ἡ αἴσθησις εἶδος αἰσθητῶν. It is not literally that the object of thought is the form of forms, or that the object of sensation is the form of sensible bodies. Yet as aforesaid, reason is in a sense, the same as the object of thought, and sense is the same as the object of sensation. The context suggests this, otherwise these words have no significance.

[5] De An. III. 4. 429 a 27-29. Cf. Plato, Parm. 132 B, 133 C, 134 A. The form here meant must be the rational form only, which is distinguished from the others in De An. III. 4. 432 a 1. To call reason the place of forms does not conflict with calling it the form of forms; the former is the substantial, and the latter the formal aspect of it. Reason is, in a sense, rational forms, since it receives rational forms and is itself those forms in potentiality.

[6] Plato, already, admitted the mediating function of imagination for thinking, e.g., Phil. 39 A-C; Rep. VI. 510 C.

nation presupposes sensation.¹ Now, sensation is the form of things, which is perceived by sense through the body, while image is the same form which is kept in the soul.² So that, imagination does not require in each case a sensible individual; it makes an image by itself.³ To those forms primarily acquired through sensation and imagination, reason gives a further formalization, and produces thought through the apprehension and combination of these higher forms.⁴ This supposition may be proved by Aristotle's own statement: "But, since apart from sensible magnitudes there is nothing, as it would seem, independently existent, it is in the sensible forms that the intelligible forms exist, both those which are referred to by abstractions and all the habits and affections of sensible things. And for this reason, as without sensation a man would not learn or understand anything, so at the very time when he is actually thinking he must have an image before him. For images are like sensations except that they are immaterial."⁵ Needless to say, the object of thought is not the same as the object of sensation, either in the intention or in the extention of these terms. Some things are merely the object of thought and never of sensation, e.g. God as a pure form.⁶ But generally speaking, a thing may be the object of thought as well as of sensation. Mathematical forms, which are called "abstractions" in the previous quotation, and the attributes of other, sensible, things are of this kind.⁷ But though both relate to the same object, thinking differs from sensation in that the former is concerned with the universal while the latter is concerned with the individual.⁸ None the less, in such a case, the universal does not exist apart from the individual, but is immanent to it.⁹ That

---

¹ De An. III. 3. 427 b 14-16; 428 b 10-16; 429 a 1-4. Cf. Plato, Soph.264 A.
² De An. III. 3. 429 a 4-6; 2. 425 b 24; De Somn. 2. 460 b 2; 459 a 24. Cf. Plato, Phil. 34 A-C. ³ De An. III. 3. 428 a 5-16.
⁴ The intuition of form is the act of reason, their combination and separation is that of $\dot{\epsilon}\pi\iota\sigma\tau\acute{\eta}\mu\eta$ in the strict sense. Cf. An. Post. III. 23; 85 a 1, 33; 88 b 35; IV. 19. 100 b 22; Eth. Nic. VI. 6. 1141 a 7; 9. 1142 a 26; 12. 1143 a 35 ff.
⁵ De An. III. 8. 432 a 3. ⁶ De An. I. 1. 403 b 15.
⁷ De An. III. 8. 432 a4-6. Proof of the real agreement of the object of thought with that of sensation, is the fact that thought presupposes imagination.
⁸ De An. II. 5. 417 b 22 f.; An. Pr. III. 18. 81 b 6; 24. 86 a 29; Phys. I. 5. 189 a 8; Eth. Nic. II. 9. 1109 b 23; VII. 5. 1147 a 26; VI. 9. 1142 a 27; Met. III. 6. 1003 a 15; XI. 1. 1059 b 26; 2. 1060 b20.
⁹ Met. VII. 13; VII. 16. 1040 b 26 f.; 1041 a 4; 7. 1049 28; X. 2. 1053 b 16; XI. 2. 1060 b 23-28; An. Post. I. 24. 85 a 31; De An. III. 7. 431 b 12-16; Met. VII. 8. 1033 b 20.

which is perceived through sensation and kept and reproduced by imagination is the form of the individual, e.g. the form of a certain triangle or a certain man, Kallias.[1] Still they are surely the form, and do not include the matter itself. Sensation does not involve the matter of this individual triangle, e.g. the paper it is drawn on or the traces of a pencil it is drawn with. As for Kallias, his body itself does not come into our sensation. What is perceived by sense is the form of a triangle upon the paper, or the form of Kallias who has a body. What is imagined is the form of a special triangle and the figure of Kallias. Seeing that sensation and imagination are related to the individual, and what makes the individual an individual is matter, we must not contend that sensation and imagination have no bearing on matter. Yet they receive the form that is accompanied by matter as materialized form, but not as matter itself. If they receive the matter itself, it would destroy the sense, and the cognition of the object would never be attained. How then should we distinguish sensation from imagination? Aristotle says: "Images are like sensations except that they are immaterial."[2] Should we understand this literally to mean that image does not include matter, but sensation does?[3] This assumption would contradict the above statement that sensation receives the form of object, but does not include matter. Aristotle's remark probably means that sensation receives various accidental forms which accompany the matter, if not the matter itself, together with the essential form in question, while imagination, being the act of keeping and reproducing the forms which are abstracted by sensation, does not include such accidental forms of the matter. For instance, on receiving the figure of a triangle drawn on a sheet of paper by a pencil, sensation receives the form of the paper and the traces of the pencil, but the content of imagination is limited to the figure of this triangle, excluding that of the paper and pencil, or abstracting some of the material attributes of the sensation. Both sensation and imagination do not include the matter itself, but imagination lacks the accidental forms of the matter, while sensation has all of them. Such would be the real meaning of this sentence. Next we should take note of the statement: "The reason which actually thinks is the same as the things which are thought of",[4] or "The actuality of the sensible object is one and

---

[1] Cf. p. 59, n. 8; also, Eth. Nic. VII. 5. 1147 b 5.
[2] De An. III. 8. 432 a 9.   [3] Cf. p.58,n.1.   [4] De An. III. 7. 431 b 16.

the same with that of the sense."[1] These propositions might also appear to be inconsistent with the previous statement that sensation abstracts the form of things excepting the matter. But actuality here means rather the mode of existence of the individual which has both matter and form.[2] That sensation is the same as the actuality of the sensible object merely means that in sensation sense receives the form of the sensible object.

Sensation receives the form which accompanies the matter, e.g. the triangle, even though not together with the matter; and yet surely this form is received together with the accidental attributes of the matter. Wherefore such a form has the individuality of the material body, but remains as much the form as ever. The form which is perceived by sensation cannot be applied to any other thing but to this individual object on account of its concreteness and individuality. For instance, the sensible form of Kallias applies only to Kallias, not to Socrates. It is the form which can be apprehended on the face of the individual existent Kallias. But in imagination, all or some parts of the accidental attributes are abandoned. In proportion to the extent of this abstraction, imagination is differentiated into several degrees, the most concrete of which is hardly distinguished from sensation. Still, imagination reserves the speciality of the form, however abstract it may become.[3] The image may allow a free variation, and may represent other individuals, to be sure, yet it has no real universality. Essentially, it remains the form of things. Sensible form or imaginary form having such a character, rational form or the form of forms must be the universal form which unifies these individual or special forms. The rational form of the triangle would be the triangle in general, that of Kallias man in general. That sensation is concerned with the individual, while thought is concerned with the universal, means no more than this. Now, sensible form does not include matter itself, yet is accompanied by matter, viz. it is a somewhat materialized form. (Even imagination presupposes, though more indirectly, the specialization of the form through the matter.) This form is the principle which, e.g. organizes the matter into Kallias. Accordingly, the rational form which is admitted in the

---

[1] De An. III. 2. 425 b 26; 426 a 9; III. 8. 431 b 23; 432 a 2; II. 12. 424 a 18.
[2] Met. VII. 2. 1042 b 10; 1043 a 6 ff.; 3. 1043 a 30;   IX. 8. 1050 a 16; b 2; 1051 b 31; XII. 5. 1071 a 8; 7. 1072 a 25.
[3] De Memor. 1. 449 b 31-450 a 5.

sensible form[1] must be the principle which makes this sensible form a form, viz. the essence of this material form. The form of forms must be the pure form which has thrown away the whole of the materiality that was remaining in the form of things. It is the essence of the triangle, or the essence of man.[2] Thus we have learnt that form as the active principle of thought is the universal form, or the meaning which is expressed in the form of a concept.[3] From the psycho-genetic point of view, such a universal form, i.e. the concept or the meaning as its content, might seem to be nothing but the secondary object which is abstracted from the sensation of a concrete individual. But from the logical and philosophical point of view, or the so-called absolute-unconditional point of view, every human cognition is, on the contrary, possible by such a conceptual form.[4] Essentially, a rational form precedes a sensible form, and the object of sensation or thought precedes sensation or thinking. As for sensation and its object, let them be dismissed for the present. The active principle necessary for human thinking is the object of thought, and this object, the form of forms, is the conceptual form or the meaning itself. Moreover, as aforesaid, this form of forms must be the same as the active reason, or at least it has an essential reference to it. In truth, they are neither quite different, nor absolutely identical. Let us remind ourselves that we have previously enquired about the difference between the divine and the active reason. At that time, we have asserted that they are essentially one and the same, rejecting thereby Brentano's theory which makes them absolutely different. But we have not yet studied the relation in detail. On this point, we say also that they are one and two or two and one respectively.[5] Divine reason, active reason, and

[1] De An. III. 8. 432 a 5.
[2] Met. VII. 7. 1032 b 1 f.; VII. 10. 1035 b 32; 1036 a 1; VII. 8. 1033 b 5; VIII. 4. 1044 a 36; V. 2. 1013 b 23; Phys. II. 2. 194 a 20; II. 3. 194 b 26; Met. V. 2. 1013 a 27 f.
[3] Met. VII. 10. 1035 b 14-16; XIII. 8. 1084 b 10; III. 1. 996 b 8; VII. 10. 1035 a 21; VII. 11. 1036 b 5; VIII. 4. 1044 b 12; XII. 2. 1069 b 34; Phys. II. 1. 193 a 31; IV. 1. 209 a 21; De An. I. 1. 403 b 1.
[4] Met. IV. 5. 1010 a 25.
[5] In the De Anima, Aristotle does not speak about God or the divine reason. Although the active reason is called holy, it is not equal to the divine reason. In trying to systematize Aristotle's theory of reason from the statements about the divine reason in Met. XII. 1 and the active reason in the De Anima, we must expect an attack from the philologist. According to Jaeger, both of these

SOLUTION OF THE PROBLEM 63

the form of forms are neither quite different from, nor quite the same as, each other. What does this mean? To be sure, they all are the principles of thought in a wider sense. Now Aristotle

statements may have been formulated in Aristotle's early age, so that there would not be any objection to making them associate with each other. For us, on the contrary, since we assume the notion of active reason to be the most developed stage of Aristotle's reason theory, and since we throw doubt on the early formation of De An. III, there remain only two courses. Either we may deny the early formation of Met. XII, and make it comparatively a late work like the De Anima, or we may admit that it is an early work, and recognize the continuance of the thought it contains. A guarantee for the possibility of the former hypothesis is that Jaeger himself considered the formation of De An. III to be later in his previous work, Die Entstehungsgeschichte des Aristotelischen Metaphysik, p. 173. The latter hypothesis finds powerful security in the fact that there is also the same theory of the divine reason in the Ethica Nicomachea, which Jaeger considered to belong to the later period. Jaeger also assumes that it is Aristotle's later theory that the soul is the form of the body, and that thinking is an uninscribed faculty which receives the conceptual form of an object through imagination. It is true that the active reason is related to the divine reason, but it is none the less impossible unless one presuppose the passive faculty of cognition. Hence we have assumed a later formation for De Anima III. 5, which involves the theory of active reason. The same considerations apply to Met. XII, though there is a difference as to degree. E.g., Met. XII. 7. 1072 b 20-24: νοητὸς γὰρ γίγνεται θιγγάνων καὶ νοῶν, ὥστε ταὐτὸν νοῦς καὶ νοητόν. τὸ γὰρ δεκτικὸν τοῦ νοητοῦ καὶ τῆς οὐσίας νοῦς, ἐνεργεῖ δὲ ἔχων, ὥστ' ἐκείνου μᾶλλον τοῦτο ὃ δοκεῖ ὁ νοῦς θεῖον ἔχειν, καὶ ἡ θεωρία τὸ ἥδιστον καὶ ἄριστον. The last phrase might mean either "the divine belongs to the prime mover rather than to the human mind", or "this (actuality) rather than that (potentiality) is what reason is thought to have of the divine"; cf. Ross's commentary *ad loc.*, also Met. XII. 9. 1074 b 15-22; 1075 a 5 ff.

All the above statements seem to show that though no technical terms such as νοῦς ποιητικός or νοῦς παθητικός are used, Aristotle substantially recognized the distinction between the two reasons. This theory, which admits the speciality of reason, and distinguishes the human reason from the reason of God, by no means agrees with early Platonism. In contrast, emphasis upon the corporeality of the soul and the passivity of the human reason is more suitable to the next period, as the antithesis to early Platonism which admits the soul in general to be immortal. The notion of the actual reason seems, at least from a logical point of view, to be a most natural concept for Aristotle to formulate. At present, we would refrain from deciding the age of Met. XII. and consequently, we refrain from deciding between the two hypotheses.

In either case, it is not unreasonable to explain the theory of the active reason in the De Anima in reference to the theory of the divine reason in the Metaphysica. But it is not our real intention to identify the active reason with the divine or with that of God. God is an unmoved mover, not an agent or an efficient cause. But

admitted kinds of cause to all change and movement. They are, *causa materialis, causa efficiens, causa formalis,* and *causa finalis.*[1] The other causes except *causa materialis* were summerized in the active principle in a wider sense, and were set in opposition to *causa materialis*, the former being referred to form and the latter to matter.[2] Is it then, really an adventurous attempt to assign these four causes to those four concepts respectively, viz., to the passive reason, the active reason, the form of forms, and the divine reason ? Rather we cannot but wonder why such a natural interpretation should never have been attempted. In the first place, it was already proved, by Aristotle's own statement, that passive reason is the material cause from which actual knowledge is formed just as a product is formed from its material. There is also no doubt that active reason, being, as its name shows, the agent, the producer that makes all things, is the efficient cause of thought. As for formal cause, the object of thought was the form of forms or the conceptual form, which gives an actual form to passive reason. It was said that reason when it actually thinks is one and the same as the object of thought. What, then, does this mean but that the object of thought is the formal cause of thought ? Lastly, cocerning the object of thought and active reason, object as far as it is an object, is beyond dispute objective, while active reason, even though it might be derived from God, as far as it is reason, cannot be but subjective. The argument of those who adopt the immanent theory of active reason is founded upon this. Here, taking into consideration the transcendent theory, we must ask ourselves if efficient cause may also be an immanent principle.

if God contents himself with his self-contemplation, being indifferent to the world, and having no activity at all, how then is it possible that He is called an "unmoved mover" or a "prime mover" ? Those who deprive God of all influences upon the world, show a lack of understanding of Aristotle's God, who moves the world through being loved; cf. Met. I. 2. 983 a 8; XI. 7. 1064 a 37; XII. 7. 1072 a 26 ff.; De Cael. I. 9. 279 a 32; Phys. VIII. 6. 259 a 14 etc. They are no less mistaken than those who take Him as an agent and an efficient cause like the Creator in Christianity; cf. Brentano, Arist. Lehre v. Ursp. d. mensch. Geistes, 121-140.

[1] Phys. II. 3. 194 b 23-33; Met. V. 2. 1013 a 24 ff.; Phys. II. 3. 195 a 15; II. 7. 198 a 16; III. 7. 207 b 34; IV. 1. 209 a 20; De Somn. 2. 455 b 14; Gen. An. I. 1. 715 a 4; V. 1. 778 b 8; An. Post. IV. 11. 94 a 21; Met. I. 3. 983 a 26.

[2] Phys. II. 7. 198 a 24-27; cf. De An. II. 4. 415 b 9; Gen. An. I. 1. 715 a 6; II. 1. 732 a 4. Zeller op. cit. 328 n. 1.

Certainly, cause was seen to be external in production, but immanent in natural generation.[1] Now, thinking is not an external production, but is in one sense immanent, in another transcendent. So also with actual reason. To understand this more fully, let us recall of the metaphor of light as describing active reason. As we have explained above, sight was the result of the acting of a coloured object upon the pupil, through the medium of light.[2] The object gives a colour to the light which is the actuality of a transparent medium. This metaphor is quite apt.[3] Let us assign passive reason to the eye, active reason to the light, and the object of thought to the colour—there consists a complete analogy between the two phenomena. The object of thought is received by passive reason through the medium of active reason, and hereby the form of the object is realized in passive reason. Brentano has also regarded active reason as a medium like light, but he has lost sight of the completeness of this analogy, and considered that light is not active upon the object, but, being acted upon by the object, acts

[1] Phys. II. 1. 192 b 21; IV. 4. 254 b 17; De Cael. 2. 268 b 16; Met. V. 4. 1015 a 14; 1014 b 19. [2] Cf. p. 34, n. 2.
[3] T. Ide argues (Tetugakuzassi, No.622) that light is the transparent state of the medium which exists between the sight or the eye and its object, i.e. a coloured thing, whereas the passive reason and its object come into contact immediately, and the active reason is not a real medium. The active reason having nothing to make transparent between thought and its object, may merely shine as the complete actuality of thought just as the sun always shines. Thus, in spite of his opposition to the attempt to combine the God in Met. XII and the active reason in De An. III, he does identify God with the active reason. After all, he is compelled to acknowledge, that just as light is a third element distinct from sight and its object, so also the reason as an agent would have to be taken, in a sense, as a third element together with the passive reason and its object. His failure to understand this analogy made him take the theory of the active reason to be nothing but a "paradox" and "a falling into transcendent idealism". As we shall prove in the following, the active reason is to be understood as knowledge. The form or the object of thought does not come into contact immediately with the passive reason as the cognitive subject. If they did meet immediately, not only would there have been no use of a medium, but also man would have been endowed with eternal thinking. The active reason, which was compared to light, is nothing but the medium of thinking. If one asks us for a potential medium like air as the substratum of light, we would answer him, on behalf of Aristotle, that it is human culture. Culture or a tradition of knowledge is necessary for an individual to think. One might no more see forms or participate in the divine reason in a primitive or savage society, than a pupil might see the colour of a body in darkness.

upon the eye, while active reason acts upon the object.[1] Thus in Brentano's interpretation the fine analogy has unfortunately been marred, and the concepts of active and passive reasons have fallen into absurdity. Now for the first time through our interpretation, the complete adequency of this analogy is made clear. The coherency of Aristotle's theory shines out of the mist of his ambiguous expression.

What, then, does it mean to say that the object of thought is received by passive reason through the medium of active reason? What sort of existence is this active reason in reality? The form of forms, being the object of thought, was in itself a meaning transcendent in relation to the subject, not in relation to things. But the absolutely transcendent meaning cannot act directly upon the reason as the faculty of thought. Transcendent meaning is eternal, while the human being who has passive reason is not always acted upon by this object. In order that he may think actually, the object of thought must already in a sense be immanent in him. In order that a man may think of something, some one must have thought of it already. Plato explained human thought as the immortal soul's reminiscence of knowledge which was acquired in a previous life.[2] Aristotle does not admit the immortality of the individual soul, but requires at least the immortality of super-individual reason as the active principle of human thought. An individual can only think in a tradition of learning. Though man is by nature able to think, it is only in the sense that he is by nature a general.[3] There is in him the possibility of thought only in the first sense of the term $δύναμις$, viz., in the sense of logical or ideal potentiality.[4] Man is by nature able to think, in the sense that he belongs to the genus that thinks. This possibility is not $δύναμις$ in the superior sense, but only $ἐνδεχόμενον$.[5] Such a potentiality can by no

[1] Brentano, op. cit. 173. De Corte misunderstands both the act of light and that of the active reason; viz., he assumes, as it seems, that light acts upon the object and makes it really coloured, and that the active reason likewise acts upon the object of intellect instead of upon the passive reason; cf. op. cit. 47. Needless to say, his interpretation as well as Brentano's depends upon St. Thomas' Paragr. 730, though Thomas is not responsible for De Corte's mistake as regards the part of light in vision.
[2] Meno 81 ff., 98 A; Phil. 34; Phaed. 73 A; Phaedr. 275 A.
[3] De An. II. 5. 417 b 31.
[4] De An. II. 5. 417 a 21-28.
[5] Cf. p. 6, n. 6.

means become actual by itself, but must at first become a potentiality in the second sense, viz. potency or ἕξις. Its development is mediated by an actual being.[1] The potency that can develop by itself into actual thinking is not such an innate faculty that a man is possessed of in so far as he is a man, but a habitual knowledge which is acquired through learning. It is developed through education by those who have acquired knowledge by means of actual thinking.[2] Only those who have been educated and who have

---

[1] De An. II. 5. 417 a 30-b 2; 417 b 12-16; 417 b 2 ff. De An. III. 5. 430 a 19-21. τὸ δ' αὐτό ἐστιν ἡ ἐνέργειαν ἐπιστήμη τῷ πράγματι· ἡ δὲ κατὰ δύναμιν χρόνῳ προτέρα ἐν τῷ ἑνί, ὅλως δὲ οὐ χρόνῳ· Brentano declares those persons to be quite ignorant of Aristotle's thought, who take this sentence as follows: "Since the human being exists without beginning, an individual may have knowledge potentially before he has it in actuality; yet the actual knowledge is as old as the potential, because another man would have had the knowledge actually before him" (Arist. Lehre v. Ursp. d. menschl. Geistes. 22 ff.). As the proof for his argument he quotes Met. IX. 8. 1049 b 17-25: τῷδε χρόνῳ πρότερον ὧδε· τὸ τῷ εἴδει τὸ αὐτὸ ἐνεργοῦν πρότερον, ἀριθμῷ δ' οὔ. λέγω δὲ τοῦτο ὅτι τοῦδε μὲν τοῦ ἀνθρώπου τοῦ ἤδη ὄντος κατ' ἐνέργειαν καὶ τοῦ σίτου καὶ τοῦ ὁρῶντος πρότερον τῷ χρόνῳ ἡ ὕλη καὶ τὸ σπέρμα καὶ τὸ ὁρατικόν, ἃ δυνάμει μέν ἐστιν ἄνθρωπος καὶ σῖτος καὶ ὁρῶν, ἐνεργείᾳ δ' οὔπω· ἀλλ' τούτων πρότερα τῷ χρόνῳ ἕτερα ὄντα ἐνεργείᾳ ἐξ ὧν ταῦτα ἐγένετο· ἀεὶ γὰρ ἐκ τοῦ δυνάμει ὄντος, ... This is not sufficient evidence for denying the interpretation that a particular cognition of an individual presupposes a preceding thought. Rather, Brentano falls into dogmatism through inferring from the above quotation that God as the creator makes potential knowledge actual. For he cuts short the quotation with an evident intention, whereas what we meet in the following is quite a different idea from that of the creative action of God, viz., ἄνθρωπος ἐξ ἀνθρώπου, ἀεὶ κινοῦντός τινος πρώτου· τὸ δὲ κινοῦν ἐνεργείᾳ ἤδη ἔστιν. It is not the Creator, but a man who makes a man; it is not God, but a cultivated man who makes a cultivated man. The phrase, ἀεὶ κινοῦντός τινος πρώτου would mean that there is always a preceding efficient cause which exists in actuality. Even if one prefers to understand this to mean that there is an eternal first mover or God, it does not follow of necessity that God acts as an agent, much less does it make our interpretation impossible. Admitted that a man begets a man, and a man of culture makes a man cultural, it is analogically necessary that he who produces from a cognitive faculty of an individual an actual instance of knowledge is rather a teacher than a Creator.

[2] Similarly with generation. The man in active potentiality, exists in the father's seed, while in passive potentiality, it is involved in the mother's menstrual blood (Met. VIII. 4. 1044a 35). These potentialities are actualized only through the combination of a particular father and a particular mother (Pol. I. 2. 1252 a 26). From a fertilized egg thus generated, comes an embryo, which thenceforth grows through its innate principle into manhood (Met. IX. 7. 1049 a

learned can think by themselves.[1] Even the boy in Plato's Meno required the leading of Socrates as the efficient cause to make him think. Consequently, the active reason, that mediates between the passive reason—a mere innate faculty of thinking—and the transcendent meaning, and realizes an actual thought, must be knowledge. The mediating act of this active reason may be found in education, wherein the uninscribed reason of a student receives knowledge from the reason of a teacher who has already learned. This act of education is at once both the thinking activity of the teacher and the realization of the habitual potency of his reason. The active reason in the teacher acts upon the passive reason of the student, and this delivery of knowledge may be deemed as the preservation and development of truth itself. The form of forms is revealed through the active reason in human thought. In educa-

14). The mother corresponds to the body, the menstrual blood to the passive reason, and the form of man to the concept as the object of thought. Just as there must be an actual seed or an actual father in generation, so there must be an element of knowledge and a teacher in thinking (Mot. An. 5. 700 b 2; Met. XII. 7. 1073 a 3). We need not be afraid, as Mr. Ide is, that the fallacy of the so-called "third man", which Aristotle applied to the idealist, will be found in Aristotle himself. It is rather a matter of common knowledge that Aristotle introduced the concept of efficient cause, in order to get rid of the difficulty of the third man, which would be necessary for the idealism that assumes man's participation in the absolute transcendent idea. But there may be another objection. If the active reason is the knowledge, which must be implanted in a student's soul by a teacher, how is it possible that it is separable from the human soul and is immortal? If, on the contrary, it be separable and immortal, it seems to be rather probable that what mediates between this knowledge and the human soul is something like the "third man". Our answer to this is as follows:—The active reason is separable from an individual soul, therefore it is immortal. The ideal of generation is just the realization of this immortality of genus (Gen. An. II. 1. 732 b 32; De An. II. 4. 415 a 26; cf. Plato, Symp. 206 E; 207A-D). Knowledge is not a mere fact of subjective consciousness, but its essential being rather constitutes the world of culture, which is beyond individual lives. But it is not an absolute transcendent reality like the ideas of the Platonist, which individual souls should participate in. It is rather an actual knowledge which is transmitted from one individual to another, just as the form of man is transmitted from one actual man to another.

[1] De An. II. 5. 417 b 16-26. The object of thought is sometimes immanent in the soul, and in this respect it may be said that "the passive reason comes into contact immediately with its object" (cf. p. 64,n.3). But this is a learned state and not innate like the sensitive faculty. Learning requires education by a scholar through which the transcendent forms become immanent in the soul. Cf. Plato, Theaet. 186 C; Tim. 44 A,B.

tion, active reason is presented by the teacher, and acts upon the passive reason of the student, so that both reason are forming the two moments of human reason, but are not yet combined in one and the same subject. But when a student has learned, he has acquired hereupon the qualification of a teacher, and the two reasons have come into combination. Now he can think independently of the teacher. Knowledge is conditioned by the object in so far as it is the cognition of an object, but when it becomes a habit, it is already an immanent principle. Knowledge mediates the law of the world with human reason, but once acquired, it acts independently of external objects. Thus we can dispose of the contradiction between the transcendent and the immanent theory of active reason.

Having shown that one can assign the passive reason, the form of forms, and the active reason, to the material, the formal, and the efficient cause, respectively, we shall pursue further the analogy of sight and assign the divine reason to the final cause. Specifically, the analogy is that between fire, viz., the sun, as the origin of light, and the divine reason as the origin of active reason.[1] The potentially transparent medium becomes actually transparent through the sun-fire. This is light, which mediates between the colour and the eye. In just the same way is the active reason related to the divine. The divine reason does not immediately act upon human reason,[2] while the passive reason is merely potential and uninscribed. The reason *par excellence* must have an actual form like the divine reason, but in order to be active (upon the passive reason of man), it must be not only actual but also itself a kind of potency. Such a potency which is founded upon an actual existence is nothing but so-called ἕξις or habit. Therefore, the active reason which acts upon the passive reason must be a ἕξις. And that which makes the active reason what it is is the divine reason. Whereas, on the other hand, that which makes the efficient cause what it is is the final cause. Hence the final cause is called the first cause. But the final cause makes the efficient cause what it is, only through being mediated by the formal cause. The formal cause is, so to say, the final cause in so far as it appears in the stage

---

[1] Cf. De An. II. 7 (p. 34, n. 2); Plato, Rep. VI. 507 E-509 A.

[2] However strange it may appear, and in spite of Brentano's opposition, the final cause or the prime mover is different from the efficient cause or the agent, as Zeller asserts; cf. Zeller, op. cit. II. 2. 374 n. 2; Brentano, Arist. Lehre v. Ursp. d. menschl. Geistes, 29 ff. Psych. d. Arist. 235 ff.

of individual movements, or in other words, the former is the self-limitation of the latter. The efficient cause, then precedes the formal cause, and is the holder of the potency which organizes the matter into a concrete individual. Thus the divine reason makes the form of forms determine the active reason. God thinks only on himself, just as the sun shines by itself. The air is illuminated by the sun and becomes itself light. Being in this light, everything gives colours to the light and generates the sight in the eye. Similarly, God is content with his contemplation, while the active reason organizes the form of forms into the system of human knowledge, and gives it to the reason of a concrete person;—thus the thought of man is actualized. All these activities are aiming at the complete actuality of forms in God. Being illuminated by the divine reason, or aiming at the complete actuality of God, and stepping into the world of knowledge, our reason participates in eternity. Man is mortal together with his individual soul, but in so far as he lives in science, he is immortal.[1] We might rather say that the immortal reason is science itself. And yet, science becomes rich through the thinking of man. It is the accumulation of thought or the habitual contemplation of mankind. The passive reason of man is like the earth, which receives the seeds, nourishes the trees, and brings forth new seeds. The passive reason does the same with knowledge. The knowledge of man becomes possible through God, hence man loves Him and tends towards Him. Aristotle says that man comes to think about thought itself in accordance with his acquisition of knowledge,[2] which amounts to saying that in accordance with the act of active reason, thought becomes its own object. When active reason is thought of as such, it is the reflection of Divinity in man. At the same time, when man understands that he is not only an active reason, but also a passive reason and further an inferior soul and a body, he becomes aware of the fact that he is a finite creature. The active reason is the reason of God that appears in man. Yet the reason of God is not homogeneous with human reason, but differs in the degree of its potency. God, to Aristotle, is a pure metaphysical principle which rises above the anthropomorphism of Greek mythology and is beyond the personality of the Christian

[1] Cf. Plato Tim. 90.
[2] De An. III. 4. 429 b 5-10; 430 a2-4; Met. XII. 7. 1072 b 20; cf. Hicks's note *ad loc.*

God. He has neither will nor human thinking.¹ Aristotle says that God is reason or that His act is thinking,² to be sure, but since this reason of God is pure actuality, it is not like human reason which "sometimes thinks, and sometimes does not", but is an eternal thinking.³ Such an eternal thinking is not possible for a reason which is concerned with an object other than thinking itself, because such a reason is passive and conditioned by an objective form.⁴ Consequently, the object of divine reason is nothing but thinking itself, viz. it is *νόησις νοήσεως*.⁵ This thinking of thinking, as the act of the divine reason, corresponds exactly to the form of forms as the object of human reason. We may easily see the relation between them through the following comparison: The meaning means itself; the form of forms is the objective, and the thinking of thinking is the subjective, side of this transcendent meaning. The former is meaning as the object of passive reason, the latter is the same meaning, which, however, is perceived retrospectively by reflective intellect. The world which is governed by God or prevailed over by the divine reason is the world which is organized by meanings, viz. the world of *λόγοι* or concepts. Thinking of thinking is not only the reflection upon itself of human thinking as it appears to man, but also in its essential being, the act of God who makes man reflect upon himself.

Of course, human reflection, i.e., man's thinking of his own thinking, is the most divine of all human activities. Man does not reflect his own dignity as far as his thinking is concerned to exterior objects. In such a condition, he is not yet man *par excellence*. It is only through knowing himself as a man, that he becomes a real man. When he turns his eyes from the object to himself, he finds out the *self* as the subject of thinking. The essence of man is to be

---

¹ As is well known, Plato yet admitted a god who acts as a personal creator. But Brentano's attempt to explain Aristotle's god as an almighty creator ultimately fails; cf. Psych. Arist. 234 ff.; Arist. Lehre v. Ursp. d. menschl. Geistes.

² Met. XII. 7. 1072 b 18; 9. 1074 b 21; Eth. Eud. VII. 12. 1245 b 17; cf. also Met. I. 2. 983 a 5; [Mag. Mor. II. 15. 1212 b 39;] Pol. III. 16. 1287 a 29; Top. IV. 4. 132 b 11; 6. 136 b 7; Fr. 46. 1483 a 27.

³ Met. XII. 7. 1072 b 15 ff.

⁴ Met. XII. 9. 1074 b 21 ff.

⁵ Met. XII. 9. 1074 b 33-35. αὐτὸν ἄρα νοεῖ, εἴπερ ἐστὶ τὸ κράτιστον, καὶ ἔστιν ἡ νόησις νοήσεως νόησις. According to Brentano (Arist. Lehre v. Ursp. d. menschl. Geistes 133 ff.), *νοεῖν* is the act of *νοῦς* in the strict sense, i.e. intellectual intuition, and as the object of intellectual intuition, God has only

a reflecting subject.[1] The Greek has in fact apprehended human being as ζῷον λόγον ἔχων, viz. a rational animal.

Although it was a philosopher of the Greek πόλις that first recognized the human essence in reason, the idea of *homo sapiens* is not limited to a certain race or class, but holds a wider applicability. The anthropological view of man as *homo faber* is a mere objective view. Its supporters say that human intellect is a higher mental function developed through the use of instruments, since man is generated not as *homo sapiens*, but as *homo faber*. But *homo faber* does not yet reflect himself as human being. It is not himself but the philosopher who calls him a man, while the philosopher is never a *homo faber*, but always a *homo sapiens*. It may be, as Engels or Spengler says,[2] when man has begun to walk standing upright, i.e. when he has become an animal possessed of hands, that he has become the master of nature. Still it is only when he has discovered reason, or has begun to reflect upon himself as a rational being, that he has appeared on the stage of the spiritual world. Already in the antiquity of Greece, Anaxagoras maintained the view of *homo faber*, i.e., the assumption that man became a rational being through having hands. Against him, our philosopher replies:[3] "Rather he has come to possess hands on account of his reason. Before reason reflects upon itself as reason, it has been acting as the principle which makes hands of forefeet. Here also is applied the principle, that what is posterior in generation is prior in essence.[4] Human pro-

---

himself, but as the object of another kind of cognition, e.g. that of ἐπιστήμη, he has other things. Brentano maintains moreover that what cannot exist as an object may still be recognized. This argument by no means persuades us.

[1] Whence Aristotle estimated ontology, epistemology (Met. I. 2. 983 a 5), psychology (De An. I. 1. 402 a 1), and theology (Met. VI. 1. 1026 a 16), to be higher than physics. But the being which reflects oneself is not a mere individual subject like the *Existenz* in our century. The subject of reflection is not an individual, but a man or a political animal, (Pol. I. 2. 1253 a 2), and politics was not a theoretical science, but an architectonic or master art (Eth. Nic. I. 1. 1094 a 27). Stoicism, in which an individual become the subject of reflective consciousness, was a kind of decadence, as well as a development of humanity.

[2] Spengler, Der Mensch und die Technik, ch. 5.

[3] Part. An. IV. 10. 687 a 5-21.

[4] Met. I. 8. 989 a 15 f; IX. 8. 1050 a 5; XIII. 2. 1077 a 19, 27; Phys. VIII. 7. 261 a 14; Gen. An. II. 6. 742 a 21; I. 18. 722 a 24; Met. V. 11. 1019 a 2; De Cael. II.4. 286 b 16.

duction is essentially technical,[1] and art is knowledge that acts with the body. *Homo faber* is already *per se, homo sapiens*. Man may have been generated naturally as *homo faber*, but essentially he is *homo sapiens*. Besides, when he began to reflect upon himself as a rational being, he also found out God. Man did not reflect upon himself as anything else than a creature. Likewise, God was able to be God, only in creating human being. The birth of man is simultaneous with the birth of God. If God had not created man, what might he have been to himself? Zarathustra of Nietzsche calls upon the sun, *"Du grosses Gestirn! Was wäre dein Glück, wenn du nicht Die hättest, welchen du leuchtest!"* Man *par excellence* is the son of God. There has been no race that knows no god. The primitive man becomes a spiritual being by finding out his god.

Now, in the Greek ideal of *homo sapiens*, both art and religion had a fine harmony with intellect. But in the bare *homo religiosus'* view in which this harmony is split into discrepancy, nothing but passion can mediate between God and man. To the Greeks, passion is too human, if not brutal. If man should face God through passion, he would either fall into that mysticism wherein he is intoxicated with the immediate union of man and God, or else he would be separated from Him and degraded to being His servant. Such a kind of reflection would be either the autohyponotism of a conceited hermit or the self-abasement of a failure, but it is not suited for the strong. The free citizen of Greece admitted the inferiority of man to God, but was too proud to submit to Him as a slave. In the ideal of πόλις, *homo sapiens* was also *homo religiosus* and *vice versa*. If we let the *homo faber*, who has not yet arrived at the self-consciousness of intellect, be the primitive man, the *homo religiosus* who has lost his intellect exemplifies in another form the decadence of humanity. Further, just as the intellect which is separated from production is powerless, so the intellect which has lost religion is apt to become aimless. The former decends through its powerlessness, and the latter is steeped in nihility. Those who have more or less both faults are the tragic *intelligenzia* of modern times, or the σοφιστής who was a cause of the fall of the πόλις, or the κοσμοπολίτης who was cast loose in accordance to that fall. But the *homo sapiens* as the Greek ideal, and consequently the ideal

[1] In Aristotle, ποίησις in the strict sense always presupposes τέχνη, which is a kind of ἐπιστήμη in the wider sense, or one of practical knowledge. Whenever ποιεῖν is used of a process of natural generation, it should not be taken as a technical term; cf. ch. III.

type of man for Aristotle, was the godlike man[1] who was far beyond these morbid types. Man *par excellence* is *homo sapiens*. He perceives his own essence through thinking. And the highest thinking is the thinking of thinking. Man enters into connection with God through reflection, but however closely his reflection might resemble that of God, it is human thinking after all. Man resembles God through thinking his own thought, yet he does not become God himself. Rather he is convinced of his finiteness through this reflection, which, though it is the revelation of divine reason in man, yet is finite none the less. He cannot but admit his finiteness through reflection, because his reflection is always related to thinking of objects, while these objects of thought are the *data* with which we have nothing to do. Human thinking is by nature passive and finite; so is his reflection. It cannot rest upon pure contemplation, but is ever apt to be pulled back to thinking of an external object.[2] Human reason is not a pure contemplative reason, but a contemplative-practical reason. In this respect, it is distinguished from the divine reason, which is itself the eternal thinking of its own thought. But the thinking of an external object is not of necessity separate from divine reason: the object of thought is the form of forms, which may be said to be the objectified God. The case is merely that here human reason as the subject of thinking is yet absolutely opposed to the object: in spite of their common origin of Divinity, they are not yet conscious of this fundamental unity. For all that, both human thinking and its objects are impossible apart from God.

We can herein recognize one origine of the λόγος theory which appears in Philo's philosophy and the Gospel of St. John. God, the word, the light, and man in St. John's Gospel correspond respectively to God, the form of forms, the active reason, and the passive reason in Aristotle. At the beginning of St. John's Gospel, we read, "In the beginning was the Word, and the Word was with God, and the Word was God. The same was in the beginning with God. All things were made by him; and without him was not anything made that was made." Here, the Word and God are both two and one simultaneously. The Word is not wholly identical with God,

[1] Cf. p. 42, n. 2; Plato, Prot. 315 E; Soph. 216 B; Phil. 18 B; Rep. 331 E; Men. 99 D; Phaedr. 238 C.
[2] Met. XII. 9. 1074 b 33-36. In mankind, even the thinking of thought is possible through the thinking of an object. Met. XII. 7. 1072 b 18-21.

yet divine in its essence. And the creation of the world by God is performed through the determinating action of the Word. This is exactly parallel to the organization of matter by God through the form. Further St. John says, "In him was life; and the life was the light of men"; thus life is assigned to the act of λόγος which is compared to light, and made the active principle of human knowledge. This also corresponds to Aristotle's analogy between active reason and light, the former being considered to be that which mediates between objective form and passive reason. Who is it then, that perceives the word through being illuminated by the light? It is "a man sent from God, whose name was John. The same came for a witness, ...He was not that Light, but was sent to bear witness of that Light." Corresponding to this state of affairs, Aristotle's active reason brings forms to passive reason, this latter nevertheless being a human faculty and something which cannot be separated from the body. The prophet John corresponds, in Greece, to the philosopher in general. But though we have pursued thus far the resemblance of Aristotle and St. John, we must bid farewell to the latter when we meet with Jesus as the incarnation of the light. Here lies a great gulf fixed between Greek philosophy and Christian belief. Aristotle's philosophy never admits to man a being superior to the prophet John. The active reason which is compared by Aristotle to light is not a personal being. The relation of Aristotle's philosophy to Christianity might be said to be similar to that of the prophet John to Jesus.

It is surely a very interesting theme to follow the development of Aristotle's theory of knowledge in religious philosophers, especially in Philo and Plotinus, who supplied Greek philosophy to Christianity, or to pursue the relation of his theory of reason to the dogma of trinity in medieval theology, wherein Aristotle was made the servant of Jesus. But it would be beyond the limit of this study. We think it rather a more urgent necessity to compare Aristotle's theory of reason with Plato's theory of the soul.

§ 5. COMPARISON WITH PLATO'S THOUGHT

We have explained the four concepts of Aristotle, viz., the divine reason, the form of forms, the active reason, and the passive reason, as each being parallel respectively to the final, the formal, the efficient, and the material cause. But we find also in Plato analogous concepts in reference to the generation of the world and the formation of knowledge. They are God, the ideas, the good, and the reason or the soul. It is not quite evident how these concepts are related to each other in Plato. His statement of God and the universe, being very much of mythological character, is far from being a strictly scientific theory. Moreover, various myths are told about the creation and government of the universe by God. The most important of them is the variation story similar to the theory of Hesiod in the *Statesman*,[1] and the creation story in the *Timaeus*.[2] These two dialogues are both regarded as belonging to the later period and though the former probably precedes the latter, there is probably no great interval between them. From the fact that in such close sequence these quite different stories of creation are told, we might guess that these myths are to be taken as expressions of phantastic imagination rather than as scientific theory.[3] Of these two stories, no doubt the latter is by far the more important. In the *Statesman*, the myth is more accidental to the main theme, while in the *Timaeus*, it forms the principal subject, and is far more detailed in its contents. It is in the latter that we find an intimate relation to Aristotle's theory.

Now, according to the myth in the *Timaeus*, the universe is the product of a creation which originates in the beneficence of God.[4] This creation begins at first with the production of the universe, which is itself the created God, a body pervaded by the soul. Then, the universe is divided into heavenly bodies.[5] The created god is trusted by the one Creator to produce the lower beings. He produces mortal bodies and mortal souls, into which the one Creator inspires immortal souls homogeneous with the created god.[6] The creation by God is performed following the model of immortal ideas,[7] and these ideas compose a scale, which is ruled by the idea of the good.[8] How then, should we conceive the relation holding among the Creator, the ideas, and the idea of the good, all of which are the principles of creation? If the idea of the good

---

[1] Pol. 269 ff.   [2] Tim. 28 ff.
[3] Cf. Cornford, Plato's Cosmology, 28 ff.; Taylor, Comm. on Plato's Tim. 59.
[4] Tim. 29 E.   [5] Ibid. 34, 36, 40.
[6] Tim. 41. But in Phil. 30, the human soul is derived from the soul of the universe.   [7] Tim. 27 E.
[8] Rep. VI. 508 B-C.

is the uniting principle of the ideas, while God creates everything through imitating the ideas, are God and the idea of the good the same ? If they are different, how do they relate to each other ? If the idea of the good is the real principle of unification, God would no longer be the real creator or the ruler. But if on the contrary, God is the real creator, the idea of the good can no longer be an independent principle. Further, if the ideas are the model of the creation, yet different from God, then neither could God be the real creator, nor could the idea of the good be the uniting principle of the ideas. It would be inconsistent to say, on the one hand, that God creates ideas, while saying on the other hand, that the creation cannot dispense with models. In consideration of these difficulties, Zeller identified God, the ideas, and the idea of the good altogether.[1] But if they are all identical, whence comes the conceptual independence ? — May we not solve these difficulties through analogy with our previous interpretation of Aristotle's concepts ? And if we should succeed in setting up an analogy between them, may we not thereby guarantee our interpretation of Aristotle's theory ?[2]

To this end, let us compare the two theories with each other. To begin with, in Aristotle, God is an unmoved mover or a final cause, its essence being pure reason, and its act thinking; compared to visionary phenomena, it is like the sun as the source of light. But in Plato, there is not yet the division of cause into kinds. Though Aristotle's criticism that Plato acknowledged only formal cause and material cause cannot be admitted without qualification,[3] at least it is undeniable that there is lacking in Plato any clear-cut

[1] Zeller, op. cit. II. 1. 694-712.

[2] Needless to say, Aristotle admitted no creation whatever. Both the world and the divine reason are eternal and exist without beginning. What has come to be must sometime pass away: cf. Zeller, op. cit. 380 f. It is only what is eternal that is immortal. Immortality means for him eternity *a parte ante* as well as *a parte post*: cf. Nuyens, op. cit. 307 f. I cannot nevertheless consent to the opinion that it was a defect of Aristotle's philosophy that it is lacking in a theory of creation (Nuyens, op. cit. 318; Joivet, Essai sur les rapports entre la pensée greque et la pensée chrétienne: Aristote et Saint Thomas ou l'idée de création, 77). It was by no means owing to ignorance that Aristotle did not hold the creation theory which surely existed in his predecessors.

[3] Met. I. 6. 988 a 8. Against Aristotle's opinion, Ross points out as the expression of Plato's concept of efficient cause, Phaedr. 245 C, D; Legg. 891-899; Soph. 265 B -D; Tim. 28 C ff.; Phil. 23 D; 26 E-27; as the suggestion of the final cause, Phil. 20 D; 53 E; Tim. 19 D ff.; Legg. 903 C.

concepts of final cause and efficient cause. He also makes God reason[1] and the cause of being and cognition,[2] but the essence of this cause is not distinct. He makes the self movent precede the moved movent,[3] and takes it for the essence of life and the first agent.[4] But the self movent, if not moved by another, yet has in itself the two moments of activity and passivity. And even though it may be automatic, it cannot be eternal or unchangeable as far as it is movable. That the absolute being should be eternal and unchangeable, is not sufficiently brought into accordance with the requirement that it should be the final cause of movement.[5] This was attained for the first time when Aristotle admitted the final cause, which moves everything, to be itself unmovable.

Secondly, the idea which is used by the Creator as the model, would correspond to the form of forms or conceptual form of Aristotle. The idea of Plato is not the subjective image or the content of consciousness, but the objective form or the *noematic* object, just as is the form of forms of Aristotle.[6] It is a transcendent meaning, and human reason can think only through participating in it. It is the active principle of human thinking. At the same time, everything that may become the object of sensation, holds its existence only through participating in idea; so that idea is the principle of things.[7] The Creator formed indefinite matter through ideas.[8] In these respect, the idea is not different from the conceptual form. One might, however, oppose our explanation which combines Aristotle's conceptual form with Plato's idea. Aristotle's criticism of the idea theory is one of the most familiar things in the history of philosophy. But it does not of necessity amount to the complete rejection of this theory. Aristotle rejected the theory of ideas mainly because it makes the idea another entity parallel to the sensible object, and apprehends the former by analogy with the latter.[9] Nevertheless, what he called the form was nothing but the idea which is transcendent above the subject, yet immanent in the object. Of course, it was far from his intention to assume infinite meanings corresponding to all sensible

[1] Phil. 30, 28.   [2] Phaed. 95 E-100 B.   [3] Legg. 894-896.
[4] Phil. 26; Tim. 46 D, E; cf. Met. XII. 6. 1072 a 1.
[5] Zeller, op. cit. II. 1. 689. 696.   [6] Phaedr. 247; Tim. 51; Phaed. 100, 102.   [7] Phaed. 102; 100 C-E; Parm. 130.
[8] Cf. Baeumker, Das Problem der Materie, 193 ff.
[9] Met. III. 2. 997 b 3; VII. 13. 1039 a 24 ff.; X. 10. 1059 a 10; XIII. 9. 1086 a 35 ff.

objects. Now the object of rational cognition may be immanent in the sensible object in respect of reality, but logically it is separable, and the logical point of view is superior to the real. Consequently, the ideas which are immanent in the subject, must logically presuppose transcendent meanings. This was the common belief of Aristotle as well as Plato. It would by no means a strained interpretation to make Aristotle's conceptual form correspond to Plato's idea.

Even if the active principle of human thought were reduced to a transcendent idea or an objective form, it does not lead to the denial of subjective activity. The thinking of thinking and the form of forms in Aristotle are two sides of one transcendent being. The former is the subjective, and the latter the objective, apprehension of it. The one, being the act of reason, is the interior aspect of God, while the other, being the essence of the world, is His exterior aspect. The relation between God and the idea in Plato would be similar to this. The thinking of thinking is a simple consciousness, while the form of forms contains plurality. So with God and the idea: God is simple, but the idea, though it too may be simple when compared to sensible images, yet is *eo ipso* coordinated with other ideas. For instance, man itself is one compared with Kallias and Socrates, but it is only one special concept which is coordinate with horse itself or colour itself. It might seem as if this speciality or multiplicity of forms or ideas is quite different from pure and simple act such as the thinking of thinking, or from a single and absolute God. But just as the thinking of thinking develops into objective cognition by making itself the form of forms, and then comes back to the absolute subjective consciousness through the negation of that objective cognition,[1] so God as a single Creator may create the world only through manifesting Himself as multiple ideas. The idea is not a reality which exists apart from God and precedes His creation as its model, but the other being (*Anderssein*) of the one God. On this account, God remains the absolute being, while ideas are what make other things, though being themselves not made by others.

It is an extraordinarily difficult question, how this simplicity and multiplicity of the absolute being consist at the same time. If we search for that which mediates between the one God and many forms, and between the absolute Creator and multiple ideas, it

[1] Cf. p. 70, n. 2.

can be nothing but the active reason of Aristotle and the idea of the good in Plato. Neither the forms of Aristotle nor the idea of Plato are a random multitude, but there is in them some organization of the general and the special, or at least some distinction as to degree of generality. The scale of Plato's ideas was far from complete, yet the idea of the good was no doubt the highest unity of ideas.[1] In Aristotle, conceptual forms are summed up in ten categories, which are practically the fundamental forms of being and of its rational cognition. The idea of the good in Plato is, no doubt, the principle which mediates the simple consciousness of God with many ideas. Being itself the highest idea, it partakes in divinity as far as it is good. Similarly, the active reason of Aristotle may be understood not only as the medium between many conceptual forms and human reason, but also as the principle which differentiates the single consciousness of God into the multitude of forms.[2] The form generates a thought in the human soul through the active reason, while various forms are derived from the reason of God, in so far as God manifests Himself as the system of knowledge. This would be the reason why Trendelenburg considers that God is an active reason, even if not all active reasons belong to God. But strictly speaking, the idea of the good in Plato is not the medium between ideas and the human soul, but between ideas and God, whereas Aristotle's active reason mediates between ideas and passive reason, but not between God and forms. This difference is due to the fact that God in Aristotle is what is looked upon and loved from beneath, while God in Plato is what creates and loves others from above. Assuming the multitude, Aristotle searched for the one, while Plato's main interest was, on the contrary, to deduce the former from the latter. Moreover, in Plato, the soul was not differentiated completely, so that ideas and the soul were combined directly without requiring any medium. In spite of such differences, generally speaking, the divine reason, the active reason, and the form of forms in Aristotle are analogous to the God as the creator, the idea of the good, and the ideas, respectively, in Plato. They are all in a wider sense the formal principle of being or cognition, and in this respect, they are one and three at the same time.

There remain for us to consider the passive reason of Aristotle and the soul of Plato. These are in a sense analogous, but not so

---

[1] Soph. 253 D.
[2] Cf. Bergson, L'évolution créatrice, 348.

similar as the other concepts are. In Aristotle, the active reason as the system of knowledge being super-individual and immortal, gives the form of forms or the transcendent meaning to the passive reason of man. Whereas in Plato, the eternity of ideas directly leads to the immortality of the soul which knows them.[1] The soul is regarded as absolutely simple; such problems as the passivity of human reason and the finiteness of the individual soul are neglected entirely.

That there is an immortal soul was a traditional ideal of the Greeks,[2] and it was also the lifelong belief of Plato, which he held together with the transmigration-theory of the Orphics and Pythagorians.[3] It continued in his thinking until the middle and late period, which are represented by the *Republic* and the *Laws*,[4] but the most eminent expression of it is found in his early work, the *Phaedo*, wherein Socrates states it with a tone of enthusiasm.[5] The belief, briefly stated, is as follows: The soul cannot attain a complete cognition of truth, because it is bound with the body. Sensation is the obstacle of cognition, rather than its pre-requisite. Eyes and ears are, as Heraclitus said, nothing but evil witnesses. The soul is able to see truth only when it has got rid of the body, which is achieved through death. Hence death is the ideal of the philosopher who loves truth.[6] Nevertheless, in this world, the soul can neither exist nor think entirely apart from the body. Our thinking is in fact mediated by the body; otherwise, the soul would not even be disturbed by the body. Accordingly, the soul may be separable from the body, but is not as yet separated from it. The separability of the soul is compatible with the dependence of thought upon physical conditions. The difficulty about the inseparable $\pi\acute{\alpha}\theta\eta$ of the soul and the separable reason is thus solved. Even when the $\pi\acute{\alpha}\theta\eta$ of the soul is taken in a wider sense which includes thinking, its inseparability is not of necessity inconsistent with the separability of the soul. It is not, however, the whole soul that is separable; it would be absurd to assume that the sensible part is separable from the body. Even in the *Phaedo*, where the separability of soul is affirmed, the func-

---

[1] Phaed. 75 f.; 100; cf. Grote, Plato, 190 n.
[2] De Coulange, La cité antique, 7 ff.   [3] Grote, Plato, II. 202 n.
[4] Rep. 10. 609 ff.; Tim. 41, 43, 69; Legg. 859 B, 967 E.
[5] Phaed. 64, 66 f., 80, 83; cf. Phaedr. 245; Meno 81, 86.
[6] Phaed. 64; Theaet. 176 A.

tion of the separated soul is a pure thinking[1] and no other lower consciousness or phenomenon of life. Therefore, if the soul in general mean the principle of life, such a separable part of it should be distinguished from the rest by the name of reason. Only the rational part of soul is separable, and yet in actuality, it is combined with the body.[2] Already in the *Timaeus* Plato divided the soul into immortal reason and other mortal parts. Aristotle's division is simply a natural development of this theory.

But how can it be that, what is separable from the body is bound with it ? As far as it is separable, it must essentially be quite independent. How is it possible that such an independent being is seized by another ? This is a problem which Plato was presumably unable to solve, and it should have been a difficulty even for Aristotle who limited the immortal part of soul to reason. Maybe it was as a last attempt to solve this question, that he distinguished the active and the passive reason in *De Anima* III. 5. The separability of reason from the body and its dependence upon the body are harmonized by limiting soul to reason, and dividing it into active and passive. What is essentially independent is active reason, which is the only divine element. It enters into connection with the human soul in so long as it is active towards the passive reason of man, and in this respect only, it forms a moment of human reason. Now, the human soul, including passive reason, is by nature the actuality of the body and inseparable from it. So that, strictly speaking, there cannot be any restraint of the soul through the body. At most, the soul is limited by the body only to the extent that man is unable to continue a pure scientific contemplation; this limitation amounts to no more than the difference between man as a knowing, rational being and man as a concrete individual subject. For Plato, such an explanation was impossible. But we may find even in him, the embryo of an idea which could grow into Aristotle's theory of the reason. Plato distinguished two ways in which the soul is bound by the body. The soul is essentially different from the body; hence the two are separable. The essential function of the soul is thinking, but the soul is not completely separable from the body, because it is bound with the

---

[1] Phaed. 66 - 68; cf. Grote, Plato, II. 161 n.

[2] Tim. 30, 69. This distinction does not imply that Plato abandoned the dualism of soul and body and the immortality of the personal soul; cf. Nuyens, op. cit. 141.

body, and even thinking is mediated through sensation. Still, that the soul operates through the body in thinking, is not the same as its being bound with the body through sensation and desire. In sensation and desire, the soul is employed by the body, while in thinking, the soul rather employs the body, though it is mediated by sensation. Man is unable in this world to think as a pure soul. But even if he thinks through the medium of body, soul is the master, body the servant,[1] in so far as he thinks. Thinking is the highest life of mankind. It is the life of the philosopher, the exercise of death in life, the life which is most contiguous to death.

Thus Plato admitted that thinking in this world operates through the body. If, then, the soul without the body thinks after death, is this posthumous thinking homogeneous with the thinking which occurs in life? Plato admitted no essential difference between them, but Aristotle, as we have seen above, denied memory to the active reason which is separated. He not only divided reason from soul, but also distinguished in reason the active and the passive, and limiting immortality, unmixedness, etc. to the former, reconciled the contradictory requirements of transcendency and immanency of reason, and at the same time, recognized the essential difference between the thinking which depends upon the body and that which is independent of it. Passive reason thinks through the body, so that, it is essentially conscious and has memory. Active reason, however, is separable, and not the subject of consciousness, but the objective mind which mediates between transcendent meaning and the thinking subject. Such a reason is really acting even in our lifetime. Human thinking is impossible without it. Nevertheless, this reason is immortal and separable from the body. Being separable, it will be separated from the body, and once separated, it has no longer memory or consciousness. This actual separateness of active reason seems, in Aristotle, to be confined to the case of death. Therefore, the primitive belief in the immortality of the individual soul which has memory and consciousness has now been given up.

But what is the nature of this immortal reason? We interpreted it as the system of knowledge, or rather more widely, culture in general, as the expression of transcendent meaning. Indeed, active reason is essentially super-individual and divine, even when it makes human thinking act in man's lifetime by giving conceptual

[1] Phaed. 66, 83.

forms to passive reason. We think not as mere individual or a natural being. As far as we are conscious, we cannot dispense with the body, yet as far as we are concerned with forms, we live in the world-mind, or rather the world-mind is living in us.[1]

Aristotle seems to have admitted the separation of active reason only when the body dies. But, in our view, this separation is not confined uniquely to the moment of death. To express our thought means that the thought makes itself objective and eternal, emancipating itself from consciousness. In this sense, expression is the separation of active reason from the body, step by step. And since conscious thinking is done through participating in active reason, the world-mind is returning every moment to its independent existence, through passive reason. We are living and dying every moment, dying in life and living in death. The death of the body, being the extinction of a subject, in which the development of the world-mind takes place, or the ending of a special system of this development, has, of course, an important significance. But such an event is taking place, more or less, every moment in our life. Thus considered, Plato's saying, "Philosophy is the study of death", would gain a more profound significance.

We may resume the above arguments as follows: —Putting forward later Platonism against the early theory of the immortal soul, Aristotle at first restricted the immortal part to reason. But his positivistic mind compelled him, on the other hand, to admit the fact, that reason is combined with the body through imagination and sensation. With this recognition of the fact alone, the immortality and independence of reason would have been endangered. Aristotle seems to have endeavoured to rescue it through dividing reason into the active and the passive, and confining divinity and immortality to the former. But he did not succeed in giving his thought a fully logical and systematic expression, and sometimes the necessity of imagination in human thinking, sometimes the separability of reason is emphasized; Aristotle's reflection about the species of reason, which was intended to unite the two charac-

[1] The active reason has been thinking before a man's birth, losing its memory at his birth when it unites with the body, and then it acquires abstract ideas through sensible experiences. This career of the active reason appeared to Brentano to be an uncomprehensible process (Arist. Lehre v. Ursp. d. menschl. Geistes 81). This is because he took the active reason as a mere psychological phenomenon. There is no unreasonableness for us, who are acquainted with Kant's transcendental idealism and Hegel's philosophy of spirit.

ters, appeared only once, in *De Anima* III. 5, and in quite an unsatisfactory form. This want of clear statement has presented great difficulties to the history of philosophy. We must notice in particular, that this sequence of Aristotle's thought is never distant from Platonism, but rather develops Plato's theory of idea and soul, differentiating the concepts more thoroughly and remedying the theory's difficulties.

§ 6. PARTS OF THE SOUL

As is evident from the above investigation, what is really separable from the body is only reason and specifically the active reason, which, in this respect, is essentially different from the other parts of the soul. And if active reason is separable from the body in reality, it will be separable from the other parts of the soul in reality as well. So that, the parts of the soul are not parts in a conceptual and functional sense only, but also in a real sense. Needless to say, it is not always in respect of reality, that the soul is separable from the body or the parts of the soul from each other, though this does not necessarily amount to our saying that any other separation than a functional or conceptual should be denied. It is true that when we cut certain plants and animals, the parts of their soul are also divided along with their body, whereas the parts of the soul themselves are not divided from each other.[1] For instance, when we cut the body of an earthworm, each part of the body has all of the nutritive, the sensitive, and the moving faculty, but these parts of soul do not separate from each other in reality through this division. Such a phenomenon is, however, not universal to all kinds of living beings. Besides, comparing one kind to another, if the one has a function which is wanting in the other, these different parts might be separate from each other, and this separation would not be merely conceptual; e.g., the nutritive faculty may exist apart from the sensitive, and sensation apart from reason. Among sensations, a lower faculty such as touch, may exist apart from a higher faculty such as sight.[2] Generally speaking, a lower function is separable from a higher, in the sense that the one may act apart from the other. How then

[1] De An. I. 5. 411 b 19 ff.; 413 b 16.
[2] De An. II. 2. 413 a31 ff.; II. 3; I. 5. 410 b 18.

is this possible ? Is it because each function has its proper subject, and the real separation of such subjects makes possible the separation of these functions ? But we cannot find such a real separation except between active reason and the soul which is bound with the body. For the soul other than active reason is the actuality of the body, so that its subject is nothing but the body. If, then, each part of the soul has its proper subject, these subjects must be different parts of the body. Is it then the case that to head belongs its proper part of soul, to heart its proper part, to limbs their proper part, and so on ? What is it, then, that unites these parts of body and soul, and makes one living being ? According to Aristotle, it is not body that unifies the parts of the soul, but on the contrary, the soul that unifies the parts of the body. The soul being thus the principle of unification, at least it must exist as a whole in an individual; the parts of the soul must not be distributed to each part of the body, but pervade the whole body.[1] This is proved by the fact that when we cut a certain plant or animal, each of the divided parts has various functions in the same manner.[2] Assuming that the subject of psychical functions is the body, and that the soul pervades the body, it seems much more necessary that the parts of the soul means the kinds of its functions. But there remains another possibility, viz., if a certain function is always accompanied by another certain one, and *vice versa*, we may assume such a complex of functions to be an independent part. This may be called a secondary division, as against the first or real separation. No doubt, among the moments of such complexes there is no longer a divisibility in the sense of separate existence. The only possible divisibility is mere difference of function, and mere conceptual distinction, which, however, constitutes the third kind of division. Which of these three does Aristotle really mean when he talks about the parts of the soul ? We must inquire about this directly from his own statements.

Concerning the division of the soul, there was, as aforesaid, already before Plato, the duopartite theory of the rational and the irrational, while Plato himself took the tripartite theory of the reasoning, the passionate, and the appetitive, and further he assumed these parts to be really separable. In his early age, Aristotle followed this tripartite theory, but afterwards turned to criticize it.

[1] De An. I. 5. 411 b 9; II. 4. 416 a 8.   [2] De An. I. 5. 411 b 24.

For instance, in *De Anima* III. 9, delcaring both the doupartite and the tripartite theory to be insufficient, he adds other parts to them. Here he takes the principle of these divisions to be the difference of function, and argues that, if we take such a principle, we should further add to these parts the nutritive, the sensitive, the imaginative, and the desiring part. He does not, however, give a clear exposition as to whether it is suitable to divide the soul through its functions, so that it remains yet doubtful whether he affirms all these added parts to be independent ones. Besides, the parts of the soul which Aristotle mentions here and there are not always definite, both in respect of number and species. Let us, then, compare the main statements in the *De Anima* about this point.

1) *De An.* I. 5. 411 a 26: "Now, cognition belongs to the soul and so do sensation, opinion, appetite, wish, and desires in general; locomotion also occurs in living beings through the soul; and likewise growth, maturity, and decay. Does, then, each of these belong to the whole soul, so that we think, perceive, are moved, and in each of the other operations act and acted upon with the whole soul, or are different operations to be assigned to different parts"?

Herein Aristotle counts as the functions of the soul, cognition, sensation, desires (including appetite and wish), locomotion, growth, maturity, and decay, which are all somewhat closely related with each other. But there is no account how these parts are related with the soul and its parts.

2) *De An.* II. 2. 413 a 22: "But the term life is used in many ways, and if life is present in but a single one of these senses, we say that this thing is living, e.g., reason, sensation, motion and rest in respect to place, and the motion involved in nutrition, and further decay and growth." —This also should be taken as a mere enumeration of functions.

3) *De An.* II. 2. 413 b 11: "For the present, let us say so much that the soul is the principle of these functions above mentioned, and is determined by them, namely, by the nutritive, the sensitive, the intellectual, and the motive. But whether each of these is a soul or a part of a soul, and if a part, whether it is separable only conceptually or also in respect to place, these are questions some of which are not difficult to see, but the others have difficul-

ties." —These parts are also explicitly enumerated as mere functions, not as parts of the soul.

4) *De An.* II. 3. 414 a 31: "Of the powers of soul above mentioned, namely, the nutritive, the desiring, the sensitive, the locomotive, and the intellectual," —This passage is concerned explicitely with the functions.

5) Also in *De An.* II. 3. 415 a 1, Aristotle enumerates as the functions of the soul such parts as the nutritive, the locomotive, the reasoning or intellectual, and imagination.

6) But *De An.* III. 9. 432 a 26, reflecting about the division of the soul, he condemns the duopartite and the tripartite theory to be insufficient, and continues as follows: "For in respect of the differences by which these parts are separated, there appear also other parts which have among them a greater distance than these, namely the parts which we have just discussed, the nutritive, which belongs also to plants and to all living beings, and the sensitive, which cannot easily be classed either as rational or irrational. Further, the imaginative is in its essence different from them all, while it is very difficult to decide with which of these it is identical or not identical, if one may assume separate parts in the soul. Then besides these there is the desiring, which would seem to be different both in concept and in capacity from all the foregoing."

These parts are enumerated on the assumption that the parts of soul coincide with its functions; the expression might appear as if the parts added by Aristotle were taken as forming parts of the whole together with the three maintained by Plato. But in fact, the three parts of Plato are not so independent as the additional parts; the passionate and the appetitive part having no clean-cut distinction with each other. Aristotle seems to have intended to reserve only the reasoning part out of Plato's three, and add to it his four parts. This is evident from the next quotation.

7) *De An.* III. 10. 433 b 1: "But those who divide the parts of the soul, if they divide and separate them in respect of powers, will find that such parts tend to become very numerous: the nutritive, the sensitive, the thinking, the deliberative, and the desiring, for these differ more widely from one another than the appetitive does from the passionate."

Though the principles of division in the above quotation are

numerous and indefinite, we might reduce them to six:
- the nutritive (nutrition, growth, decay)
- the sensitive
- the imaginative
- the desiring (appetite, wish)
- the motive
- the intellectual (reason or rational intuition, opinion, deliberation, reasoning)

Of these six kinds, imagination or the imaginative part appears only once in 6), and besides, its independency is doubtful. Desire is lacking in 1), 2), 3), and 5); motion in 6), and 7). No quotation comprises all these six. This makes us suspect that Aristotle did not intend a complete division of the soul or at least did not attach much importance to it. What are found everywhere are nutrition, sensation, and intellect. Hence we might guess that desire, imagination, and motion have less importance or have no clearly distinct status. Indeed, imagination and sensation have as intimate an inter-relation as desire and motion do. Imagination would be in most cases omitted, because it may be reduced to sensation in a wider sense, and further because it is sometimes counted in the modes of intellect. As for desire and motion, an indication of their incomplete separation is the fact that they are never omitted at the same time though either of the two may drop. According to Brentano,[1] Aristotle may not have enumerated all of the parts, partly because one may easily supply the rest if one knows the principle involved, partly because he intended to reduce these parts into the three main parts of nutritive, sensitive, and intellectual. For Brentano's assumption to stand, there should be at least a single place in which only the so-called three main parts are enumerated. But in fact, there are always more than four, and besides, they are not definite in kind.

Brentano denies the agreement between the faculties or functions and the parts of the soul. Different faculties, he thinks, might belong to the same part just as sensation and sensitive desire do to the same part. The parts of the soul would then not correspond to difference of functions, but would rather depend upon functional complexes. He assumes also that Aristotle admitted firstly the part which accounts for nutrition, reproduction, and lower sensation such as taste and touch, secondly, the part which accounts

[1] Brentano, Psych. d. Arist. 59.

for such higher sensation as sight or hearing, together with locomotion, thirdly, the part which accounts for intellectual thinking; and he assumes that they are divided as the parts of the soul, because they are found separately in different genera of living beings. If, however, Aristotle really divided these three parts, he would have given names to each of them; moreover, these parts do not agree in their contents with the three parts that Brentano mentioned, viz., the nutritive, the sensitive, and the intellectual: for sensation extends both over the first and the second, and desire both over the sensitive and the intellectual part.

Brenatno attributes many functions to the three. To the nutritive part belongs only unconscious assimilation of nourishment, but to both the sensitive and the intellectual part belong perception in a wider sense, desire, and behavior; and of behavior, some is conscious and some unconscious, so that these parts would possess three or four faculties.[1] It is because he deprived the desiring part of independency that he was obliged to attribute desire etc. to the sensitive and the intellectual part. This is pointed out by Aristotle himself as the inconsistency that may result unless we admit an independency to the desiring part.[2] In truth, appetite is not the act of the sensitive part only, but of the desiring part as mediated by sensation.

Generally speaking, it would be by far more natural to identify the parts of the soul with its functions, than to attribute many functions to limited parts and to admit some community between the functions which belong to different parts. That the parts are related with one another, is compatible with dividing soul into parts, but the division of the soul would have no meaning as far as the soul itself is concerned, unless the functions were divided distinctly. Moreover, Aristotle never distinguishes the parts from the functions, and mentions as the parts of soul, sometimes the rational and the irrational, sometimes so-called functions such as the nutritive, sensitive, desiring, motive, etc.

According to Brentano, the soul is divided into parts either from a physical or from a logical point of view. The physical division is the separation of faculties through being distributed to the parts of a substance; such, for example, is the division of the immortal from the mortal part of man. And the logical division is the separation of powers, such that all living beings do not partake both of this and

[1] Ibid. 61 - 69. [2] De An. III. 9. 432 b 3-7.

of that power; in this respect the vegetative faculty is divided from sensation, lower sensations from higher ones, higher sensations from locomotion, and further, locomotion from intellectual faculties. Aristotle talks about the parts of soul in this last sense.[1] But as stated above, we would take the logical division rather as the second kind of division, assuming it to be a distinction of fucntions. The division which Brentano identifies with the logical one is situated between the first or physical division and a functional one. It is the division which acts as the principle of classification of living beings, and may be called biological division. The authenticity of this division is beyond doubt, but it is only one kind of division made by Aristotle. We would adopt all of the three points of view, rather than limiting ourselves to any one as the scholars have done in the past. Aristotle would have divided the soul, physically or rather metaphysically, into the rational and the irrational, or more minutely, into active reason and other parts comprising passive reason; biologically, into the mainly nutritive, the mainly sensitive, and the mainly intellectual complexes of functions—the view Brentano adopted; and further, logically, into an indefinite multitude of parts, as often enumerated by Aristotle. In short, the division of parts of the soul is not confined to the logical, but may be sometimes logical, sometimes biological, and sometimes physico-metaphysical.

This would explain the fact that Aristotle, who seems to have proposed in the *De Anima* the multipartite theory in the place of the traditional duopartite theory, restores the latter and tries to arbitrate both theories in the *Nicomachean Ethics*. He has admitted from the outset that soul is divisible in many ways from different points of view. Only he asserts that it should be divided into more parts than two or three if we choose a division according to faculties. Thus the duopartite theory and the multipartite theory are compatible without any contradiction.

The synthesis which was tried in the *Nicomachean Ethics*, is as follows: The soul is, at first, divided into the rational and the irrational part. Within the latter, there is the vegetative part, which accounts for assimilation and growth. This is possessed by all living beings, having no reference to reason. Sensation is treated in like manner. There is, in the second place, another part of the irrational soul, which sometimes obeys and sometimes

[1] Brentano, Psych. d. Arist. 57.

disobeys reason, namely, the desiring part. Aristotle says that, in accordance with the subdivision of the irrational part, the rational part is also divided into a superior sense, which has reason in itself, and an inferior, which obeys the other just as a son obeys his father.[1]

But this rational part in the secondary sense is in its contents not different from the irrational part in the secondary sense. They are similarly the same desiring part, only distinguished through a difference of viewpoint. In so far as it has not reason in itself, it is irrational, yet in so far as it may obey reason, it is rational. In order to get a more essential division, we might rather more appropriately distinguish the rational part into the part which orders like a father, and that part which is contented in itself, and make both of them correspond to the aforesaid two parts of the irrational soul. This correction would explain the real thought of Aristotle, seeing that, in a certain place, he divides the soul into the rational and the irrational, and assignes the ethical virtue to the former, then subdividing the rational part into the scientific or self-sufficient rational part and the reasoning or epitactic rational part,[2] he assigns science and wisdom to the former, and prudence to the latter.[3]

The duopartite theory which divides the soul into the rational and the irrational, originates from the metaphysical point of view, but in the *Ethics* it has lost its metaphysical sense and acquired a practical meaning. Herein the division is due to a consideration of the essence of the virtues in each part, and the method of their rearing. The virtues of the irrational part are ethical, consisting in moderation, and are formed through habituation; whereas the virtues of the rational part are intellectual, which, having in themselves reason and being formal, have no need of further determination by reason. They are not moderate in their essence, and are developed by teaching. With the positing of these distinctions, the duopartite theory of the soul would seem to have reappeared on the stage with an ethical significane.

To those who do not admit the multiplicity of dividing principles, it might appear quite curious that the duopartite theory which seems to have been once given up in the *De Anima*, should reappear in the *Ethica Nicomachea* though this is a later work.

[1] Eth. Nic. I. 13. 1102 b 28 ff.; cf. ibid. I. 7. 1098 a 3.
[2] Eth. Nic. VI. 2. 1138 b 35 -1139 a 12.
[3] Eth. Nic. VI. 3; 5. 1140 b 1, 25; VI. 7; VI. 13. 1144 b 14 ff.; X. 7; Pol. VII. 14. 1333 a 25.

Hence appears quite naturally the theory which maintains that the *Ethica Nicomachea* is founded upon the old duopartite theory. For instance, Jaeger considers[1] that the *(Nicomachean) Ethics* is yet founded upon the primitive view of the soul which admits only rational and irrational parts. Only he does not conclude from this, that the Ethics has been formed earlier than the *De Anima*, rather he explains that though Aristotle reached, in the psychological study, an extremely advanced scientific view by the aid of his biological study, yet, being unable to apply this new knowledge to the area of practical philosophy, he still remained in the Platonic tradition. Actually, the charge would seem to be mainly due to Aristotle's intention to simplify the problem. As he says in the *Nicomachean Ethics*, the moral philosopher should have knowledge about the soul only in order to understand the fundamental phenomena of the objects of his inquiry and in so far as it is needed for those objects; any further precision would be more than his purposes call for. Thus in the *Ethics*, we might suppose that he avoided complicating the problem by introducing the new idea of soul which he attained in the *De Anima*. But this hypothesis amounts to assuming that in the *Nicomachean Ethics*, Aristotle failed to master thoroughly the theory of the *De Anima*.

Y. Huzii has followed Jaeger's theory and advanced further, deeming the formation of the *Nicomachean Ethics* to be prior to that of the *De Anima*. In his study of Aristotle he says, "We may infer with sufficient reason that *Ethica Nicomachea* VI must have been composed remarkably earlier than these parts of the *De Anima;* its fundamental thought places it in the age of the *Ethica Eudemia*. For the fundamental concepts in the *(Nicomachean) Ethics* are founded upon the Platonic scheme, which was given up as incomplete already in the *De Anima*. This was the scheme of Aristotle's early thought, which admits to the soul two parts, the rational and the irrational, without referring to the parts posited later, viz., the θρεπτικόν, αἰσθητικόν, διανοητικόν, and the concept of the soul as the first ἐντελέχεια of the organism.[2] This assumption seems directly to be referring only to the date of the book VI or at most to the three books, V, VI, and VII. In fact, where Huzii differs from Jaeger is in not admitting book VI to be original in the *Nicomachean Ethics*. He hesitates to

[1] Jaeger, Aristoteles, 355 ff.
[2] Y. Huzii, Aristoteles Kenkyu (A study of Aristotle), 186.

decide this point, conjecturing that either the book might originally have belonged to the *Eudemian Ethics* except for the revision of the definition of φρόνησις, or that the three books V, VI, and VII of the *Nicomachean Ethics* might have been composed earlier than the rest of this book.[1] But in the footnote[2] to his proposition that the concepts in the *Ethics* are founded upon the early thought of the duopartite theory, this interpreter asks us to compare *De An.* III. 9. 432 a 24- 7 not with *Eth. Nic.* VI, but with *Eth. Nic.* I. 13. 1102 a 26-1103 a 10. Besides, the fundamental concepts of the intellectual and ethical virtues are founded upon this duopartite theory, not merely in book VI, but also in the whole *Nicomachean Ethics*. Consequently, if he wishes to set the date of *Eth. Nic.* VI, "remarkably earlier than the *De Anima*", on account of the duopartite theory in book VI, he should rather infer that the whole *Nicomachean Ethics* was formed remarkably earlier than the *De Anima*. And this, in fact, was his last conclusion:—"That Aristotle did not, in this place, have in mind the definition of the soul in the *De Anima*, is evident from the fact that he followed Plato's thought, which strictly distinguishes the soul from the body, rather than taking the soul as the ἐνέργεια of the body. So that it is at least a more natural interpretation to infer that the *Nicomachean Ethics* has been formed earlier than any part of the *De Anima*."[3]

We can, however, by no means agree with this interpreter. In the first place, *Eth. Nic.* I and II, which Huzii asks us to compare with the *De Anima*, does not only depend upon the assumption of two parts in the soul, but also admits various parts such as the nutritive, the desiring, the appetitive, and the intellectual; even the sensitive part is admitted in this book as a part of the soul. Hence, it is not because Aristotle did not think of the stricter concepts in the *De Anima*, that he established in the *Nicomachean Ethics* the concepts of virtues upon the duopartite theory. It is true that in book VI, we find only the two concepts of the rational and irrational parts instead of such concepts as the nutritive part, the sensitive, the desiring, etc. We might possibly assume from this fact that book VI, is earlier than the *De Anima*. But it is too hasty to conclude that it was formed in the period of the *Eudemian Ethics*, or is borrowed from that work, for we find even in the

---

[1] Ibid. 184.   [2] Ibid. 188, n.2.

[3] Ibid. 188 n. 3. Nuyens actually reached this conclusion, cf. op. cit. 193. His agrument, though very ingenious, does not persuade me completely.

Eudemian Ethics the concepts of the nutritive, the sensitive, and the desiring, evidently enumerated as parts of the soul.[1] If we admit Huzii's reasoning, we shall reach the conclusion that book VI of the *Nicomachean Ethics* must have been formed at least remarkably earlier than *Eth. Nic.* II. 1.—Even the interpreter, who assumes that *Eth. Nic.* VI. expresses Aristotle's earlier thought in the period of the *Eudemian Ethics*, would not dare to assert such a bold conclusion. Hence we must adopt a different interpretation of the fact that *Eth. Nic.* VI, or rather the whole *Nicomachean Ethics*, has adopted the duopartite theory of the rational and the irrational parts of the soul.

We have seen that in *Eth. Nic.* I various functions proper to the *De Anima* were enumerated along with the two parts. These heterogeneous groups of concepts are not employed unsystematically, but are coordinated rather well. In *Eth. Nic.* VI, especially, the intellectual part is divided into the scientific and the reasoning, the former being called absolutely rational, and the latter epitactic-rational. This subdivision of the intellectual part gives evidence, no doubt, of the mature reflection of Aristotle's later period; other functions or parts are not enumerated only because the problem at present is confined to the intellectual virtues and there is no need of referring to them. The problem of the sensitive part is not in the center of attention, but it is by no means neglected; in 1098 a 2, it is attributed to the irrational part, being common to animals, as is the nutritive part. Elaboration is lacking, because the matter is almost irrelevant to the problem of virtue. The functional division in the *De Anima*, being made mainly from the psycho-

---

[1] Eth. Eud. II. I. 1219 b 20 - 32. So it is entirely unfair for Jaeger to say that Aristotle yet follows Plato quite faithfully in Eth. Eud. II. 1. 1219 b 28: ἐπεὶ δ' ἀνθρωπίνην ἀρετὴν ζητοῦμεν, ὑποκείσθω δύο μέρη ψυχῆς τὰ λόγου μετέχοντα, οὐ τὸν αὐτὸν δὲ τρόπον μετέχειν λόγου ἄμφω, ἀλλὰ τὸ μὲν τῷ ἐπιτάττειν, τὸ δὲ τῷ πείθεσθαι καὶ ἀκούειν πεφυκέναι· εἰ δέ τί ἐστιν ἑτέρως ἄλογον, ἀφείσθω τοῦτο τὸ μόριον. It is evident from the context, that this is not a case of following Plato's scheme as Jaeger says, to say nothing of the fact that even the duopartite theory does not belong primarily to Plato, as we have seen above. Now Aristotle continues, ibid. 36-1220 a2: ἀφῄρηται δὲ καὶ εἴ τι ἄλλο ἐστὶ μέρος ψυχῆς, οἷον τὸ φυτικόν. ἀνθρωπίνης γὰρ ψυχῆς τὰ εἰρημένα μόρια ἴδια· διὸ οὐδ' αἱ ἀρεταὶ αἱ τοῦ θρεπτικοῦ καὶ αὐξητικοῦ ἀνθρώπου· δεῖ γὰρ, εἰ ᾗ ἄνθρωπος, λογισμὸν ἐνεῖναι (καὶ) ἀρχὴν καὶ πρᾶξιν, ἄρχει δ' ὁ λογισμὸς οὐ λογισμοῦ ἀλλ' ὀρέξεως καὶ παθημάτων, ἀνάγκη ἄρα ταῦτ' ἔχειν τὰ μέρη.

logical point of view, has no more significance to ethical theory than the biological division through functional complexes. What is important for ethics, is the practical value, rather than the real classification, of psychical functions. Nor has the definition of the soul as the first actuality of the body as much importance for ethics, which aims at practice, as it has for metaphysics. In short, Aristotle synthesized in the *Nicomachean Ethics* the traditional duopartite theory with the multipartite theory, which shows rather a more mature thought than would the absolute renunciation of the duopartite theory.

Yet, as we can find this plan of synthesis already in the *Eudemian Ethics*, we would not venture to conclude from this, that the *Nicomachean Ethics* is posterior to the *De Anima*, any more than we would conclude that the *Eudemian Ethics* itself is posterior to the *De Anima*. Such a philological presumption is far from our intention, as we believe that the duopartite theory is not given up even in the *De Anima*. We only assume that Aristotle, who presented in the *De Anima* the multipartite theory from the theoretical point of view, was obliged and endeavoured in both Ethics to synthesize the two kinds of classification from the practical point of view. Therefore, it is impossible to decide the period of these three works from these considerations.

The second argument which Huzii depends upon in assuming the *Nicomachean Ethics* to be earlier than the *De Anima*, seems to be more persuasive. It points out that in the *Nicomachean Ethics*, what is prevalent is the Platonic view, in which the soul is contrasted with the body, instead of the new theory of the *De Anima*, which defines the souls the actuality of the body. This neglect of the relation between soul and body, surely results in a defect in ethical theory, especially in the argument concerning ethical virtues. For all that, it would be a too hasty conclusion to decide from this the period of these works. For, we find this very thought in *Met.* VIII. 3. 1043a 34 as well; so that, according to Huzii's way of argument, *Met.* VIII. together with the *De Anima* should be assumed to be later than the *Nicomachean Ethics*. Taken independently, this hypothesis involes no difficulty. But compared with Met. VII, VIII, and IX, the *Nicomachean Ethics* appears to have some mark of development[1] e.g., with regard to such concept as

---

[1] Cf. p. 6, n. 6; Ando, Aristoteles no Sonzairon (Aristotle's Ontology), 234 ff.

δύναμις or ἕξις, and so we must refrain from such an inference from he above data alone. At any rate, since these three works all belong to Aristotle's last twelve years, it would be an act *ultra vires* of philology to suppose a too remarkable development of thought during this period without any sufficient reason.

In short, on this problem, we should like to conclude that Aristotle has divided the soul in many ways, from such various points of view as the logical-psychological, the biological, the metaphysical-physical, and the ethical.

CHAPTER II

THE FUNCTIONS OF THE SOUL

§ 1. THE DEVELOPMENT OF FUNCTIONS

WE have reached, in the previous chapter, the conclusion that the principle of dividing the soul is not always the same, but that there are various sorts of divisions, such as the logical-psychological, biological, metaphysical-physical, or ethical, and that we should neither restrict Aristotle to any one, nor construe differences as due to changes in his thought. Many of these schemes of division may have been derived from his predecessors, while some of them were originated by himself. Instead of insisting on a single scheme of division, Aristotle would seem rather to have synthesized these various schemes, assigning each one its particular meaning. The attempt to prove a transition in his thought through the philological-chronological study of his works has not succeeded, at least so far.[1] Besides, we must take care lest the abuse of the philological method reduce the system to poverty. The way to solve apparent contradictions and heterogeneous expressions is not simply to assume a transition in his thought; we should rather endeavour to find a logical sequence in these elements, unless there are philological reasons for proceeding otherwise. For, the thought of an eminent philosopher is neither an incoherent chaos "like an unskilful tragedy"[2], nor so abstract and simple a scheme as to be blind to any possible antagonism between reality and logic. It is rather a process of presenting abundant difficulties and solving the resulting problems by ascending to a more comprehensive and penetrating standpoint. And this is in fact the most remarkable merit of Aristotle's way of thinking. The method of Aristotle's philosophy is not confined to the *aporematic*, yet the presentation of ἀπορίαι being its essential moment, we should not always avoid these difficulties by presuming differences of date or the confusion of materials. Even if philological research attained the highest success, it would by no means prove that Aristotle simply altered the opinion and abandoned the attempt at collaboration. Aristotle was not

---

[1] Cf. p. 18, n. 2.   [2] Met. XIV. 3. 1090 b 19.

only a unique scholar who ranks with Plato and other philosophers in the Academy, but the very man who brought Greek Philosophy to perfection. To be an opponent of Plato was one of his aspects, to be a successor to Plato was another. In truth, he was not a successor or an oponent, but successor and oponent at the same time. We should not suppose him a pure original thinker in his later period, by regarding all Platonic or traditional elements in him as belonging to his early work. The later Aristotle should be rather regarded as the systematizer of a most comprehensive and synthetic philosophy.

Now the soul is divided into rational and irrational parts, either from a metaphysical or an ethical point of view. Metaphysically, it is divided according as the parts possess substantial independency and eternity, while ethically, the practical interest in what manner the virtues of each part of the soul are generated or acquired gives another meaning to this division. There are also many other kinds of divisions, the most important of all being the biological-psychological one, which is peculiar to Aristotle. But we think that these divisions made from various points of view are synthesized and united in the *Ethica Nicomachea*,[1] a work of Aristotle's last years. Firstly, it is evident that the nutritive part in the psycho-biological division is irrational, while the intellectual part is rational. The other four parts, the sensible, the imaginative, the appetitive, and the motive are in one sense irrational, but in another rational. In order to subsume these intermediate parts under the two concepts rational and irrational, Aristotle distinguishes two different meanings for these terms. Just as there are rational parts in the primary and the secondary sense, so are there irrational parts in both senses.

The irrational part in the primary sense acts quite independently of reason; to it belongs the so-called vegetative soul[2] that manages purely physiological and unconscious functions such as nutrition, growth, and reproduction. Whereas the irrational part in the secondary sense is that which obeys or resists the commands and prohibitions of reason, just as a man obeys or resists his father's words.[3] The function of this intermediate part is here represented by desire,[4] but more exactly, it should also include sensation, imagination, and movement, which are all closely connected with desire.

[1] Eth. Nic. I. 13. 1102 a 26.   [2] Eth. Nic. I. 13. 1102 a 32; De An. II. 2. 413 b 8.
[3] Eth. Nic. I. 13. 1102 b 13.   [4] Eth. Nic. I. 13. 1102 b 30; cf. Pol. III. 4. 1277 a 6.

Certainly, these functions are not so intimate as nutrition, growth, and reproduction, which are united in a single nutritive part. There are some differences of degree among them, and they do not always accompany each other. Nevertheless owing to their close connexion, they are treated by the practical interest of ethics almost as a single part. Of course, sensation and imagination are not only principles of action, but also may be moments of theoretical knowledge.[1] Yet they are generally attributed to all or most animals,[2] and are not confined to those which are rational. Those animals move on the occasion of sensation or imagination,[3] while the immediate efficient cause of their locomotion is desire.[4] So the representative faculty of this part is not desire only, but sometimes is sensation instead. Taking special notice of the latter, Brentano has divided the soul into the nutritive, sensitive, and rational parts.[5] In short, the irrational part in the secondary sense is the conscious soul of animals which implies sensation, imagination, and movement.[6] It is because of its practical importance, that ethics emphasizes desire, regarding the other functions as something preliminary or auxiliary to the activity of this representative function. Since such a part of the soul may be, again, regarded rational in so far as it shares in reason, Aristotle calls it the rational part in the

---

[1] Sensation is a kind of cognition (Gen. An. I. 23. 731 a 33). It is discriminating, like intellect (Motu An. 6. 700 b 20; An. Post. II. 19. 99 b 35; De An. III. 9. 432 a 16; Top. II. 4. 111 a 19; cf. De An. III. 2. 426 b 10; III. 3. 427 a16), and analogous to simple assertion or thinking (De An. III. 7. 431 a 8). It is the beginning of induction or the principle of knowledge, in so far as it is discriminating (An. Post. I. 18. 81 b 8; Top. I. 12. 105 a 18). So that it is not a practical principle *per se* (Eth. Nic. V. 2. 1139 a 20; De An. III. 9. 432 b 19). Sometimes the animal soul is divided into a locomotive faculty on the one hand, and a cognitive faculty which includes sensation and intellect on the other (De An. III. 9. 432 a 15; III. 3. 427 a 17). This would be a distinction from the standpoint of whether a soul is active or passive with respect to the object. This is, so to say, the ideal aspect, not the real. Sensation may be a principle of theoretical knowledge, but from a genetic point of view, it is without doubt practical as a preserving function of the body. It is not a practical principle, only in the sense that it is not an active and immediate principle like desire. Nevertheless, as desire presupposes sensation or imagination, it is an indirect principle of conduct.

[2] Part. An. III. 4. 666 a 34; II. 1. 647 a 21; 10. 656 a 3; IV. 5. 681 a 19. Gen. An. I. 23. 731 a 33; b 4; II. 1. 732 a 13; 5. 741 a 9; III. 7. 757 b 16; VI. 1. 778 b 32; De An. II. 2. 413 b 1; De Sensu. 1. 436 b 11; V. 1. 467 b 24; Met. I. 1. 980 a 26.   [3] Motu An. 6. 701 a 5.

[4] De An. III. 10. 433 b 16; Motu An. 6. 701 a 1; 10. 703 a 5.

[5] Brentano, Psych. d. Arist. 58-60.   [6] Ibid.

secondary sense.[1] while the rational part in the superior sense is the thinking part which involves reason in itself. But in this point, as we have said above,[2] we might rather divide, more strictly and consistently, the rational part into theoretical intellect, which engages in its thinking activity quite independently, and practical intellect, which guides the irrational part in the secondary sense, just as a father does his son. The rational part in the secondary sense corresponds to the irrational part in the secondary sense; they are, so to say, the two sides of one and the same thing, but are themselves not quite identical. For to order is one thing, to obey another: the former is essentially rational, while the latter essentially irrational. It is only accidentally that the former is irrational and the latter rational. Aristotle himself makes this distinction.[3] The two species of rational parts in the first division are διανοητικόν and ἠθικόν, while those of the second division are θεωρητικόν and πρακτικόν. If we may distinguish between rational parts and reasoning parts, the former pair would be the two species of rational parts and the latter pair the two species of reasoning parts.

Through the combination of the functional parts of the soul, and the two parts, rational and irrational, in the traditional division, Aristotle found a way to give a practical meaning to the theoretical division. For the motive of the so-called psychological division is theoretical, and that of the ethical division is practical.[4] Yet the synthesis of these heterogeneous divisions is hardly accomplished as far as *Nicomachean Ethics* is concerned. On this account, Jaeger's criticism[5] that in Aristotle's ethics the duopartite theory is dominant, while the functional division that was worked out in his psychology is neglected, is right to some extent. But it is not because, as he thinks, Aristotle's ethical thought was constrained by the preceding theory of Plato, so that the results of his psychological study could not be applied completely, nor, as Fuzii conjectures, is it because the former was formed before the latter; it is rather because of the difference in scientific interest or viewpoint between these two sides of the philosopher's thought. Psychology as a part of natural science is chiefly theoretical, whereas ethics, being a kind of practical science, is governed by a practical interest. The division and investigation of virtues is not a mere observation of

[1] Eth. Nic. I. 13. 1103 a 1 ff.
[2] Ch. I. § 6.
[3] Eth. Nic. VI. 2. 1138 b 35 ff.
[4] Cf. Zeller, Ph. d. Gr. II. 2. 499 n 5.
[5] Jaeger, Aristoteles, 355 ff.

natural functions, but a research into the ways of conducting human affairs. Excellence in nutrition, or sight, or imagination, is not inquired into, only because it has no importance for ethical practice. The ethical writings inquire about the soul in order to clarify the virtues,[1] and inquires about the virtues in order to define the essence of happiness and thereby to bring to individuals and states the highest happiness. To require that ethical works should be described in accordance with psychological functions is due to an ignorance of methodology: in Aristotle's words, it betrays one's lack of παιδεία.[2] As far as human conduct is concerned, however, it is in fact desirable to study the relations between the psychological functions of the human soul more fully. This will also contribute much to our understanding of conduct and virtue. But we should not limit this study to his psychology and ethics, but rather ought to extend it to all of his works. Aristotle's ethics indeed presupposes such a systematic connection.

Now the soul was defined as the form of a natural body having in it the capacity of life.[3] It is by nature the activity of the body and the very principle which makes it a living body. The body lives because of the soul, without which it is only a material object.[4] Consequently the primitive functions of life, such as nutrition or reproduction, are not simply the functions of the body as a mere material object, but rather in fact those of the soul as the principle of life.[5] Since such is the relation of soul and body, there would be no function of the soul which is independent of the body; what we call a function of the body is in fact an act of the soul in the body, and an act of the soul is nothing but a function of the body that appears as the soul. A true physicist who wants to perceive a psychological phenomenon completely, should not content himself with seeing it as mere consciousness, but also ought to explain its physiological basis.[6] But a possible distinction to be drawn is that the body's conditioning of the soul is direct in a

[1] Eth. Nic. I. 13. 1102 a 18-25.
[2] Met. IV.4. 1006 a 6 ff; Eth. Nic. I. 1. 1094 b 19-1095 a 2.
[3] De An. II. 1. 429 a 19; ch. II. § 1.   [4] De An. I. 5. 411 b 8-10.
[5] De An. I. 4. 416 a 18 f.;   416 b 9-11;   De An. III. 12. 434 a 22, 26;   II. 4. 415 a 23; Gen. An. II. 7. 745 b 24; III. 7. 757 b 16; II. 3. 736 a 35; 4. 740 b 36; 740 b 29; De Juvent. 2. 468 b 2; De Resp 8. 474 a 31; 18, 479 a 30. Nutrition the lowest and the most general function of the soul common to plants: De An. II. 2. 413 b 7; 4. 415 a 23; III. 9. 432 a 29; 12.434 a 22, 26.
[6] De An. I. 1. 403 b 11 f.

lower stage, but indirect in a higher. A lower psychical phenomenon makes contact directly with the body, while a higher one is conditioned by lower psychical functions. Thus nutrition and reproduction appear as mere bodily functions, while thinking is apt to be considered as if it were independent of bodily conditions, though it is comparatively easy to perceive the necessity to it of imagination and sensation. Still this is a mere difference of degree: as a rule, no functions of the soul are possible without some accompanying bodily changes. The active reason, which appears to be the only exception, is not, as we have seen, a part of the soul, in so far as it is the form of the body, but the objective spirit which gives a form to the passive reason.

Body and soul are not related to each other as two heterogeneous principles, but are conjoined as matter and form, so that they are strictly correlative: the central organ of the body is at the same time the place of the soul and the condition of its unity. Seeing that the soul is nothing but the principle of life, it is evident that it is situated at the centre of the body.[1] Such a central organ of the body, and consequently also of the soul, is found in the heart,[2] for it is at the same time the starting point and the end of blood-vessels,[3] the distributing centre of blood,[4] the origin of heat[5] which is necessary for life;[6] once the movement of heart is stopped,

---

[1] De Juvent. 1. 467 b 14-17. According to Nuyens, the localization-theory of the soul is peculiar to Aristotle's transitional period, to which belong De Partibus Animalium, De Juventute et Senectute, as well as De Respiratione. But we do not find it so incompatible as he says, to assume on the one hand that the soul is the form of the whole body, and on the other hand that its central organ is the heart. Cf. op. cit. 164 together with Rolfes's note on this point. Besides, Nuyens finds it difficult to prove the antecedency of De Respiratione to De Anima because of the reference of the former to the latter in 474 b 11; cf. op. cit. 168 f.

[2] De Resp. 17. 479 a 1; De Juvent. 4. 469 a 28; De Somno. 2. 456 a 6; Part. An. III. 3. 665 a 12; 4. 666 b 14; Met. VI. 10. 1035 b 26.

[3] Part. An. II. 647 b 4; 9. 654 b 11; III. 4. 665 b 15; 17. 666 a 8, 31; 5. 667 a 16; Gen. An. II. 4. 740 a 22, 28; 6. 744 a 5; 6. 743 a 1; IV. 8. 776 b 12; V. 7. 787 b 28; De Somno. 3. 456 b 1; De Juvent. 3. 469 b 1. 468 b 32; De Memor. 8. 474 b 7; De Resp. 8. 474 b 7; Hist. An. III. 3. 513 a 22; 4. 514 b 22.

[4] Part. An. III. 3. 665 a 11, 18; 665 b 20; 666 a 15; De Resp. 17. 478 b 35; De Juvent. 4. 469 a 33; 1. 468 a 1; 2. 468 a 21.

[5] De Juvent. 6. 470 a 19; 4. 469 b 8; 5. 470 a 6; Part. An. II. 3. 650 a 5.

[6] De Juvent. 4. 469 b 9-20; De Resp. 17. 478 a 24; 478 b 32; Part. An. II. 7. 652;b 27; III. 7. 670 a 24; II. 7. 653 b 5; IV. 13. 696 b 17; Gen. An. II. 6. 743 b 28.

the temperature cools, the circulation of blood ceases, and the death of the animal ensues.[1] Thus the heart is, on the one hand, the first in the sequence of individual generation,[2] on the other hand, it is the central organ of nutrition in sanguine animals;[3] the blood that circulates through it is responsible for supplying nutriment to the whole body.[4] Food is first taken through the mouth, then digested by the stomach and excreted at the end of the body, but what presides over the whole nutritive process is the heart, the other parts being only ancillary to it.[5]

Properly speaking, the uniting principle of an animal is not the body, but the soul.[6] Yet, as far as the soul is the form and actuality of the body, the correlation of psychical functions must correspond to that of bodily organs. The heart is not only the centre of nutrition, but also that of sensation,[7] imagination,[8] feeling,[9] desire,[10] and motion,[11] and further even of prudence.[12] Generally speaking, the differentiation and development of psychical functions correspond to those of bodily parts, and both of them are proportionate to the complexity of life.[13] But the differentiation and development of life and body are so continuous, as often to make us unable to decide in classification to which genus a species should belong.[14] If such a continuity should be admitted between living beings and lifeless things,[15] as well as between animals and

[1] De Juvent. 4. 469 b 13-20.
[2] De Juvent. 3. 468 b 28; 469 b 30; Gen. An. II. 4. 740 a 8, 13; 740 b 3; 5. 741 b 16; 1. 735 a 24; 4. 738 b 16; 740 a 17; II. 6. 743 b 26; III. 2. 753 b 19; Motu An. III. 4. 666 a 10, 21; cf. Gen. An. IV. 1. 766 b 2; Met. V. 1. 1013 a 5; Part. An. 4. 665 a 33; 665 b 1; 666 a 20; II. 6. 742 b 36.
[3] De Juvent. 3. 469 a 5; Part. An. II. 1. 647 a 25.
[4] De Juvent. 3. 469 a 2; Part. An. II. 3. 650 b 12; 651 a 15, 10; III. 5. 668 a 20.
[5] De Juvent. 3. 469 a 2; 469 b 11.
[6] De An. I. 5. 411 b 5; Part. An. I. 1. 641 a 17-21
[7] De Juvent. 3. 469 a 5, 10; 1. 467 b 28; Part. An. II. 1. 647 a 25; 3. 469 a 10; III. 3. 665 a 12, 17; 4. 666 b 14; II. 10. 656 a 28; IV. 5. 681 b 15, 32; Motu An. II. 702 b 24; Gen. An. II. 6. 743 b 25.
[8] Motu An. 6. 700 b 19.   [9] Part. An. III. 4. 666 a 12.
[10] De An. I. 1. 403 a 31; III. 9. 433 a 1; cf. Motu An. 7. 701 b 1-8; 702 a 20.
[11] Part. An. II. 1. 647a 25; III. 3. 665 a 12, 17; 4. 666 b 14; De Somno. 2. 456 b 4.
[12] Part. An. II. 2. 648 a 3 ff.; Gen. An. II. 6. 744 a 27; cf. Teichmüller, Neue Studien zur Geschichte der Begriffe, III. 133-145.
[13] Part. An. II. 10. 656 a 1-8; Gen. An. I. 23. 731 a 24 ff.; De Cael. II. 12. 292 b 7 ff.   [14] Hist. An. VIII. 1. 588 b 4-589 a 2; Part. An. IV. 5. 681 a 12; 10. 686 b 20 ff.   [15] Hist. An. VIII. 1. 588 b 6.

plants, not only the difference of psychical functions but also that of soul and body would be only relative. In this very point, we may find the characteristic of Aristotle's metaphysical principles, form and matter, which are radically different from the heterogeneous principles of matter and soul employed by Descartes or Spinoza. And in this respect also, Leibniz's monadology may be regarded as the revival of Aristotle's theory. Not only does matter always accompany form as its substratum, but also they are related to each other as potentiality to actuality. On the one hand, the body is the substratum of the soul, but on the other hand, life develops continuously from the corporeal to the psychical. The limit of this continuous series is, on the one side, the material area which is almost deprived of the psychical, and, on the other side, the pure spiritual area which has scarcely any corporeal moment. The former is the so-called *prima materia*, and the latter God.[1] But if this series should be really continuous, even a lifeless thing must have a faint and indefinite potentiality of life, and a spirit must have a corporeal substratum. Thus the whole universe is assumed to be a system of continuous development full of life.[2] Even the movement of a thing lifeless in an ordinary sense, is not quite heterogeneous with living phenomena. Just as the movements of elements such as earth, water, fire, and air follow a definite rule in accordance with their nature, so those of animals also follow their own nature, only differing in their degree of complexity.[3] Besides, the movements of animals or the complexity of life is after all due to the complexity of the organs which constitute the living

---

[1] Cf. Zeller, op. cit. 505 n. 1. Zeller regards the meridian of the development to be mankind, but according to Aristotle, man is neither the highest being nor even the highest animal. Heavenly bodies and gods are also regarded as living beings; e.g. Met. XII. 7. 1072 b 29; Top. V. 1. 128 b 19; V. 6. 136 b 7; De Cael. II. 2. 285 a 29. 3. 286 a 9; cf. II. 12; II. 2. 284 b 32; Part. An. I. 1. 641 b 15 ff. This is admitted by Zeller op. cit. 467. On the other hand, life is attributed to the elements as well. Gen. An. III. 11. 762 a 18-26.

[2] Aristotle admits life in a wider sense to all beings; e.g. he talks about the life of air and wind in Gen. An. IV. 10. 778 a 2, and the life of the sea in Meteor. II. 2. 355 b 4 ff.; 356 a 33 ff. Further, all inorganic natural phenomena are explained by analogy with organism; cf. Zeller, op. cit. 506 f.

[3] Aristotle rejects the theories of natural philosophers who explained the soul by supposing it to be constituted of such a simple element as earth, water, fire, or air (De An. I. 2). But as the soul is the form of the body, and the body is an organism which is constituted of these elements, the functions of the soul must be, after all, the complex functions of these elements.

body.[1] Consequently, we may say that psychical phenomena, like the activities of organisms, are nothing but the complex activity of the elements which constitute the organs. When the term "life" is applied beyond its usual limit to a divine being, some sort of material is assigned to such a being on the analogy of an organism. Where all the matter of an organism is formalized, and there remains only the potentiality of locomotion—such beings, viz. the heavenly bodies, are considered to be the very bodies of superorganic souls.[2] Beyond them there is only a pure form which has no matter or potentiality — a spirit in complete actuality, i.e. God.[3] All beings and all phenomena in the universe compose such a complete system of development, continuity being its fundamental principle.[4] The government[5] of God is not His voluntary practice or production.[6] Practice and production are acts or movements from desire,[7] whereas desire and movement are peculiar to incomplete beings.[8] God as the complete being, must be absolutely unmovable,[9] the contemplation of himself being his only activity.[10] All living and lifeless things are moved by Him, through loving and longing for this Supreme Being,[11] who, how-

[1] Cf. p. 104, n. 13.

[2] De Cael. II. 12. 292 a 18 ff.; II. 2. 285 a 25; 284 b 32; Part. An. I. 1. 641 b 15; Eth. Nic. VI. 7. 1141 a 35; cf. Met. XII. 8. 1073 a 26. The organs and functions of lower animals are simple, but the higher the animals, the more complex the functions. Thus the living functions of heavenly bodies which are superior to man, appear to be more complex. But Aristotle does not think so. According to him, lower creatures require only simple functions, because their life is also simple, but man requires far more complex functions to share in higher values. Whereas heavenly bodies and gods may be simple in another sense, owing to their independent existence and self-sufficient life (De Cael. II. 12). This is ingenious thought indeed, but it does not get rid of the difficulties that follow from regarding heavenly bodies as divine animals.

[3] Met. XII. 6. 1071 b 21; 8. 1072 a 26, 35; 1074 a 35; De Cael. I. 9. 279 a 16, 32; cf. Met. V. 7. 1072 b 29; Top. V. 1. 128 b 19.   [4] Cf. p. 104, n. 14.

[5] Met. XII. 7. 1072 b 7; 8. 1078 b 7 ff; XII. 10. De Cael. I. 9. 279 a 16; Met. XII. 7. 1072 b 7.

[6] Eth. Nic. X. 8. 1178 b 20; cf. 1178 a 9; 1178 b 5; VIII. 1. 1145 a 25; Zeller, op. cit. 368 n. 1; Brentano, Psych. d. Arist. 238 ff.

[7] Eth. Nic. VI. 2. 1139 a 17 ff.; 30 ff.

[8] Eth. Eud. VII. 12. 1244 b 8; 15. 1249 b 16; [Mag. Mor. II. 15. 1212 b 35].

[9] Met. XI. 7. 1064 a 37; XII. 7. 1072 a 26; De Cael. I. 9. 279 a 32; II. 12. 292 a 18; 292 b 5; Phys. VIII. 5. 250 b 20; De An. III. 10. 433 b 13.

[10] Met. XII. 7. 1072 b 18; 9. 1074 b 21; Eth. Eud. VII. 12. 1245 b 17.

[11] Pol. III. 16. 1287 a 29; Top. V. 4. 132 b 3; Gen. et Corr. I. 6. 323 a 12.

ever, does not move others through his own movement. Hence every activity of all creatures in accordance with their nature is holy.[1] What is called providence is nothing but the power of nature.[2] Is this not an excellent archetype of Leibniz's monadology and of the theory of preestablished harmony?

With this magnificient view of the universe before us, let us return to the present question, viz. the inter-relations of psychical functions. Needless to say, the correlative concepts of matter and form, or the potential and the actual, being the fundamental principles of Aristotle's metaphysics, are applicable to everything. They are applied to the relation between the parts of the soul, as well as to the relation of the soul to the body. Just as a concrete living being consists of body and soul, as matter and form, the former developing into the latter as from potentiality to actuality, likewise the lower part of the soul is related to the higher part as matter to form, and the former develops into the latter as from potentiality to actuality. This differentiation and development of psychical functions illustrates in itself the scale of biological evolution. The higher function presupposes the lower, and can not exist without it, while the lower function does not necessarily require the higher, and may exist without it.[3] The lowest functions are nutrition, growth and generation;[4] the part of the soul which is engaged in these functions is called the nutritive part[5] or nutritive soul,[6] which is most necessary and fundamental for

---

[1] De Cael. I. 4. 271 a 33; Gen. et Corr. II. 10. 336 b 27 ff.; Pol. VII. 4. 1326 a 32; Eth. Nic. X. 10. 1179 b 21; VII. 14. 1153 b 32.

[2] In Part. An. II. 10. 656 a 7, IV. 10. 686 a 27, Eth. Nic. X. 7. 1177 a 13 etc., only reason is assumed to be θεῖον while in De Divin. 463 b 12, other natural powers are said to be δαιμόνια; cf. Zeller, op. cit. 387 f. It is evident through comparison with the preceding note, that this difference too cannot be explained philologically as a development of Aristotle's thought. He may have been led to the distinction through an effort at strictness, and we may still take the view that what is δαιμόνιον is θεῖον in a wider sense.

[3] De An. II. 2. 413 b 7; 414 a 33; 415 a 23; III. 9. 432 a 29; 12. 434 a 22, 26; De An. II. 3. 414 b 28-415 a 11.

[4] Nutrition and growth are attributed to the same part. De An. II. 2. 413 a 25; 4. 416 b 12; III. 12. 434 a 24; Eth. Nic. I. 6. 1098 a 1. So with nutrition and reproduction. De An. II. 4. 416 a 19; Gen. An. II. 4. 740 b 36.

[5] De An. II. 2. 413 a 31; 413 b 5,7,12; 3. 414 a 31; 414 b 31; III. 9. 432 a 29; De Somno. 1. 454 a 13; De Juvent. 2. 468. a 28; Eth. Nic. I. 13. 1102 b 11; VI. 13. 1144 a 10.

[6] De An. II. 4. 415 a 23; III. 12. 434 a 22; De Juvent. 2. 468; b 2; De Resp. 8. 474 a 31; 18. 479 a 30; Gen. An. II. 3. 736 a 35; 4. 740 b 36.

life, and can exist without the others, while the latter cannot exist without the former.[1] The living beings which have only this lowest type of soul are plants.[2]

Now living beings have different functions in accordance with their modes of nutrition, some of these modes requiring higher functions of the soul.[3] Thus living beings that eat other living beings, are possessed of sensation, which is the function of leading nutrition, and is the characteristic of all animals. Aristotle says,[4] "But the animal must of necessity possess sensation, if nature makes nothing in vain: for everything in nature subserves an end, or else will be an accessory of things which subserve an end. Now every living body having the power of progression and yet lacking sensation would be destroyed and never reach full development, which is its natural function. For how in such a case is it to obtain nutriment? Motionless animals, it is true, have for nutriment that from which they have been developed. But a body, not stationary, but produced by generation, cannot possibly have a soul and an intelligence capable of judging without also having sensation. This proposition of Aristotle indeed expresses completely the teleological character of his biology. But, the idea that sensation is teleologically determined by an animal's mode of nutrition, does not of necessity lead to the theistic conception. Aristotle's teleology is not a theory of creation which presumes the conscious purpose of a personal god, but a theory of the development of a formal principle which is immanent in life.[5] The evolution of life is neither due to the mechanical action of elements nor to the regulation of a personal god; it is rather a natural generation from the creative principle which is immanent in life.[6] A modern pragmatist, such as Bergson, is inclined to condemn Aristotle as a mere rationalist, but we might rather conclude from the foregoing investigation, that Aristotle in fact anticipates prag-

---

[1] De An. II. 2. 413 a 31; 413 b 5; 3. 414 b 31; De Somno 1. 454 a 13; De Resp. 8. 474 b 11.

[2] De An. II. 2. 413 b 7; 4. 415 a 23; III. 9. 432 a 29; 12. 434 a 22, 26.

[3] De Juvent. 1. 468 a 9-12. Plants take nourishment from the earth, while animals nourish themselves through eating other living beings. Hist. An. VIII. 1. 588 a 16-33.

[4] De An. III. 12. 434 a 30-b4; De Sensu 1. 436 b 12-437a 1.

[5] Zeller, op. cit. 381.

[6] Part. An. I. 1. 641 b 12-26; Phys. II. 8. 199 b 26-33; Met. XII. 8. 1065 a 26 f.

matism in reducing the origin and essence of sensation and intellect to the necessities of life.[1] Aristotle, however, talks in some places of sensation as a pure discriminating faculty like knowledge, and refuses to make it the principle of conduct. This might easily be taken as an assertion of an intellectualism which would assume sensation to be an element of theoretical knowledge. But discrimination is an act or attribute of sensation taken purely *in abstracto*, rather than a concrete sensation. *In concreto*, as we have seen above, it depends on the one hand, upon the nutritive function as its substratum, and is conditioned by the mode of nutrition. On the other, as we shall observe later on, it conditions desire and conduct through the medium of feeling. These two opinions might seem at first sight to contradict each other, but in truth, the contradiction is a mere appearance which results from a difference of viewpoint. Sensation is pragmatic in its generation, but theoretical in its end. It is evident merely from the fact that sensation is a living phenomenon common to all animals, that it is pragmatic in its generation, in its primitive form, or in its usual activity *in concreto*.[2] Needless to say, the sensitive perception of an animal is not a pure theoretical cognition, but a practical one that serves directly for the preservation and development of life, i.e. for nutrition and generation.[3] Therefore, the very centre of sensation is found in the heart,[4] which is also the central organ of nutrition. Nevertheless, sensation is not desire or conduct, but a mere cognition as far as it is taken *in abstracto* as sensation: the very fact that it receives forms makes it the fundamental element of theoretical knowledge. This double character of sensatior will be made clear through the following observation on the development of special sensations.

Just as sensation is founded upon nutrition, there are also hierarchical differences among sensations. Touch and taste are the lowest of all,[5] and in addition, taste is considered to be a kind

[1] Cf. Bergson, L'évolution créatrice. 115 ff.
[2] Eth. Nic. VII. 6. 1149 a 10; Part. An. I. 5. 651 b 5; III. 4. 666 a 34; II. 1. 647 a 21; 10. 656 a 3; IV. 5. 681 a 19; Gen. An. I. 23. 731 a 33; 731 b 4. II. 1. 732 a 12; II. 5. 741 a 9; III. 7. 757 b 16; V. 1. 778 b 32; De An. II. 2. 413 b 1; De Sensu 436 b 11; De Juvent. 1. 467 b 24; Met. I. 1. 980 a 28; Eth. Nic. IX. 9. 1170 a 16; VI. 2. 1139 a 20.   [3] Hist. An. VIII. 1. 589 a 2-5.
[4] De Juvent. 3. 469 a 5-8; Part. An. IV. 4. 678 b 1-4.
[5] De An. II. 2. 413 b 4-7; 414 a 2-4; 3. 414 b 3; Hist. An. I. 3. 489 a 17; Part. An. II. 8. 653 b 23; De Sensu 1. 436 b 13; De Somno 2. 455 a 7.

of touch, because it is a sensation which feels through directly touching food.[1] Next to taste and touch, come smell, hearing, and sight, in ascending order. The rule of progressive development of psychical functions is applied also to the interrelation of sensations. The lower sensation may exist by itself, but the higher presupposes the lower.[2] Touch and taste act by direct contact with objects, but smell and other higher senses perceive objects through media.[3] What relates directly to nutrition is of course touch and taste, or touch in the wider sense which includes taste. Animals cannot live without this sensation.[4] Generation, being a primitive function inseparable from nutrition,[5] is also mediated by touch as the lowest sensation. "These two senses (i.e. taste and touch), then, are necessary to the animal, and it is plain that without touch no animal can exist. But the other senses are means to well-being, and are necessary, not to any and every species of animal, but only to certain species, as, for example, those capable of locomotion. For if the animal capable of locomotion is to survive, it must have sensation, not only when in contact with anything, but also at a distance from it."[6] "Thus the animal has sight to see with, because it lives in air or water or speaking generally, in a transparent medium...... It has hearing in order that information may be conveyed to it."[7] Higher sensations are also naturally necessary for life, but they are not simply needed for mere existence, but are useful for a better life. And for the sake of a better life, the animal needs a perception of distant objects. Sight and hearing are higher than taste, because they give a knowledge about distant objects and a wider perspective to life. "The senses which operate through external media, viz. smelling, hearing, and seeing, are found in all animals which possess the faculty of locomotion. To all that possess them they are a means of preservation; their final cause being that such creatures may, guided

---

[1] De An. II. 9. 421 a 18; III. 12. 434 b 18; De Sensu 4. 441 a 3; Part. An. II. 17. 660 a 21.
[2] De An. III. 12. 435 a 12-14.
[3] De An. III. 12. 435 a 14-19.
[4] De An. III. 12. 434 b 10-24; De An. II. 3. 414 b 6-9.
[5] De An. II. 4. 415 a 23; 416 b 24.
[6] De An. III. 12. 434 b 22.
[7] Ibid. 13. 435 b 19.

by antecedent perception, both pursue their food, and shun things that are bad or destructive."[1]

The distance of space between object and subject is directly proportional to the interval of time between sensation and enjoyment. This distance or interval corresponds to the degree of value of the sensation. A higher sensation is nothing other than an ability that allows us a wider observation and earlier foreknowledge of objects distant in time and space. This principle is not confined to relations among sensations, but may be extended analogically to the relation of sensation to intellect.[2]

The higher sensations not only direct the basic functions such as nutrition and generation more effectively than the lower, through giving perceptions of distant objects, but also they prepare for higher mental activities. Among the three kinds of sensations, smell, being almost subordinate to taste, is responsible for an indirect guidance to nutrition and generation; but, especially in the case of human beings, smell has the function of promoting or inhibiting health, besides being immediately concerned with nutrition. An example of this would be the smelling of the perfume of flowers.[3] Hearing and sight are not irrelevant to nutrition, but they also guide it indirectly, and were developed for the purpose of the preservation of existence and for generation.[4] But these higher sensations are already freeing themselves of the immediate interests of life. Especially, hearing and sight are the *sine qua non* of our higher cognition. Of course they are themselves kinds of sensation, yet they form the beginning of intellectual cognition beyond mere sensations. "Such sensations are a means of preservation to all that possess them......But in animals which have also intelligence they serve for the attainment of a higher perfection. They bring in tidings of many distinctive qualities of things, from which the knowledge of truth, speculative and practical, is generated in the soul. Of the two last mentioned, seeing, regarded as being supplied for the primary wants of life and considered in its direct effects, is the superior sense; but for developing of intelligence, and in its indirect consequences, hearing takes the precedence. The faculty of seeing, thanks to the fact that all bodies are coloured,

---

[1] De Sensu 1. 436 b 18.　　　　[2] Cf. De An. III. 10. 433 b 5 ff.
[3] De An. II. 3. 414 b 10 f.;　De Sensu 5. 443 b 16-30;　444 a 14 f.;　445 a 1-4;　ibid. 27-b 1;　Eth. Nic. III.13. 1118 a 16.
[4] Eth. Nic. III. 13. 1118 a 16-22.

brings tidings of multitudes of distinctive qualities of all sorts;....
while hearing announces only the distinctive qualities of sound,
and to some few animals, those also of voice. Indirectly, however,
it is hearing that contributes most to the growth of intelligence.
For rational discourse is a cause of instruction in virtue of its being
audible."[1] We find the same thought at the beginning of the
Metaphysics: "All men by nature desire to know. An indication
of this is the delight we take in our senses; for even apart from
their usefulness they are loved for themselves; and above all others
the sense of sight. For not only with a view to action, but even
when we are not going to do anything, we prefer seeing (one might
say) to everything else. The reason is that this, most of all the
senses, makes us know and brings to light many differences between
things."

Whether hearing or sight be superior, in stating that these
higher sensations act for the sake of a higher life above the mere
discrimination of nutriments, Aristotle often repeats that they make
us discriminate the qualities of many things. Though every sensation is the discrimination of some differences, these higher sensations prepare the remarkable progress of reason beyond the direct
interests of life. It is not necessary to discriminate many differences
in objects, in order to preserve a mere natural existence. Hence
the sensations of lower animals are comparatively simple and discriminate only in so far as is necessary for a bare existence.[2] Whereas, for the sake of well-being, one requires more enjoyment and
consequently a more distinct discrimination of minute differences.
Concurrent with the expansion of environment, higher sensations
gradually develop in order to discriminate many objects, and in
further dependance on these intellect grows. These basic sensations being necessary for the growth of intellect, the loss of any
sense entails a defect in the corresponding portion of knowledge.[3]
Sensation and reason are not heterogeneous functions which oppose
each other, but homogeneous instruments of life on different stages.
It is fundamental to the thought of Plato,[4] and here he is followed
by Aristotle, to make the object of sensation individual and acciden-

---

[1] De Sensu 1. 437 a 1 ff. φρόνησις is used here in the wider sense, and means knowledge in general comprising both practical and theoretical knowledge.
[2] Cf. p. 104, n. 13; p. 106, n. 2.
[3] An. Post. I. 18. 81. a 38 - b 9.
[4] Theaet. 160, 151 ff., 163 ff., 165, 179, 187, 192 ff.

tal, and that of knowledge universal and necessary.[1] On the other hand, sensation is regarded as a cognition which is homogeneous with reason;[2] they are distinguished as different stages of development. Just as sensation originates from the direct necessity of nutrition, and differentiates itself in accordance with the modes of the latter, reason also can be thought of as being an instrument for a more complicated life,[3] and presupposes sensation as its foundation either genetically or functionally.[4] The cognition of cause and principle, which is the function of reason, means mediated cognition that enables us to perceive objects distant in time and space, which might be perceived through sensation, if we were present there at that moment.[5] Sensation, on the one side, tending in its pure activity towards intellectual cognition, is regarded as a kind of theoretical knowledge; but reason, on the other side, also presupposes sensation as its *sine qua non* of generation, and is continuous with it. Taking rational cognition in the ideal sense, we come to such a concept as that of immortal active reason, or further, to that of divine transcendent reason; but taking it as a real psycho-physiological action, we ought to admit in it a sensitive element common to lower animals. In Aristotle's thought, man is an intermediate being between God and animals; he is rather a higher animal which has acquired intellect out of sensibility, than a mixture of intellect *and* sensibility.

Generally speaking, those who make sensation an element of intellectual knowledge are rationalists, while those who make the former the cause of the latter are called empiricists. Though the two theories oppose each other in the modern age, there would seem not be a real inconcistency between them. According to Aristotle, sensation is not only an element of intellectual knowledge,

---

[1] De An. II. 5. 417 b 22; An. Post. I. 18. 81 b 6; 24. 86 a 29; Phys. I. 5. 189 a 7; Eth. Nic. II. 9. 1109 b 23; V. 5. 1147 a 26; VI. 9. 1142 a 27; cf. De Juvent. 2. 468 a 22; Met. I. 5. 986 a 32; V. II. 1018 b 32; Gen. An. I. 2. 716 a 19; Gen. et Corr. I. 3. 318 b 29; Eth. Nic. IX. I. 1172 a 36; [De Spirit. 4. 482 b 19, 21] etc.

[2] Motu An. 6. 700 b 20; An. Post. II. 19. 99 b 35; De An. III. 9. 432 a 16; Gen. An. I. 23. 731 a 33 - b 2.

[3] Probl. XI (XXX). 5. 955 b 23-28. In spite of the spuriousness of this book, the thought is no doubt in accordance with Aristotle. Cf. Part. An. IV. 10. 687 a 7 - 23; Hicks's note on 432 a 2; Rhet. I. 6. 1362 a 21 - 24.

[4] De An. III. 3. 432 a 3- 8; 427 b 15 f.; 12. 434 b 3 - 8.

[5] An Post. II. 2. 90. a 24 - 30.

but also the cause of intellect. In spite of his rationalistic ideal of knowledge, he chooses the empirical explanation of its growth and reality. Herein also we find a fine harmony of his metaphysics and his positive science. Sensibility is rather the ground of the intellect than the origin of evil and falsehood. Intellect is not only a transcendent principle, but also leads the body and aims at the purest contemplation. To be a transitional or dual being is not a mere negative quality of human nature. Man, standing on the earth and conscious of his kinship with all other creatures, looks up to heaven and enjoys a mental homogeneity with spirits and God. A fine harmony of reality and ideal, of piety and pride—*homo sapiens* with a complete body—that was Aristotle's idea of man.

Since sensation is the origin of intellect, and since the ideal action of intellect is pure theoretical knowledge or contemplation, our mind never leaps immediately from sensation to contemplation. Both ontogenetically and phylogenetically, we start from the sensation and at first form a memory, which keeps the impression of that sensation, then organizing the memory construct an experience, and through finding out the universal principle in it, acquire an art. That which organizes and employs the art thus acquired, is practical intellect such as prudence or politics. Absolutely free contemplation is only possible for individuals and societies that are governed by such a practical intellect.[1] But such a process expresses only the stages of generation and not an essential sequence. It is quite doubtful whether Aristotle considered that theoretical knowledge is essentially mediated by practical or productive knowledge. We will have to postpone the solution of this problem for the present. At any rate, the next function above sensation being imagination, which is evidently the substratum of both thought and desire, our next problem must be, without doubt, the relation of sensation and imagination.

§ 2. THE REFERENCE OF FUNCTIONS

The foregoing considerations have been restricted to the accumulative progress of psychical functions, and did not refer

[1] Met. I. 1. 980 a 27-b 12. 981 b 13-25; An Post. II. 19. 100 a 3 ff.; Eth Nic. I. 1. 1094 a 18 - b 11.

to the essential difference and correlation of them. We must therefore reflect once more upon the essential relation between nutrition and sensation. It is also necessary to solve the difficulty of definition which we shall encounter on the way from sensation to imagination. For, as we have seen above, imagination is in a sense higher than sensation, and is intermediate between sensation and intellect. Their essential difference is that while sensation (αἴσθησις) grasps the matter together with the form of an object, imagination (φαντασία) does not include the matter.[1] But the exclusion of matter was the mark of sensation, through which it was distinguished from nutrition. The same distinguishing mark should not be applied once more to other higher functions. Hence we have avoided a literal interpretation, and have argued that sensation receives the subordinate forms which accompany the matter together with the principal form, while imagination receives only the principal form.[2] Such being the case, we should at first investigate the essential difference of sensation and nutrition.

According to Aristotle, the act that accepts an external object with its matter included is nutrition,[3] while sensation receives only the form without the matter. The object keeping its independence, only its form is introduced to the inside of an animal; and this is the sensation.[4] We hear from Bergson[5] who is one of the most original thinkers in our time, that the sensation of an object is

---

[1] De An. III. 8. 432 a 9.
[2] Cf. ch. I. § 3. Most scholars find no difficulty in the sentence just quoted. They usually take it to be that the object of sensation has matter. But this explains nothing, because Aristotle distinguishes herewith not αἰσθητά and φαντάσματα, viz. the objects of sensation and the contents of imagination, but αἰσθήματα and φαντάσματα viz. the contents of sensation and those of imagination. One might alter αἰσθήματα to αἰσθητά, but then, the contrast of αἰσθήματα and φαντάσματα would disappear. Whereas Aristotle tries to prove that intellectual knowledge is imppossible without sensation, saying that intellect thinks with image (De An. III. 8. 432 a 9). For that purpose, he might have wanted to say that intellect does not think without sensation; but as this is against the fact, he chose to say intellect thinks with image intending to suggest thereby that φάντασμα is essentially the same as αἴσθημα. Consequently, we ought rather to recognize that here is found the distinction of sensation and imagination. Cf. De Memor. 1. 450 a 30.
[3] De An. II. 1. 424 a 32.
[4] De An. III. 8. 431 b 26; III. 2. 425 b 23; II. 12. 424 a 17.
[5] Bergson, Matière et mémoire, 25.

formed by the diminution which the act of an image suffers when it encounters a subject of automatic reaction, or by the virtual image that happens through the reflexion of the act. But even this novel expression would in its contents scarcely surpass Aristotle's theory of sensation. When Aristotle says that sensation receives the form of a thing without the matter, the abstraction or the exclusion of the matter is nothing but this so-called diminution. In Aristotle also, sensation is not an addition of something to the object, but rather a diminution of something from it. Besides, this diminution is not a mere negative limitation, but in a sense the preparation for managing the object.

That sensation receives the form of a body without the matter, certainly means that sensation is regarded as abstraction. But to take sensation as a kind of abstraction is not to have an abstract theory of sensation. This is by no means a paradox; I only reject a shallow attack of *Lebensphilosophen* against abstraction. To abstract the form and leave the matter is of course an operation of mind upon an object. It is onthing more and nothing less. Nothing more, because we (with Aristotle) do not presuppose matter and form as independent elements and then construct reality from them. Nothing less, because cognition always requires some active operation upon the object, and where there is no abstraction, there cannot be any cognition. A concrete cognition, in the literal sense, is a *contradictio in adjecto*. A concrete thing does exist, and might be experienced, but could never be known. For to experience is one thing, but to know another. And even experience, in so far as it is human, is impossible without presupposing some cognition, and accordingly abstraction too. Therefore if the expression "concrete cognition" is to have any meaning, we can only take it as the ideal of synthesis mediated by abstraction. In other words, it is the end of the efforts to comprehend reality through a minute analysis and an exhaustive synthesis.

Now Aristotle merely regards sensation as a kind of passivity;[1] he never confines it to mere inaction. Thus he argues that sensation, though concerned with individuals, does not accept the individuals themselves, but perceives a primitive universality therein.[2] The act of sensation that abstracts the form from a concrete thing, is nothing but a preparation for managing a body at one's

[1] De An. II. 11. 423 b 31.
[2] An. Post. II. 19. 100 a 15 - b 1; 31. 87 b 28 - 31.

pleasure. Matter remains the same through all the transition of forms; it is the substratum or constant medium of many forms and is never created, nor does it ever perish. In this sense matter is something we have nothing to do with, and may be said to be the obstacle to the will, or its negative principle.[1] Yet the will never opposes matter as such. The opposition of the will must be to some form or to a qualified matter. Matter as such is something indefinite,[2] the material on which some form is pressed. Reducing a body to matter, the mind acquires the potentiality of impressing its own form upon it. On the other hand, mind in its turn receives the form of that body. And since form is a definite and eternal being,[3] all mind can do is to deprive something of its form, and then give that form to another thing.[4] The former act is cognition, and the latter production. To abstract a form from a body means to catch the essence of it, or to submit oneself to the negation that that body exerts over the mind. The self-negation of this mind is also the necessary moment of its self-affirmation. Form is the principle that makes a thing itself, but whenever a thing is perceived through its form, it is reduced to mere matter, while the form itself is made the mind's own.[5] Mind acquires the faculty of dominating a thing through perceiving its form. We may act upon a thing only through knowing it, that is to say, through depriving a thing of its actual form and replacing that form with another,

---

[1] Cf. Baeumker, Problem der Materie, 280 f.; Dilthey, Beiträge zur Lösung der Frage vom Ursprung unseres Glaubens an der Realitat der Aussenwelt (Gesamm. Schr. V), 104 ff.

[2] Phys. IV. 2. 209 b 9; Met. IV. 4. 1007 b 28; VII. 11. 1037 a 27; IX. 7. 1049 b 1; Met. XII. 10. 1087 a 16; cf. Met. VII. 3. 1029 a 20; De An. II. 1. 412 a 7; Met. VII. 1. 1042 a 27.

[3] Met. VII. 8. 1033 b 17; 9. 1034 b 8, 13; VIII. 3. 1043 b 17; 5. 1044 b 2; XII. 3. 1069 b 35; 1070 a 15; Phys. V. 1. 224 b 5, 11; Met. XI. 11. 1067 b 9.

[4] Generally speaking, there is neither absolute generation nor passing away: the generation of one thing is the passing away of another, and *vice versa*. Cf. Gen. et. Corr. I. 3; Zeller, op. cit. 391. Production is a kind of qualitative change, and the form which constitutes the essence of art derives itself from the productive exercise which precedes the mastery. Just as a man is begot of a man, so a house comes out of a house, i.e., we learn the art of building by building a house. Art and producer are the mediators of this form. Cf. Eth. Nic. II. 1. 1103 a 33; 1103 b 11; Met. IX. 1. 1048 a 26; VI. 7. 1032 a 32; 1032 b 21.

[5] De An. III. 8. 432 a 1 - 3. The tool is taken as an examle, not only in an analogical sense, but also implying the practical significance of the holding of forms through intellect and sensation.

which the mind has acquired elsewhere and kept in itself. This is the very essence of art, of which we shall speak later on.[1]

Sensation is the lowest cognition and the minimum requisite of art, while the higher arts require knowledge or science as well. But it is quite evident that it is impossible for the soul that lacks even sensation to produce anything. Nutrition, which accepts both the matter and the form of a body is quite passive, while sensation is active by its abstraction. That sensation as well as imagination and intellect is discriminating and descriptive, means that they apprehend the form of an object and distinguish it from the other forms. But in order that this may be possible, it is requisite at first to discriminate the form from the matter. So we must here recognize two kinds of discrimination.

Even nutrition, however, is not a mere passivity, in so far as it is a kind of living function. A living being accepts food, matter and form together; then the object loses its actual form and takes another form, viz., food is digested and nourishes the living body or becomes the body itself.[2] But, while the form-giving act of nutrition is unconscious, the separating act of sensation is followed by consciousness. In nutrition, the object is at first received as a whole, and then is separated, but in sensation, the object remains as it is, independently, and the two moments are separated. In the former, transformation is direct and actual, but in the latter, indirect and potential. In other words, nutrition performs passion and reaction at a stroke, but sensation reserves the action for the future. This agrees fundamentally with Bergson's thought,[3] which explains sensation as the scheme of potential actions. But the expression of Bergson is lacking in accuracy; while Aristotle, who is more analytical and aims at clearness, admitting the teleological connection among the reception of impressions, their synthesis, their preservation, their modification, and the activity towards the realization of them, yet assigns to each of these moments respectively such different concepts as sensation, *sensus communis*, memory, imagination, and desire. Be that as it may, it is just because sensation has such a nature, that it guides the function of nutrition. The

[1] Met. VI. 9. 1034 a 23 f.; 7. 1032 a 32 f.; 1032 b 13 f.; XII. 3. 1070 a 15, 30; 4. 1070 b 33; Gen. An. II. 1. 735 a 2; II. 4. 740 b 28; Part. An. I. 1. 640 a 31 f.; 639 b 15; cf. Gen. An. II. 1. 734 b 21; 734 a 31.
[2] De An. II. 4. 416 a 34 - b 1; 416 b 3, 12, 20; III. 12. 434 b 19.
[3] Bergson, Matière et mémoire, 48.

nutrition of animals is by no means blind, but of necessity is mediated by some sensation. Before taking food, animals perceive what and how the objects are, viz., whether they may eat those things or not. Thus the difference between nutrition and sensation is after all a comparative difference between direct and indirect reactions, between actuality and potentiality, and likewise a difference as to distance in time and space. It is founded on the same principle as that which we can perceive differentiating sensation, imagination, and intellect. The qualitative difference of living functions is reduced to the quantitative difference of the temporal and the spacial distance between object and subject.[1]

This relation found among sensation, imagination, and intellect, applies also to the objects of these faculties. Imagination being distinguished from sensation in the respect that it leaves out accidental forms, its object, viz. image or φάντασμα, must be also more abstract than sense impression or αἴσθημα; in abstraction, it approaches to concept, which is of course the object of intellect. Now the relation among sense impression, image, and concept is that the first is individual, the second is special, and the third is universal; and this relation being continuous, the distinction between its terms also must be a relative one. We have however noticed that the individual in Aristotle is the product of the mutual determination of matter and form, and these two principles are related to each other interconvertibly, each acting either as the universal or the special; the above mentioned order is only the formal side of this dual interrelation.[2] From this point of view, imagination might be taken either as the process in which sensation sifts out its accidental forms, or as that in which concept determines its universal character gradually, the former being formalization and abstraction, and the latter materialization and combination.

The above mentioned relation among sensation, imagination and intellect, or that among sense impression, image, and concept, may be recognized everywhere in Aristotle's writing though we do not find such a concise expression of it. For instance, the thinking faculty is found only in the animal which has sensation and imagination, and whenever one thinks he must have an image before him.[3] This indicates on the one hand, that the thinking faculty,

[1] Bergson, op. cit. 18 f.   [2] Ando, Aristoteles no Sonzairon, 214.
[3] De An. III. 7. 431 a 17; 8. 432 a 8, 13; De Memor. 1. 449 b 31; De Sensu 6. 445 b 16; cf. Ch. II. § 1.

being developed from imagination and sensation, is a more delicate instrument of life which aims at the same end as do they, and on the other hand, that concept is homogeneous with image, only more general and formal. Nevertheless the very fact that human thinking cannot operate without images indicates that, even in theoretical contemplation, it maintains the practical inclination to return to the conrete reality through the medium of imagination. Imagination is just as much the middle term in the descent from intellect to conduct, as it is in the ascent from sense impression to concept. A sense impression being received from a present object,[1] it remains in the soul after the real object has gone away,[2] forms the experience, and becomes the principle of art and science.[3] On account of this intermediate character, imagination is sometimes said to be a mere residue of sensation or inert sensation,[4] sometimes not only attendant to conceptual thinking, but also itself a kind of thinking.[5] It is also said that of instances of imagination, some come from sensation and some from intellect,[6] the former sort being sensitive imagination, the latter called deliberative, reasoning, or intellectual imagination,[7] which is of course confined to human beings. Further, these imaginations are all accompanied by pleasure and pain, whereby they arouse desire as the originative power of conduct. In short, imagination is on the one hand the process through which sensation proceeds towards contemplation, and on the other hand, the medium through which intellect guides conduct.

The relation of general : special : individual exists not only among concept, image, and sense impression, but also among various particular kinds of concepts. Properly speaking, it is actually primarily to the order of concepts that it applies. How then is this relation differentiated in the two regions ? In limiting a genus to a species, the differentiae are definite and essential for this genus[8]

---

[1] De Memor. 1. 449 b 14.
[2] De Memor. 1. 449 b 24 f.
[3] An. Post. II. 19. 100 a 3- 14; Met. I. 1. 980 a 28 ff.
[4] De An. III. 3. 429 a 1; De Somno. 1. 456 a 17; Rhet. I. 11. 1370 a 28.
[5] De An. III. 3. 427 b 27 - 29; 428 a 2-5; De An. I. 1. 403 a 8; III. 3. 437 b 28; 10. 433 a 10;   cf. Motu An. 6. 700 b 17, 7 701 a 30, 36; 701 b 18; b 35; 11. 703 b 18.
[6] Motu An. 8. 702 a 19
[7] De An. III. 10. 433 b 29; 11. 434 a 6;
[8] Top. VI. 6. 144 a 24 - 27; 144 b 16 f.; Part. An. I. 3. 643 a 27-30.

while in determining or delimiting a concept to a particular image, the determinants are accidental forms. In the former case, we must add the essential attributes in a certain order, but in the latter case, the attributes to be added are accidental and indefinite. The species subsumes individual examples, but does not represent the genus. Whereas it is the most important mark of the image, that it represents not only the individuals, but also the genus or the general concept. For instance, a portrait, being an image, represents an individual, while an image of a triangle with certain sides and angles represents a genus of triangle.[1] This difference as to mediations, viz., the dual mediation of image on the one hand, and the single mediation of concept on the other, proves that the relation among concept, image, and sense impression, is concrete, while the subordination of concepts is abstract.

Though sensation and imagination are different functions, they are sometimes reduced to a single part of the soul.[2] Imagination is the fundamental function common to memory, dreaming, and fantasy[3]—these are distinguished from one another through the mode of time—and belongs to the part of the soul which manages the so-called *sensus communis*.[4] This *sensus communis* holds a unique situation among other sensations. Special sensations act through special organs such as the eye, ear, nose, etc., while *sensus communis* has no special organ,[5] but is rather the function of the heart,[6] which is the central organ common to all special sensations. It is also called the first sense[7] or the origin of sensations;[8] it compares,[9] discriminates,[10] makes unity of special sensations,[11] and further perceives or imagines general forms, such as

[1] De Memor. 1. 450 a 1.
[2] De Somniis 3. 462 a 8 - 12; 459 a 16; 458 b 30.
[3] De Memor. 1. 450 a 22 - 25, 12; De Somniis 1. 459 a 21 f.
[4] De Memor. 1. 450 a 10 f.
[5] De An. III. 1. 425 a 13.
[6] De Somno 2. 456 a 6; De Juvent. 1. 467 b 28-30; 469 a 20; 3. 469 a 10-12; Part. An. II. 10. 656 a 28; 656 b 25; III. 3. 665 a 12; 4. 666 a 11-20, 33; Part. An. II. 1. 647 a 23-31; III. 10. 672 b 16; IV. 5. 678 b 2; Gen. An II. 6. 743 b 26; VI. 2. 781 a 21.
[7] De Memor. 1. 450 a 10; De Somniis 3. 641 a 6; 641 b 4.
[8] De Somno 2. 455 a 15-20; De An. III. 2. 426 b 14; 425 b 12-25; Eth. Nic. IX. 7. 1170 a 31; Eth. Eud. V. 12. 1244 b 26.
[9] De Somno 2. 455 a 15 ff.
[10] De An. III. 2. 426 b 8 ff.
[11] De An. III. 1. 425 b 1.

motion, rest, figure, magnitude (extension), number or unity;[1] time also belongs to its function.[2]

Special sense impressions are momentary phenomena which take place between present objects and certain senses;[3] they are elementary impressions which are experienced independently through different special senses. They disappear as soon as the objects disappear, or as the connection between sense and object is interrupted. Whereas our concrete perception is not a random succession or aggregation of actual and elemental impressions, but rather a synthetic unity of them. For instance, this substance is at once red, hard, sweet, spherical, small, and resting. A special sense does not make us known that a red thing is also hard and sweet, or that it is spherical and small. It is the function of *sensus communis* to make such references among them—it is thus an intermediate intuitive faculty between special sensation and conceptual thinking.[4]

Besides, a momentary impression falls short of the synthetic perception of an object. In order to unite impression A with impression B, one must hold A till B happens. We need memory to form a coordinate perception out of the homogeneous or heterogeneous impressions experienced successively. *Sensus communis* must therefore be engaged in time perception as well as in space perception. It is not coordinate with special sensations, but is the synthetic and dominant moment of perception. It is the psychological denomination of the synthesizing function of the heart, which being the central organ of sense, accepts and organizes the impressions which come from special senses.[5] When it acquires a kind of independence of the exterior world, it is called imagination.

We are reminded immediately, by this function of *sensus communis* and imagination, of the *Einbildungskraft* and the *reine Anschauung* of Kant. Aristotle's *sensus communis* being, as we have just mentioned, the imaginative faculty *vis à vis* time and space, it thus resembles

---

[1] De An. III. 1. 425 a 14; 425 b 4; De Somniis 1. 458 b 5; De Sensu 4. 442 b 4; Eth. Nic VI. 9. 1142 a 27.   [2] De Memor. 1. 450 a 9-23.
[3] De Memor. 1. 449 b 14.   [4] De An. III. 1. 425 a 30-b 3.

[5] The concept *sensus communis* originates in Aristotle. Plato, in his early period, regarded sensation as a function of the body, while the act of synthesis or apperception was assumed to be intellect (Phaed. 65). In his later period, he considered sensation to be a functon of soul through body, and the unification of impressions was attributed to soul (Theaet. 186 D; 184 D). But, there was not yet the concept of *sensus communis*.

Kant's intuition of time and space, as *reine Anschauung* or *Anschauungsformen*. But the image of *sensus communis* is more concrete than time and space as the form of intuition, and rather more akin to the *Schema* of *transcendentale Einbildungskraft*. For Kant, elemental sensations are opposed to *reine Anschauung* as matter to form. This opposition, no doubt, is nothing but a heritage from Aristotle, to which Kant has succeeded through the Scholastic philosophy. Yet the two concepts are combined rather more closely in Aristotle. Special sensations and *sensus communis* are not mere heterogeneous principles, but rather moments of the same perception, and there is no distinction of the one being *a posteriori* and empirical, the other *a priori* and transcendental.

This relation becomes more evident if we compare *sensus communis* and imagination: they belong to the same part of the soul, only differing in name. An image persists somehow independently of actual and present perception, and may appear either as a dream or as a memory; but sensation cannot persist apart from reality. Concrete perception cannot but accept the conditions of present existence, though it presupposes a synthetic function of *sensus communis* besides special sensations. It is a phenomenon that happens from the actual contact of subject and object, while in imagination, the soul is more distant from the object. Hence imagination is the principle of freer conduct. Kant divided his *Einbildungskraft* into the productive and the reproductive;[1] *sensus communis*

---

[1] Kant, K. d. r. V. II. 1. 2. WW. Cass. III. 126. Kant defines the imaginative faculty thus: — "*Einbidungskraft ist das Vermögen, einen Gegenstand auch ohne dessen Gegenwart in der Anschauung vorzustellen*". He further explains, "*Da nun alle unsere Anschauung sinnlich ist, so gehört die Einbildungskraft der subjectiven Bedingung wegen, unter der sie allein den Verstandesbegriffen eine korrespondierende Anschauung geben kann, zur Sinnlichkeit; sofern aber doch ihre Synthesis eine Ausübung der Spontaneität ist, welche bestimmend und nicht, wie der Sinn, bloss bestimmbar ist, mithin a priori den Sinn seiner Form nach der Einheit der Apperzeption gemäss bestimmen kann, so ist die Einbildungskraft sofern ein Vermögen, die Sinnlichkeit a priori zu bestimmen, und ihre Synthesis der Anschauungen den Kategorien gemäss muss die transzendentale -Synthesis der Einbildungskraft sein, welches eine Wirkung des Verstandes auf die Sinnlichkeit und die erste Anwendung desselben, (zugleich der Grund aller übrigen), auf Gegenstände der uns möglichen Anschauung ist. Sie ist als figürlich von der intellectuellen Synthesis (ohne alle Einbildungskraft, bloss durch den Verstand) unterschieden*". Following to this comes distinction in question:—"*Sofern die Einbildungskraft nun Spontaneität ist, nenne ich auch bisweilen die produktive Einbildungskraft und unterscheide sie dadurch von der reproduktiven, deren Synthesis*

resembles the former, and imagination is akin to the latter,[1] though the analogy between them is not complete. For *sensus communis* is the condition of perception,[2] while imagination presupposes

lediglich empirischen Gesetzen, nämlich denen der Assoziation, unterworfen ist, und welche daher zur Erklärung der Möglichkeit der Erkenntnis a priori nichts beiträgt und um deswillen nicht in die Transzentalphilosophie, sondern in die Psychologie gehört." In the first paragraph, Kant attributed *Einbildungskraft* to *Sinnlichkeit,* and in the second paragraph he makes it "*eine Wirkung des Verstandes*", and "*die erste Anwendung desselben (d.h. des Verstandes)*". Similarly, ibid. 164: "*Nun ist das, was das Manniffaltige der sinnlichen Anschauung verknüpft, Einbildungskraft, die vom Verstande der Einheit ihrer intellektuellen Synthesis und von der Sinnlichkeit der Manningfaltigkeit der Apprehension nach abhängt.*" If this be literally taken, it would be a paradox to assign *Einbildungskraft* both to *Verstand* and *Sinnlichkeit*. This seeming paradox comes from the intermediate character of *Einbildungskraft*. In other words, it is due to the too narrow definition that what is *a priori* is intellectual and what is intuitive is sensible. *Einbildungskraft* involves both apriority and intuitiveness without contradiction. Kant leaves the study of *reproductive Einbildungskraft* to psychology, but the observation of the empirical fact that the cognitive faculty of the human soul develops from sensation to imagination, and from imagination to thinking, is by no means useless in explaining the mediating function of imagination with respect to sensibility and intellect.

[1] K. Nisitani assignes memory to the *reproductive,* and dreaming to the *productive Einbildungskraft.* cf. Aristoteles Ronko (A study of Aristotle).

[2] Kant, K. d. r.V. 1 ed. 120: "*Das erste, was uns gegeben wird, ist Erscheinung, welche, wenn sie mit Bewusstsein verbunden ist, Wahrenhmung heisst, ... Weil aber jede Erscheinung ein Mannigfaltiges enthält, mithin verschiedene Wahrnehmungen im Gemüte an sich zerstreut und einzeln angetroffen werden, so ist eine Verbindung derselben nötig, welche sie in dem Sinnen selbst nicht haben können. Es ist also in uns ein tätiges Vermögen der Synthesis dieses Mannigfaltigen, welches wir Einbildungskraft nennen und deren unmittlbar an den Wahrnehmungen ausgeübte Handlung ich Apprehension nenne. Die Einbildungskraft soll nämlich das Mannigfaltige der Anschauung in ein Bild bringen; vorher muss sie also die Eindrücke in ihre Tätigkeit aufnehmen, d.i. apprehendieren.*" Ibid. 123: "*Die Einbildungskraft ist also auch ein Vermögen einer Synthesis a priori, weswegen wir ihr den Namen der produktiven Einbildungskraft geben; und sofern sie in Ansehung alles Mannigfaltigen der Erscheinung nichts weiter als die notwendige Einheit in der Synthesis derselben zu ihrer Absicht hat, kann diese die transzendentale Funktion der Einbildungskraft genannt werden.*" Kant is proud of his discovery of this synthetic act: ibid. 120 n. But as mentioned above, nothing is farther from truth than to say that no psychologist has ever thought that imagination is the necessary ingredient of perception itself. This is just what Aristotle, the founder of psychology, has quite clearly stated. On the other hand, *sensus communis*, which produces all memory, dreaming, and imagination, was considered to be the faculty of giving unity to special sensations, and making a uniform perception out of

actual perception. In regard to this, the relation between them might appear to be more distant than that between special sensations and *sensus communis*, yet they are not so heterogeneous as those *Einbildungskräfte* are with each other. They are, in the last analysis the aspects of one faculty.

Now imagination, being the function of *sensus communis*, is in a sense homogeneous with sensation, but in another sense is distinguished from it. Sometimes, it is not admitted equally to all animals, but is limited to higher animals.[1] Sometimes, however, it is also attributed to lower animals, as when Aristotle says that when we cut the body of an insect, sensation, movement, imagination, and desire are all found in each part alike.[2] We cannot but declare that theory a little extravagant that admits imagination and desire to each divided part of an insect; but a view that limits imagination to some animals only, and one which admits it generally to all, might be reconciled through distinguishing some difference of degree in imagination. For instance, in one place, Aristotle actually allows imagination even to the lowest animals which have only the sense of touch—but with the qualification that such animals have imagination ἀορίστως,[3] i.e. in an indefinite manner.

Now since *sensus communis* is in a sense the necessary condition of all concrete perceptions, it is no doubt common to all animals in some degree.[4] Imagination also, being a function homogeneous with *sensus communis*, belonging to the same organ, and being something like a remnant of sensation, would be duly attributed to all animals. But since there are various kinds of imagination, not all of them are necessarily common to all animals. Memory, for instance, being a kind of imagination, is confined only to those animals which have time perception.[5] It is not necessarily confined

---

elemental sensations. Aristotle never limited it to a mere reproductive faculty. He believed in a certain sense that "*die Sinne liefern uns nicht allein Eindrücke, sondern setzen solche auch sogar zusammen und brächten Bilder der Gegenstände zu Wege*". But he attributed this faculty not to an elemental and special sensation, but to the faculty of synthetic perception called *sensus communis*.

[1] De An. III. 3. 428 a 8-11; cf. Hicks's note *ad loc.*; ibid. 3. 415 a 10 f.; III. 3. 428 a 21 f.
[2] De An. II. 2. 413 b 16.
[3] De An. III. 11. 434 a 4.
[4] De Somno 2. 455 a 22-24.
[5] De Memor. 1. 449 b 28-30; 2. 453 a 6-9; Hist. An. I. 1. 488 b 24-26. Zeller points out Aristotle's inconsistency in sometimes confining memory to rational

to man, but at least to a comparatively higher species of animals. So also with the imaginative grasp of number.

The reason why Aristotle thus admits indefinite images to lower animals is, according to his own statement, that such animals also feel pleasure and pain, and consequently have appetites. Hence we learn the relation of appetite or desire in general with sensation and imagination. Sensation and desire are so closely connected, that whenever one exists, the other also exists of necessity, and one cannot exist apart from the other.[1] Neither does he who has no sensation have desire, nor does he who has no desire have sensation. In this respect, those two parts are related to each other, not as the sensitive part is to the nutritive but as nutrition is to reproduction.[2] They are not in a subordinate, but in a coordinate, relation, so that the sensitive part and the desiring part may have different functions, conceptually or psychologically, yet they can never be the classificatory principles of living beings. The so-called conceptual or psychological difference is that, while sensation is the faculty of receiving forms,[3] desire is that of realizing[4] them— the difference of passivity and activity. Therefore, though they are accompanied by each other of necessity, the relation is not convertible without qualification. In fact, sensation on the one hand presupposes desire teleologically: the animal has sensation in order to desire something. On the other hand, desire also presupposes sensation, as its efficient cause:[5] the animal desires only through sensation.

---

being, sometimes also granting it to other animals (Ph. d. Gr. II. 2. 401 n. 4). He quotes as an example of the former, De An. III. 10. 433 b 5-7. ἐπεὶ δὲ ὀρέξεις γίνονται ἐναντίαι ἀλλήλαις, τοῦτο δὲ συμβαίνει ὅταν ὁ λόγος καὶ αἱ ἐπιθυμίαι ἐναντίαι ὦσι, γίνεται δ' ἐν τοῖς χρόνου αἴσθησιν ἔχουσιν κτλ. But we may easily notice that this sentence means only that conflict among desires, or the antagonism of reason and appetite, occurs only in an animal having time-perception; it does not follow of necessity that the converse is also right. It is possible that an animal having time-perception has no reason and follows only imagination. It should also be noticed that here are used the words, perception of time.

1 De An. II. 3. 414 b 4-6; III. 7. 431 a 13 f.
2 De An. II. 4. 416 a 19.
3 De An. II. 5. 416 b 33 f.; I. 4. 408 b 16; II. 4. 415 b 24; De Sonmiis 2. 459 b 5; Phys. V. 2. 244 b 11, 25; Met. IV. 5. 1009 b 13; De An. II. 12. 424 a 18 f.; III. 8. 431 b 23; 432 a 2.
4 Motu An. 6. 701 a 1; 10. 703 a 5; De An. III. 10.
5 Motu An. 8. 701 a 35.

Thus sensation is a faculty given to animals to perceive the forms of objects in order that they might desire and act through it. Sensation is the faculty of passive cognition, and desire that of active conduct; the former arouses the latter through the feeling of pleasure and pain. Sensation as mere cognition may be an element of theoretical knowledge, but when it is accompanied by pleasure and pain, it becomes the efficient cause of disire and conduct. A pleasant thing naturally generates the desire for it, and a painful thing is avoided of necessity.[1] But the feeling of pleasure and pain is not added to the sensation from without, but is originally combined with it. Sensation and feeling are in truth differentiations of what is originally the same activity. Sensation without feeling results only through the self-negation of natural experience. Such is the special phenomenon of a highly developed mentality, peculiar to man.

Now, feeling appears sometimes to be experienced immediately with sensation, sometimes to accompany imagination.[2] But it is doubtful whether a desire is possible when feeling coincides directly with sensation. There may be an impulsive and reflexive pursuit or avoidance, but no conscious desire or evasion. A lower animal would at once stretch its tentacle, whenever it perceives any food, but would not particularly be conscious of a desire. A conscious desire or evasion presupposes an image rather than a sensation. Aristotle himself says, that there must be an image in order that a desire may exist.[3] Is it not, then, spurious that there is a desire wherever there is a sensation? Should we not rather say that mere sensation is not sufficient for the existence of desire?

Speaking more strictly, the feelings of pleasure and pain already presuppose some distance between sensation and act. Or in other words, sensation happens where there is some distance between stimulus and reaction, so that lower animals scarcely have any conscious sensation. Thus, sensation consists in the distance between stimulus and reaction, and feeling accompanies of necessity this independence of sensation, its independence being proportionate to that of sensation. Consequently, there ought to be the feelings of pleasure and pain, wherever there is the faculty of sensation, and there ought to be desires, wherever there are the feelings of pleasure and pain. But, evidently imagination is more

---

[1] De An. III. 7. 431 a 8-12.   [2] De An. III. 7. 431 b 6-10.
[3] De An. III. 7. 431 a 14-17; III. 10. 433 b 28.

independent of the object than sensation is, the former depending upon the distance between sensation and act, the latter upon that between stimulus and reflex. The more complex the manner of acting becomes, the more the importance of imagination increases.

There is desire, where there is independence of sensation. But as sensation is a passive impression received from a present object, or the system of such impressions, it does not contain the form of future action or its result, which is rather the content of imagination. Consequently, there cannot be the disjunctive question, whether sensation or imagination is the real cause of desire. Desire is possible whenever sensation becomes independent, and wherever there is a desire, there must be an imagination as its moment. The act of the animal is its reaction against the outside world which gives the stimulus to it; sensation is the passive side of this experience, and imagination the active side, both of them being mediated by the feelings of pleasure and pain. When united with the feeling, imagination appears as a desire.[1] Thus considered, Aristotle's statement, on the one hand, that sensation produces desire, is not different from his statement, on the other hand, that imagination is the *sine qua non* of desire. Sensation and imagination are continuous and cannot be divided distinctly, hence Aristotle sometimes admits imagination to all animals, sometimes confines it to higher animals. That lower animals have imagination and desire "in an indefinite manner" means that their sole sensation, i.e. that of touch, involves the minimum potentiality of these faculties. Imagination is at a minimum when sensation immediately produces desire, but at a maximum, when desire is mediated by practical reason.

Strictly speaking, every desire presupposes imagination, and there must be a minimum image even when it seems to come immediately from sensation. Thus imagination admits some difference of degree. It is divided into the rational imagination peculiar to man, and the sensible imagination common to animals.[2] Since

[1] Motu An. 8. 702 a 17-19: τὰ μὲν γὰρ ὀργανικὰ μέρη παρασκευάζει ἐπιτηδείως τὰ πάθη, ἡ δ' ὄρεξις τὰ πάθη, τὴν δ' ὄρεξιν ἡ φαντασία· αὕτη δὲ γίνεται ἢ διὰ νοήσεως ἢ δι' αἰσθήσεως. Herewith, the conditional sequence would be, sensation or thinking—imagination—desire—affect—organ. This appears to be different from our interpretation in that affect is placed between desire and the motion of the organ, instead of between imagination and desire. But in truth, affect would rather seem to prevail throughout the above series.

[2] De An. III. 10. 433 b 29 f.; II. 11. 434 a 5-7.

sensation and imagination are common to all animals, and desire always accompanies them, desire is also common to all animals, only being either low or high, in accordance with the sort of corresponding sensation or in proportion to its intimacy with sensation. The sensation itself is proportional to the intimacy between the object and the subject of action, the lower sensation being immediate and the higher mediated, for the former is the most indispensable instrument of life, while the latter is not so necessary, yet useful for a higher and richer life. All sensations form the initiative moment of action through giving us the perception of present objects, but when an animal then desires, it must of necessity predict some future states that are to be realized. This predictive consciousness is no longer a sensation, but an imagination.[1] When the reaction is contiguous to the stimulus and the act is so simple that one proceeds to enjoy the object at once, the perception of the present object and the imagination of future conduct are so close together that in some extreme cases we can hardly discriminate them from each other. On the contrary, when the intention is only realized through a complex operation, viz. in the case of the desires that fulfil the demands of a complicated life, imagination makes its appearance between sensation and desire.

Imagination may be regarded to be a primitive form of thought in so far as it perceives an abstract from.—"But to the thinking soul images serve as sense impressions and when it affirms or denies good or evil, it avoids or pursues."[2] That "the soul never thinks without an image"[3] also suggests that the proper function of reason is the guidance of action. Such a reason unites itself with imagination, and becomes the determining principle of desires. Its difference from sensitive desire or appetite is that "the reason bids us resist because of the future, while appetite regards only the immediate present".[4] The so-called theoretical resaon or theoretical intellect is nothing but the state where the relation between object and subject becomes so indifferent that imagination no longer is accom-

---

[1] De Memor. 1. 449 b 27 f. No details are given about expectation; but as imagination produces in consciousness the image of an object when this object does not present itself, expectation as well as memory must be regarded as a mode of imagination; cf. De An. III. 3. 428 a 7, 16; 2. 435 b 25.

[2] De An. III. 7. 431 a 15.

[3] De An. III. 7. 431 a 17; 8. 432 a 8; De Memor. 1. 449 b 31.

[4] De An. III. 10. 433 b 7.

panied by a strong emotion that might evoke a desire. Aristotle seemes to have recognized this real genealogy connecting practical and theoretical intellcet, when in determining the grades of knowledge he supposes sensation, experience, art, and prudence to be a gradual accumlation, and above all of them sets theoretical knowlege, which he assumes to be an uninterested cognition that is possible through leisure.[1]

The most sensitive of all imaginations is the indefinite imagination of lower animals, which almost agrees with sensation. About rational imagination,[2] on the other hand, Aristotle speaks as follows: "The sensitive imagination, then as we have said, is found in the other animals also but the deliberative one only in the rational animals. For to decide whether to do this or that is already the task of reasoning. And one must measure through a single standard, for one pursues the greater good. Hence one can form a single image out of many images."[3] — From what has been said, the so-called deliberative image would be a special image chosen out of many possible images through deliberation. Aristotle further continues:[4] "And the reason why the lower animals are thought not

[1] Met. I. 1, 2; cf. Eth. Nic. X. 7.

[2] De An. III. 10: 433 a 10. Here calculation or reasoning is opposed to imagination. We must understand imgaination here to be restricted to sensible imagination. But though there is rational imagination, none the less reasoning is different from imagination. Practical imagination means the imagination which results from reasoning rather than the imagination that reasons.

[3] De An. III. 11. 434 a 5-10.

[4] The ἕν in the sentence ὥστε δύναται ἓν ἐκ πλειόνων φαντασμάτων ποιεῖν, is usually taken as meaning an image. But K. Nisitani, making it identical with the πρῶτα νοήματα in De An. III. 8. 432 a 12, and the πρῶτον καθόλου in An. Post. II. 19. 100 a 16, explains it to be the first step in the process wherein a general concept is formed from accidental images (Aristoteles no Kosoron, i.e. Aristotle's theory of imagination). But Aristotle's statement is concerned with practical deliberation and with the adjudication of desires. It does not have to do at all with the subsumption of images into a general concept. The ἕν might well be taken as an image, yet it is by no means a general concept that subsumes special images, but an image calculated through practical estimation. Nisitani does not admit that this statement is concerned with the relation of imagination and desire. He insists nevertheless, upon his interpretation, saying that the same things could be said of this relation in the theoretical area as in the practical area. In evidence whereof, he quotes De An. III. 7. 431 b 10-12: καὶ τὸ ἄνευ δὲ πράξεως, τὸ ἀληθὲς καὶ τὸ ψεῦδος, ἐν τῷ αὐτῷ γένει ἐστὶ τῷ ἀγαθῷ καὶ κακῷ· ἀλλὰ τῷ γε ἁπλῶς διαφέρει καὶ τινί. Hence he concludes that the truth, being a kind of good, is an object of desire. But the text in question proves only that reason uses images as its material

to have opinion is that they do not possess that form of imagination which comes from syllogism, while the latter (i.e., deliberative imagination) implies the former (i.e., opinion). Hence desire contains no deliberative faculty."[1] We may learn very much from these words: in the first place, that deliberation takes the form of syllogism; in the second, that opinion presupposes deliberation or prac-

medium in practice as well as in cognition; we cannot infer from this that what is derived from such an image must be a general concept. Much less does it imply, as Nisitani says, that "the truth, being a kind of the good, becomes the object of desire". The object of desire is the good and never the truth. What the last quotation really means is that just as true and false are the measure of theoretical thinking, so good and bad are the measure of practical thinking, and just as sensation desires what is the more pleasant, so practical intellect desires what appears to be the best. Nisitani maintains his previous interpretation in his Aristoteles Ronko (A study of Aristotle), p. 160 ff., adding a more detailed proof, which fails however, to persuade us. Deliberating imagination must be either imagination founded upon deliberation or imagination that deliberates something. Whereas deliberation (βούλευσις) is concerned in the first place with affairs that are in our power and can be otherwise, and in the second place, with means rather than ends, and constitutes a moment of προαίρεσις or will (Eth. Nic. III. 5. 1112 a 30; 1112 b 11; VI. 2. 1139 a 13; Mag. Mor. I. 35. 1196 b 29; Rhet. I. 2. 1357 a 4; 6. 1362 a 18; II. 5. 1383 a 7). So προαίρεσις is said to be βουλευτικὴ ὄρεξις. (Eth. Nic. III. 5. 1113 a 11; VI. 2. 1139 a 23; Eth. Eud. II. 10. 1226 b 17; Mag. Mor. I. 17. 1189 a 31). We shall analyse the structure of βούλευσις more fully later on. In short, it is a practical reasoning searching for a concrete means to an end, and forms a syllogism. Now συλλογισμός is naturally opposed to ἐπαγωγή; the former proceeds from the general to the particular, the latter from the particular to the general (Eth. Nic. VI. 3. 1139 b 29; An. Pr. I. 24. 43 a 3; An. Post. I. 1. 71 a 5; Top. I. 12. VIII. 2. 157 a 18). The example of practical reasoning which follows the above quotation is also such a reductive inference (De An. III. 11. 434 a 15 ff.).

Thus, we cannot agree with Nisitani, who maintains that deliberative imagination (which was formed from deliberation) which, when it acts in practice, makes a universal image of a greater and better thing out of other apparent goods, has an analogous part when it acts in a pure contemplation. We admit without hesitation that the contemplation of reason is mediated by images, and there are differences of degrees among images. But the text in question does not refer to such a thing. The expression φαντασία corresponds to βουλευτικὴ ὄρεξις, which is the paraphrase of προαίρεσις. But βουλευτικὴ ὄρεξις implies an ὄρεξις which follows from deliberation rather than an ὄρεξις which deliberates. Analogically, the so-called φαντασία βουλευτική should mean the φαντασία which follows from βούλευσις. St. Thomas takes the ἕν as the third image which is a standard of estimation, though not a right one. It is rather an image chosen according to a standard than a standard itself.

[1] De An. III. 11. 434 a 10.

tical syllogism. Let us examine these points later on; but the more remarkable point is that, in the third place, the imagination peculiar to man is the deliberative one, which is the imagination inferred from (practical) syllogism, and a special image chosen out of many possible images. The choice of this image is of course the result of a practical syllogism or at least conditioned by it. As desire presupposes imagination, and imagination is divided into the rational and the irrational, so desire also should be divided into the rational and the irrational. Aristotle, in fact, dividing the besire into these two species, makes appetite and passion irrational desires, and wish a rational desire which pursues the good.[1] He even substitutes for "wish" the term λογισμός, which may be rendered as "calculation" or "reasoning". But there is another concept of προαίρεσις or will, which is paraphrased by the words βουλευτικὴ ὄρεξις, i.e., "desire determined through deliberation". These two concepts are not to be directly identified: will is said to consist of desire and reason,[2] while wish is treated merely as a kind of desire.[3] In the *Ethica Nicomachea*, they are clearly distinguished in such a way that while wish relates to the end, will does to the means, and that the former relates also to immpossibles, while the latter only to possibles.[4] Thence it seems that wish is not a volition determined through deliberative reasoning, but a material desire which ought to be further determined through deliberation.

Now, there are some difficulties about the rationality of wish. According to J. Walter, wish must be irrational, since it is a kind of desire. Aristotle's real meaning in saying wish belongs to the reasonable soul,[5] is, he thinks, that it depends upon the possessor of reason, rather than that it is itself a mode of reason or that its content is conceptual.[6] Against this interpretation, Teichmüller maintains that wish must be rational, because, the reason which corresponds to wish is rational (λογιστικόν).[7] The resolution of these

[1] Rhet. I. 10. 1368 b 37-1369 a 7.
[2] Eth. Nic. III. 5. 1113 a 9-12; VI. 2. 1139 a 23; Eth. Eud. II. 10. 1226 b 17; [Mag. Mor. I. 17. 1189 a 3;] Eth. Nic. VI. 2. 1139 b 4 f.; 1139 a 31-33.
[3] De An. III. 10. 433 a 23; Motu An. 6. 700 b 22.
[4] Eth. Nic. III. 4. 1111 b 19-30; 5. 1112 b 11; 1113 a 2; [Mag. Mor. I. 17. 1189 a 7;] Eth. Eud. II. 10. 1226 b 9.
[5] Top. IV. 5. 126 a 12; De An. III. 9. 432 b 5.
[6] Walter, Die Lehre von der praktischen Vernunft in der griechischen Philosophie, 204 f.
[7] Teichmüller, Neue Studien zur Geschichte der Begriffe, III: Die praktische Vernunft bei Aristoteles, 93 n. 2.

opposite interpretations may be found in Aristotle's own statements. Criticizing the duopartite theory that divides the soul into the rational and the irrational, and the tripartite theory that divides it into the cognitive, the passionate, and the appetitive, Aristotle says: "Then besides these there is the desiring, which would seem to be different both in concept and in capacity from all the others. And surely it is absurd to split this up. For wish takes place in the rational part, while appetite and passion occur in the irrational part. And, if the soul is three, desire would take place in each of these parts."[1] This is a criticism made from the standpoint of one who divides the soul into many parts according to its different functions. But, as we have seen above, this multipartite theory was synthesized with the duopartite theory, and the desiring part was reduced to the irrational part, so that, as Aristotle clearly recognized, it would be impossible to reduce the desiring part to the irrational part in a purely functional sense. An irrational part which included the desiring part completely, would have to be a metaphysical and ethical concept rather than a functional one. Wish is a function of the desiring part, and not itself the function of reason. Yet, since the desiring part does not act alone, but cooperates with other parts, wish might be said to be the form of desiring part's action through the aid of the rational part, and to this extent it could be called rational. The basic function might be, as Walter assumed, irrational, yet its relation upon the intellect cannot be said to be merely accidental. Strictly speaking, rationality may be accidental to the desiring part, yet reason must be a necessary attribute of wish, since wish involves in itself a rational moment. Walter says, not that the intellect determines desire itself, but that it only acts as the motive bringing the object to the desire.[2] That is to say, the image or representation that accompanies the intellectual action begets the desire, through the medium of pleasure and pain. But if we grant that intellect begets a desire through an image, the desire which appears in such a way must be specifically a rational desire. If it be admitted that wish is the act of the desiring part mediated by the intellectual part, the difference of this wish from will is not yet distinct enough. A wish is in a sense a rational desire, to be sure, but how then is it distinguished from will, which is desire mediated by deliberation concerning means? On the one hand, wish is said to

[1] De An. III. 9. 432b 2-5.   [2] Walter, op. cit. 198 f.

be a kind of reasoning, or to be a kind of desire which results from rational imagination or from practical syllogism; on the other hand, it is regarded as an immediate desire distinguished from will, which is the desire mediated by deliberation or reasoning. To solve this difficulty, we must, in the first place, ask whether rationality as the moment of wish conditions in some way or other the rationality of will, and in the second place, how rationality as the moment of will relates to that of wish.

As is evident from the paraphrase "deliberating desire", will is composed of the two moments of deliberation and desire. What sort of desire is this, then ? We have seen that desire is divided into wish, passion, and appetite. May all of these three equally be moments of will ? If we provisionally take the rationality which is the moment of will to be practical intellect in general, desire surely partakes of this rationality as far as it obeys reason. Thus it seems, so far, that all desires may be equally moments of will. Proof of this is, that in the character of a temperate man, appetite obeys reason, and desires in accordance with it.[1] But on the other side, seeing that courage is said not to venture a risk when driven by passion, but to obey reason,[2] even passion could not be a moment of will. Besides, passion and appetite were defined as irrational desires from the outset.[3] Thus Walter says that wish must be more intimate to will than the other desires, but being unable to reject appetite and passion altogether, he admits them to be moments of will as far as they co-operate with reason.[4]

This, however, is a very ambiguous and insufficient solution, and we cannot understand from this, whether will includes various appetites as well as wish or not. At any rate, wish is considered to be rational in some sense. What is then, this rationality of wish, or of desire in general ? One might say that it consists in a harmony with deliberation.[5] But as far as deliberation presupposes the end and relates only to the means of realization, we cannot but find ourselves in a vicious circle in making this supposition. Being mindful of such difficulties, we would rather acknowledge the consistency of Teichmüller's theory, which refuses rationality to desire itself as a moment of will, and maintains that every desire may become a will, if it is accompanied by deliberation as to means.[6] In

---

[1] Eth. Nic. III. 15. 1119 b 11 ff. 7; cf. ibid. 10. 1115 b 11 ff.; 17 ff. [2] Eth. Nic. III. 11. 1116 b 23-1117 a [3] Rhet.I. 10. 1369 a 4. [4] Walter, op. cit. 214. [5] Walter, op. cit. 254, 496; Eth. Nic. VI. 2. 1139 a 26 ff. [6] Teichmüller, op. cit. 94.

fact, it is stated that a wicked man follows an appetite with his own will, e.g. an indulgent man pursues an excessive pleasure with will and deliberation, making it his maxim to seek bodily pleasure. Does not, then, the rationality of will condition the rationality of wish by any means whatever? In other words, is deliberation a thinking about means which may combine with any desire, but which has no special intimacy with wish? Surely this is not the case, because, as we have seen above, a wish is a desire founded upon a deliberative or rational image. Yet, if that deliberation were nothing but a mere searching for means, we should simply have arrived at the result of confusing wish and will. So the only possible way of solving this difficulty is to distinguish different meanings for "deliberation" or "reasoning". The deliberation, the reasoning, and the practical syllogism that are the moment of wish must be different from those that are the moment of will. The former must be the estimation of the end itself, while the latter must be the search for the means to realize a certain end. In fact, in talking about the image or the reason as the moment of wish, it is always said by Aristotle that it teaches us the good and bad of the end,[1] while deliberation as the moment of will is said almost always to be the search for the means.[2]

Thus we have distinguished two meanings for "deliberation" or "reasoning": on the one hand they are the estimation about the end; on the other, the search for the means to realize a desire. Wish presupposes deliberation in the former sense; but deliberation in the latter sense rather presupposes wish, and through the co-operation of this deliberation and the wish results the will which is called a deliberated desire. Will and wish are rational in different senses and both coexist without contradiction. Since deliberation as the moment of wish is the estimation of the end. A mere wish is not always a possible desire: it may relate to an impossible thing. For instance, the immortality of an individual life being impossible, it cannot become an object of will, when one considers the means of its realization; yet immortality itself keeps

---

[1] De An. III. 7. 431 a 14; 432 b 6. In Ethica Nicomachea, III. 7. 1114 a 31, it is stated that images lead us to a good or to a bad end, while we are ourselves the cause of these images, and responsible for what kind of image we have. This implies that the image which precedes a desire is the estimation of an end. Cf. ibid. III. 6. 1113 a 23 f.; 1113 a 29-33; VIII. 2. 1155 b 23 -27.
[2] Eth Nic. III. 5. 1112 b 11-24; Rhet. I. 6. 1362 a 18-20.

its value none the less. Whereas wish, though presupposing deliberation, yet concerns the end, and not the means.

§ 3. DESIRE AND PLEASURE

Desire follows sensation or imagination, and is divided into the rational and the irrational, in accordance with the division of images into those direct and sensitive, and those indirect and intelligible. The rationality of desire is not due to the cognition of means, as is the rationality of will, but to the estimation of the end. Such a rational desire is called βούλησις or wish. θυμός or passion, as the other kind of desire, is in a sense rational, but in another irrational. It is compared to hasty servants, who run out before hearing out the matter, and mistake the orders afterwards, or a dog which barks even at a familiar visitor as soon as it hears a knock. It listens to an argument to some extent, but mishears it.[1] It occupies the same place in desire, as that which desire in general occupies in the whole soul. The most irrational of all desires is appetite: yet even this has some connection with reason in so far as it obeys the orders of reason,[2] this fact being due to the essence of desire in general.

All these three kinds of desires tend to action through being prompted by sensation or imagination,[3] so that they are passive as compared with the latter. In the relation of the animal to its circumstances, the passive side is sensation and imagination, and the active side desire. The animal makes an act, which is a kind of locomotion, through a passive perception. Thus, desire being the principle of animal locomotion, what cannot move its place can have also no desire.[4] Plants take nourishment, but never desire; and the animals that do not move, have only a germ of desire. Desire is the potentiality of locomotion, while sensation and imagination are the potentiality of desire. In other words, desire is the determining principle of the act which was imagined through perception. Thence it may appear that what sensation and imagination are to desire, is just what the formal principle is

---

[1] Eth. Nic. VIII. 7. 1149 a 24; 1149 b 1, 6.
[2] Eth. Nic. III. 15. 1119 b 11- 17.   [3] Motu An. 7. 701 a 29-b 1.
[4] De An. III. 10. 433 b 27 f.; 11. 433 b 31-434 a 5; De An. III. 9. 432 b 15-17.

to the material one. But strictly speaking, it is a desiring faculty rather than a desire that is really a material principle. For desire must already involve in itself the sensible or imaginative form as its moment.

Sensation, imagination, desire, and act form a group, in which they are connected with one another in the order of potentiality and actuality. This whole group forms the irrational part in the secondary sense, and is contiguous on its lower limit with the irrational part in the primary sense, which manages nutrition and reproduction: while on its upper limit, it is contiguous with the rational part in the secondary sense, which orders and leads the others like a father. So, generally speaking, this part presupposes on the one side, the nutritive part as its matter or substratum, and on the other, requires the rational part as its form or substance in the sense of essence. Thus, desire comes into being to subserve the preservation of life, and yet its ideal is realized as the so-called ethical virtues.

As is well known, not only to Aristotle but also to the Greeks in general, virtue means the excellence of any function or its effective character.[1] So the virtue of man in the superior sense, is the excellence of the soul, which is of course the essence of man.[2] Now, the functions of the human soul are vegetative functions, such as nutrition, growth, and reproduction; animalistic functions, such as sensation, imagination, desire and movement; and the pure human or super-biological function of thinking. But the human soul was divided from the metaphysical and ethical point of view into double irrational and double rational parts. Consequently, the virtues of man should be divided into two kinds of irrational and two kinds of rational virtues, or rather more minutely, each function of the soul should have its corresponding virtue. But, as we have stated in reference to Jaeger's theory, the virtues in Aristotle's ethics do not necessarily correspond to psychological functions. And this is neither due to the fact that his ethics has failed to make use of the results of his psychology, nor is it due to early formation of his ethical books, but chiefly due to their difference from his psychology in scientific interest. Ethics asks for virtues mainly for the sake of practice, being itself the very development of practical intellect such as prudence or deliberation. There-

[1] Eth. Nic. II. 5. 1106 a 15-19.
[2] Eth. Nic. I. 13. 1102 a 16; Pol. I. 2. 1253 a 36.

fore, what man has nothing to do with, or what does not matter at all to human welfare is quite out of ethical question. This is indeed the reason why, e.g., the virtues of the irrational part in the primary sense are not discussed at all, and only those of the irrational part in the secondary sense are admitted as human virtues.[1] Not that the irrational part in the primary sense has no virtues, but that the mark of the human soul was taken to be its rationality. The irrational virtues belong to man only in so far as he is an animal, and not in so far as he is a rational being. The distinctively human virtues are restricted to the functions that partake somehow of reason, even if they should fundamentally belong to the irrational part.[2] The irrational functions dominated by reason are esteemed as particularly human, because just those actions constitute the realm of human freedom, while the mere excellence of the nutritive function remains a natural necessity, with which we have ethically nothing to do. We can manage only those activities of life that are mediated by desire. Consequently, the virtues lower than those of the irrational part in the secondary sense are not worthy of investigation for ethics that aims at practical effects. Virtue is the habit of the effective activity of a function, but we can manage only those functions which are somewhat rational. The virtue of the desiring part is that state of desire in which it tends to realize various effects through being managed by reason. This is the practical reason, the virtue of which is represented by the concept of $\varphi\rho\acute{o}\nu\eta\sigma\iota\varsigma$ or prudence. Prudence accompanies of necessity the ethical virtues, or rather we might say, that prudence is the formal principle of ethical virtues.[3]

The essence of ethical virtue is the control of desire or the obedience of the irrational soul to practical intellect. All kinds of desires may be the substrata of such virtues, and there is no discrepancy between Aristotle's psychology and his ethics in this respect. While in his psychology only the natural functions of the human soul were analysed, in the ethics, we are asked to reflect about the modes in which these natural functions are realized in society. What seems at first to be a discrepancy between these two parts of Aristotle's work is in truth nothing but a mere appearance due to the complexity of the latter.

[1] Eth. Nic. I. 13. 1102 b 11 f.
[2] $\delta\iota\alpha\nu o\eta\tau\iota\varkappa\grave{\eta}$ $\dot{\alpha}\varrho\varepsilon\tau\acute{\eta}$ being the virtue of the rational part in the proper sense, $\dot{\eta}\theta\iota\varkappa\grave{\eta}$ $\dot{\alpha}\varrho\varepsilon\tau\acute{\eta}$ that of the rational part in the secondary sense. Cf. § 1.
[3] Eth. Nic. VI. 13. 1144 b 17-32; cf. Trendelenburg, op. cit. II. 384 ff.

Desires aim at various objects through the medium of sensation and imagination; they extend to a wide realm ascending from direct vital values through the material up to the spiritual. The sensations of taste and touch, and the corresponding nutritive and sexual appetites, exist on the boundary between the vegetative soul and the irrational part in the secondary sense, the latter including desire as well as sensation and imagination. These two kinds of sensation and their corresponding appetites form the realm of temperance and indulgence, together with continence and incontinence.[1] The vegetative soul as a mere irrational faculty falls short of having a human virtue, but it participates in reason in so far as it acts through a desire, and to this extent it may have an ethical virtue. Needless to say, temperance is an ethical virtue, indulgence a vice, the former being the character which holds in moderation the nutritive and sexual appetites, the latter being the want of rational regulation, allowing excessive appetites to prevail. (There may be a character which is lacking in appetite at all, but it has no ethical significance.) Continence and incontinence resemble the above two characters, only in this case excessive desires are present and struggle with reason. We need not enter into details here; but generally speaking, in these lowest desires, it is necessary to maintain moderation in order to conserve and promote the activity of life. Just as with regard to the sense of touch, an excessive stimulus destroys the organ[2] and endangers life, while in higher sensations, there is but little danger of such a kind, so the moderation of these lower desires is the most fundamental of all ethical virtues, and the *sine qua non* of a good life. Hence Plato regarded temperance as the fundamental virtue to all citizens, while courage or prudence was considered to be rather proper for a higher class.[3] Among special sensations, smell, hearing, and sight are more refined senses, which originally arose for the sake of preservation and reproduction, yet with the expansion of their environment they are developed gradually into pure cognition beyond the immediate interest of life. The desires which accompany these sensations also require moderation, which is, however, not indispensable to the preservation of life. Temperance and

---

[1] Eth. Nic. III. 13. 1118 a 23-26; VII. 6. 1147 b 26-31; 1148 a 4-10, cf. Stewart's note *ad loc.*; Eth. Nic. VII. 1. 1145 a 35 - b 2; 1145 a 16-18; VII. 6. 1148 a 4 ff.; III. 13. 1117 b 23 f.
[2] De An. III. 13. 435 b 15-19.   [3] Rep. 432 A.

indulgence, as well as continence and incontinence, are found only conditionally in such regions. For instance, those who love the smell of an apple, of roast meat or of cosmetic matter, love in fact the lower pleasures which are associated with these sensations,[1] rather than the enjoyment of these smells themselves. Similar phenomena are also found in hearing and sight. Only in such an accidental sense may we admit temperance and other kindred characters to these higher sensations,[2] or rather, such characters reveal themselves accidentally through them.

The desires that are conditioned by the vegetative-nutritive function are confined to nutritive and sexual appetites, which are accompanied by touch and taste, and the moderation of them forms the virtue of temperance. The other desires that are accompanied by higher sensations aim at higher values beyond the immediate needs of nutrition and reproduction. Even taste, when it wants not much wine or food, but delights in deliciousness, is not of necessity to be blamed as indulgence or incontinence.[3] As for smell, man is alone able to enjoy it for its own sake, unlike animals, which enjoy it only for the sake of expected food.[4] The delight in music or play may be in a sense the enjoyment of hearing and sight,[5] but just as these higher sensations are the beginning of intellectual cognition, their objects involve more or less a spiritual meaning, and tend towards some spiritual values.

Generally speaking, desire is the efficient cause of act, and is divided into appetite, passion, and wish.[6] The division is no doubt derived from Plato's tripartite theory of the soul. Appetite in the strict sense is the sensitive desire which longs for bodily pleasure, especially for the natural and necessary pleasures of eating, drinking, and sexual activity.[7] But in its wider sense, it

---

[1] Eth. Nic. X. 13. 1118 a 1-13.   [2] Eth. Nic. VII. 6. 1148 b 2-9.
[3] Eth. Nic. III. 13. 1118 a 26-32.   [4] Eth. Nic. III. 13. 1118 a 16.
[5] Eth. Nic. III. 13. 1118 a 6.
[6] De An. II. 3. 414 b 2; III. 10. 433 a 23. Motu An. 6. 700 b 19, 22; 7. 701 b 1; Eth. Eud. II. 7. 1223 a 26; [Mag. Mor. I. 12. 1187 b 37.]

[7] ἐπιθυμία is defined as: τοῦ ἡδέος ὄρεξις· Top. VI. 3. 140 b 27; De An. II. 3. 414 b 5; III. 10. 433 a 25; Part. An. II. 17. 661 a 8; Rhet. II. 11. 1370 a 17; Eth. Nic. III. 3. 1111. a 32; 4. 111 b 16; VII. 10. 1151 b 11; Eth. Eud. II. 7. 1223 a 34; VII. 2. 1235 b 22. The concept τὸ ἡδύ has also wider and narrower senses. The narrower sense of a lower, sensible pleasure is more usual. A desire in an animal or a child is always called ἐπιθυμία. Eth Nic. III. 13. 1118 b 8; 15. 1119 b 5; Pol. VII. 15. 1334 b 23; III. 16. 1287 a 31; De An. III. 10. 433 b 6; 433 a 3. It is essentially an irrational desire: Rhet. II. 19. 1393 a 2; 10. 1369 a 4.

extends to the region of higher values such as property or honour:[1] Aristotle's concept of ἐπιθυμία μετὰ λόγον, i.e. "appetite with reason", probably means such a desire.[2] Both property and honour are more or less indirect values: they have utility rather than value itself,[3] and may lead to vulgar enjoyment as well as spiritual satisfaction. They are intermediate values, and rather should be regarded as the objects of passion or wish.[4]

With regard to these desires of higher values, moderation is none the less the essence of virtue, and excess or defficiency that of vice. Moderation concerning the desire for property is liberality and magnificience, the corresponding vice of excess being prodigality and vulgarity, the vice of deficiency meanness and niggardliness respectively.[5] The virtue relevant to honour is pride, and the corresponding vices are vanity and humility,[6] to which are analogous ambition and unambitiousness.[7] The emotion against libel is anger, which is the negative expression of passion, and with regard to which there are the virtue of good temper, the vices of irascibility and excessive meekness.[8] Among other ethical virtues, the chief ones are courage and justice. They are also founded upon vital and material values, being attitudes towards the latter. Courage is not concerned directly with vegetative functions such as nutrition or reproduction, but is grounded more profoundly upon the desire for existence. Even nutrition itself

---

[1] Eth. Nic. VII. 6. 1148 a 22, 27.   [2] Rhet. I. 11. 1370 a 17-27.
[3] Eth. Nic. I. 3. 1095 b 26-28; 1096 a 6 f. Honour is the highest of external goods; it is merit for virtues; Eth. Nic. IV. 7. 1123 b 35, 20; V. 10. 1134 b 7; VIII. 16. 1163 b 4. The distribution of it is the chief problem of politics: Pol. II. 8. 1268 a 21; III. 5. 1278 a 20; IV. 4. 1290 b 12; 13. 1297 b 7; V. 6. 1305 b 4; 8. 1308 b 13. Needless to say, wealth is of such a nature: Eth. Nic. V. 5. 1130 b 30 - 32.
[4] Though θυμός is considered to be a kind of ὄρεξις, it has no verbal form. We can easily perceive from Aristotle's discussion of the dispositions μεγαλοψυχία and φιλοτιμία that honour is the object of θυμός, but owing to the lack of verbal form for this word, one ought to say ὀρεγεῖν ἐφίεσθαι or φιλεῖν τὴν τιμίαν. Such a disposition is also said to "wish" (βούλεσθαι) for honour (Eth. Nic. VIII. 9. 1159 a 12). The expression θυμός mainly takes the negative form of anger. Wherefore it is sometimes omitted from the enumeration of the kinds of desires.
[5] Eth. Nic. II. 7. 1107 b 16; IV. 1 - 6.
[6] Eth. Nic. II. 7. 1107 b 21; IV. 7 - 9.
[7] Eth. Nic. II. 7. 1107 b 25; IV. 10.
[8] Eth. Nic. II. 7. 1108 a 4; IV. 11.

is nothing but a function of this fundamental instinct. It may have been on account of this immediateness and radicality, that courage was discussed by Aristotle before temperance. Of course courage is more than a mere desire for existence, since its essence is to actualize a higher social value through the denial of this basic and, so to say, blind volition. Courage is especially the virtue of not fearing death in war for the sake of one's own state.[1] But service for the state does not of necessity require one to die in war. The more essential mark of courage is the subjugation of the fear of death; and the will to serve for one's own state or the subjugation of the fear of death can form the virtue of courage only because the attachment to life presupposes the value of life. Death in war would not be a virtue, unless life itself is something good.[2] And yet, just through death in war, we shall get a higher life; or we may rather say that the animalistic and biological life is thereby raised to the national life. Courage is nothing but the fit use of life-value. Only, in this case, as the will to life is elevated through negation, it concerns not appetite, but passion and affect. Just as moderate enjoyment of appetites, being the positive expression of vegetative life, forms the virtue of temperance, so its negative expression appears as the feeling of fear, the moderation of which forms the virtue of courage. Courage is rightness of avoidance rather than that of pursuit: it might have been treated next to temperance, because it is in a sense temperance's other side.

As for justice, though it is a virtue of extraordinary importance, its basis is nothing more than the pursuit of external good such as property or honour.[3] The distribution of property among nations or in human society should be proportionate to qualities of personality, e.g. virtue or birth. The appropriate distribution is justice. It bears some resemblance to generosity or magnificence so far as both of these are commonly founded upon the desire for property or the use of it, differing only in that the latter are con-

---

[1] Eth. Nic. III. 9. 1115 a 35. Häcker, in Das Eintheilungs-und Anordnugsprincip der moralischen Tugendlehre in der nicomachischen Ethik, tried to divide the Aristotelian virtues according to the principles of life. He ranked courage in the first class with temperance, the former being the vitue of θυμός the latter that of ἐπιθυμία. Zeller was opposed to this theory (Ph. d. Gr. II. 2. 634 n. 1), and emphasized the social character of this virtue.

[2] Cf. N. Hartmann, Ethik. II. 3.

[3] Eth. Nic. VI. 5. 1130 b 26; 1130 b 3.

cerned with individual acts, and the former with social relations.[1] Let us, however, for the present postpone consideration of the details of ethical virtues and of the desires upon which they are based.

In short, then the three kinds of desires, appetite, passion, and wish, are divided according to the varieties of their object's utility for life: the natural and necessary is the object of appetite, the spiritual and rational is that of wish, while power, being intermediate between the two, is the object of passion. One may see from the foregoing statement, that rational value, which is *per se* the object of wish, stands upon the basis of natural and social values. For instance, though all desires for virtues are wishes, yet temperance has its basis in appetite. Herein we find the explanation for the complication of the objects of desire and wish, viz., although appetite is by nature the instinctive and irrational desire for natural needs, yet in its enjoyment, it may be and must be obedient to rational regulation,[2] and in this respect, appetite may be bestowed with a sort of rationality. On the other side, wish, inspite of its essential rationality and its intention upon spiritual values, may have a more immediate irrational object as its basis.

Ethical virtues, as the virtues of the desiring part, are the right states of desires which pursue the values of life, property, honour, etc., and are dominated by practical intellect. A mere desire is neither good nor bad; it is nothing more than indefinite matter from the moral point of view. Honour and property are themselves something good,[3] and even nutritive and sexual appetites are recognized to be necessary for human nature.[4] The asceticism that would establish morality at the sacrifice of natural desires, is far from the intention of Aristotle, who esteems reproduction as a holy act through which all living creatures partake in eternity.[5] But the material desires may become either good or bad, in accordance with their modes of appearance. The formal principle of these desires is reason, their determination through right reason

[1] Eth. Nic. V.4. 1130 b 1.
[2] Eth. Nic. III. 15. 1119 b 9 - 15.
[3] Eth. Nic. VII. 6. 1147 b 23-29; 1148 a 22 - 28.
[4] Eth. Nic. III. 14. 1119 a 5; VII. 6. 1148 b 15.
[5] De An. II. 4. 415 a 28 - b 7; Eth. Nic. VII. 14. 1153 b 32; Plato, Symp. 206 E; 207 A; Legg. IV. 721 B, C; Teichmüller, Studien Zur Geschichte der Begriffe, 351.

moderation, and the habits which are qualified by it ethical virtues.[1]

Every desire is able to be the "matter", in this sense, of ethical virtue. Not only spiritual values, but also vital or material values may be the basis of them. Temperance, for instance, is the moderation of desires in nutritive and sexual affairs, good temper in that of passion or anger. Does not then moderation or right reason make the desire itself rational? If rational desire is wish, and irrational desire passion and appetite, does it not follow that a good man has only wish and is free from passion and appetite of any kind? Indeed, the realization of bare appetite or passion would not be virtuous: ethical virtue must be a habit reared by reason.[2] A character that is dominated unconditionally by natural desire is brutal; and a habit wherein desire is not obedient to reason is incontinence, or something analogous to it. In ethical virtue, desire itself must be made rational, and rational desire is either wish or will. Now the rationality of will has to do merely with the means for an end, while the estimation of an end itself is allowed only to wish. Therefore, the ultimate principle of ethical virtue must be wish or the desire for the good. This does not mean, however, that appetite and passion are rejected altogether, rather they are acknowledged by wish and converted to it. The matter of ethical virtue is desire in general only in so far as it is regulated by and assimilated to wish.[3] On the other hand, wish is not always good, but sometimes good and sometimes bad. We do not wish something unless we take it to be good,[4] but not all that seem to be good is really good. It is possible to wish something bad or disgraceful, mistaking it for a good thing, e.g., in the case of an indulgent person: his act is not only opposed to right reason, but also led by a wrong opinion,[5] and being thus founded upon such a vicious principle, his character itself becomes positively vicious. Such a bad desire convinced of its rightness would be a wish, rather than an appetite or a passion. It may possibly presuppose an

[1] Eth. Nic. II. 5. 1106 a 26 - 32; 1106 b 18 - 28; 6. 1106 b 36 - 1107 a 2; II. 9. 1109 a 20; III. 8. 1114 b 27; IV. 13. 1127 a 16; Eth. Eud. II. 3. 1220 b 35; 5. 1222 a 11, 13; Pol. IV. 11. 1295 a 37; Eth. Nic. II. 2. 1104 a 26; VI. 13. 1144 b 26 f.
[2] Eth. Nic. II. 1. 1103 a 23 - 26.
[3] Eth. Nic. III. 15. 1119 b 11 ff.; 6. 1113 b 1; 14. 1119 a 11.
[4] Eth. Nic. VI. 11. 1136 b 7 f.; Eth. Eud. II. 7. 1223 b 6 f.; Eth. Nic. III. 6.
[5] Eth. Nic. VII. 4. 1146 b 22 f.; VII. 9. 1151 a 11 - 14, 20-24; VII. 8. 1150 a 19; 3. 1146 a 31.

appetite, but here it is not that a strong appetite supersedes the reason, but rather that one wishes an excessive pleasure and pursues it with convinced calculation, even though the appetite may be comparatively weak.[1] Ethical virtue should not be defined as character determined by wish. Right reason does not always agree with wish, for not all that one believes to be good, is really so. In his early works such as *Metaphysica* XII or the *Ethica Eudemia*, Aristotle referred appetite and passion to the apparent good, and wish to the absolute good,[2] but in the *Ethica Nicomachea*, he turned to a division of wish itself into the ideal and the actual, and assumed that every one cannot but wish what appears good to his image or opinion.[3] The absolute difference of value between appetite,

[1] Eth. Nic. VIII. 6. 1148 a 17-22.
[2] Met. XII. 7. 1072 a 27 f.; Eth. Eud. VII. 2. 1235 b 21-23.
[3] In Eth. Nic. III. 6. 1113 a 15-b 2, Aristotle distinguishes an absolute object and an incidental object of wish, the one as real good, the other as apparent good. In Eth. Eud. VII. 2. 1235 b 26-29, imagination and opinion are distinguished from each other, the one gives the apparent good, the other the real good. Yet, this thought was also abandoned. Both imagination and opinion cannot get rid of subjective finiteness. We must also refer to Eth. Nic. VIII. 2. 1155 b 21-26, where we find similar distinction in regard to the object of love. Of course the object of desire and that of love are not the same, since desire is somewhat different from love; yet the solution of dividing the object of love into the absolute ideal and the relative fact, is analogous to the case of desire (cf. Top. VI. 8. 147 a 1 ff.). Here there is no detailed treatment of pleasure, but he seems to imply a division of pleasure also into the absolute and the relative. In what manner these two meanings of good and the pleasant related to each other? In Eth. Eud. VII. 2. 1236 a 9, the absolute good is identified with the absolutely pleasant, and the relative good with the relatively pleasant. Further it seems to be discordant to the distinction between the good and the apparent good, that at the end of the statement in Eth. Eud. above referred, the author denies the difference of the lovable and the apparently lovable. But there is no real inconsistency between the two statements. The good is objective, and may subsist whether a man admits it or not. Even if it may appear manifold to various subjects, it never loses its essence, only its applicability is restricted. On the other hand, the object of love has no significance apart from affection. Desire and pleasure also being essentially subjective feelings, we cannot distinguish τὸ βουλητόν from τὸ φαινομένον βουλητόν or τὸ ἡδύ from τὸ φαινομένον ἡδύ even if we may distinguish τὸ ἀγαθόν and τὸ φαινομένον ἀγαθόν. Therefore, the division of the object of desire in Mag. Mor. II. 11. 1208 b 37 seems to be beyond Aristotle's real intention. About the absolute and the relative good, cf. Eth. Nic. VII. 13. 1152 b 26.

Next to be noticed is that the pleasant is mistaken to be good. This statement proves our hypothesis that βούλησις being itself a rational desire, may be concerned

passion, and wish was thus mitigated. The distinction that the first two are immediate desire, and the last a desire which tends towards a remoter object through the medium of intellect, is reserved, yet they are all the same the desires of a finite human being who is not free from fault.

Just as all desires presuppose pleasure and pain, so are the satisfaction and lack of satisfaction of them followed by the same feelings. The imagined feelings as the agent of desires are potential, and the feelings as the result of conduct are an actual experience. Being potential, the former would involve a kind of material element and are somehow mixed. The experiences of desires themselves, at least of some of them, being actual want and discontent, are followed by a kind of pain.[1] They are pleasant[2] only through the potential pleasure which accompanies imagination as the content of desire, viz., owing to the expectation of enjoyment. At any rate, the type of pleasure and pain correspond to various types of desires and their objects. We may consider either that the feeling is differentiated by desire, or conversely that the quality of desire is determined by that of feeling. Aristotle in fact takes the concept of pleasure in a double meaning: in its strict sense, it is a lower value that is opposed to good and utility,[3] but in a wider sense, it means the feeling of satisfaction that accompanies all undisturbed actions.[4] Among desires, appetite especially pursues pleasure in the strict sense, while wish aims at the good, which is more precious and of higher value.[5] In general, pleasure is divided into the corporeal and the mental.[6] Evidently, a mere body cannot

with the object of so-called sensible pleasure. Namely, wish may consent to or refuse the enjoyment of lower appetites. As far as we desire something as good, it is certainly a wish. The above cited statement would show us that βούλησις does not always imply a true estimation.

[1] Eth. Nic. III. 14. 1119 a 4; VII. 13. 1153 a 31 f.

[2] Cf. Eth. Nic. IX. 1. 1164 a 13 ff.; X. 7. 1177 a 25. In the former, the expectation of profit, in the latter, the love of knowledge is said to be pleasure. Cf. Eth. Eud. II. 8. 1124 b 16; Rhet. I. 11. 1370 a 27; 1370 b 10, 30; II. 2. 1378 b 7.

[3] Eth. Nic. I. 2. 1095 a 22 f.; Eth. Eud. VII. 2. 1235 b 22; Eth. Nic. II. 7. 1107. b 7.

[4] Eth. Nic. VII. 13. 1153 a 12.

[5] Rhet. I. 10. 1369 a 3; Eth. Nic. VIII. 9. 1159 a 12; V. 11. 1136 b 7; Eth. Eud. II. 7. 1223 b 6; cf. Eth. Nic. III. 13. 1118 a 1-13.

[6] Eth. Nic. III. 13. 1117 b 28 f. Following this, pleasures that accompany sight, hearing, smelling, are enumerated as bodily pleasures, besides lower pleasures that accompany taste and touch.

feel any pleasure:[1] bodily pleasure really means only the feeling in which bodily determination is comparatively noticeable. This bodily pleasure corresponds to the so-called sensitive appetite, which is further divided into various kinds of sensations or appetites. There is on the one hand the pleasure that accompanies the satisfaction of nutritive or sexual appetite, i.e., the pleasure of touch and taste, and on the other hand, the pleasure that accompanies higher sensation or desire. Nutrition and reproduction being the most fundamental and indispensable functions of life, the satisfaction of the appetites of which they are the ends is also the most natural and necessary pleasure of living beings.[2] Such pleasure presupposes bodily needs which make us uneasy and which are in a way unpleasant or painful. The fulfilment of sensitive desire is the process in which bodily needs are satisfied and what is incomplete becomes complete. It is when one takes notice of these natural and necessary appetites, that one takes pleasure to be motion or generation.[3]

In its wider sense, as aforesaid, pleasure is not limited to the satisfaction of such a necessary desire, but may as well be the pleasure that accompanies a higher sensation or rational activity. Such a pleasure is not the result of any need or want, but of undisturbed exercise of one's proper function, and consequently consists not in motion but in action.[4] Aristotle even goes so far as to say that just such a pleasure is pleasure *par excellence*, and the before described necessary pleasure is nothing more than an accidental one, for the essence of pleasure is the action of nature, and necessary pleasure is in fact the consciousness of motion which is experienced by the healthy part of the soul in the process of recovering its injured nature.[5] To conceive the satisfaction of sensitive desire as pleasure (Aristotle's pleasure in the strict sense), is the view of common sense, while to take spiritual satisfaction as the real pleasure is to form a philosophical or ideal concept of it.

The very best of all ideal pleasures is that of pure contemplation,[6] which is the most self-sufficient and complete activity of reason.[7]

[1] Eth. Nic. X. 2. 1173 b 11.
[2] Eth. Nic. VII. 6. 1147 b 23-31; VII. 8. 1150 a 16-18.
[3] Eth. Nic. VII. 12. 1152 b 12-14; [Mag. Mor. II. 7. 1204 a 33.]
[4] Eth. Nic. VII. 13. 1153 a 7-15; X. 2. 1173 b 7-20.
[5] Eth. Nic. VII. 15. 1154 b 15-20.
[6] Eth. Nic. X. 7. 1177 a 22-25.
[7] Eth. Nic. X. 7. 1177 a 27; b 1.

To admit contemplation as the highest and purest pleasure means no doubt to raise it beyond the area of act and desire. But in human being even cognition or contemplation may be regarded as a kind of satisfaction of desire. For man is not a pure reason, but is emotional as well as intellectual, and corporeal as well as spiritual.[1] Such a being does desire to know;[2] the desire to know is a wish, and a kind of rational desire. The pleasure that accompanies a cognitive action may be regarded as the satisfaction of this desire.[3] Therefore, pleasure in the widest sense is necessary for all human acts, and to reject it would lead to the denial of desire and action themselves.[4] Of course, even if the satisfaction of a desire is pleasure, desire is not of necessity the pursuit of pleasure. The conscious content of a desire is the end, pleasure being the concomitant phenomenon of its attainment.[5] The pleasure that enters into the content of desire is of lower nature, but the pleasure that follows the satisfaction of desire may have different degrees of value;[6] because, as pleasure is correlative to desire, a dog has his pleasure and a horse his, and so has man his own proper pleasure.[7]

Now man is on the one hand a rational being and resembles God, but on the other hand, he is a kind of animal and living being. His desires and actions range from the vegetative to the divine, and his pleasures are also various in proportion to them.[8] Pleasures are different in accordance with man's ways of living. The most

---

[1] Eth. Nic. VII. 13. 1152 b 36-1153 a 2. The "naturally pleasant" is considered to be a spiritual and higher pleasure, but it is not the satisfaction of a natural desire, which is rather a usual appetite or a normal sexual desire. Cf. ibid. III. 13. 1118 b 19; Part. An. I. 5. 645 a 8; Met. XII 7. 1072 b 14-16; Eth. Nic. X. 7. 1177 b 26-29; Met. I. 1. 980 a 20 f.

[2] Met. I. 1. 980 a 22.

[3] Eth. Nic. X. 7. 1177 a 25-27.

[4] Eth. Nic. II. 2. 1104 b 13-16; ibid. 34-1105 a 1; 1105 a 4 f.; VII. 14. 1153 b 30; VIII. 4. 1156 b 16 f.

[5] Eth. Nic. VIII. 14. 1153 b 29-32; Pol. VIII. 5. 1339 b 31-38; II. 9. 1271 b 7-10; cf. Trendelenburg, Beiträge zur Philosophie, III. 185, 205, 211; Scheler, Der Formalismus in der Ethik und die materiale Wertethik, 94 f.

[6] Eth. Eud. VII. 2. 1235 b 21-23. Pleasure may be the object only of lower desires. Yet, as a result, it may follow a higher act, which is *per se* the object of wish. Rhet. II. 4. 1381 a 6-8; Eth. Nic. VII. 6 1148 a 22-26; V.10 1151 b 19; VII. 14. 1153 b 7-13; X. 2. 1173 b 20-23; 28-31. 5. 1175 b 24-27; ibid. 36-1176 a 3.

[7] Eth. Nic. X. 5. 1176 a 3.

[8] Eth. Nic. I. 6. 1097 b 32; 1098 _ 12.

human mode of living is the spiritual or intellectual action[1] which is proper to man, viz. contemplation and conduct. Of the two, the former is essentially divine, and man can only occasionally partake in it. It is rather a divine life than a human one, and one might deem it advisable for men, being men, to think of human things, and being mortal, of mortal things; viz., one might assume conduct to be more suitable to man than contemplation, and political affairs than science. Aristotle, however, insists upon the idealistic view of man against such a realistic view. According to him, man ought to make himself immortal as far as possible, and do everything to live in accordance with the highest part in himself, and he even says that "This would seem, too, to be each man himself, since it is the authoritative and better part of him."[2] In the same way, the pleasure that is suitable to man is that with which a wise man would be delighted,[3] viz., the pleasure of contemplation in the first place, and the pleasure that follows moral conduct in the second place.

Thus all animals feel their particular pleasure in the actions that arise from their own nature or habit, so that it is the mark of one's character in what thing he feels pleasure and in what pain. The pleasure that follows the satisfaction of desire by no means detracts from the moral value of the act, rather it proves it. He who does good conduct with pain, is of inferior character, and one who does it with pleasure is a man of virtue. Moral elevation as the end of education, is nothing but the rearing of a character that will feel pleasure in good conduct and pain in a bad one.[4]

Herein we find a remarkable peculiarity of Aristotle's eudaemonism as against the rigoristic theory of Kant. Kant should have correctly said that conduct the content of which is pleasure, viz., that which aims at the enjoyment, is impure, instead of saying, as he actually did, that the conduct which has a material ground makes the pleasure its content. He misunderstood the fact that the realization of a desire for a material end is accompanied by pleasure, to signify that the pursuit of pleasure is itself the motive

---

[1] Eth. Nic. I. 6. 1098 a 7.
[2] Eth. Nic. X. 7. 1177 b 26; 1178 a 3; X. 5. 1176 a 24-29.
[3] Eth. Nic. X. 5. 1176 a 15; Pol. VIII. 3. 1338 a 4-9.
[4] Met. VII. 4. 1029 b 5-7; Eth. Eud. V. 2. 1237 a 1; 1236 b 39-1237 a 9; Eth. Nic. II. 2. 1104 b 3-13; I. 9. 1099 a 7-21.

of such a desire.[1] In truth, however, to have a material ground for conduct is not always the same as to pursue pleasure.[2] It presupposes, indeed, a natural or acquired disposition of man, but while Kant absolutely rejects all kinds of inclination, Aristotle rather distinguishes the qualitative difference among them, and would admit moral value to conduct which arises from an excellent inclination. Ethical virtue is just such a rationalized disposition and nothing else. Kant, by deeming obligation the essence of morals, radically rejected happiness or pleasure, and therefore encountered a difficulty in making the moral ideal accord with human nature. But at once an idealist and a man of common sense as he was, Kant could not advise man to sacrifice the general wish for happiness to moral purity. The only solution that he could present was to offer the old-fashioned religious consolations of the highest good and the immortality of the individual soul.[3] There is no essential relation between virtue and happiness. God alone can combine the two heterogeneous requirements through His benevolence or providence. Immortality of the soul is nothing more than a promissory note that postpones the harmony which is not satisfied in the lifetime, and moreover, there is no proof that guarantees the payment of this bill, all being left to our faith and belief. In this way, life would, in the last analysis, amount to mere betting.

It is otherwise with Aristotle. According to him, happiness is not such an element external to morality, that can be combined with it only through God or through faith in Him, but is essential to morality. It is not the grace of God, but rather itself the end of conduct and, so to say, a part of oughtness. It is not of a definite quality as in Kant, but indefinite.

With what kind of quality we should fill it is the problem of our moral endeavourment. In other words, it is not that happiness is given in charity for good conduct, but that it is our duty or ideal to feel happiness in good conduct. It is not that a man of virtue should *become* happy, but rather that a happy man is just that man who is a man of virtue.

[1] Kant, K. d. p. V. I. 1. § 2. Lehrsatz 1. WW. Cass. V. 23; ibid. Lehrsatz II. & Folgerung. WW. V. 24 f.; He neglects the difference of value among material desires (cf. ibid. Anmerkung), but it is not right to assume that every material rule has reference to an expected pleasure.
[2] Trendelenburg, Beiträge etc. III. 184 f.; Scherer, Formalismus etc. I. 2.
[3] **Trendelenburg**, op. cit. 189 f.

We have stated that Aristotle's concept of the highest happiness involves lower values like Kant's concept of the highest good, and therewith shows the necessary limitation of man as a finite rational being. Nevertheless the essential of ideal happiness is after all the spiritual satisfaction that follows virtuous conduct. The Epicurians and the Stoics assumed the harmony of virtue and happiness, only differing in the element they emphasized. According to Kant, "The Epicurians said that to be conscious of the maxim which leads to happiness, that is virtue, while the Stoics said that to be conscious of one's virtue, that is happiness. To the former cleverness is the same as morality, while to the latter, who preferred a higher name for virtue, only morality was the true wisdom." Whereupon he regrets[1] that their sharp wit....was unhappily applied to making out the identity of the two extremely unequal concepts of happiness and virtue. But through separating these concepts so absolutely, he only arrived at the insufficient solution, which we have just examined, to the problem of their relation. Seeing thus, we cannot repress our hearty approval of Trendelenburg,[2] who finds the most complete solution of this problem, in Aristotle's theory that assumes gradual development to the ideal harmony of virtue and happiness, as well as of reason and feeling; —neigher making virtue a means to lower pleasure, nor making the consciousness of virtue equal to happiness and thus neglecting human nature, nor appealing to a *deus ex machina* in order to bring together a virtue and a happiness quite heterogeneously conceived.

On the one hand, however, even Kant, who made duty the essence of morality, could not deny the deep satisfaction that follows moral conduct,[3] and on the other hand, there would be a ground for reflection whether it is suitable for Aristotle to have conceived the satisfaction of desire in general as pleasure. In order that he might avoid the suspicion of hedonism, he should have rather called it, e.g. joy, or at least be content himself in calling it happiness. Indeed, happiness was for him a concept of quite an extensive meaning. It may comprise sensitive pleasure, the satisfaction of possessive desire and desire for honour, and further the bliss

---

[1] Kant, K. d. p. V. I. 2. 2. Cass. WW. V. 121.
[2] Trendelenburg, op. cit. 210 f.
[3] Kant, K. d. p. V. I.2. § 2. WW. V. 128; K.d.U.K. Einl. III. WW. V. 247, 264.

deriving from moral conduct and pure contemplation.[1] What one would regard as the content of happiness, or what one would feel happy about, expresses his character. Happiness is a value concept *par excellence*, but pleasure is a natural concept. Pleasure may also have some value—but only in so far as it is considered to be happiness.[2] And to think something to be happiness means to esteem it; the proof is that happiness is considered to be respectable and not praisable,[3] for to be praisable is to partake in a value, while to be respectable means to be the value itself as the measure of estimation. Happiness is almost synonymous with the good, so that everyone would agree in taking the good for happiness, except that to say "the good is happiness" might be a mere tautology or a formal answer.[4] The only difference between the two is that the one is the subjective, and the other the objective, aspect of value. Why, then, was Aristotle not content himself merely with calling the satisfaction of desire happiness? Why, on the one hand, did he criticise hedonism, while on the other hand, enlarging the concept of desire so as to speak of pleasure as the satisfaction of desire in general? Perhaps this is not without its reason. The satisfaction of

[1] Eth. Nic. I. 3.
[2] Eth. Nic. I. 5. 1097 b 2-5; 3. 1095 b 16; III. 6. 1113 a 34 f.
[3] Eth. Nic. I. 12. 1101 b 12-14; 21-23; 1101 b 35-1102 a 1. τιμίον is different from Kant's *Achtung* which is accompanied by a kind of pain.
[4] Eth. Nic. I. 4. 1095 a 14-22. As to the indefiniteness of happiness, cf. Kant, K.d.p.V.I.1. § 3. Lehrsatz II. WW. V. 28: *Glücklich zu sein, ist notwending das Verlangen jedes Vernünftigen, aber endlichen Wesens und also ein unvermeidlicher Bestimmungsgrund seines Begehrungsvermögens. Denn obgleich der Begriff der Glückseligkeit der praktischen Beziehung der Objekte aufs Begehrungsvermögen allerwärts zum Grunde liegt, so ist er doch nur der allgemeine Titel der subjektiven Bestimmungsgründe und bestimmt nichts spezifisch, darum es doch in dieser praktischen Aufgabe allein zu tun ist, und ohne welche Bestimmung sie gar nicht aufgelöset werden kann. Worin nämlich jeder seine Glückseligkeit zu setzen habe, kommt auf jedes sein besonders Gefühl der Lust und Unlust an, und selbst in einem und demselben Subjekt auf die Verschiedenheit der Bedürfnis nach den Abänderungen dieses Gefühls, und ein subjektiv notwendiges Gesetz (als Naturgesetz) ist also objektiv ein gar sehr zufälliges praktisches Prinzip, dass in verschiedenen Subjekten sehr verschieden sein kann und muss, mithin niemals ein Gesetz abgeben kann, welches bei der Begierde nach Glückseligkeit nicht auf die Form der Gesetzmässigkeit, sondern lediglich auf die Materie ankommt, nämlich ob und wieviel Vermögen ich in der Befolgung des Gesetzes zu erwarten habe.*—A mere concept of happiness never gives a moral rule, still a character which feels happiness in a good act has by feeling so a moral value. Not a mere subjective satisfaction, but the satisfaction in a certain situation, expresses the moral value of a man's character.

a desire has two aspects: the one being valuable, the other natural. Seen from the valuable side, it is happiness, but from the natural side, it is a kind of pleasure. The experience of moral conduct may be happiness, as far as the subject is a moral person, but the same experience is pleasure in so far as he is an animal. We should not neglect this natural aspect, since morality is not only a transcendent ideal, but also involves an actual power that dominates a concrete person. This power is rather the ground of morality itself.[1] It attests to the eminence of Aristotle's thought rather than its deficiency, that he, who was a psychologist and biologist as well as a moralist, could not remain at the mere axiological point of view.

It is not a hedonistic assertion but a psychological expression of eudaemonism in Aristotle, that he considered pleasure to be the satisfaction of desire in general. But can this eudaemonism avoid critisism from Kantian ethics? To make happiness the ultimate end of conducts would mean to reduce morality to inclination. When one seeks happiness as his ultimate end, if not pleasure, would this not be after all a spiritual egoism, being no different from Epicurianism? Is the true morality not the actualization of a will determined by the feeling of duty? Does eudaemonism not injure the dignity of morality? We shall state the details of Aristotle's concept of end, and try thereby to confront Kant's ethics, at a later point in this inquiry when we consider what is the essence of practice and production. Anticipating our conclusion for the present, we say that the end is not a subjective but an objective one. That every act aims at happiness means not that man makes this his conscious purpose, but that it acts as the objective and regulative principle of all instances of conduct. It is the end for a philosopher as a reflective mind, but not always the end for the practical subject. So, a biologist may rightly recognize self-preservation as the end of all living activities, though animals and plants are not conscious of this end.

If happiness is the objective end and not the subjective purpose, it will never detract from the moral value of practice. Man does not always pursue satisfaction with consciousness, yet the satisfaction of a desire will naturally result in happiness none the less. Moreover, even if happiness should be made the subjective end, it does not of necessity harm the dignity of morality. For happi-

[1] Eth. Nic. X. 1. 1172 a 20-26; cf. Trendelenburg, op. cit. 200 f., 209 ff.

ness, being, as aforesaid, the highest value, is not the same as the natural feeling of satisfaction. To pursue happiness is after all to pursue the highest good, or to intend to realize the highest value. Of course a mere desire for happiness is not more praiseable than blamable, but it is morally indifferent. Being a bare natural tendency, such a desire may be either good or bad. Its moral value depends upon the substance of happiness.

§ 4. VOLUNTARY ACT

Now that we have observed the material aspect of desires in order to explain the species and essence of them, we must next investigate the formal aspect, in which desire actualizes itself into conduct. Generally speaking, desire is the effort to acquire or realize the object which is recognized through sensation, imagination, or intellect. Voluntarity simply means the causality of desires, and an animal is said to have acted voluntarily when its movement is caused by a conscious desire. Though all living activities are in a sense movements, movement in respect of place, which is the essence of conduct, is found only in some kinds of animals.[1] The principle of this movement must be either body or soul. And as body is passive, such an active principle must be the soul.[2] It is evident moreover that it does not belong to the nutritive part, because this part involves exclusively the function of accepting and assimilating external matter. This movement also aims at a certain end, and is accompanied by imagination and desire, which is not the function of the nutritive part.[3] Besides, if nutrition were the principle of this motion, even plants would move themselves.[4] Nor is sensation the direct principle of motion, for there are some animals that have sensations yet do not exhibit locomotion.[5] How then is it with reason or intellect? Aristotle considers herein three modes of reason. Firstly, theoretical reason without doubt is not the principle we are seeking, for it thinks nothing about practical matters, and cannot tell whether an object should be pursued or avoided, while motion is some kind of pursuit

---

[1] De An. I. 5. 410 b 20; II. 3. 415 a 7; 415 b 22; III. 9. 432 b 19-21.
[2] De An. I. 5. 410 b 19-21; II. 3. 415 b 21-22.
[3] De An. III. 9. 432 b 14. [4] De An. III. 9. 432 b 17.
[5] Ibid.

or avoidance.[1] Secondly, there are cases, when reason, even though thinking about practical affairs, yet does not command pursuit or avoidance, while the heart or some other part of the body acts as the direct moving principle of fear or desire.[2] How should this second kind of reason be called—theoretical or practical ? It seems to be practical in so far as the object of cognition is practical affairs, but it seems also to be theoretical as far as this cognition does not determine conduct. Aristotle himself gives here no decision : presumably it might correspond to the habit called σύνεσις or γνώμη, i.e., insight or judgement, which is somewhat inert konwledge of practice.[3] An indifferent judgement about practical affairs would

---

[1] De An. III. 9. 432 b 26.   [2] Ibid. 29 ff.
[3] Eth. Nic. VI. 11. 1142 b 34-1143 a 24: ἔστι δὲ ἡ σύνεσις καὶ ἡ εὐσυνεσία, καθ' ἃς λέγομεν συνετοὺς καὶ εὐσυνέτους οὔθ' ὅλως τὸ αὐτὸ ἐπιστήμη ἢ δόξῃ (πάντες γὰρ ἂν ἦσαν συνετοί) οὔτε τις μία τῶν κατὰ μέρος ἐπιστημῶν, οἷον ἡ ἰατρικὴ περὶ ὑγιεινῶν, ἡ γεωμετρία περὶ μεγέθη· οὔτε γὰρ περὶ τῶν ἀεὶ ὄντων καὶ ἀκινήτων ἡ σύνεσίς ἐστιν οὔτε περὶ τῶν γιγνομένων ὁτουοῦν, ἀλλὰ περὶ ὧν ἀπορήσειεν ἄν τις καὶ βουλεύσαιτο. διὸ περὶ τὰ αὐτὰ μὲν τῇ φρονήσει ἐστίν, οὐκ ἔστι δὲ τὸ αὐτὸ σύνεσις καὶ φρόνησις. ἡ μὲν γὰρ φρόνησις ἐπιτακτική ἐστιν· τί γὰρ δεῖ πράττειν ἢ μή, τὸ τέλος αὐτῆς ἐστίν· ἡ δὲ σύνεσις κριτικὴ μόνον.... ἡ δὲ καλουμένη γνώμη, ... ἡ τοῦ ἐπιεικοῦς ἐστὶ κρίσις ὀρθή· σημεῖον δέ· τὸν γὰρ ἐπιεικῆ μάλιστά φαμεν εἶναι συγγνωμονικόν ... ἡ δὲ συγγνώμη γνώμη ἐστὶ κριτικὴ τοῦ ἐπιεικοῦς ὀρθή· ὀρθὴ δ' ἡ τοῦ ἀληθοῦς. ibid. 12. 1143 a 25-35: εἰσὶ δέ πᾶσαι αἱ ἕξεις εὐλόγως εἰς ταὐτὸ τείνουσαι· λέγομεν γὰρ γνώμην καὶ σύνεσιν καὶ φρόνησιν καὶ νοῦν ἐπὶ τοὺς αὐτοὺς ἐπιφέροντες γνώμην ἔχειν καὶ νοῦν ἤδη καὶ φρονίμους καὶ συνετούς. πᾶσαι γὰρ αἱ δυνάμεις αὗται τῶν ἐσχάτων εἰσὶ καὶ τῶν καθ' ἕκαστον· καὶ ἐν μὲν τῷ κριτικὸς εἶναι περὶ ὧν ὁ φρόνιμος, συνετὸς καὶ εὐγνώμων ἢ συγγνώμων· τὰ γὰρ ἐπιεικῆ κοινὰ τῶν ἀγαθῶν ἁπάντων ἐστὶν ἐν τῷ πρὸς ἄλλον. ἔστι δὲ τῶν καθ' ἕκαστα καὶ τῶν ἐσχάτων ἅπαντα τὰ πρακτά· καὶ γὰρ τὸν φρόνιμον δεῖ γινώσκειν αὐτά, καὶ ἡ σύνεσις καὶ ἡ γνώμη περὶ τὰ πρακτά, ταῦτα δ' ἔσχατα. Hence we understand that σύνεσις and γνώμη are concerned with practical objects, and are distinguished not only from ἐπιστήμη but also from δόξα. They must be kinds of practical knowledge, for δόξα may be sometimes theoretical, though it is concerned with individuals. One might suppose it to be rather theoretical, from the definition that it is critical and not imperative. But, in fact, it means only to judge rightly another man's speech about practical affairs. Cf. ibid. 11. 1143 a 11-15. This knowledge is not imperative, presumably because it is concerned with the affairs of another man and not with one's own. Yet it is none the less a kind of practical knowledge, and may become imperative. A sympathetic person who understands another man's words, is rather a worldly-wise man than a scientist. This σύνεσις or γνώμη would become imperative, when one is obliged to act, and feels an inner desire; otherwise he would remain a mere observer of life. In Eth. Nic. X. 10. 1181 a 18, these words are used to

remind us of a theoretical kind of knowledge such as ethics. Here is indeed the most favourable ground for Zeller's interpretation, that Aristotle admitted the theoretical knowledge about practice,[1] and for Walter's opinion that the content of ethics and polititcs is in fact theoretical knowledge.[2] Yet this kind of knowledge has no importance for Aristotle either from a theoretical or a practical point of view, but it is a mere variation of knowledge which is transitional or intermediate between the practical and the theoretical. Ethics, on the contrary, is by no means the action of σύνεσις or γνώμη, but it is rather the action of φρόνησις which is the practical knowledge *par execllence*. It is never an indifferent observing intellect that gives no command about practical matters, but the very source of power which should foster the virtues of man and bring both to individuals and society the highest good.[3] It was the Greek view of ethics, and at the same time Aristotle's belief thereof that ethics should be *architectonic* prudence — prudence of the most general and fundamental sort—and the moral philosopher should be a man of widsom *par excellence*.[4] But to emphasize the practical utility of ethics in such a way does not amount to despising theoretical knowledge. To make the latter identical with that inert practical knowledge would be a serious misunderstanding and an intolerable debasement of it. If theoretical knowledge were such a thing, it would certainly be inferior to practical knowledge.

mean something like a righteous judgement through experience. A little farther on, ibid. b 10, it is said that an amateur who cannot estimate properly, may survey the laws and constitutions, yet to him, τὰ τοιαῦτα δειξιοῦσι τὸ μὲν κρίνειν καλῶς οὐκ ἂν ὑπάρχοι, ... εὐσυνετώτεροι δ' εἰς ταῦτα τάχ' ἂν γένοιντο. This does not necessarily deny that σύνεσις is a kind of empirical knowledge, provided that it is external and indifferent.

In the area of theoretical knowledge, we find also a non-professional culture or παιδεία, which is not a special and autonomic faculty of research, but a cognition of an observer who appreciates professional works. σύνεσις or the critical knowledge of practice would correspond to παιδεία in the theoretical area. These indifferent and critical faculties have only a secondary importance both in the theoretical and the practical areas. Part. An. I. 1. 639 a 1 ff. Eth. Nic. I. 1. 1094 b 23. 1095 a 1. Cf. Pol. III. 11. 1282 a 6; Pol. I. 5. 1254 b 20-24.

[1] Zeller, Ph. d. Gr. II. 2. 77 n. 5.
[2] Walter, op. cit, 157 ff., 537 ff. cf.; Teichmüller, Neue Studien zur Geschichte der Begriffe, III. Die praktische Vernunft bei Aristoteles, ch. 1. We shall study this point later on.
[3] Eth. Nic. II. 2. 1103 b 26-30; I. 1. 1095 a 5 f.
[4] Cf. Teichmüller, Neue Studien, etc. 24 ff.

But in reality, theoretical knowledge is regarded as more precious on account of such properties it has as generality and necessariness.[1] Thus theoretical intellect is concerned with its proper objects such as God, nature, or mathematical princiles,—knowledge of which being metaphysics, physics, mathematics, etc. They are higher than practical science such as ethics or politics.[2] This, however, is not our problem for the moment. Aristotle is only inquiring about the *sine qua non* of conduct, and endevouring to prove that it is not reason. For this purpose he enumerates various forms of intellectual activity which are wanting in practical efficiency. Of the two above mentioned, the one is purely theoretical, and the other is practical yet powerlesss, resembling theoretical knowledge, but lacking in the positive marks peculiar to the latter. Neither of them is the efficient cause of conduct. But there is further in the third place, a reason that does order a man to pursue or avoid something, yet is wanting in practical power.[3] In this case, reason is no doubt practical, and not only knows pracical matter, but also commands to do something, only this command is not obeyed but rather the opposite desire is realized instead of it, as in the case of an incontinent person. Generally speaking, the fact that not all who know medical art are always successful at healing, is the proof that something else than knowledge has dominating power over conduct.[4] It might therefore appear as if intellect cannot be the efficient cause of conduct. But it does not follow of necessity, that only appetite is the dominating power of conduct. For instance, a continent man obeys the command of his intellect in spite of his appetite;[5] thence it seems conversely as if intellect were the true agent, or at least so in some cases. Therefore, either intellect or desire must be the agent of conduct.[6]

Aristotle admits both of them at once to be the principle of motion or conduct. Of course not intellect in general: at least theo-

[1] Eth. Nic. I. 1. 1094 b 11-27; VI. 7. 1141 a 20; Met. VI. 1. 1026 a 21; XI. 7. 1064 b 1; Met. I. 2. 981 b 17; 982 a 1; X. 9. 1074 b 27; Top. VIII. 1. 157 a 9.
[2] Met. VI. 1. 1026 a 13; 1. 1069 a 30; 6. 1071 b 3; De An. I. 1. 403 b 7; Phys. II. 2. 193 b 31; An. Post. I. 10. 76 b 3; 13. 79 a 7; An. Pr. I. 41. 49 b 35; Met VII. 10. 1036 a 8; XIII. 2. 1077 a 9; III. 2. 997 b 20; 996 a 27; De An. III. 7.
[3] De An. III. 9. 433 a 1.
[4] Cf. Met. IX. 5. 1048 a 8; 8. 1050 b 30. Cf. Ando, Aristoteles no Sonzairon, 221.
[5] De An. III. 9. 433 a 8.   [6] De An. III. 10. 433 a 9.

retical intellect must be excluded. The intellect that acts as the principle of motion is that which calculates about some purpose,[1] viz., practical intellect. Desire also intends some end, for the object of desire is the beginning of practical reason, and the end of practical reason is the beginning of conduct. Thus, both desire and practical intellect are reasonably regarded as the principle of motion. At first, the object of desire moves, and through it the intellect: the intellect is moved through the object of desire. Even when not intellect but imagination moves, it does not move by itself, but requires desire in addition.

Arguing thus, Aristotle concludes that the more radical and general agent, which precedes intellect and desire, is the object of desire. For, if both intellect and desire move a man in act, they move through a common principle. Whereas intellect does not move without desire, wish, though intellectual, is yet itself a kind of desire. And when some one moves through reasoning, he moves not only through mere reasoning but also through wish. On the other hand, desire may be an agent without intellect,[2] for there is a kind of desire which moves contrary to reasoning, viz. appetite. It will follow then, that what always moves is the object of desire.

Now since reason is always true, but imagination and desire are sometimes right and sometimes not, the object of desire will be either the good or the apparent good.[3] That is to say, the object of desire is sometimes intended through mere imagination, and sometimes appreciated through practical intellect, and one may commit an error in the former case. Needless to say, the one case is that of passion and appetite, and the other that of so-called wish.[4]

The object of desire is the good or the apparent good, it is not the good in general, but the practcal good, viz. one which may exist or not.[5] The most fundamental principle of motion is thus

---

[1] De An. III. 10. 433 a 14. There is a question as to how to translate ἕνεκά του λογιζόμενος. If we translate this like Trendelenburg, as "calculating the end", the practical reason would be a thinking about the means, thus modifying the formation of the end. If on the other hand, we translate this like Walter and many others as "calculating the means to an end", the practical reason would consider only the means, supposing the end unconditionally. We prefer the theory of Loening, who takes it as meaning calculation about conduct; cf. Zurechnungslehre des Aristoteles, 30.

[2] Part. An. I. 1. 641 b 7.

[3] De An. III. 10. 433 a 26; Met. XI. 1. 1059 a 36-38.

[4] Rhet. I. 10. 1368 b 37-1369 a 7.   [5] De An. III. 10. 433 a 29.

the object of desire, and next to it, desire is more necessary than intellect,[1] the latter partaking only indirectly in it. Aristotle, excepting at first the nutritive faculty, next supposing for a time intellect and desire to be the principle of conduct, then found the common principle in the object of desire, and at last decided that the desiring faculty is the direct efficient cause of conduct. In the *De Motu Animalium*,[2] almost the same thought is stated, where intellect, imagination, and sensation are all summed up in the concept of *reason;* appetite, passion, and wish in that of *desire;* while will is regarded to be composed of reason and desire. Thus the two generic faculties of reason and desire being admitted in a sense as the principles of motion, the ultimate efficient cause is reduced to the object of them. Here also, in the succeeding statement, the immediate agent of conduct is assumed to be desire. But why is the final principle that makes the agent an agent, i.e. the *causa finalis* said to be the object of desire and that of intellect? Presumably it is because desire always intends its object through the reason in the generic sense. Namely, the object of desire is given to the desiring faculty either through sensation, imagination, or reason in a narrower sense. In this respect the object of desire is the same as the object of reason. It moves at first reason, and then, the desiring faculty.[3] The immediate agent of conduct may be desire, but the object of intellect, viz. the object of sensation, of imagination, and of reason must precede to it, in respect of the sequence of phenomena. Herein we can also find an important suggestion about the function of practical reason. It is clearly stated that reason, or generally the faculty of knowing practical affairs, not only searches for the means to realize a given desire, but also determines the desire itself.

The process, in which the desiring part arouses movement is as follows. —Motion contains three moments; one is that which moves, next the means through which it moves, and then that which is moved.[4] The first is further divided into that which does not move itself, and that which moves itself and moves others. The unmoved mover is the valuable object which is the *causa finalis* of motion. In human conduct, it is the practical good and the object of desire as well as of reason or imagination.[5] The moved

---

[1] De An. III. 10. 433 b 11.   [2] Motu An. 6. 700 b 15-28.
[3] Motu An. 6. 701 a 2-6. 33-b 1.   [4] De An. III. 10. 433 b 13.
[5] Met. XII. 7. 1072 a 23-31. Teichmüler is not right in taking (op. cit. 207)

movent is the desiring part of the soul,[1] which is the *causa efficiens* of motion. It moves in so far as it desires, for desire is a kind of motion and action.[2] Only it belongs to the motion in a wider sense, as a qualitative change, yet compared with the act as a kind of locomotion, it is not the moved but the movent.[3] We may easily see that the medium between the object and the soul, which lets the *causa finalis* determine the *causa efficiens*, is the cognitive functions such as sensation, imagination, and intellect, or generally, the reason in a wider sense. In the third place, the moved is the animal as an organism, and the instrument through which desire moves others is the body as a corporeal thing.[4] Through what process then does desire move the body to realize its object given by intellect and imagination?

Desire is no doubt a function of the soul; but since the soul is the form of the body, there should be no function of soul apart from body, except the active reason that was analysed in the first chapter. Desire is more or less correlative with the body, and always follows some bodily change.[5] The central organ of sensation was seen to be the heart, its uniting function being the so-called *sensus communis*, and imagination was also attributed to it. Along with the psychological determination of desire through sensation and imagination, the central organ of desire is also sought in the heart. Seen from the physiological point of view, the determination of desire through sensation or imagination is nothing but the process wherewith the stimuli which come from the nerve endings are carried to the heart and arouse in it a delicate expansion and contraction through heating and cooling, which being further transmitted to the periphery give rise to the motions and changes

the unmovable movent as practical reason in a wider sense. Practical reason is also a kind of efficient cause, i.e., a thing which is moved by another and moves another. It is the first medium, that supplies the good as an unmoved movent to consciousness. Teichmüller's mistake seems to arise from the fact that Aristotle here mentions merely the appetitive part as the second moment of movement. But following the sequence more carefully, we see that the cognitive part of the soul comes between these moments, as we state in our text.

[1] De An. III. 10. 433 b 16; Motu An. 6. 701 a 1; 10. 703 a 5.
[2] De An. I. 4. 408 b 16; III. 10. 433 b 17 f.; cf. Hicks's note *ad loc.*; Desire itself is not a locomotion, but a mental action, as Plutarchus also holds.
[3] Phys. VIII. 2. 253 a 12.
[4] De An. III. 10. 433 b 19.
[5] De An. I. 1. 403 a 5-403 b 19.

in limbs, skin, etc.[1] It is not that desire as a pure mental function moves the purely physical body, but rather that desire can move the body through being itself a physiological phenomenon.[2] The heart is precisely the unifying point of the functions such as nutrition, sensation, imagination, desire, and motion.

There are, however, desires and desires, as we know: appetite being the irrational desire, wish, the rational, and between them passion, which is partly rational and partly irrational. The relation of these desires to the body naturally differs. Generally speaking, the more irrational the desire, the nearer is it to the body; the lowest of desires is appetite, which aims at sensual pleasure and immediately serves self-preservation and reproduction. But as for wish, although, being rational, it is distant from the body, still it cannot exist apart from the body. For even the contemplation of theoretical intellect, which is the purest and most transcendent of all mental functions, is impossible without imagination, and therefore not independent of the body.[3] Much more so with desire, which is a practical function through and through. However rational it may be, it must of necessity exist under bodily conditions. That wish is distant from the body, is only a relative matter, and nothing more. It is merely that the object of such a rational desire is not such as might satisfy an immediate bodily need, but one of a higher order; it is not a mere nutriment of the body, but a higher good that makes a good life possible. Instead of evoking sensible pleasure or pain, it is imagined with the feeling that it is good or bad, beautiful or ugly. Hence the object of wish is said to be good or beautiful, while that of appetite to be pleasant. But however beautiful and good the ideal may be, it is only realized through bodily movement or action, so that it must of necessity be mediated through the movement of the heart. Even a rational image acts upon the central organ of sensation and desire through pleasure and pain. Hence, as aforesaid, the good and beautiful does not exist independently as a mere spiritual value, but requires to be pleasant, and the absolute good is identified with the absolutely pleasant.[4] As far as thinking and imagination are not accompanied by the feelings

[1] Motu An. 7. 701 b 13-32; 8. 701 b 33-702 a 19; 11. 703 b 26-36
[2] Part. An II. 1. 647 a 23-31; III. 4. 666 b 15.
[3] De An. I. 1. 403 a 9; III. 7. 431 a 16; 8. 432 a 8, 13; De Memor. 1. 449 b 31; De Sensu 6. 445 b 16.   [4] Eth Eud. VII. 2. 1235 b 32; 1236 b 26; 1237 a 27.

of pleasure and pain and produce no desire, they cannot move the body and can never act. The body is dominated, in this case, by another appetite that moves the heart with a stronger emotion.[1] This is a physiological explanation of the so-called incontinent act, or more generally, of unvirtuous character. Ethical virtue is nothing but the harmony of reason and sensibility, of soul and body. For the good and beautiful to remain a mere spiritual value is the mark of powerless reason. In order that such an ideal may become actual, it must first be realized in a bodily habit. The spiritualization of the body is at once the embodiment of the spirit.

Whether it aims at a bodily need or a spiritual value, every desire is an efficient cause that moves the body through the physiological function of the heart, which, in its turn, is aroused by an image followed by an emotion. Desire moves through being moved, making itself a kind of movement, as far as it is affected by an object, yet it moves a concrete person through the instrument of body. Desire expresses, on the one hand, an actual form, in so far as it is the act of the desiring part; yet it is on the other hand an efficient cause which involves a principle of movement tending to action upon the external world. It is an active potency, or more explicitly, a ἕξις in the particular sense previously indicated.[2] We might define it as a ἕξις to an act. Aristotle himself in fact calls it a habit in one place,[3] but in most cases "habit" is applied rather to virtue or vice, which underlie desire and conduct.[4] This is because desire is more temporal than character; and moreover, the interest of ethics is in the process from character to desire or will, rather than from desire to act. Let us limit ourselves to distinguishing ἕξις as an ontological concept from ἦθος as a practical concept, and taking notice of the fact that the former is a relative concept like δύναμις and ἐνέργεια.[5] At any rate, this ἕξις-ness of desire determines the notion of voluntary as a fundamental concept of practical philosophy. Desire, originating from a special character produces an external act. This internal

---

[1] Eth. Nic. VIII. 4. 1156 b 22, 15; [Mag. Mor. II. 11. 1209 a 7; b 32.]
[2] Cf. p. 6, n. 6.　　　　　　　[3] Pol. VIII. 15. 1334 b 17-20.
[4] Cat. 8. 8 b 29; Eth. Nic. II. 4; Eth. Eud. II. 2; Mag. Mor. III. 7; Phys. VII. 3. 246 a 12, 30; Pol. I. 13. 1259 b 25; II. 6. 1265 a 35; Rhet. I. 6. 1362 b 13; II. 12. 1388 b 34; III. 7. 1408 a 29; Eth. Nic. II. 6. 1106 b 36; VI. 4. 1140 a 4; Eth. Nic. II. 4. 1105 b 19-26.　　　　[5] Cf. p. 6 n. 6

VOLUNTARY ACT

origin of an outward-turning action is the essence of voluntarity. As is often said by Aristotle, the object of an act, or the practical affair, is that which may be otherwise than as it is. This possibility of being otherwise does not consist of contrary ἕξις or δύναμις, but of contradictory ἐνδεχόμενα, not of real potencies, but of ideal possibilities of being thus and not being thus.[1] In this way one member of the contradictory opposition has no more reality than another. In order that something which lacks an active principle may realize itself, it must have some efficient cause. This truth is not confined to human beings, but applies to all living and non-living beings.[2] But only when a conscious subject involves such an active principle, is its act said to be voluntary.[3] Things may occur either from nature, from necessity, or from accident.[4] Such things are all outside of our responsibility. We are responsible only for what is caused by us and depends upon us; on account of this we submit to praise and blame, and in this consist virtue and vice.[5] In short, voluntarity means the freedom of an act, and this the fundamental principle of all moral estimations. Are, then, all our acts voluntary, or is there any involuntary act? On this point the *Eudemian Ethics* asks directly for the positive mark of voluntarity, while the *Nicomachean Ethics*, making a detour, tries to explain it through the characteristic of involuntarity. In the former work, the mark of voluntarily is sought in desire, will, and intellect. Now desire is divided into wish, passion, and appetite, and it would seem as if any act that is originated in them were equally voluntary. But when we take any one of them as essential to voluntarity, we shall encounter the contradiction that a desire is at once voluntary and involuntary whenever heterogeneous desires conflict with each other. If we make will the essence of voluntarity, there occurs another difficulty, viz., that an act which arises from a voluntary wish may arise without deliberation, which is essential to will. If neither desire nor will can be the essence of voluntarity, there remains only intellect. Intellect here is regarded as recognizing the individual conditions of an act, e.g. its object, means, end, etc.[6] But Aristotle here reflects, and points out that desire and will appeared not to be the essence of voluntarity, only because he

---

[1] Cf. p. 6, n. 6.   [2] Eth. Eud. II. 10. 1226 a 22-25.
[3] Eth. Eud. II. 6. 1223 a 1-9.
[4] Part. An. I. 1. 639 b 20-640 a 12; 642 a 1-13; 30-b 2
[5] Eth. Eud II. 6. 1223 a 10-20.   [6] Eth. Eud. II. 9. 1225 b 2.

had tried to make just one of them the sole principle of voluntarity. In lifeless beings, the principle of movement is either interior or exterior; if the former, it is in a sense free, but if the latter, constrained. In the animal, the interior principle does not remain as a mere nature, but becomes an appetite; yet, the animal having in it no conflict between appetite and intellect, its construction is near to that of lifeless beings. But this is not so with man, who has a conflict between irrational desires such as appetite or passion, and rational desires such as wish or will, all of which equally belong to his essence and are not differentiated in such a way that the one group of desires is interior and the other exterior. Therefore, as aforesaid, if we only take account of one kind of them, we cannot but fall into a dilemma: viz., we must conclude that we are voluntary as far as we follow an appetite, yet involuntary as far as we oppose wish. Now as all belong to the essence of man, we should argue the problem of voluntarity taking account of man as a whole; and if we do so, we will conclude that from whatever desire and whatever will an act may arise, it should none the less be regarded as a voluntary act.[1] In the *Ethica Nicomachea*[2] also, Aristotle argues against the sophistry that claims praise for good deeds because of their voluntariness, yet refuses the blame for disgraceful conduct, on the ground that it has been compelled by appetite and so is involuntary; here he asserts that all our acts that arise from our desires are equally voluntary, and that if one admits the good conduct to be voluntary, the disgraceful must also be voluntary none the less.

Generally speaking, all animals, including man, are moved movents and the agents of action. They exhibit locomotion, which, however, originates from their circumstance.[3] But the exterior stimulus sometimes moves at first intellect and desire, and next through them the body of the animal, and sometimes moves the body directly without being mediated by perception or desire, as e.g. in sleeping.[4] When the domination of circumstantial power is indirect, the act is voluntary, but when it is direct, it is involuntary. Whether the desire be rational or irrational, is a matter which is irrelevant to voluntarity. Man is apt to complain of pleasure's compulsion when he yields to a lower appetite, but compulsion is

[1] Eth. Eud. II. 7. 1223 a 21 ff.
[2] Eth. Nic. III. 3. 1111 a 22-b 3.
[3] Phys. VIII. 21. 252 b 17-28; 253 a 7-21; VIII. 6. 259 b 1-20.
[4] Phys. VIII. 2. 253 a 11-21.

limited to that which is accompanied by pain,[1] pleasure being rather the motive of all human conducts. Even a noble wish does not become actual without being combined with a kind of pleasure. Man is neither a mere rational being, nor a merely sensitive one, but a unity of both at the same time. Consequently, all higher or lower acts are equally due to his voluntary; it does not matter whether they are committed in the pursuit of sensitive pleasure or of moral goodness. Voluntarity consists in the process wherein the power of circumstances translates itself into actual conduct through the medium of desire; it does not concern the setting up of desire or the intellectual activity required for the realization of desire. After all, voluntarity means that the efficient cause of an act is immanent in the subject; it is the activity of a desire in its realization in conduct.

As we have seen above, the *Nicomachean Ethics*, defining voluntarity from the reverse side, makes the first moment of involuntarity compulsion by an external power. Compulsion means that the origin of an act is quite external, and there is no activity of the subject, e.g., when a storm blows a ship off its course to a land which is not its intended destination.[2] In such a case, the desire of the subject contributes nothing to the actual result; the one is quite accidental to the other. But not all phenomena to which the subject contributes nothing are involuntary: for instance, a mere natural phenomenon is not involuntary, whether it be merely external, or a physiological function of his body.[3] What is involuntary is that which might possibly or rather probably be done by a person, yet is not really done by him, when his actual desire is overcome by an external force. On this account, a compulsory phenomenon is accompanied by pain, and a voluntary act is followed by pleasure.[4] Voluntarity is the activity of desire in general, and involuntarity through compulsion is its negation. Involuntarity is a kind of negative attribute, not the privation of desire, but its disturbance.

Compulsion thus means a physical enforcement, and this is the principle of an involuntary act. Resembling this is a mental enforcement, which occurs, e.g. when a powerful man threatens

---

[1] Met. V. 5. 1015 a 26-33. Here also ἀνάγκη and βία are not distinguished. Rhet. I. 11. 1370 a 10.
[2] Eth. Nic. III. 1. 1109 b 35-1110 a 4; 1110 b 15-17.
[3] Eth. Nic. V. 10. 1135 a 31-b 2.
[4] Eth. Eud. I. 8. 1224 a 30; Eth. Nic. III. 1. 1110 b 11.

one with such a serious injury as to compel one to do what he naturally never wants, or when a mighty power causes one to give up property that he usually values, in order to avoid a danger. It might be doubtful whether such conduct be voluntary or involuntary. Aristotle, first admitting in it a mixture of voluntarity and involuntarity, then decides its essential part to be voluntary. For, seen with all its concrete conditions in the moment of action, it is voluntary in the final analysis. There is, indeed, an element of voluntarity in so far as one is willing to submit to an enforcement to do something which is *per se* undesirable, through the consideration of injuries or pain that may arise from refusal. In such an act also the origin of his organs' movements is in himself, and it is in his power to decide whether to act or not, so that this act is surely voluntary. But considered in the abstract, it may be involuntary; for no one would like to do such an act for its own sake.[1]

This interpretation of enforcement proves that voluntarity consists not in the origin of desire, but in its process of realization. Through whatever enforcement or temptation a desire may arise, it does not fail to be the voluntary principle of an act, as far as it is a man's own desire. The voluntarity of an act suffers nothing from the origin of desire.

But if we must say that an act performed through enforcement is not voluntary without qualification, does it follow that voluntarity should belong only to a special kind of desire? Does this mean that what arises without enforcement is a voluntary desire, and what occurs through enforcement is an involuntary desire? In truth, we should attribute voluntarity and involuntarity to acts rather than to desires. Voluntarity being the property of an act originated in one's own desire, it is nonsense to say a desire itself is involuntary: it would be to commit a *contradictio in adjecto*, i.e., to assume a desire without desiring. It is possible to do something without desiring it, but impossible to desire without desiring. The statement in question must only mean, that, disregarding all concrete circumstances and observing the mere fact of an act, the thing is not desirable by itself. And since there is no such desire

[1] Eth. Nic. III. 1. 1110 a 4 ff. In the Nicomachean Ethics, βία is distinguished from ἀνάγκη, but in the Eudemina Ethics, there is no such distinction, and βία is treated generally as the principle of compulsion or enforcement. Though physical enforcement is distinguished from psychical compulsion, this distinction is reduced to a difference of degree, so that we can find no decision of the problem. Cf. Eth. Eud. II. 8. 1225 a 1-34.

by nature, the corresponding act must also be involuntary abstractly (ἁπλῶς). An enforced act is regarded to be involuntary from an abstract point of view. ἁπλῶς may be translated either "absolutely" or "abstractly". Whatever cause or motive it may have, an act is considered to be voluntary, as far as we refer it to the desire as its efficient cause. What is not desired abstractly, may be desired in the concrete conditions as comparatively better, so that the act which originates in such a calculative desire is none the less voluntary.

In short, the first moment of voluntarity is spontaneity which is common to every kind of desire. Under whatever reason and form a desire may arise, its undisturbed realization is equally voluntary. The rational moment such as the reflection of the moral meaning of an end or the search for the means is not involved in the voluntarity of an act. Wish or will is, of course, a kind of voluntarity, but voluntarity involves also the act that arises from an entirely irrational appetite. Hence it is recognized not only in an adult, but also in a child, and not only in man, but in animals as well.

Now voluntarity involves an intellectual moment besides spontaneity. What sort of intellect is it then, if it is neither will nor wish? The *Nicomachean Ethics* here again tries to explain it from its opposite, ignorance.

The second condition that makes an act involuntary is ignorance. But an act through mere ignorance is not yet involuntary, though it is not-voluntary. To be involuntary, it must be further followed by repentance.[1] We may see the contents of this not-voluntary

[1] Eth. Nic. III. 2. 1110 b 18-24. Scholars have found an extraordinary difficulty in the theory that repentance constitutes the difference between ἀκουσία and οὐκ ἑκουσία, Hildenbrandt (Geschichte und System der Recht-und Staatsphilosophie, II. 275), and Siebeck (Geschichte der Psychologie, I. 2. 102), considered that Aristotle made the previous act non-voluntary through repentance. Kastil (Willensfreiheit 4), classed conduct without repentance as voluntary. On the contrary, Stewart (Notes on Aristotle's Nicomachean Ethics) and Loening (Zurechnungslehre des Aristoteles, 174), point out a discordance with ibid. III. 1. 1110 a 14 f., which admits that "voluntary" and "involuntary", being contradictory with each other, have no intermediate term. Therefore, Loening argues, the presence of repentance has no relation to responsibility, and non-voluntarity is heterogeneous with voluntarity, which are the conditions of moral responsibility. He also considered that the non-voluntary movement in the De Motu Animalium, which we quoted for our interpretation, has no connection with this. We can by no means agree with him. Firstly, that voluntarity or involuntarity is

act in the *De Motu Animalium*, where Aristotle, dividing certain kinds of physiological phenomena into the involuntary and the not-voluntary, presents, as an example of the former, the movement of the heart and the sexual organs, and of the latter sleeping, awaking, or respiration.[1] The former are called involuntary, because such organs move through imagination without reason's command. This does not mean that all acts which follow imagination and oppose intellect are involuntary; rather the term "involuntary" is used on negative ground that a higher wish is overcome by such an irrational affect. The latter actions are called not-voluntary, since they are not caused by imagination or desire, but are mere physiological movements and changes of the body.[2]

An act that occurs through ignorance, yet is not followed by repentance or pain, is thus not-voluntary. On the contrary, even when accompanied by knowledge, a mere natural phenomenon, e.g. decay or death, is neither voluntary nor involuntary.[3] Similarly, heating and hunger, being not conscious and spontaneous, are not voluntary, but they are not-voluntary rather than involuntary.[4] This substantiates our foregoing statement that involuntarity is not the privation, but rather the negation, of spontaneity. What is naturally outside of our spontaneous desire is not involun-

determined on the moment of act, means only that an act is voluntary in so far as one desires and acts what is most desirable in the concrete situation of the act. In saying an act that is accompanied by repentance is involuntary, and that that which is not is voluntary, Aristotle does not mean that what was voluntary at the moment of conduct, becomes afterwards involuntary on account of repentance or the contrary. Repentance was rather admitted as a mark by which we discriminate the voluntarity of an act. An involuntary act produces repentance owing to the discrepancy of one's general purpose and the result of that act, while a non-voluntary act is not followed by repentance, because it has never aimed at a certain end. Secondly, the accompaniment of pleasure with a voluntary act, pain with an involuntary one, and apathy with a non-voluntary one is not accidental, but is because pleasure and pain are the emotional sides of success and failure. So that, thirdly, the non-voluntary physiological phenomena cited in the De Motu Animalium, are nothing but the "non-voluntary" here at issue.

[1] Motu An. 11. 703 b 5.   [2] Cf. De An. III. 9. 432 b 29 ff.

[3] Eth. Nic. V.10. 1135 a 31; b 1. According to Rassow, Spengel, and Stewart, such a phenomenon is involuntary, and not οὐκ ἀκούσιον. So, Rassow alters ὧν οὐθὲν οὔθ' ἑκούσιον οὔτ' ἀκούσιόν ἐστιν to ὧν οὐθὲν οὔτ' ἐφ' ἡμῖν οὔθ' ἑκούσιόν ἐστιν and Spengel to ὧν οὐθὲν ἑκούσιόν ἐστιν, Stewart also takes οὔτ' ἀκούσιον as an interpolation. cf. Stewart's note *ad loc*. But these alterations would be unnecessary, because decay and death are neither ἑκουσία nor ἀκουσία but μὴ ἑκουσία.   [4] Eth. Nic. III. 7. 1113 b 26-30.

tary, although it is not-voluntary. What is involuntary is such an act which might by nature be made otherwise by us and yet is actually compelled by an external force. We feel pain and repentance, because we are compelled to act against our desire. This is evident in the case of physical compulsion, but the same analysis is also applicable to involuntarity through ignorance: the subject does not know the real meaning of what he is doing; when a result comes about which he would not have wanted but rather would have prevented, if he had had cognition of it, he regrets that his general wish was obstructed by it. There are plenty of examples[1] of such involuntary action through ignorance, viz. wishing to explain the construction of a catapult, one lets it go off through an error, or one kills one's own son, mistaking him for an enemy, or being ignorant of the fact that a spear is pointed, one unintentionally kills a man, or taking a stone for a pumice stone, harms a man with it, or giving a draught to save a man, one really kills him, etc. In every case, an unintended result happens, on account of one's ignorance about the individual conditions of the act.

Further proceeding with these considerations, Aristotle distinguishes δι' ἄγνοια, acting through ignorance, from ἀγνοῦντα, acting in ignorance.[2] The former is the case, when the subject is ignorant of individual facts, and a result comes about which is different from his desire and intention;[3] the latter is the case, when the knowledge that one ought to have, is disturbed or want-

[1] Eth. Nic. III. 2. 1111a 6-18; Eth. Eud. II. 8. 1225 b 1-6.
[2] Eth. Nic. III. 2. 1110 b 24-27: ἕτερον δ' ἔοικε καὶ τὸ δι' ἄγνοιαν πράττειν τοῦ ἀγνοοῦντα· ὁ γὰρ μεθύων ἢ ὀργιζόμενος, οὐ δοκεῖ δι' ἄγνοιαν πράττειν ἀλλὰ διά τι τῶν εἰρημένων, οὐκ εἰδὼς δὲ ἀλλ' ἀγνοῶν. In Eth. Eud., this distinction about ignorance is obscure. Also Eth. Nic. V.10.1135 a 23 f.; ibid. 32. Eth. Nic. V. 10. 1136 a 5-9: τῶν δ' ἀκουσίων τὰ μὲν ἐστι συγγνωμοικὰ τὰ δ' οὐ συγγνωμονικά. ὅσα μὲν γὰρ μὴ μόνον ἀγνοοῦντες ἀλλὰ καὶ δι' ἄγνοιαν ἁμαρτάτουσι, συγγνωμονικά, ὅσα δὲ μὴ δι' ἄγνοιαν, ἀλλ' ἀγνοοῦντες μὲν διὰ πάθος δὲ μήτε φυσικὸν μήτ' ἀνθρώπινον, οὐ συγγνωμονικά, A mistake from ignorance might well be called involuntary, but we can by no means consent to assume to be involuntary an act done in ignorance and arising from a passion which is admittedly unnatural and unhuman. It is acknowledged that such an act is not free from responsibility. Therefore, it must be voluntary. This would seem to be the brutal habit which is distinguished from vice in the proper sense: Eth. Nic. VII. 6. 1149 a 1 ff. But even if it be not vice, it is not involuntary, for the acts of children and beasts are also said to be voluntary. Therefore, such an act appears to be called involuntary by Aristotle, simply because it does not originate in one's will. Cf. Stewart's note *ad loc*.
[3] Eth. Nic. V. 10. 1135 b 11-16.

ing on account of an enduring character or temporary state of mind. Sometimes, one may be careless of his usual knowledge[1] through drunkenness or anger, sometimes he may be ignorant of the general norm of practice as to what one ought to do and not, viz., in the case of ignorance in the will, τῇ προαιρέσει ἄγνοια.[2] This distinction corresponds to that of incontinence and indulgence. The former is the case, when will itself, being good, yet is overcome by a stronger appetite, and a result happens that is undesirable and disagreeable to reason. The latter is the case, when will itself is in ignorance of the norm. The one is the disturbance, and the other the privation, of reason. In both cases ignorance belongs to the very character of the subject, so that an act in ignorance is by no means involuntary. The kind of ignorance which is the real cause of an involuntary or not-voluntary act is that which is exterior and accidental to the character of the subject, and does not concern such a universal principle as the law of morality or legal law, but concerns individual facts.

Ignorance in the will, by the way, might appear to make an act involuntary and irresponsible, because the rational activity as the moment of will is the cognition of a causal relation between the end and the means. But what Aristotle calls here ignorance in the will is rather characteristic of the wish that precedes the deliberation of means, or the will which calmly calculates about the means for satisfying an appetite; therefore it should rather be called the will which is dominated by ignorance. We may understand the function of practical intellect from the fact that such a state is called ignorance in the will; for if it is called ignorance, in spite of the fact that there is in this state a calm calculation about the means, it is evident that such a knowledge concerns, not the means, but the value of the end.

If ignorance is the cause of an involuntary act, a voluntary act should be accompanied by knowledge,[3] while not only the act that arises from a rational desire or a wish, but also that which arises from any desire whatsoever, is voluntary. Animals and children are regarded as acting voluntarily just as well as men.[4] Hence it is evident that the knowledge which is necessary for a voluntary

[1] Eth. Nic. III. 2. 1110 b 24; VII. 4. 1147 a 10 ff.
[2] Eth. Nic. III. 2. 1110 b 28-1111 a 2.
[3] Eth. Nic. III. 3. 1111 a 22-24; Eth. Eud. II. 8. 1224 a 7; 9. 1225 b 1 ff.
[4] Eth. Nic. III. 3. 1111 a 26; 4. 1111 b 7.

act, is indifferent to the origin of desire. What is, then, the knowledge that accompanies all desires, including the appetites of animals and children? Now, desire is the conscious effort of animals to realize the potential forms which are held by sensation, imagination, and intellect. Imagination sometimes opposes intellect, yet is regarded as a kind of knowledge in a wider sense; even sensation ranks with intellect as a faculty of discriminating forms. But sensation and imagination are not the knowledge that makes an act voluntary. If so, every act that arises from a desire would be voluntary without exception, and there would be no involuntary act. Whereas one may act involuntarily, though he has distinct sensation or imagination about the object or contents of his desire, and he feels a repentance when his expectation is betrayed by the real result; such a feeling would not occur if he had no cognition about his desire.[1] For instance, a woman who, wishing to give a man a medicine, gave him a poison by mistake, surely had a good wish to cure him of his illness; nevertheless she did not know the present drink to be a poison, so that mistaking it for a remedy she gave it to him, and killed him *involuntarily*. In such a sense, the cause of involuntarity is said to be the ignorance about individual facts. If this proves to be the case, conversely, the knowledge that makes an act voluntary, must also be the knowledge about individual facts which are necessary to realize the desired end. Such a knowledge of means is no longer involved in desire itself, but is the contents of βούλευσις, so-called deliberation.[2] The deliberation of means presupposes an end. We trace the series of means up to the proximate step, which we can manage immediately. The terminus of this deliberation is precisely the starting point of an act, and the desire thus mediated by the consideration of means is called προαίρεσις or will.[3] But a voluntary act is not always conduct through will or deliberation. Aristotle implicitly admits that conduct through will is voluntary in a superior grade,[4] but never excludes other kinds of conduct as not voluntary. The acts of children and animals are none the less

---

[1] Eth. Nic. III. 2. 1110 b 18-23.
[2] Eth. Nic. III. 5. 1112 a 30; b 11;.2. 1139 a 13; [Mag. Mor. I. 35. 1196 b 29;] Rhet. I. 2. 1337 a 4; 6. 1362 a 18; b 5; 1383 a 7.
[3] Eth. Nic. III. 5. 1113 a 9-12; VI. 2. 1139 a 23; Eth. Eud. II. 10. 1226 b 17; [Mag. Mor. I. 17. 1189 a 31.]
[4] Eth. Nic. I. 8. 1168 b 34.

recognized to be voluntary,[1] though they do not follow deliberation or will. Let us return once more to Aristotle's words to solve this difficulty.

Aristotle says that the ignorance which results in involuntarity, consists in what, how much, who, whom through what, why and how one should do, and he says that we are most often ignorant of the object and the end of our act.[2] Consequently the knowledge which makes an act voluntary must be about the essence, the quality, the subject and the object, the means, the reason or the end, and the method, of conduct. It is also stated that the ignorance that results in involuntarity is concerned with individual facts in the concrete circumstance and not with general affairs. For instance, Melope,[3] who killed his son through ignorance, did not kill him without knowing that he was killing an enemy, but only did not know that it happened to be his own son.

With regard to ignorance of ends, one might wonder if it is possible that a man should do something without knowing his purpose. Aristotle's true meaning would be that though an indefinite general end may be known, the individual results that might be caused by this act are unknown, e.g., when an act done for the purpose of explaining the function of a catapult happens to hurt a fellow, the direct result of that concrete act has been to hurt a man. Surely, such a result is an effect rather than a purpose. But, seeing that the concept of end in Aristotle is not of necessity that of a conscious purpose, but is rather to be taken as that of an objective form, the above effect might as well be called an end in this particular sense. At any rate, the ignorance that makes an act involuntary concerns individual facts, and involuntarity means that the general end of the subject is betrayed by individual facts on account of this ignorance. Now the individual, in so far as it is an individual, is not the object of deliberation, but of perception. We do not deliberate but perceive whether it is bread or not, and whether it is baked well or not,[4] or taking the above examples, whether the drug is a remedy or a poison, whether

---

[1] Eth. Nic. III. 4. 1112 a 14-16; V.10. 1134 a 19-21. Knowledge about individual affairs of conduct, might enable us to call an act voluntary, yet the act falls short of being willed in so far as it is not accompanied by calculation and deliberation.
[2] Eth. Nic. VI. 1. 1235 a 25.
[3] Eth. Nic. III. 2. 1111 a 12; Poet. 14. 1454 a 5.
[4] Eth. Nic. III. 5. 1113 a 1.

the spear is pointed or round, and whether the object is an enemy or one's own son.

Thus considered, the knowledge which is the principle of voluntarity seems to be the intuition of an individual fact, and not the reasoning as to cause and effect like the deliberation which is the moment of will. Herein we may find the difference between voluntary act and will. But thinking over the matter more profoundly, we see that even if there should be the imagination of the object and the perception of individual facts necessary to the realization of the desire, unless the two are not combined, no act would occur. There must be some reasoning which mediates the two. If so, voluntarity should again require some kind of deliberation after all.[1] We can only distinguish voluntarity and will—disregarding for the moment their difference of category—in the point that these two kinds of perception are not combined through so much distinct inference in the former as in the latter. In other words, deliberation is minimum in a mere voluntary act: it does not yet actualize itself as deliberation, and exists only in potentiality. This is the reason why will first appears in a mature person, while voluntarity is found in animals other than man as well, and herein we may notice also the continuous development of animals.

Voluntarity and will have no qualitative difference, and will is the development and augmentation of voluntarity. But, in will, intellect becomes really actual and dominates desire. On this account, the moral value of conduct in the most strict sense is at first recognized in conduct through will.[2] Will is not the sufficient condition of moral goodness, but is at least the necessary condition of moral estimation. A mere voluntary act may be in a sense responsible, say, in the legal sense, yet insufficient for reflective morality. The acts of children and animals are neither good nor bad in the strict sense of morality. Now since deliberation is the moment of will and a kind of practical thinking, moral goodness and badness are found only in such rational formes of conducts.[3] To be rational in such a sense has surely by itself a positive value,

---

[1] Eth. Nic. IX. 8. 1169 a 1; cf. Rhet. II. 9. 1369 b 21.
[2] Rhet. I. 9. 1367 b 21-23.
[3] Eth. Eud. II. 11. 1228 a 11-15; Rhet. I. 13. 1374 a 11-13; 1374 b 14; Top. IV. 5. 126 a 36; Eth. Nic. VII. 11. 1152 a 17; VI. 13. 1144 a 20; VIII. 15. 1163 a 23; III. 4. 1111 b 34; 1111 b 6; Rhet. I. 10. 1368 b 6-14; cf. Eth. Nic. III. 4. 1111 b 7, 13.

only not a moral value. Moral value is not the value of the rational as such, but the value that is attached to rationality; viz., it is because the conduct that is mediated by such a kind of reason has a higher spontaneity, being a more constant expression of one's character.[1] Yet, since practical intellect dominates and leads the desiring part, and ethical virtue consists in the *ratio* or moderation of desire and conduct, there must be some function of practical intellect other than the aforesaid deliberation which is the moment of will. In such a practical intellect, the virtue of intellect would at once be the essence of moral goodness. This must be just that deliberation which we have previously distinguished from the deliberation as the moment of will and made the essential moment of wish. The deliberation in will was a mere search for the means to realize desire, while the deliberation in wish is such an intellect as gives desire itself a rational value, viz., the estimating intellect.

Theoretical intellect remains in an indifferent contemplation about the natural order, and has no direct reference to practice.[2] Practical virtue serves it by enabling man to partake in such a pure contemplation, and the theoretical intellect on its side contributes nothing to the practical virtue.[3] But practical intellect is further divided into two species: one, presupposing a desire, is concerned only with the means; while the other makes desire itself rational and gives it a positive value. In order, however, to inquire more minutely into these two forms of practical intellect, we must analyse the structure of conduct. Conduct is a kind of animal behavior in so far as it is guided by intellect, practice and production being its two main forms. Our next problem, then, should be the study of practice and production, πρᾶξις and ποίησις, and our inquiry about the soul will be thus combined with the investigation of conduct.

[1] Eth. Nic. III. 4. 1111 b 5 f.   [2] De An. III. 9. 432 b 27.
[3] Eth. Nic. VI. 7. 1141 a 20; Eth. Eud. VII. 15. 1249 b 9 ff.

CHAPTER III

PRACTICE AND PRODUCTION

§ 1. PRACTICE AND PRODUCTION

THE human soul is divided into the rational and the irrational parts; and both of these, furthermore, have a two-part structure. The rational part is subdivided into the theoreticcal and practical intellect, while the irrational part is subdivided into the vegetable soul, which is quite unconscious, and the animal soul, which either obeys or disobeys the practical intellect. Of this irrational soul in the secondary sense, the passive moment is sensation and imagination, and the active moment, desire. Sensation and imagination, being accompanied by pleasure and pain, give rise to pursuit and avoidance, i.e., to active and passive desires. But, more strictly speaking, Aristotle's concept of $αἴσθησις$ is not limited to elementary sensation, but comprises a more figural perception. And a concrete perception is in some degree organized through the so-called *sensus communis*, which is homogeneous with imagination. Even if perception be regarded as the organization of present stimuli concerning present objects, desire, at least, presupposes the expectation of future conduct, so that its immediate agent is imagination rather than sensation; whereas sensation is a mere indirect efficient cause. Desire is nothing but imagination taken in the dynamic aspect. But imagination is either sensitive or intellectual; the desire founded upon the fomer is appetite, and that founded upon the latter is wish, passion being situated between the two.

In reflex, where stimulus and reaction are in a close contact with each other, there may be an elementary sensation, but no perception that gives rise to a desire. It is only where there is a distance between stimulus and emotion, that the cognitive form of desire takes place, called sensible imagination. It is a primitive imagination and a stage in the process from sensation to imagination. In such a simple desire, its realization is also direct, involving no intellectual function, either in the setting up of end or in its realization. Therefore appetite and passion are called irrational desires, or desires against calculation. Whereas a complex act, which instead of pursuing an instantaneous pleasure, chooses a certain end among various possibilities, and realizes its end, through some means, must be mediated by intellect. This is a transitional phenomenon between the irrational part and the rational. Fundamentally, desire is irrational, but it is sometimes accompanied by intellect.

Rational activity in man is divided into theoretical and practical cognition. The ideal of intellect is theoretical cognition, but its original duty is the guidance of practice. Theoretical intellect is concerned with eternal and necessary beings, and performs no act other than to know these objects.[1] In theoretical cognition, human intellect is quite passive. Active reason finds its proper stage in theoretical cognition, to be sure, but as we have seen, it is the medium rather than the subject of cognition. It is a universal principle and an unconscious holder of eternal forms. It makes human thinking possible as far as it is immanent in our soul, but essentially it is rather separable from our soul. Being the medium of God and man, it is compared to light which mediates between things and the pupil of the eye. We have interpreted this reason to be science or culture *qua* objective mind.[2] Whether this interpretation be admitted or not, at least it is certain that the human reason which is combined with the body through imagination is passive, even when it engages in theoretical cognition. It receives the forms from outside and cannot create them. We only think about the forms as they exist, without being able or intending to change them. The object of theoretical cognition is a necessary being which cannot be otherwise — μή ἐνδεχόμενον καὶ ἄλλως ἔχειν. While, on the contrary, that of practical cognition is what can be otherwise; it is transient, and ontologically accidental,[3] so that the practical subject is rather active. And when practice does not remain an inpulsive act, but is mediated through intellect, rational desire as a whole is active, whether the active principle be involved in intellect or in desire[4]—intellect is active either *eo ipso* or at least accidentally.

The object of practical intellect is what can be otherwise, or an accidental being. Not all things, but at least some of them, are modified by our conduct: we impress the forms of our volition upon them. This is rational conduct, or πρᾶξις in a wider sense, which is further divided into πρᾶξις (in a narrower sense) and ποίησις, i.e. practice and production.[5] In practice the end is the

---
[1] Eth. Nic. X. 7. 1177 b 1-4; De An. III. 9. 432 b 26-28.   [2] Ch. I. § 4.
[3] Eth. Nic. VI. 2. 1139 a 6-12.   [4] Ch. II. § 4.
[5] Eth. Nic. VI. 4. 1140 a 1-6; VI. 5. 1140 b 3f.

act itself, while production aims at some other result.¹ Contemplation is absolutely non-practical,² practice makes conduct itself the end, and production aims at the result of conduct.

We must notice, however, that in Aristotle's terminology, a word may be used both in a wider and in a narrower sense, and that daily usage is often confused with a scientific use of a term.³ With regard to the word πρᾶξις, this word expresses in its wider sense the acts of all living creatures, and is applied not only to human being but also to the movements of animals, plants, and heavenly bodies.⁴ For they are all possessed of soul, which is the principle of life. Seeing that even the activities of nutrition and reproduction of lower living creatures are called πρᾶξις as far as they are the acts of soul, it is no wonder that the sensation which appears in animals should be called πρᾶξις.⁵ On the other hand, a superhuman rational being is also assumed to perform πρᾶξις, as far as it is possessed of soul and is in a sense a living creature. For instance, the essence of happiness is εὐπραξία; yet God lives in "happiness" in this sense, though being employed only in the contemplation of Himself. Thus mere contemplation is also πρᾶξις, and sometimes may even be called πρᾶξις in the most excellent sense.⁶ This is of course the widest sense of the word. Next in a slightly narrower sense, contemplation is excluded from the notion, so that God would not share in "practice" in this sense.⁷ At last, in the most strict sense, absolutely irrational functions such as sensation or nutrition are also excluded,⁸

---

[1] Eth. Nic. VI. 5. 1140 b 6 f.; X. 6. 1176 b 6-9; Eth. Nic. VI. 2. 1139 b 1-4; cf. Mag. Mor. I. 35. 1197 a 11.   [2] Eth. Nic. X. 7. 1177 b 1 ff.

[3] Cf. Nuyens, op. cit. 205 f.   [4] De Cael. II. 12. 292 b 1-8; 292 a 18-21.

[5] Hist. An. I. 1. 487 a 11-17; Hist. An. VIII. 1. 589 a 2-5; 12. 596 b 20 f.; Gen. An. I. 23. 731 a 25 f.; Pol. VII. 14. 1333 a 34 f.

[6] Pol. VII. 3. 1325 b 14-23; Phys. II. 6. 197 b 5: ἡ δ' εὐδαιμονία πρᾶξις τις· εὐπραξία γάρ. Zeller is right in taking the ποίησις which is predicated of contemplation in a wider sense, but wrong in making it opose ποίησις, quoting Eth. Nic. VI. 2. 1139 b 3; 3. 1140 b 6 etc. (Ph. d. Gr. II. 2. 368 n.1). The πρᾶξις which is thus predicated of happiness and contemplation, should be taken as act in general.

[7] Eth. Nic. X. 8. 1178. b 8-22; cf. Met. XIII. 7. 1072 b 18; Pol. VII. 1. 1323 b 23; Eth. Eud. VII. 12. 1244 b 8; De Cael. II. 2. 292 b 5.

[8] Eth. Nic. VI. 2. 1139 a 19 f. It is quite another matter that sensation is said in De An. III. 9. 432 b 19, not to be the principle of locomotion. For in the first place, conduct is not a mere locomotion, and in the second place, the reason for this statement in De An. is that there are some animals that do not exhibit locomotion.

and πρᾶξις is restricted to human conduct alone.¹

Being distinguished from sensation, πρᾶξις might seem to be attributed to the part of the soul which governs locomotion.² Not only man, however, but also most animals move in space. To what part of the soul, then, belongs πρᾶξις in the strict sense? Nutrition, sensation, and imagination, as well as thinking, being excluded, the only remaining part is the desiring part. Yet desire does not act by itself, but presupposes sensation or intellect; and an animal, also, acts through desire mediated by sensation and imagination. Therefore the πρᾶξις which is proper to man must be a locomotion through intellectual desire. Thus we have arrived at πρᾶξις *qua* human practice. But in spite of this restriction, πρᾶξις in this meaning yet contains both practice and production. And while πρᾶξις or πράττειν is applied to production, ποίησις or ποιεῖν is applied to practice as well.

It is by no means an undue expansion of its meaning to use the verb ποιεῖν not only for production but also for conduct in general including practice. It means moreover, like πράττειν, living activity in general, and furthermore even the act in general of all things. This is not astonishing but rather quite natural, because ποιεῖν in the primary sense is the most general sort of concept, which forms a kind of category along with πάσχειν.³ It is an aspect of movement, or its active moment.⁴ But the notions of active and passive are applicable not to every movement, but particularly only to qualitative change. They are applied neither to increase and decrease, nor to locomtion.⁵

Active and passive are aspects of the movement that takes place between opposite qualities imposed upon the same substratum.⁶ ποίησις in such a wide sense is applied not only to

[1] Eth. Eud. II. 6. 1222 b 18 - 20; 1224 a 28-30.

[2] De An. III. 9. 432 a 17.

[3] Cat. 4. 2 a 3 f.; 9. 11 b 1; Top. I. 9. 103 b 23; Met. V. 7. 1017 a 28; Gen. et Corr. I. 7 - 9.

[4] Gen. et Corr. I. 7. 323 a 15 ff.

[5] Phys. II. 1. 192 b 14; V. I. 225 b 7; 2. 226 a 25; VII. 2. 243 a 6; VIII. 7. 260 a 27; 261 a 32 ff.; De Cael. IV. 3. 310 a 23; Met. IX. 1. 1042 a 32; XI. 12. 1068 a 10; b 17; XII. 2. 1069 b 9; cf. Phys. V. 2. 225 b 10 - 226 a 26; Gen. et Corr. I. 4. 319 b 31; De An. I. 3. 406 a 12; Long. 3. 465 b 30; Cat. 14. 15 a 13.

[6] Gen. et Corr. I. 6. 322 b 18, 23; 7. 323 b 31; 324 a 2, 34; b 16; De An. III. 4. 429 b 26; De Cael. II. 3. 286 a 33; Long. 3. 465 b 16; cf. Gen. An .I. 21. 729 b 10.

human production, but also to sensation,[1] memory,[2] desire,[3] or emotion,[4] and further to all living activities[5] such as locomotion,[6] nutrition,[7] reproduction,[8] and even to the movements of lifeless bodies.[9] In such an ordinary use, the term ποιεῖν even surpasses the limitation of designating the moment of qualitative change. But not only is it applicable to the irrational phenomena above mentioned, it is also extended to theoretical cognition[10] in the same way as is πρᾶξις or πράττειν. Accordingly, it may be regarded as even more comprehensive than πρᾶξις.

Since πρᾶξις and ποίησις or πράττειν and ποιεῖν are used in various meanings, we must treat them with extreme prudence and distinguish the scientific terminology from the ordinary. To those who read Aristotle without this prudence, the system of this father of logic would appear as a mere heap of confusion and paradox. Indeed for modern dialecticians, there would be no novel opinion that might not be constructed from Aristotle.

Let us then express the strict scientific sense of the terms πρᾶξις and ποίησις by the words "practice" and "production". They

---

[1] De Sensu 3. 440 a 17; Met. XI. 6. 1063 b 4; Part. An. II. 3. 650 b 4; 17. 661 a 9.
[2] Pol. II. 8. 1268 b 31; IV. 2. 1289 b 23; 8. 1293 b 28.
[3] Eth. Nic. I. 1. 1095 a 10.   [4] Eth. Eud. III. 1. 1228 b 15.
[5] For example, an animal catches its prey (Hist. An. VIII. 20. 603 a 2; IX. 32. 619 a 31), digs a hole (ibid. 2. 590 b 23), hides itself (ibid. VIII. 17. 601 a 15; 13. 599 a 7; IX. 5. 611 a 20), bees make their combs (ibid. V. 22. 554 a 16), a spider bites a prey (ibid. I. 39. 623 a 1), hairs grow (ibid. VII. 4. 504 a 23), and milk is produced (ibid. III. 21. 522 b 32).
[6] De Cael. IV. 4. 312 a 5; Inc. An. 15. 713 a 13; Hist. An. IV. 4. 530 a 9; V. 6. 541 b 16; VIII. 12. 597 a 20; 13. 599 a 4; IX. 37. 622 b 7; VI. 29. 579 a 13.
[7] De Sensu 10. 475 b 27; Hist. An. I. 1. 487 a 16 ff.; 24 IV. 8. 534 a 11; VIII. 2. 589 a 17; 591 a 9; 3. 593 a 27; 10. 596 a 14; IX. 1. 608 b 20; 19. 617 a 17.
[8] Hist. An. I. 1. 488 b 6; V. 2. 540 a 17; 4. 540 b 5; 5. 540 b 7; VI. 14. 568 a 17; 18 573 a 29; 29. 578 b 6, 16; VII. 2. 583 a 2; 4. 584 a 34; X. 29. 618 a 28.
[9] Various phenomena are called ποιεῖν such as the confusion of colours (Meteor. I. 5. 342 b 7), the change of quantity and figure (ibid. I.6. 343 b 35), qualitative change (Gen. An. II. 2. 735 b 18), the coming of night (Meteor. II. 1 354 a 31), or the occurrence of noise (ibid. 8. 368 a 14; Hist. An. IV. 8. 533 b 16; IX. 37. 621 a 29), of burning and of fire (Meteor. II. 5. 361 b 19; IV. 9. 387 b 30; Part. An. II. 2. 649 b 5), etc.
[10] An. Pr. I. 8. 30 a 10; 15. 34 b 9; 25. 42 a 22; 27. 43 a 24; 28. 44 b 26; 6.28 a 23; Top. V. 2. 130 a 7; Poet. 16. 1455 a 15; cf. Pol. VII. 17. 1336 a 5; Eth. Nic. I. 3. 1096 a 5; Part. An. I.1. 640 a 11; Hist. An. V. 1. 539 a 5; I. 6. 491 a 12; Top. VI. 4. 142 a 2; 141 b 18; VII. 2. 129 b 18 etc.

are distinguished in that the one has its end in itself, and the other its end outside of itself. The end is usually taken as the contents of will or as the imagination which precedes the result and leads the act. But, taking the end thus as a conscious purpose, the difference between practice and production would, after all, become merely subjective. If practice were the act that aims at nothing other than itself, while production aims at some other result, such a subjective end being dependent upon the individual subject, an act may be either practice or production in accordance with personal arbitrariness, and production would be always subordinate to practice. For instance, the accumulation of wealth would be practice to a miser who aims at money-making, but the same act would be production to a man who makes money for the purpose of education or some political end. Whereas it is a matter of arbitrariness whether one regards an act as the end or the means. Consequently, as far as we take the end subjectively, the distinction of practice and production will be merely relative to our choice. And if the distinction be thus relative, a practice would be sometimes regarded as a production, and a production as a practice; further, practice would be impossible apart from production, and *vice versa*. Moreover, practice involves an external act as well as production does. For such an act is not attained at a stroke, but requires some means. But as far as an act is concerned with the means, *ex hypothesi* it is not a practice, but a production. If practice *par excellence* is not mediated by production, it must be restricted to a most simple act. E.g. seeing might be regarded as a practice *par excellence*, as far as it does not go through a process and aims at no other end than itself. In fact, Aristotle himself is hinting at such a view.

Even in these cases, however, if it be necessary to resort to a complicated means, in order to see the object, this process, being not the end itself, must be a production. Conduct which has no means and no external end, is nothing but simple sensation. But it is absurd to identify practice *par excellence* with such simple sensation. Aristotle, not only distinguished practice from sensation, but also regarded moral conduct to be more than mere voluntary act. It was assumed to be an act which comes from προαίρεσις or βουλευτικὴ ὄρεξις,[1] i.e., from will or a deliberated desire. On the other hand, βούλευσις and προαίρεσις are said to be

[1] Eth. Nic. III. 4. 1112 a 14 f.

concerned not with the end, but with the means.[1] Accordingly, an act which bears moral significance must be a complex act mediated by many means, and not independent of production. Hence one might say that practice and production are distinguished in their extension, yet considering more profoundly, practice is mediated by production, and production is only possible through practice. Though this very conclusion is not unallowable, the relation of practice and production is by no means so superficial. We must take care lest we be deceived by words. The aforesaid relation of practice and production requires the independency of the opposite terms. The "dialectic synthesis" involves more than a distinction of aspects. Be that as it may, let us dismiss for the moment, the paradoxical terms of dialecticians, lest we should lose our way into "the darkness wherein every ox becomes black".

Now, Aristotle assumes that practice aims at an end, and admits no practice which has no end besides the activity itself. Further a practice is made the means for another practice, which, in its turn, serves for another practice and so on. Similarly with regard to production. For instance, all conduct concerning war is subordinated to strategy.[2] But, if an act which has an exterior end be a production instead of a practice, such subordinate conduct would be a production rather than a practice. Nevertheless, Aristotle always speaks of conduct as concerned not with a universal end, but with particular facts.[3] Further, admitting that both practice and production require instruments, he divides the instruments into two kinds, the instrument in the strict sense, which

[1] Eth. Nic. III. 5. 1112 b 11; 1113 a 2; 4. 1111 b 27; Eth. Eud. II. 10. 1226 b 9; [Mag. Mor. I. 17. 1189 a 7;] Eth. Nic. VII. 5. 1140 a 30.

[2] Top. VI. 12. 149 b 31 f.; Eth. Nic. I. 1. 1094 a 14-18. The distinction between the act which has no end other than itself and that which has such an end (1094 a 5 ff.), is of course that of practice and production. Whereas there is the same relation between the domination and the subordination, both in practice and in production, namely a relation of end and means. This would be quite paradoxical, if we take the end which is realized in the act itself as a subjective purpose (cf. Loening, Die Zurechnungslehre des Aristoteles, 7. n. 13). How is it possible that a practice which is essentially the end itself, should be subordinate to another master practice? It is comprehensible only when we take the end which is actual in practice, to be an objective form and a moral value. A practice which subordinates itself to another practice as its means, realizes its objective form always in complete actuality.

[3] Met. I. 1. 981 a 17; Eth. Nic. III. 1. 1110 a 13, b 6; VI. 8. 1141 b 16; Pol. II. 8. 1269 a 12.

belongs to production, and the instrument of practice such as wealth. The productive instrument is, e.g. a reed, which produces some other result, whereas the instrument of practice, e.g. clothes or beds, produce no result besides their use. The slave is also assumed to belong to wealth, and consequently it is an instrument of practice. For, life is not a production but a practice, and the slave is the means of life.[1] From what has been said, it is evident that Aristotle admitted that there are means of practice as well as means of production. Even Teichmüller seems to have stuck to the modern sense of practice and instrument, when he opposed Aristotle by saying that instrument belongs naturally to art and that there can be no instrument of practice.[2] We ought rather to endeavour to find out the particular meaning of practice that possesses such an instrument. Aristotle surely admits that instruments naturally belong to art and production. Hence wealth such as a slave is called the instrument of practice only in an analogical way.

According to Teichmüller, the action of a slave is not measured by his intention, but by his performance of the master's order; that he opens the door or washes his master's clothes is a pure technical activity instead of a practice. Indeed, the act of a slave is not in accordance with his own purpose, but is for the sake of his master's wish. But it does not necessarily follow from that that the act of a slave should be a production. An act which serves for another man's purpose, is not of necessity a production. Teichmüller's criticism appears to be founded upon the misunderstanding of taking the end-concept which distinguishes practice and production for a mere subjective purpose. Whereas we admit that the act of a slave who opens a door or washes clothes for his master is a production rather than a practice, not because he obeys his master but just because it is the opening of a door or washing of clothes. If we take the end as a subjective purpose, and distinguish practice and production through it, opening the door or washing clothes should be regarded as practice when the master himself does these things. This is, however, against Aristotle's real meaning. An act is a production for the master, if it is at all so for the slave. What is a practice for the master is similarly a practice for the slave, even if he perform it through his master's order. Hence it was said that the slave is the instrument of prac-

[1] Pol. I. 4. 1254 a 1 ff.   [2] Teichmüller, op. cit. 53.

tice, but not that of production. What distinguishes practice from production is not whether the act is the direct or the indirect object of the will. The difference is not relative, but essential and absolute. An act is either practice or production by its essence, and needs a means in either case. If a master uses a slave in his life, and if life be essentially a practice,[1] it will follow that a slave is the instrument not of production, but that of practice. Consequently, the end through which practice is distinguished from production, must be an objective form rather than a subjective purpose. Let us then, investigate the concept of end, which is a fundamental idea of Aristotle's metaphysics.

It is usually admitted that Aristotle's philosophy is a teleological system. Teleology is of course a type of thought which regards the world as the realization of an end. And we moderns are apt to suppose a teleological world as ruled by a conscious subject analogous to us, e.g., a world which is dominated by a divine Providence. In fact, there are, in Aristotle, some remnants of Platonic myths which tend in this direction, for instance, the theory of cosmological souls.[2] Aristotle, nevertheless, was the greatest positivist and scientist in his period. Aristotle the dogmatic metaphysician, who was attacked by the thinkers of early modern age, was the idol of scholastic philosophers rather than the historical Aristotle. Aristotle should be called a scientist so much the more, if he be compared with Democritus and Epicurus, to say nothing of Plato and Plotinus. Even with regard to the hackneyed expression, "Nature makes nothing in vain",[3] it is not unusual to find its like in the works of modern scientists. For all that, we are not so malicious as to interpret such expressions as acknowledgements of Divine Providence. Whereas it was just Aristotle's idea of God, that he thinks only himself without having any reference to variable things. He not only never meddles in human affairs, but also engages in no practice or production, having neither desire nor will.[4] So that, even if there be some anthropomorphic expres-

[1] Met. IX. 6. 1048 b 25.
[2] Met. XII. cf. Ross's Introduction to his Aristotle's Metaphysica.
[3] De Cael. I. 4. 271 a 33; II. 8. 290 a 31; 11. 291 b 13; De An. III. 9. 432 b 21; De Resp. 10. 476 a 13; Part. An. II. 13. 658 a 8; III. 1. 661 b 24; IV. 6. 683 a 24; 11.691 b 4; 12. 694 a 15; 13. 695 b 19; Motu An. 2. 704 b 15; 8. 708 a 9; 12. 711 a 18; Gen. An. II. 4. 739 b 19; 5. 741 b 4; 6. 744 a 37; V. 4. 788 b 20; Pol. I. 2, 1253 a 9; 8. 1256 b 21; Fr. 221; 1518 b 20.
[4] Eth. Nic X. 8. 1178 b 8.

sions in Aristotle, they must not be taken literally, but rather as ordinary or rhetorical expressions.

Aristotle's teleology is by no means a naive anthropomorphism that admits a personal god who creates and dominates the world through his arbitrary will.[1] Its principle is an objective end rather than a subjective purpose. Intention or purpose is actually a kind of end or the appearance thereof. And it is not unreasonable that the moderns should call it the end *par excellence*, since consciousness is an activity of the end. Still, purpose is after all, an appearance, not the substance of the end. Everything must be the appearance or the realization of an end, but there will not always be a subject which is conscious of this end.[2] The end may be the principle of nature as well as of art. Rather, nature is the main area of the end, and art is merely an incomplete imitation of it.[3] Such an end is the essential form[4] of an appearance, viz., the form which appears as the result of a movement and a change.[5] The tree is the end of the seed, in the sense that a tree grows out of a seed. Man's purpose is a form of this end, but it is not the end *par excellence*, since it is merely an appearance of the end, i.e., an image supposed before the result. While τέλος is a πέρας[6] and a perfection,[7] the purpose or the image of an end is yet a bare form and an incomplete existence. It will be a real end only when it is realized through acts. In modern philosophers since Descartes and Locke, there is a steadfast inclination to admit

---

[1] Breantano's theory that takes Aristotle's God as an almighty creator, is a Christian misinterpretation; cf. Brentano, Psych. d. Arist. 234 ff.

[2] Phys .II. 8. 199 b 26.

[3] Phys. II. 8. 199 a 5-20. Nature is similar to art in its construction. They are both teleological, viz., it is not the case that an imcomplete cause determines a complete form, but on the contrary, a complete form guides the realization of a potential form. What is mentioned here is only the analogy between natural growth and production, but the statement is also applicable to moral conduct. Cf. Pol. VII. 13. 1331 b 28; Eth. Nic. I. 1. 1094 a 18; also, De An. II. 4. 415 b 16 f. It is not, however, an anthropomorphic interpretation to elucidate nature through the analogy of human conduct. Part. An. I. 1. 639 b 19 - 21. Namely, the native land of the end is rather nature than production or practice, the latter developed from the former to supply the deficiency of nature.

[4] Met. VIII. 4. 1044 b 1; V. 4. 1015 a 11; Phys. II. 8. 199 a 30; 9. 200 a 34; Gen. et Corr. I. 7. 324 b 18; [Meteor. IV. 2. 379 b 25,] Gen. An. I. 1. 715 a 8.

[5] Part. An. I. 1. 641 b 24.   [6] Met. II. 2. 994 b 16.

[7] Met. IX.8. 1050 a 9, 21; Eth. Eud. II. 1. 1219 a 8; [Mag. Mor. II. 12. 1211 b 27]

supremacy to consciousness, which was the main obstacle to understanding of Hegel's objective rationalism. In Aristotle's philosophy, an end is an objective form rather than an idea which is only the undeveloped stage of an end like a seed. An end is someho v immanent in every process of movement: if there were in a seed no potential form of a tree, its germination would be impossible. Nevertheless the tree is not yet actual in the seed, so that there is not yet the actual end of the tree.

Assuming that Aristotle's end is an objective form rather than a subjective purpose, the distinction between practice and production must be whether the form is always actual throughout the process of an act, or becomes actual only in the result, rather than whether this form is a direct or an indirect purpose. But such a distinction as to objective form is just what Aristotle recognized as existing between movement and actuality.

According to Aristotle, $κίνησις$ or "movement" is an incomplete process tending to realize an end-form,[1] while $ἐνέργεια$ "actuality" or "actualization", is the constant realization of this form.[2] Thus learning or walking is a movement, while seeing or thinking is an actuality. Man completes the form of learning and walking only when he has finished learning or walking; he has not learned at the same time that he is learning, or has he walked when he is walking. Whereas in seeing and thinking, an actual form is always present and man sees and thinks throughout the whole process. He has seen and is seeing, has thought and is thinking at the same time, so that there is in reality no process.

Is the distinction of practice and production the same as that of actuality and movement? Aristotle calls practice sometimes an actuality,[3] sometimes a movement.[4] But such an ambiguity is not limited to this case: what properly should be called actuality is not infrequently called movement. Hence we may suppose that strictly speaking, practice is an actuality, though it is sometimes called movement. In fact, Aristotle says: "Since of the actions which have a limit none is an end but all are relative to the end,.... this is not a practice or at least not a complete one, for it is not an end,.... but that movement in which the end is present is a practice.

[1] Met. XI. 9. 1065 b 14-23, 33 ff.; Met. XI. 9. 1066 a 17-24.
[2] Eth. Nic. X. 3. 1174 a 14 ff.; 1174 b 2-9; Eth. Nic. I. 4. 1096 b 16 ff.
[3] Eth. Nic. I.1. 1094 a 5; 6. 1098 a 13; Pol. VII. 3. 1325 a 32; [Mag. Mor. I. 35. 1197 a 10.]   [4] Met. II. 2. 996 a 22-27; Eth. Eud. II. 3. 1220 b 27.

E.g., at the same time we are seeing and have seen, are understanding and have understood, are thinking and have thought (while it is not true that at the same time we are learning and have learnt, or are being cured and have been cured).... Of these processes, then, we must call the one set movements, and the other actualities."[1]

The above statement seems in the first place to distinguish actuality as the complete reality of the end, and movement as the incomplete, and then to make practice *par excellence* an actuality. But, there is some discrepancy between the two parts of the above quotation, viz., while the first part deals with πρᾶξις, the examples in the second part are related immediately to ἐνέργεια and κίνησις. From this statement alone, it is not evident how practice and production are related to actuality and movement. Even if practice were an actuality, production would not of necessity be a movement. It is also probable that neither is every actuality a practice, nor is every movement a production.

In the first place, it is evident that not every movement is a production. The movement of an automatic subject is not a procuction. The nutrition and reproduction of living creatures are not productions in the strict sense, to say nothing of the natural movements of lifeless things, e.g., the burning of fire or rain-fall. Production in the strict sense, is not a natural movement, but a technical act, which has its principle in the art of human beings.

Next, we must inquire whether every actuality be a practice. Aristotle mentions seeing and thinking as examples of actuality, but he does not regard such acts as practices. We have learnt from Aristotle that practice is concerned with what can be otherwise. Whereas not all objects of sight and thought are variable things. For instance, heavenly bodies are eternal and yet seen, numbers are what cannot be otherwise and yet thought of. The objects of pure contemplation, which are actual beings *par excellence*, are necessary and cannot be otherwise. Such constant and eternal things not being πρακτά, the acts that relate to them can not be πρᾶξις. Seeing is an αἴσθησις and thinking is θεωρία; neither of them is a πρᾶξις; the contemplation of God is not a practice, though it is called εὐπραξία. It would be a hasty conclusion to make seeing and thinking practices, because of their being called actualities. Much the more absurd is the opinion[2] that takes the

[1] Met. VIII. 6. 1048 b 19-35; cf. Met. VIII. 9. 1050 a 21 ff.
[2] K. Miki, Gizyutu no Tetugaku (philosophy of art), 72.

practice that is distinguished from production as identical with contemplation, and neglects that peculiarity of practice against both production and contemplation. In this way, not only does the division of intellect into the theoretical, practical, and productive, become vain, but also the situation of Aristotle's important works, such as his Politics and Ethics, in his system becomes ambiguous. However highly appreciated contemplation may be, we cannot afford to neglect the importance of practice as the basis of all cultures. As for production, Aristotle admitted it to a rank by far lower than that of practice. It is a view quite contrary to correct to substitute production for practice. Practice is similar to contemplation in that they are both without process and are actual *eo ipso*. Not every actuality, however, is contemplation. Sensation is also an actuality and yet is by no means contemplation. Practice is only *a kind* of actuality, along with sensation and contemplation. It is a particular act of a rational being mediated by desire and locomotion, being independent of both contemplation and production.

Thus far we have seen that practice in the strict sense is an actuality, but not every actuality is a practice. There remains the question whether every production is a movement, or whether there be a production which is not a movement but an actuality. No doubt, most productions are movements, but there is a question whether those performances which produce no results other than acts, such as playing on the harp or dancing, are actualities or movements. The author of the *Magna Moralia* makes them not only actualities but also practices in the strict sense,[1] while Aristotle himself makes them rather productions.[2] Certainly, such productions are actualities rather than movements, for they realize constant forms like seeing and thinking, and do not approach the results by degrees. In spite of such exceptions, generally speaking, most practices are actualities and most productions are movements, but the reverse is not true. Practice is a species of actuality and production is one of movement; they belong to different genera, but both originate in the human soul, especially in its rational part. They are different from contemplation in that they act upon the outside world and bring about some change in it.

[1] [Mag. Mor. I. 34. 1197 a 9.] Eth. Nic. I. 6. 1098 a 11. Here the playing of a harp is cited as an analogy of rational act or practice, but it is not mentioned whether the playing of harp is a practice or a production.   [2] Eth. Nic. II. 1. 1103 a 34 b 8.

Let us then sum up the distinction between practice and production. These two kinds of human conduct were distinguished through the immanence, not of a subjective purpose but of the objective form in the act. What is then the kind of conduct, in which such an objective end or form is actually realized? Aristotle endeavoured to explain it through reducing practice to actuality, but the relation of practice and actuality was not distinct enough. He avoided presenting an example of practice, and merely contented himself with presenting examples of a more universal concept of act or actuality. But, seeing and thinking were not practices in the strict sense. To play on the harp or to dance is essentially an artificial act rather than a practice. Eating and drinking as well as curing, which are mentioned as examples of practical syllogism, belong rather to production than to practice.[1] What remains, as that which would seem most likely to be accounted a practice, is simply "living" itself, and nothing more.[2] But life is the most indefinite of all concepts. It comprises all living activities, viz., vegetable functions such as nutrition and reproduction, animal functions such as sensation, imagination, desire, and movement, as well as human and partly superhuman functions such as production, practice, and pure contemplation. So that life would be unsuitable as an example of practice. But it was not Aristotle's negligence that he did not state a suitable example of practice; this would rather seem to be due to the difficulty essential to the concept of practice.

When we try to illustrate practice through a real form of it, we always fail to seize its essence. Take for example, an act like murder or money making: we find that such an act is named through its result just as we speak of killing a man or accumulating money. In such a real determination every act is a process towards a production. As we have repeated, practice in the strict sense, i.e., the act which bears its form always in actuality, is the realization, not of a subjective purpose, but of an objective form. Whereas the actualization of a subjective purpose is a voluntary act which is the basis of both production and practice. When the real form is other than the subjective end, an act is accidental to the actor's desire and is involuntary, much less rational. What is then, the objective end which is required as the essence of practice? What is the form which realizes itself without process and in eternity, the ob-

---

[1] Met. IX. 6. 1048 b 25.   [2] Ibid.

jective end through which a practice takes place without falling into involuntarity? That, we say, is not a mere fact, but a thing of moral significance.¹ The real form of a practice is the subjective end which is realized through a process, while the moral significance of it is actual in eternity and forms the objective end. One might suspect our theory of a Neo-Kantian misconstruction which brings into Aristotle the dualism of value and fact. Certainly, Aristotle was not yet aware of the clear distinction between value and fact. The reason why he was at a loss to determine and exemplify the concept of practice, was that he did not clearly conceive the objective end in practice to be a moral value. The mistake of the *Magna Moralia*, which makes performance a practice, might have originated in Aristotle himself. The explicit distinction of value and fact must be looked for in Kant, or rather in Neo-Kantains. For all that, we are not embarrassed in finding examples of this distinction to vindicate our supposition. In Eth. Nic. II. 1. 1103 a 32, Aristotle, regarding on the one hand playing on the harp a technical movement or a production, explains on the other hand practice *par excellence* as just or temperate conduct. Such virtuous conduct is nothing but the content of εὐ ζῆν or living well as previously mentioned.² Therefore living, which we said to be the most indefinite of concepts, should be taken not as mere physiological activity, but as moral practice. Practice *par excellence* would be bravery, cowardice, generosity, or niggardliness, etc., rather than fighting, escaping, giving or taking. From the aspect of fact, every instance of conduct is in process and incomplete, but from the aspect of value, it is actual throughout the whole process. Nay, it is already complete in the will.³ The Sermon on the Mount thoroughly declared this essence of practice. No doubt, it was Kant who made it the foundation of ethics; but we may find the germ of this thought in the foregoing statement of Aristotle. And it is not difficult to add other examples of this kind.—

Eth. Nic. X. 6. 1176 b 6: "Now those activities are desirable in themselves from which nothing is sought beyond the activity.

---

¹ Eth. Nic. VI. 5. 1140 b 6 f.; 7. 1168 a 15-17; Pol. VII. 14. 1333 a 9-11; Eth. Nic. X.6. 1176 b 2 - 9.
² Part. An. II. 10. 656 a 6; Pol. III. 9. 1281 a 2; cf. Eth. Eud. I. 1. 1214 a 31; 2. 1214 b 8, 16, 17; 3. 1215 a 10, 13; Pol. III. 6. 1278 b 23; 9. 1281 a 2; Eth. Nic. I. 10. 1170 b 27; I. 8. 1098 b 21; VI. 5. 1140 a 28; cf. p. 188, n. 1.
³ Top. VI. 12. 149 b 29 f. IV. 5. 126 a 36. Rhet. I. 13. 1374 a 11 - 17.

And of this nature virtuous actions are thought to be, for to do noble and good deeds is a thing desirable for its own sake."[1]

Also Eth. Nic. II. 3. 1105 a 26: "Again, the case of the arts and that of the virtues are not similar; for the products of the arts have their goodness in themselves, so that it is enough that they should have a certain character, but if the acts that are in accordance with the virtues have themselves a certain character it does not follow that they are done justly or temperately."[2]

These passages all mean that production is the actualization of a certain fact, while practice is rather the expression of the moral character of a subject. The former is the realization of a sujective end, while the latter is the expression of an objective form.

§ 2. COMPARISON WITH KANT'S THEORY

Let us presume that the above interpretation is not far from truth. Thus, production is a movement and practice is an actuality in the sense that the one is the realization of a fact and the other the expression of a value. That which distinguishes actuality from motion must be an objective end rather than a subjective purpose. Granted that production is the realization of a fact and practice that of a value, we must remark in addition that in production, the objective end agrees with the subjective purpose, but in practice they do not agree as a rule. We have seen that a fact becomes a subjective purpose as far as it forms the principle of a voluntary act, and that a production is distinguished from a mere movement in that it is performed through a subjective purpose. For instance, natural movements such as the growth or the reproduction of animals and plants are the process in which their natural forms, as the objective end, are gradually realized, still they never form the subjective purpose of these living beings. Animals neither take nourishment with the intention to sustain life, nor perform sexual acts in order to preserve their species. Whereas in human production, the end is also the purpose that guides the conduct, and in this respect production is distinguished from mere movement. The consciousness of this purpose is just the cogni-

---

[1] Cf. Eth. Nic. VI. 2. 1139 b 1 ff.; 5. 1140 b 7 ff.
[2] Eth. Nic. VI. 10. 1134 a 20; 10. 1135 b 25; VI. 13. 1144 a 20.

tion which was assumed to be necessary for a voluntary act.[1] In practice, on the contrary, the value which ought to be realized is usually an objective end instead of a subjective purpose. For while a subjective purpose is realized in a process, practice is, from its definition, a realization without any process.

Once we talk about a subjective end and objective end, we must compare them with Kant's usage of these concepts. According to Kant, a subjective end is the content of any will, while an objective end is the moral ideal at which everyone should aim.[2] The subject of an objective end, being also an ideal, is a rational being *qua* rational, yet it keeps its conscious character in spite of this idealization. At any rate, Kant admitted that the end is generally an image which is supposed as the result of an act,[3] whereas what we have called the objective end was the complete actuality of a form, which is neither conscious nor an ideal. Thus the end was conceived mainly psychologically by Kant as it had not been in ancient teleology. This gave a subjective inclination to his ethical theory. According to Kant, the good will, which is the necessary and sufficient condition of morality, is a will which is determined mainly through the consciousness of duty. Whenever a will has any material ground, it is always egoistic and unmoral, no matter what may be the value in the result of the act.

Thus, for instance, the conduct of a soldier who fights to help his fatherland may be courageous and beautiful, yet it falls short of moral approbation, as far as it is dependent on passion or attachment. In order to be morally good, one ought to act not through a passion such as patriotism, but only through the command of reason that orders one to go to the war.[4] The moral value of an act is determined only through the subjective form of resolution. This idea of Kant's respectable as it was as an attempt to reserve the purity of morality, could not but arouse the discontent of many tender minded persons[5] owing to its rigorous formalism.

---

[1] Ch. II. § 4.
[2] Kant, Gr. z. Met. d. Sitt. WW. Cass. IV. 287.
[3] Kant, K.d.U.K.Einl. IV. WW. Cass. V. 249: *Weil nun der Begriff von eimen Objekt, sofern er zugleich den Grund der Wirklichkeit dieses Objekts enthält, der Zweck,*; Ibid. 505; Met. d. Sitt. WW. VII. 194; Rel. 3. 1. A. 2. Anm. WW. VI. 144.
[4] Kant, K.d.p.V. WW. IV. 145 - 158.
[5] Schiller, Werke. Meyer's Kl. I. 178; cf. Scheler, Formalismus etc. 233.

A really moral mind, on the contrary is not concerned with duty, as Max Scheler says,[1] for the consciousness of duty is nothing but the phenomenon of inward struggle with an immoral desire. The subjective end of moral conduct exists not in the consciousness of duty, but in a concrete fact, or according to our terminology, in the real form, while the objective end or the moral significance of it is in its accordance with the moral law. A moral will should rather devote itself to realizing a real end without regarding duty. For instance, a true charity should not be accompanied by the consciousness of duty, but should be an endeavour to help the miserable with pity and love for the weak and poor. It is not unreasonable that Kant's morality should be condemned by Scheler as a Pharisaism, or ridiculed by Hegel as the morality of a chamberlain. No doubt, it is too harsh to condemn Kant as a proud hypocrite. We must withhold abuse, and reflect on the finiteness of human love. Only a genius of love who rarely appears in history, can afford to despise the ethics of duty.

Nevertheless, we dare say that Kant mistook the essence of moral conduct in confusing the objective and the subjective end. In truth, as Kant said, to a being whose will is not determined solely through practical rules, these appear as imperatives, but there is an actual consciousness of duty, only when they are asserted against an irrational desire. In other words, the consciousness of duty is the negative aspect of law, to which there must correspond a positive aspect. Where there is no positive desire to obey the law, there cannot be any resistance against unlawful desires:[2] such a will would be a mere heteronomic will.[3] Kant himself assumed man to be not only a subject of law, but also a rational being who gives it. Moral conduct which is entirely free from the consciousness of duty, would be impossible to a finite rational being,[4] yet it would be none the less false to assume that only the consciousness of duty makes moral conduct possible. This is just mistaken as to substitute a body with its shadow, or assume fever to be a condition of health for the reason that it is a kind of antitoxic function of a living body.

Of course the positive aspect of law does not necessarily appear in the subjective consciousness. Laws may be implicitly con-

---

[1] Scheler, op. cit. 196 ff.; N. Hartmann, Ethik, 234.
[2] Scheler, op. cit. 67; Trendelenburg, Beiträge etc. III. 196 ff.
[3] Kant, Gr. z. Met. d. Sitt. WW. IV. 290 ff.
[4] Kant, K.d.p.V. I.I.1. WW. V. 37.

tained in the intention rather than asserting themselves explicitly as duties. Consciousness of moral laws is their reflective appearance, or in Hegel's terminology, the *für sich Sein* of laws. Whereas the consciousness of duty is the appearance of the conflict between a moral wish and a natural desire. It is an accident, rather than the essence, of laws.

It is well known, that Kant distinguished the goodness of moral intention from that of conduct, calling the value of the former morality, that of the latter legality, and admitting the superiority of the former.[1] We might be suspected of neglecting the immortal merit of Kant and reducing morality again to mere legality, when we reject Kant's theory that makes duty the subjective end of moral conduct. But, we do not confuse legality with moral goodness, in saying good conduct to be the realization of an objective end or a valuable form. We assert that a moral conduct which surpasses legality can exist without making duty the subjective end, and further that this is the real *Sittlichkeit*, rather than mere subjective and formal *Moralität*.[2] Methinks, when Kant defined legality as the character of conduct which is objectively in accordance with the law, he meant in reality what we now call the satisfaction of a real form. This only means that the external fact of conduct conforms to the law which is itself an external norm. Whereas according to our view, not all objective thing are mere facts, but value also may be objective in significance. Needless to say, the legality which is nothing but the external agreement with legislative facts, is morally valueless. But what we call the satisfaction of an objective form is the realization of a value. According to Kant, an act which is performed not through the consciousness of duty, but through the love for a man or devotion to social order, is morally impure.[3] Even Kant admitted that an act which is performed through fear or the calculation of one's interest is base, and that which is performed through love is beautiful, only he held that they differ in degree and in their aesthetic rather than in their moral aspect. A pure moral act is, for Kant, as aforesaid, one which is done without passion and mainly in accordance with the consciousness of duty. But to resume our opinion, the consciousness of duty is the phenomenon which grows from the want of passion or from the antagonism of

[1] Ibid. I.1. 3. WW. V. 80 ff.   [2] Cf. Scheler, op.cit. 19 ff.
[3] Kant, K. d. p. V. I. 1. 3. WW. V. 91.

passion and law; there is no consciousness of duty where passion agrees with law, which is just the ideal state of morality. In such an ideal state, the subjective end of conduct, being e.g., to help the fatherland, its, objective end, i.e. its moral significance, is satisfied without any subjective consciousness of duty.[1]

The most remarkable example which characterizes the difference between the ethical thought of Aristotle and that of Kant, is the relation of temperance and continence. Both of these virtues consist in the moderation of eating and sexual appetites, temperance being the character in which appetites themselves are in accordance with the norms while in continence the appetites that are excessive are suppressed and regulated by reason. Now, for Aristotle, temperance is better than continence; the latter finds its ideal in the former, which is the state of a wise man who conforms to the laws without any effort. Kant, on the contrary, who assumed that the moral value of character consists in freedom, assigned moral goodness rather to temperance acquired through freedom —which is nothing but continence in Aristotle's terminology—rather than to temperance as a blessed dispostition. Not the harmony of reason and emotion, but the domination of the former over the latter was the essence of morality.[2] In fact, even Kant did not deny that a holy will without the consciousness of duty, has objectively a higher value than continence, only he would not have admitted to it the moral value in the strict sense. Kant emphasized the finiteness of human nature, while Aristotle set up the ideal of man. This fundamental discrepancy is, no doubt, brought about mainly through the Christianity that lies between them. The difference, however, is not so antagonistic as it appears.[3] The one depends upon the volitional attitude that aims at the improvement of character, while the other depends upon the intellectual attitude that contemplates the ideal of mind. In this respect, Aristotle might be regarded as more theoretical than Kant.

According to Kant, moral value is attached to the subject rather than to the object of conduct. The utility of conduct for society never guarantees its moral value. Morality is found mainly in the form of resolution. But, he was unable to explain how the

---

[1] Scheler, op. cit. 32; Hartmann, op. cit. 241.
[2] Trendelenburg, op. cit. III. 209 ff.
[3] Ibid. 212.

subjective function of conduct itself is valuable.[1] In reality, this value could not but be reduced to the social utility of conduct. It differs from objective values, only through the constant efficacy that is promised by the enduring intention of the subject. Fitting conduct without any firm foundation is accidental and transcient in its effect, whereas the good will of a person is the constant principle of social preservation and development. It would be nonsense to talk about the moral value of conduct apart from its effects upon society.[2] One may estimate continence more highly than temperance as far as he assumes the latter to be an accidentally favorable disposition. But what Aristotle calls σω-φροσύνη is something more than a natural disposition. It is not a natural virtue, but an ethical one. And the essence of ethical virtue is prudence or practical wisdom.

In reference to this, we must also notice that virtue for Aristotle is not confined to the value of an object. We have stated that the objective end of conduct does not always agree with the subjective end. Nevertheless they are not indifferent to each other. The objective end or the value-form depends upon the subjective end or the fact-form of conduct. When a man wishes to avoid the pain of punishment, the objective end of his conduct is negative in its value, viz., his conduct has no moral merit. On the contrary, when he wants to help the fatherland, his objective end is positive and good. The difference in value of acts depends, in the first place, upon the difference of object-value attached to their subjective ends, because the public welfare is more valuable than the individual.[3] But morality is essentially a social value. Hence it is imposed as a duty upon the individual who is apt to turn against society. Not only the matter, however, but also the form, of a subjective end conditions the objective end or the value of an act. Form and matter are correlative with each other. For instance, to avoid punishment is a resolution formed through a special sensible motive, and to help the fatherland is a resolution formed through a universal rational motive. We have been opposed

[1] Kant, Gr. z. Met. d. Sitt. WW. IV. 249 ff.
[2] Rhet. I. 9. 1366 a 36-b 11; 1366 b 36-1367 a 6; cf. ibid. 1367 b 5; Eth. Nic. I.1. 1094 b 7; IX. 8. 1168 b 31; Pol. VII. 2. 1324 a 5; 15. 1334 a 11. But, Aristotle's theory is not altruistic. In a virtuous man, the love of self and the love of others coincide: cf. Eth. Nic. IX. 8. This results from the fact that the state is essentially a community to realize a good life. Pol. III. 6. 1278 b 16; 9. 1280 a 31; b 30; II. 2. 1261 a 25.   [3] Eth. Nic. I. 1. 1094 b 7-10

to the depreciation of passionate conduct, but, passion is by no means the highest condition of moral conduct, nor its sufficient condition. There is a type of rational conduct which is higher than that which is merely passionate. The reason which appears in such conduct is not the reason which is opposed to passion, but which agrees with it. In other words, the consciousness of duty being a negative feeling which presupposes an evil desire, conduct which is determined by it falls short of the highest good, but there is a rational and moral will which is not accompanied by the consciousness of duty. Such a beautiful agreement of reason and passion was just the ideal of Aristotle's ethics.

We have also said that a conduct which aims at some material effect may agree with a norm even when one does not make duty one's subjective end. Such a conduct is the realization of socalled ethical virtue. Ethical virtue is the $\tilde{\eta}\theta o\varsigma$ or the habitual character, which is fostered through lawful conduct and does not need the consciousness of duty. It is rather the proof of moral accomplishment that one becomes free from the consciousness of duty.[1] The complete reality of ethical virtue is prudence or practical wisdom. An ideal morality requires a distinct consciousness more than merely fitting conduct. Unconscious fitting conduct is already impossible without presupposing practical wisdom. But this practical wisdom at first exists only in another person. In such a case, one's conduct is accompanied by the consciousness of duty. This consciousness changes into a positive estimation in accordance with the moral improvement of one's personality. Practical wisdom becomes purely one's own, or, rather one becomes himself pure practical intellect. Aristotle is by no means inferior to Kant in appreciating a conscious virtuous conduct.

Kant's distinction of legality and morality finds its equivalent in Aristotle's distinction of $\varkappa\alpha\tau\grave{\alpha}\ \lambda\acute{o}\gamma o\nu$ and $\mu\varepsilon\tau\grave{\alpha}\ \lambda\acute{o}\gamma o\nu$. According to Aristotle, neither is Socrates right in identifying virtue with prudence, nor is the common opinion of his contemporaries in defining virtue as a habit in accordance with right reason. They are right in assuming prudence or reason to be necessary for ethical virtues, only the former goes too far in making prudence identical with virtue, while the latter is insufficient in saying it "to be in accordance with reason"; Aristotle himself characterizes it with

[1] Eth. Nic. I. 9. 1099 a 7 - 21; II. 2. 1104 b 3-12.

the expression "habit accompanied by reason".[1] κατὰ λόγον, "in accordance with reason", means conforming to law, while μετὰ λόγου, "accompanied by reason", applies to the expression of a rational character which is acquired completely.[2] This interpretation is supported by the following statement: Eth. Nic. VI. 12. 1144 a 13:[3] "As we say that some people who do just acts are not necessarily just, i.e., those who do the acts ordained

[1] Eth. Nic. VI. 13. 1144 b 17 - 27.
[2] In Mag. Mor. I. 35. 1198 a 15 ff., κατὰ λόγον is distinguished from μετὰ λόγου in that the one signifies mere external legitimateness, while the other means accompanied by a right purpose and the knowledge of the good. This seems to be a suitable interpretation made in reference to the preceding statement (1144 a 13 - 20). But, Walter is opposed to it, because he refers it rather to Aristotle's critics of Socrates, who identified vitrue with λόγος. According to Walter, this interpretation in the Mag. Mor. would lead to supposing that Socrates had identified a mere external legitimateness with virtue, which is contrary to reality. This is also Walter's misunderstanding. For as is easily perceived from the context, the distinction of κατὰ λόγον and μετὰ λόγου has no direct reference to Socrates' identification of knowledge and virtue. Aristotle's theotry which qualifies virtue as μετὰ λόγου itself an attempt to reconcile Socrates' view with the common opinion of his contemporaries that makes virtue an external legitimateness. At any rate, Walter attaches much importance to the distinction of κατά and μετά, spending the greater part of his study on this point (cf. Julius Walter, Die Lehre von der praktischen Vernunft in der griechischn Philosophie, 84-138). His historical observations on these concepts are the most successful part of his work, yet even this part is inadequate in refusing to accept the interpretation of the Magna Moralia mentioned above.
According to Walter, μετὰ λόγου means caused by λόγος or practical reason, whereas κατὰ λόγον indicates mere objective legitimateness, not caused by reason. But what difference is there between this interpretation of μετὰ λόγου and that of the Magna Moralia, viz., between being caused by reason and depending upon conscious determination? Walter maintains that the interpretation of the Magna Moralia would lead us to admit that Socrates, having chosen κατὰ λόγον has made unconscious legitimateness virtue, which is contrary to reality. But Walter himself admits that Socrates did not describe virtue as κατὰ λόγον but used φρόνησις with διά or in the dative case, a usage which was appropriate to the intellectual theory of vitrue. It is evident from this point also that Aristotle did not imply that Socrates was included among "the moderns in general" who took virtue as κατὰ λόγον instead of μετὰ λόγου. In Walter's statement too, κατὰ λόγον always signifies external leginimateness. This proves the conscious rationality of μετὰ λόγου rather than ruling it out as impossible.
[3] Eth. Nic. VI. 13.. 1144 a 13 ff. We treat λόγος and νόμος as synonymous, on the basis of Aristotle's statement that law is reason without desire. Cf. Pol. III. 16. 1287 a 32; 15. 1286 a 19; Eth. Nic. X. 10. 1180 a 21; V. 10. 1134 a 35; Pol. VII. 14. 1333 a 6 ff.

by the laws either unwillingly or owing to ignorance or for some other reason and not for the sake of the acts themselves (though, to be sure, they do what they should and all the things that the good man ought), so is it, it seems, that in order to be good one must be in a certain state when one does the several acts, i.e., one must do them as a result of will and for the sake of the acts themselves."

Thus, action accompanied by reason is to do something which is *per se* good, but this thing does not need to be done because of its being one's duty. More strictly speaking, the above proposition only claims that right action is to do something through a good will, but not that it is to do the thing for the sake of goodness. What makes a will good is a right desire and a right deliberation. But a right desire is fundamentally rational and may be acquired only through prudence. Consequently, what makes a will good is after all reduced to right estimation. The only difference between the two theories, is that in Aristotle, the estimation is accompanied by positive value feeling, while in Kant, it is negative.

How much Aristotle attaches importance to rational will, we can see in what he says about courage. Conduct through mere anger he does not admit to be courageous, and real courage he assumes to consist in the will,[1] which aims at moral goodness and endures the pain of death.[2] Consequently, an act may be objectively useful to society, and have a positive value, yet it lacks in moral value, if it is done through passion. To be morally good, one must act through practical consideration and resolution. Needless to say, this consideration is not the calculation of interest or the mere searching for a real means, but the calculation of moral values—as N. Hartmann says: "The value of the fact which one endeavours to realize, is always selected through a moral value-feeling."[3]

This demand for the consciousness of goodness shows an approach to Kant's ethics. The value of an act is herein conditioned by the moral estimation of the act. The subjectification of the end is found in Aristotle as well. This, however, is not the same

[1] Eth. Nic. II. 3. 1105 a 31-33; 4. 1106 a 3; V. 10. 1136 a 3 f.; VI. 13. 1144 a 19 f.; Eth. Eud. II. 7. 1223 a 21 ff.; III. 1. 1230 a 27 ff.; Rhet. I. 9. 1367 b 21.
[2] Eth. Nic. III. 10. 1115 b 11-13; 11. 1116 a 28; b 30; 15. 1119 b 16; IV. 2. 1120 a 23; 4. 1122 b 8; VI. 13. 1144 a 13ff.; X. 10. 1180 a 6; cf. ibid. l. 4. 1166 a 14 ff.; Pol. VIII. 13. 1332 a 22.
[3] N. Hartmann, op. cit. II. 1. Kap. 27.

as resolution through consciousness of duty. The former is active estimation, while the latter is a negative experience of struggle between reason and desire. The consciousness of duty surely presupposes apprehension of value along with a worthless desire, but apprehension of value is not necessarily the consciousness of duty. Perhaps one often understands law as a duty, but this fact of human nature must be distinguished from ideal morality. However rare and difficult the will may be, which is determined through the positive apprehension of value, without this apprehension being accompanied by the consciousness of duty, it is none the less the ideal of morality. And morality is naturally the system of ideals, not the mere facts, of human nature. The antagonism of reason and sensibility is a fact of human nature, not its ideal. To act through the consciousness of duty is not itself a duty. It is rather the duty for man to get rid of the consciousness of duty. The consciousness of duty appears in an early stage of moral education: it gradually disappears as the exercise proceeds. Moral freedom is the harmonious state of reason and passion. It is the complete rationalization of one's desires. A development of the moral system always imposes anew upon us a difficult duty, but moral accomplishment consists in changing incessantly this new duty to a feeling of happiness. Not the discrepancy of reason and feeling, but precisely their harmony, is the measure of moral progress.

How is it, then, possible to have apprehension of value without presupposing base desires? Reason or consciousness grows in order to regulate the conflict of motives, and apprehension of value seems to be impossible if there be no opposition between value and its opposite. Indeed consciousness or reason grows from the necessity to choose the most effective act out of many possibilities. We would not deny a pragmatic view of their origin.[1] But the opposition which causes consciousness is not always that between value and its opposite, but may be an opposition between positive values.[2] When we look back from the decision, the chosen value may seem to relate to the rejected one as positive to negative. Still they may be both positive values in themselves. One might still maintain that if practical reason presupposes the opposition of values, the norm cannot but appear as a duty; for the lower value will manifest itself as an irrational attachment, against which the

[1] Bergson, L'évolution créatrice, 115 ff.   [2] Hartmann, op. cit. 339 ff.

higher value will claims itself as a duty; there will not be in truth an absolute value or negation of it, but every value will appear either positive or negative in each reference. Even if we admit these arguments, moral value need not be founded upon the consciousness of duty. For, even admitted that the conflict between value and its opposite be inevitable, it does not follow of necessity that the subject takes the part of the latter. Our conscious experience may not exhibit a complete harmony but require effort and self-restraint; yet there is all the difference in the world between obeying duty with pain and following law with pleasure. Moral accomplishment is transition from the state of mind in which moral value commands as a duty, to that in which one positively desires the value. The rigid opposition between reason and desire passes into harmony; such a harmony is found in the character of wise men as the moral ideal.

The rank of moral values is not fixed, but admits of progress, which would, however, be disturbed if one neglect the calculation of values. This is the reason why an act motivated by passion is inferior to one which is accompanied by rational insight into value. Passionate conduct may conform to the norm, but only by good luck and neither constantly nor universally. What ensures constant morality is a steady character regulated by reason. In order to sail a rough sea we need an exact compass instead of impetuous sailors. One who acts with passion, may succeed through a lucky chance, but he cannot end well. There are too many tragedies of passionate persons who erred from righteousness through personal feeling. Solon said that man's fortune cannot be known until his death. But Aristotle does not agree with him, seeing in this view a confusion of happiness and fortune. He rather assumes a happy man to be one who has a constant character such that he can endure even an unfortunate fate confidently.[1] It is a wise man whose faculties are all regulated by reason and keep a complete harmony.

§ 3. THE RELATION BETWEEN PRACTICE AND PRODUCTION

We distinguished practice and production, making the former the realization of a moral value as an objective end, and the

---

[1] Eth. Nic. III. 11. 1117 a 4-9.

latter that of a real form as a subjective end. But now we have come to recognize that objective end is not irrelevant to subjective end. The excellence of intention is adopted as the measure of moral values. What is required is not consciousness of duty, but insight into value. The moral value of practice is not measured through the usefulness of the result, but through the goodness of the conduct itself. A moral will is not merely an intention to realize an effect, but consists rather in making manifest a moral value through conduct. In Aristotle also, the goodness of practice is due to the good will. But Aristotle's good will is distinguished from the Kantian concept of the good will, which is determined by the consciousness of duty. Nor does this mean that moral value is reduced to the subjective end. Insight as to value is different from consciousness of duty in its positive character, while the subjective end of will, which is determined through this insight, is not value itself, but a valuable thing. According to Aristotle, what the will aims at, is not an abstract good, but a good thing. He repeatedly rejects Plato's idealism, which admits the idea of the good as abstract goodness and explains thereby not only moral conduct, but also the whole universe.[1] The end of conduct is said to be happiness as the highest valuable object, instead of value itself. For all that, it is not impossible to make moral value itself the subjective end.[2] To wish to be a good man or to do a virtuous act is possible, to be sure, and Aristotle himself uses the word προαίρεσις not only in the sense of a concrete particular will, but sometimes also a general intention.[3] Still, value as the subjective end of an act, is not identical with value as its objective end. To intend a moral value is the beginning of practice, not its finale. Just as a youth who sets his mind on learning is not yet thereby a scholar, so also a man who wishes to be good is not yet accomplished as a good man. A continent man, for instance, is not yet temperate in spite of his good intention. As for an incontinent man, he is far from being virtuous for all his good intention.[4] Morality as a subjective end may be realized only in process. By making moral accomplishment our subjective end, we become students of virtue who proceed to the

[1] Eth. Nic. I. 4.
[2] Cf. Hartmann, op. cit. 237 f.
[3] Cf. Teichmüller, op. cit. 96 f.
[4] Eth. Nic. VII. 2. 1145 b 12-14; 4. 1146 b 22; VII. 9. 1151 a 20-24; Eth. Nic. III. 7. 1114 a 13 - 15.

end by degrees. As an objective end, moral significance is given at once in its perfect form, but as a subjective end, it is the ideal which should be pursued and realized gradually. Hence morality is incarnate in the ideal image of a wise man. The progress towards this ideal is, strictly speaking, not practice, but production, the art that leads one to this being education or politics. Of course, the process of moral excercise consists of individual practices, and the activities of teachers and statesmen are also in a sense practices. For all that, as far as they aim at the formation of character or the accomplishment of personality, their end is attained only in the result, and according to our previous definition, the process must be called a production rather than a practice.

Thus, we have explained the meaning of $πρᾶξις$ and $ποίησις$. But in truth, Aristotle is not clear enough about the distinction of these concepts. It is not only the fault of historians, that they failed to explain the essence of these concepts and did but repeat the formal distinction between them. We would persuade ourselves that we have explained them without being guilty of a serious distortion of what Aristotle implied.

What remains for us, is the question of the relation of practice to production. But, regrettable as it is, Aristotle refers almost not at all to this matter. Here is one example of a fault in Aristotle that was noticed by Teichmüller,[1] who criticized him as being detailed in analysis but rough in synthesis. All we can do is to make some conjectures as modestly as we can.[2] Practice as well as production makes some change in objects (which are capable of being changed) through an act. Now as production is the realization of an effect, and practice that of moral significance, practice would have to be accompanied by production, since it would be impossible that the form of a value should realize itself without being mediated by a fact. An independent value without fact would be a pure internal idea rather than actual conduct. We have recognized that the Sermon on the Mount shows us the essence of practice. But this is true only in that it reveals to us the distinction between practice and production, attaching importance to the intention in practice. But taking practice in its entirety, we must return to the common sense that regards the Sermon as an exaggeration.

[1] Teichmüller, op. cit. 337.
[2] We can find some suggestion in Pol. III. 4. 1278 a 9; 18. 1288 a 38; VII. 14. 1333 a 11; Eth. Nic. V. 5. 1130 b 29 etc.; cf. ch. V.

A mere desire or will is not yet a real practice. As far as it involves the effort towards realization, it might be distinguished from theoretical thinking or imagination. But this realization is the production of a physical change in the objective world through one's bodily behavior. It is the realization of a fact-form, and may be said to be πρᾶξις or ποίησις in the wider sense. This does not, however, leads to the conclusion that every practice is mediated through a production, or that there is no practice which is not at once a production. For production as ποίησις *par excellence*, is not just any act which produces some change in the outside world. Such acts may be found in animals as well as in man, in instinctive act or in reflexive reaction. Production in the strict sense must be the realization of art, which is the ἕξις of ποίησις accompanied by reason.[1] If, therefore, there be no practice which is not a production, or if every practice be mediated by a production, moral practice would have to be followed by a technical act or mediated by it. If a practice which has a moral significance must be a voluntary and intentional act, it must be more or less accompanied by a production, since an act performed methodically following an intention, is generally a technical act or a production. But there are of course, differences of degree. Besides, the intellect essential to practice and that which is essential to production are not proportionate to each other: an act of importance may frequently be founded upon an instinctive action without art. Accordingly, there may be a kind of accompaniment, but not mediation in the strict sense. The foundation of practice is act in general rather than production. Only in so far as such an act is somewhat technical, may we say that practice accompanies production.

Is it then that production in its turn, may appear independent of practice? Or should we also admit that production is mediated by practice? The performance of an act through art, is, of course, restricted to human beings. Consequently, production being of necessity a human behavior, and man being a political animal, his behavior must have some moral significance. In this respect, we may admit that every production is a practice. But there is in fact a pure production which has the least moral significance, e.g. a creation of art for art's sake. It might seem that even the creation of a solitary artist apart from any social and moral interest,

---

[1] Eth. Nic. VI. 4. 1140 a 7.

can not be independent of society, in spite of the artist's anti-social attitude, and cannot be independent of moral significance. Yet, this is by no means Aristotle's way of thinking. According to such a view, even pure contemplation would be a moral practice as well; but Aristotle assumes it to be an anti-social activity apart from any practice and production. So that, with regard to production too, we may assume a kind of it which has the minimum of moral significance. Productive intellect is not proportionate to practical intellect, and there may be a production which is almost indifferent to morality. Production may be accompanied by some practice, but it is not mediated through the latter in the strict sense of mediation. Practice and production are neither continuous nor mediated through each other. We must be faithful to the facts at all times, and guard against the dialectic deception that admits mediation everywhere. This is the highest duty of those who think in Aristotle's way of thinking.

Let this suffice for the essence and interrelation of practice and production. They are both acts guided by practical intellect in a wider sense, which we shall investigate in the next chapter. Herewith we shall enquire about the relation of practice and production to contemplation in reference to the end.

We have repeated that practice and production are distinguished from each other through the immanence or transcendence of their objective end. Yet Aristotle, saying on the one hand, that practice aims at nothing other than the act itself, and has value in itself, states on the other hand, that ethical virtues and political activities are after all the foundations of pure theoretical thinking or contemplation, which is the highest activity of man, and that politics is like the service of a steward who guarantees the leisure of his master to enable him to be occupied with more noble engagements.[1] Thus, ethical virtue and practice are the means for contemplation. It is quite reasonable that one should find an apparent discrepancy between the two statements. Teichmüller actually pointed it out as the fatal contradiction of Aristotle's dualism.[2]

But, is it really a fatal contradiction? Does practice come to be mere production, if it refers to contemplation in this manner? This supposition would lead to the same conclusion that we rejected above, viz., to the assumption that practice without production is

---

[1] Pol. I. 7. 1255 b 20-37; Eth. Nic. VI. 13. 1145 a 6-11.
[2] Teichmüller, op. cit. 331 f.

mere contemplation. But we must once more remind ourselves that the end which divided practice and production was an objective end. This amounts to saying that, from the subjective point of view, both practice and production may be regarded either as end or as means. It is not a contradiction either to find the objective end of production in the result and to aim at the process of production subjectively, or to find the objective end of practice in itself and to make the practice subjectively the means for another practice. For instance, the act of a sculptor who makes a statue for creation's sake, is far from a practice, but a pure production, and the act of a statesman who makes a public establishment for a far-reaching aim, is not a mere production, but a practice *par excellence*. A practice, though being in a sense a self-end, may be none the less a means for another practice or contemplation.

Nevertheless, the above suspicion does not dissolve, even if we take the end in the objective sense. Practice will not be the end itself, if the value of it depends upon that of contemplation, and if it is valuable as far as it makes contemplation possible and contributes to it. Still, practice and ethical virtues may subserve theoretical virtues without being devoid of their own value. Their means-value is compatible with their self-value.[1] Aristotle never made the independence of values impossible by regarding contemplation the highest. The existence of a highest value does not deprive the lower values of their independency. Every value has its place in a scale without losing its independency. In this respect, the highest value should be distinguished from the most universal value. Contemplation is the highest value instead of the most universal. The most universal value of human life is happiness, rather than contemplation. Aristotle neither identified happiness with contemplation, as is often mistakenly supposed, nor did he refuse other activities the right of being moments of happiness. His ethical view stands by no means upon a narrow-minded scholarship, but rather displays an extremely rich and sensible humanity. Happiness is what every one desires, so that it is indefinite in its contents, and varies for each man. Moral characters are differentiated just through this variety.[2] Namely, some feel happiness in bodily pleasure, some in the accumulation of wealth, and some in social fame; none of this is wrong *a priori*. But it was the character which finds happiness in contemplation, that was

---

[1] Top. VI. 12. 149 b 35 f.   [2] Cf. p. 196, n. 1.

admitted to be the highest by Aristotle, and he really considered that this action affords us the most excellent happiness—both in quality and in quantity. Happiness is not restricted to contemplation, but may be had either in moral practice, social fame, bodily pleasure, or wealth. Hence, indeed, it is valuable to feel happy in contemplation; if on the contrary, every value subsists only as the means for contemplation, there will be no real difference among the values. They will be, at most, either nearer or farther from the final end, but will have no qualitative difference. Whereas Aristotle admitted not only various contents of happiness, but also considered the happiness of a virtuous man to be the synthesis of these values,[1] since even a saint, being man and animal cannot live apart from social or natural goods. These lower ways of living and the necessary values are subordinate to contemplation as the highest value, to be sure. Yet Aristotle's contemplation does not refuse independency to those lives and values. It is not like a tyrant who makes every one a slave, but like a philosopher-king who allows every one his liberty and allows him a life suitable to his worth. The self-endness of practice does not contradict with its utility for contemplation. As aforesaid, contemplation is an eternal and static self-end, while practice is self-end in conjunction with act, and production is the process of realizing an outward end. They are all independent respectively, and yet form the hierarchy of values.

Contemplation, practice, and production are different in their degrees of value, yet they are all spiritual activities which make a man a human being. Contemplation is the most self-sufficient, next comes practice, and production is the last. To be self-sufficient does not mean not to presuppose other activities, which are less self-sufficient. Contemplation is the most self-sufficient in the sense that its end exists in itself, not that it does not require lower functions of soul and body for its activity. Rather, on the contrary, a higher form cannot realize itself without being founded upon lower forms or matters. In order that self-sufficient contemplation may be possible, the foundation of spiritual life must be built by practice and production. All these spiritual activities

---

[1] Cf. Eth. Nic I. 5 ff.; Rhet. I. 5. 1360 b 20 ff. This relation between contemplation as the highest happiness and the synthesis of value as complete happiness is similar to the relation in Kant between *das oberste Gut* and *das höchste* Gut, viz., between *supremum* and *consummatum*; cf. Kant, K. d. p. V. I. II. 2. WW. V. 120.

involve an intellectual moment, and their rank of value is raised as the intellectual moment becomes more dominant and self-sufficient.

Practice and production are the activities of the irrational part of the soul which is dominated by the rational part. They are irrational on the material side, but rational on the formal side. In our inquiry into the correspondence of the rational and irrational parts of the soul in practice, the next problem must be the **analysis of the rational part in general.**

The object of theoretical knowledge is what is eternal and immovable, or what is movable, yet possessing the principle of motion in itself. The knowledge which is concerned with the former is metaphysics, that which is concerned with the latter, natural sciences.[1] The object of practical or productive knowledge is movable, and does not possess the principle of motion in itself, so that it may be moved and changed by human intellect.[2]

Since Aristotle does not go into detail about practical and productive knowledge, it is not evident whether they include the practical sciences such as the *Politics*, the *Ethics*, the *Poetics*, and the *Rhetoric*, which compose his works, or are confined to somewhat more pragmatic thinking. We must, at any rate, distinguish this generic sense of ἐπιστήμη from the above mentioned special one, in which it is coordinate with reason and wisdom. ἐπιστήμη as the generic concept implies knowledge in general rather than science. If we take it as a species of theoretical knowledge, we should also admit, in accordance with the foregoing statement of Aristotle, that ἐπιστήμη πρακτική is practical theoretical knowledge. Yet it would be quite absurd for practical knowledge and productive knowledge to be theoretical, because knowledge is practical or productive just so far as it is not theoretical.

For all that, we will here be confronted with a powerful objection. This conceives practical knowledge or productive knowledge as the theory of practical or productive affairs, such as the *Ethics* or the *Poetics*, rather than as a direct principle of action. These kinds of knowledge are theoretical in so far as they are reflective and universal, though their objects are practical. Zeller,[3] for example, on the ground that Aristotle calls theoretical philosophy what he should have duly called theoretical knowledge,[4] takes the ἐπιστήμη, which is divided into the theoretical, the practical, and the productive, as science rather than knowledge. Such sciences are, he argues, different from φρόνησις and τέχνη, which are merely immediate faculties of practice and production. We can find no such concept as practical philosophy or productive philosophy,[5] yet Aristotle really means under the concept of "philosophy concerning

[1] Met. XI.7. 1064 a 16 ff.   [2] Ibid.
[3] Zeller, op. cit. 177 n.5.   [4] Met. VI. 1. 1026 a 18.
[5] In Bonitz's Index Arist. 821 a 36 ff., φιλοσοφία is divided into theoretical, practical, and productive philosophy; whereas in fact, the division in the statements there mentioned is either that of διάνοια (e.g. Met. VI. 1. 1025 b 25) or of ἐπιστήμη (e.g. Met. XI. 7. 1064 b 1-14).

human affairs"[1] or "political philosophy",[2] ethics and politics, and defines φιλοσοφία as a theoretical knowledge or a knowledge which aims at truth.[3] Still, if philosophy is a kind of theoretical knowledge, θεωρητικὴ φιλοσοφία would no longer be equal to θεωρητικὴ ἐπιστήμη. If, on the contrary, we identify such ἐπιστήμη with φιλοσοφία, it would follow that philosophy is not necessarily theoretical, but merely synonymous with knowledge. The verb φιλοσοφεῖν is not only confined to the strict sense of philosophical contemplation,[4] but is also sometimes used in a wider sense to express thinking in general[5] in the same way as ἐπιστήμη, and still holds a somewhat universal character as compared with practice.[6] This is much more the case with the noun φιλοσοφία, which seems to indicate a universal thinking rather than thinking without qualification. At any rate, ἐπιστήμη and φιλοσοφία, being theoretical knowledge, are concerned only with necessary being or with nature.

Julius Walter, though he does not, like Zeller, identify the classification of knowledge with that of science or philosophy, regards the contents of the *Ethics*, the *Politics*, and the *Poetics*, which constitute the system of Aristotle, as theoretical knowledge. He admits that ἐπιστήμη and φιλοσοφία, as generic terms, implied in antiquity, including Aristotle, all faculties of intellect, their range not being limited to science and philosophy in the strict sense,[7] and he notes that Aristotle himself gives as exemplifying theoretical ἐπιστήμη is confined to physics, mathematics, and metaphysics,—excluding ethics and poetics.[8] He assumes, nevertheless, that ethics is objectively different from prudence, and poetics from art, the former in each case being theoretical, the latter practical.[9] Thus Aristotle's *Ethics* and *Poetics* would be in their contents, the product of theoretical intellect, yet lacking in independency in their form, and would be attributed rather to practical or productive faculties such as prudence and art.[10] These interpretations of Zeller's and Walter's which would reduce the *Ethics* and the *Poetics* to theo-

[1] Eth. Nic. X. 10. 1181 b 15   [2] Pol. III. 12. 1282 b 23.
[3] Met. II. 1. 993 b 20.
[4] Met. I. 2. 982 b 13; IV. 2. 1004 b 9; 5. 1009 b 37; Eth. Nic. II. 3. 1105 b 13, 19; Pol. I. 7. 1255 b 37; De Cael. III. 1. 298 b 12.
[5] Pol. VII. 11. 1331 a 14-17; De Divin. I. 463 a 4-7; Met. I. 3. 983 a 33-b3; Pol. II. 10. 1272 a 22-24; Pol. VII. 10. 1329 a 40-b2; Pol. VIII. 5. 1340 b 5 f.; Eth. Nic. VII. 12. 1152 b 1 f.
[6] Pol. III. 8. 1279 b 12-15.   [7] Walter, op. cit. 538, 542.
[8] Ibid. 543.   [9] Ibid. 540 f.   [10] Ibid. 548 f.

retical knowledge, were fiercely attacked by Teichmüller.[1]

Teichmüller proves the homogeneity of practical philosophy and prudence from the following four grounds. In the first place, ethics and politics are concerned with the same objects as prudence is; and likewise with poetics and art. Though ethics and politics are different in that the one is concerned with the happiness and virtues of individuals, and the other with those of nations or states,[2] they are similarly concerned with human conduct, and both are the knowledge which regulates conduct through rules, bringing about human good.[3] Ethical and political cognition contributes much to life, just as the archer who aims at a mark may hit upon what is right.[4] But practical intellect or prudence is also concerned with human good and evil,[5] aims at the good of human conduct,[6] and regulates or employs other practical faculties for this end.[7] In other words, prudence recognizes the worth in general of life, and is not a mere subordinate faculty of practice. Ethical and political cognitions are intellectual as well as practical, their end being to serve for conduct, i.e., to be good for individual cases;[8] the universal knowledge relevant to them must thus be applied to individual cases. For example, together with the universal knowledge about what the best constitution and the best legislation for each nation should be, there is needed the special knowledge, how a state can be governed.[9] Prudence also must involve universal knowledge and its application. If it is lacking in universal knowledge, it will remain a mere particular act and will be unable to indicate an infallible direction for our life.

In the second place, politics and ethics have the same content as prudence. Since prudence is manifest in consideration, each prudent decision forms a practical inference. But, the minor premiss of this practical inference being indefinite in each case, its essential contents must be determined by the major premiss. This major premiss exhibits the constant state of prudence, and characterizes a φρόνιμος, as distinguished from a clever man or a mediocrity. Prudence shows us the highest good. Now the practical good exists not in actuality, but only in potentiality, as the end which is aimed at. For this end, the prudent man must recognize every

---

[1] Teichmüller, Neue Studien zur Geschichte der Begriffe. III. 12-35.
[2] Eth. Nic. I. 1. 1094 b 7.   [3] Ibid. b 4.   [4] Ibid. a 22.
[5] Ibid. IV. 5. 1140 b 4.   [6] Ibid. 10. 1142 b 22.   [7] Ibid. 5. 1140 a 25.
[8] Ibid. 7. 1141 b 3.   [9] Pol. IV. 1. 1288 b 25; 1288 b 35.

means. This is the very knowledge that forms the contents of ethics, since this is what prudence has to do with, the contents of ethics and politics are contained in the activity of prudence. One would exhibit a gross ignorance of Aristotle's thought, by reducing ethics and politics to some knowledge other than prudence. It is because moderns mistakenly suppose knowledge and insight to be objectively found in books, that they are led to assume such a science of practice. Being a man of antiquity, Aristotle did not know any ἠθική or πολιτική that were not at once the virtue of φρόνησις. Thus, prudence necessarily involves knowledge of the individual as well as the universal.[1]

In the third place, ethics and politics have the same method as prudence. Unlike theoretical science, these practical sciences are wanting in exact necessity and must be content with mere probability. Richness and courage may sometimes result in harm, hence the belief arises that moral law is merely conventional and not natural.[2] Further, since ethics and politics are not self-sufficient, but aim at some sort of conduct, it would be vain only to know. This is also the reason why these sciences cannot attain a strict exactitude.[3] For, the good as the object of practical knowledge is not so definite as the object of the theoretial sciences; it depends upon the particular subject, and is different in each case; resolution requires not only a major premiss, but also a minor one, the major premiss itself is not constant, but suffers modifications in each case.[4] Consequently, ethics and politics have no more exactness than prudence has. In order to gain universal knowledge, one must have sufficient experience, moral will, continence, and virtue. Only under these conditions are political and ethical theories really appreciated. The word σωφροσύνη means to σῳζεῖν the φρόνησις, i.e. to preserve prudence. Indulgence does not corrupt mathematical insight, but ruins moral assurance,[5] because we may preserve or lose prudence through pleasure and pain. Young men have only little experience, so that they can neither appreciate or use the ideas in a book, nor have prudence. A boy may be a mathematician, but not a wise man:[6] he may speak about morality but is unable to have a firm belief in what is right.

[1] Eth. Nic. VI. 5. 1140 a 27.   [2] Ibid. I. 1. 1094 b 12.
[3] Ibid. II. 2. 1103 b 26.   [4] Ibid. 1103 b 34.
[5] Ibid. VI. 5. 1140 b 11   [6] Ibid. I. 1. 1095 a 2; VI. 9. 1142 a 11.

In the fourth place, and finally, Aristotle himself uses πολιτική and φρόνησις in the same meaning. He says in the *Ethica Nicomachea*:[1] "Politics and prudence are the same state of mind, but their essence is not the same. Of the wisdom concerned with the city, the prudence which plays a controlling part is legislative prudence, while that which is related to this as particulars to their universal is known by the general name politics; this has to do with action and deliberation, for a decree is a thing to be carried out in the form of an individual act. This is why the exponents of this art are alone said to 'take part in politics', for these alone 'do things' as manual labourers 'do things'. Prudence also is identified especially with that form of it, which is concerned with a man himself—with the individual: and this is known by the general name 'prudence'; of the other kinds, one is called household management, another legislation, the third politics, and of the latter, one part is called deliberative and the other judicial." This may be illustrated as follows:

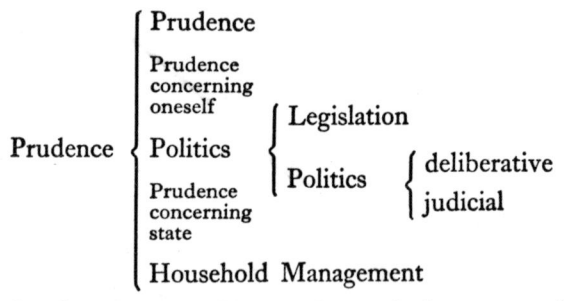

$$\text{Prudence} \begin{cases} \text{Prudence} \\ \text{Prudence concerning oneself} \\ \text{Politics} \begin{cases} \text{Legislation} \\ \text{Politics} \begin{cases} \text{deliberative} \\ \text{judicial} \end{cases} \end{cases} \\ \text{Prudence concerning state} \\ \text{Household Management} \end{cases}$$

Aristotle adopting this usual terminology as technical terms, calls attention to the fact that they are all founded upon the same habit, and censures the man who pretends to prudence without the knowledge of politics and household management. He calls ethical theory politics, in so far as individual prudence requires political wisdom.[2] There is no principle of politics and ethics other than πολιτική or φρόνησις as Walter presumes; these two sciences are regarded by Aristotle as to be studied just for the sake of conduct.[3] If, as Walter holds, ethics is a theoretical science, and πολιτική as the vitue of the statesman aims at individual act, Aristotle would by no means have identified the problems and

---

[1] Ibid. VI. 8. 1141 b 23.   [2] Ibid. 1141 b 25.
[3] Ibid. II. 2. 1103 b 26.

requirements of ethics with those of a practical statesman. In reality, Aristotle says that a true statesman is thought to endeavour especially for virtue, because he wants to make citizens good and obedient to laws[1]. Further, he says, the study of ethics is the work of πολιτική[2] and the problems of ethics require more knowledge of the soul than medical science does; accordingly, a statesman also requires the study of the soul for practical purposes. Farther precision, he adds, may be attained by strict theoretical psychology, but exceeds the area of ethical research.[3] In the first half of this statement, Aristotle states the necessity of psychological study for a statesman, and in the second half, he says that precise psychological study is beyond ethical research. There exists therefore no essential difference between the cognitions of the statesman and the cognitions of ethics. Of course, a real statesman does not always possess ethical knowledge; Aristotle only talks about the ideal of the statesman. Just as there is no medical science without the art of a physician, and there is no geometry apart from a geometrician, so there is no politics apart from the soul of a statesman. Aristotle says that every artist should, like a statesman, first, recognize the best form, secondly, consider what form is suitable for a man or a society, and thirdly, how one should produce this form and preserve it; and he observes that a practical statesman can dispense with political science[4] as little as with practical talent. These conditions, however, are not satisfied by any man, or a man of practice, but require the philosophical scholarship which has been credited since Socrates and Plato. In order to live well as a citizen or a private person, one requires philosophical contemplation about morals and politics, instead of the rhetorical art of a sophist or the mere experience of a practical statesman. It would, however, be a paradox, if it were a theoretical philosophy that is required for life. What is required must be the practical philosophy which aims at conduct or life rather than mere knowledge. Aristotle's Ethics and Politics present it; hence it is called philosophical prudence or political philosophy.[5] He maintains, none the less, that men, if they would master these sciences, also require natural endowments just as does practical wisdom or prudence.[6] For, man can neither rightly

---

[1] Ibid. I. 13. 1102 a 6.   [2] Ibid. 1102 a 12.   [3] Ibid. 1102 a 18.
[4] Pol. IV. 1. 1288 b 16; b 25.   [5] Top. VIII. 14. 163 b 9.
[6] Eth. Nic. III. 7. 1114 b 6; VI. 5. 1140 b 17; VI. 13. But, these references of Teichmüller seem to be insufficient for proving the point.

love and hate, nor recognize and choose what is good, without ethical virtues. So that in order to be good, it is not enough to obey the words of a wise man, just as one may only obey the words of a physician in order to be healthy. In moral virtue, knowledge and intention are more important than obedience. Moral intention is given through ethical virtues and makes the end of conduct right, while prudence or practical wisdom indicates the means for this end. This cognition, being philosophical, is displayed in the form of syllogism, which is found in the Ethics. The rightness of the principle or the major premiss depends upon ethical virtue, for we know what habit is the end and the highest good, only through our virtues. The principle is recognized only through moral intellect or prudence, and this syllogism is practical rather than theoretical, for its conclusion results in conduct and in one's way of life, instead of mere knowledge.[1]

These arguments of Teichmüller for the identification of the cognitive function in ethics and politics with prudence seems to me nearly perfect and satisfactory. In short, the classification of the varieties of $ἐπιστήμη$ by Aristotle is, both in its form and matter, the classification of kinds of knowledge in general and not of science. Practical and productive $ἐπιστημαί$ are by no means theoretical knowledge, but practical and productive through and through. They are different from experience only in the point that they are master-arts: they are architectonic. Now, the essence of knowledge is correlative with its object; just as knowledge about number and heavenly bodies cannot be practical, so the cognition of virtues and constitutions cannot be theoretical. Thus the analysis of knowledge agrees with that of intellect, and will be summarized as follows:[1]

$$νοῦς\ διάνοια\ ἐπιστήμη \begin{cases} ἐπιστημονική \\ (θεωρητική) \\ \\ λογιστική \\ (βουλευτική) \\ (δοξαστική) \end{cases} \begin{cases} \begin{cases} νοῦς \\ ἐπιστήμη \\ σοφία \end{cases} \begin{cases} πρώτη\ φιλοσοφία \\ μαθηματική \\ φυσική \end{cases} \\ \\ \begin{matrix} πρακτική \\ —φρόνησις \end{matrix} \begin{cases} ἠθική \\ πολιτική \\ οἰκονομική \end{cases} \\ \\ \begin{matrix} πιοητική \\ —τέχνη \end{matrix} \begin{cases} ποιητική \\ ῥητορική \end{cases} \end{cases}$$

[1] Eth. Nic. VI. 13. 1144 a 31.

§ 2. *ΔΟΞΑ* AND *ΔΟΞΑΣΤΙΚΟΝ* PART

The cognitive faculty is generally called either νοῦς, ἐπιστήμη or διάνοια in a wider sense, and is divided into the theoretical and the practical; the one being called ἐπιστημονική or θεωρητική, and the other λογιστική or δοξαστική. As for the δοξαστική, it is doubtful whether we should understand by it practical intellect or not. The distinction between ἐπιστήμη and δόξα being most emphasized by Socrates and Plato, it is quite natural that the classification of intellect into the ἐπιστημονική and the δοξαστική should have been adopted by Aristotle at first. But we must refrain from the hasty conclusion that this is a distinction between theoretical and practical knowledge. Rather we should go back to Plato and investigate the concept of δόξα in opposition to ἐπιστήμη.

This pair of concepts was a favorite subject of discussion for Socrates,[2] and it is argued that in Plato's dialogues the interpretation of these terms differed according to the date of the dialogue.[3] In the works of Plato's early or middle period, such as the *Phaedo* and the *Republic*, ἐπιστήμη and δόξα are clearly distinguished both in their objects and in their value. Besides ideas, which are real being, and perfect not-being, there are also changeable phenomena or the world of generation. The knowledge of ideas is ἐπιστήμη, and not-being is quite unknowable while the changeable world of phenomena is the object of αἴσθησις and δόξα, i.e., sensation and opinion. Opinion is a kind of cognition which comes from sensation. Consequently, sensation and opinion stand, in respect of cognitive value, between knowledge and ignorance. "They are darker than knowledge, but clearer than ignorance."[4] Considered in reference to their subjects, sensation and opinion are inferior, because they are not the pure function of the soul, but come from the impinging of bodily elements upon it.[5] In the

---

[1] Cf. the classification in Régis's L'opinion selon Aristote, 62. The qualification of λογιστικόν and δοξαστικόν is divergent from mine. This point will be examined critically further on.
[2] Phaed. 96.
[3] Burnet, Greek Philosophy, I. 248; Taylor, Plato, 339.
[4] Rep. 477, 478.   [5] Phaed 53.

Republic, ἐπιστήμη and διάνοια form νόησις as the cognition of being, while πίστις and εἰκασία form δόξα as the cognition of generation.[1]

This thought of Plato's, however, is said to have been remarkably changed after the *Theaetetus*. Sensation, being still inseparable from the function of the soul, is esteemed rather higher,[2] only it is not the function of the independent soul, but that of the soul acting through the body. On the other hand, opinion is assimilated to knowledge,[3] which is cognition through the independent soul, and its characteristic is to be seen in talking with oneself.[4] In the *Sophist*, which is written in the same period as the *Theaetetus*, monologue is assumed to be the function of intellect in general, while opinion is esteemed as the complete reality of intellect, since it, in contrast to monologue, involves affirmation and negation.[5] The expression of opinion is a sentence, which is either true or false.[6] "Opinion" seems here to express almost the same thing as "judgement" in general.

How, then should right opinion be distinguished from knowledge? We cannot find the precise answer[7] in the *Theaetetus*, except in the hypothesis[8] that "the true opinion accompanied by λόγος is knowledge, but what is without λόγος is outside of knowledge. What has no λόγος is not known, but what has λόγος is knowable." This idea is, however, already seen in the early works such as the *Meno* and the *Symposium*. According to the *Meno*, true opinion and knowledge are essentially different, though not different practically.[9] Opinion makes everything good and beautiful, as far as it remains in us, but it is apt to escape from our mind; it becomes knowledge, only when "secured" by reasoning as to cause.[10] Also in the *Symposium*, right opinion for which the holder is incapable of giving a reason, is not knowledge.[11] Opinion "is awakened into knowledge by putting questions."[12] In the *Theaetetus*, in spite of the minute investigation about the meaning of λόγος which is the mark distinguishing knowledge from true opinion, there is not a definition of this word; but it is conjectured

---

[1] Rep. 533 f.
[2] Theaet. 184. In the Republic, the subject of sensation is the body, while in the Theaetetus and the Sophist, it is the soul which acts through various kinds of sense organs.
[3] Theaet. 187.   [4] Ibid. 189 E.   [5] Soph. 263 E.
[6] Ibid. 264 A.   [7] Theaet. 201 ff.   [8] Ibid. 201 C-D.
[9] Meno. 79 C.   [10] Ibid. 98 A.   [11] Symp. 202 A.   [12] Meno. 86 E.

from the foregoing passage, that it means the process of inference or its expression, while opinion alone is nothing but an immediate assertion or a belief without reason, so that its reality would be also accidental.

Though it is said that the concept δόξα has suffered a remarkable change after Plato's middle period, we cannot recognize any conspicuous change except that the subject of opinion has come to be regarded as a pure soul. It is true that, in the *Theaetetus*, the thought in the *Phaedo* and the *Republic* that characterizes opinion as concerned with unreal objects does not come in front. No doubt, this signifies the decay of Plato's ἀνάμνησις-theory in contrast to his new higher appreciation of the phenomenal world. But we would prefer to see a change of viewpoint, rather than a transition of thought, between these two theories of opinion. In the *Phaedo*, opinion and knowledge were distinguished in that the one is concerned with provisional phenomena, and the other with eternal ideas. Whereas in the *Theaetetus*, the distinction turns on the form of cognition rather than the object. We may recognize in such a change of measure a higher estimation of phenomena and of opinion. But this does not necessarily mean that the distinction of δόξα and ἐπιστήμη through their objects was given up by Plato in his later period. We must notice that the formal distinction of opinion and knowledge through λόγος is not limited to the later period represented by the *Theaetetus*, but is also more distinctly stated in the early works such as the *Meno* and the *Symposium*. In those early works, opinion is regarded to be potential knowledge, while in the *Theaetetus* and the *Sophist*, it is called the completion of thinking. But the discrepancy here is a mere appearance, and there is no real change of thought. Opinion is potential and less complete than knowledge as far as it is not corroborated through reason, yet it is a complete thinking as far as it is presumed as a definite assertion. It involves the risk of falsehood because it is not reflective of its process of thinking, so that, being in a sense the completion of thinking, it may form a hypothesis when combined with sensation.[1]

Plato's conception of knowledge and opinion considered above makes a great contribution to our inquiry. In Aristotle too, opinion is opposed to knowledge: the latter is regarded as the cogni-

---

[1] Soph. 264 B.

tion of eternal things,[1] while the former is concerned with facts which are not necessary.[2] This is evidently a continuation of Plato's thought in the *Phaedo*. Opinion and knowledge are also distinguished not through their objects but through the modes of cognition. There is knowledge, when we recognize that something necessarily belongs to something else through its essence, but there is only opinion when we recognize that it belongs accidentally to the same thing.[3] Thus the distinction between opinion and knowledge is similar to that between false and true opinions, so that true opinion is assimilated to knowledge: this concept of opinion is just what we found in the *Theaetetus*. The first distinction, viz., through the objects, is not reconcilable with the second, viz., that through the modes of cognition. Aristotle himself admits that the object of knowledge is in a sense, though not absolutely, the same as that of opinion, just as the object of true opinion is the same as that of false opinion. For instance, the diagonal of a triangle may be either the object of knowledge, i.e., when it is studied essentially, or the object of opinion, when studied as an accidental fact. In the same way, animal is the object of knowledge when treated as the essence of man, but the object of opinion, when considered as the accidental attribute of him.[4] That is to say, the object of knowledge is, properly speaking, the necessary being which cannot be otherwise than it is, and the object of opinion is what can be otherwise; but in its subjective appearance, one may have an opinion about necessary being as well.

Opinion, being thus the cognition of things which can be otherwise, or of things considered as capable of being otherwise, may be sometimes true and sometime false,[5] but subjectively it is a judgement attended by conviction.[6] It presupposes an inference,[7] lacking only in the real ground of its conviction or in the actual pro-

---

[1] An. Post. I. 2. 71 b 9-12, 15; Eth. Nic. IV. 3. 1139 b 20-24; cf. An. Post. I. 4. 73 a 21;   I. 6. 74 b 5; I. 8. 75 b 21.

[2] An. Post. I. 33. 88 b 30-89 a 4; cf. Met. VII. 15. 1039 b 34; IX. 10. 1051 b 14; Eth. Nic. VI. 5. 1140 b 27.

[3] An. Post. I. 33. 89 a 17-b 23.

[4] An. Post. I. 33. 89 a 11 ff.

[5] An. Post. I. 33. 89 a 5;   IV. 19. 100 b 7; De An. III.3. 428 a 19; Eth. Nic. VI. 3. 1139 b 17;   Met. X. 6. 1062 b 33;   De Int. 14. 23 a 38.

[6] De An. III. 3. 428 a 20, 22;   Eth. Eud. VII. 2. 1235 b 29.

[7] De An. III. 3. 428 a 22 f.

cess of inference;[1] it is no more than a dogmatic conclusion.[2] Theoretically, it has comparatively a low value, but practically, it is as effective as knowledge,[3] because practice is concerned with the individual and what can be otherwise.[4] Yet it would be a hasty conclusion, if one should infer from this, that opinion is the cognition of individual things, or is concerned only with practical objects.

It is true that the object of knowledge is the universal,[5] whereas what moves us is opinion concerning individual things.[6] But opinion is not only concerned with individual things, as there are also some universal opinions. For instance, in Eth. Nic. VII. 5,[7] both the major and the minor premisses of theoretical and practical inferences are called opinions—the one being universal, and the other individual, opinion. The universal is such as "All sweet food should not be tasted", while the individual is such a perceptive judgement as "This is sweet". In De An. III. 11,[8] it is said that not a universal opinion but an individual one moves animals. This shows evidently that opinion should not be limited to individual judgement, but that there is also universal opinion.[9] On the other side, knowledge is taken as the cognition of the universal, and applied not only to theoretical but also to practical objects. The practical cognition which was called universal opinion is in this terminology called knowledge. For instance, in Eth. Nic. X. 9 :[10]—"But the details can be best looked after, one by one, by a doctor or gymnastic instructor or any one else who has the general knowledge of what is good for everyone or for people of a certain kind (for the sciences both are said to be and are, concerned with what is universal); .... it will perhaps be agreed that if a man does wish to become master of an art or science he must go to the universal, and come to know it as well as possible; for, as we have said, it is with this that the sciences

[1] Eth. Nic. VI. 12. 1143 b 11.
[2] Ibid. 10. 1142 b 13.   [3] Ibid. 12. 1143 b 11-14. cf. p. 218, n. 10.
[4] Met. I. 1. 981 a 17; Eth. Nic. III. 1. 1110 a 13; b 6; VI. 8. 1141 b 16; Pol. II. 8. 1269 a 12.
[5] Met. XI. 1. 1059 b 25; 2. 1060 b 19; III. 6. 1003 a 15; XIII. 9. 1089 b 5; 10. 1086 b 33; An. Post. I. 31. 87 b 38; De An. II. 5. 417 b 23; Eth. Nic. VI. 6. 1146 b 31; X. 10. 1180 b 15.
[6] De An. III. 11. 434 b 16.   [7] Eth. Nic. VII. 5. 1147 a 25.
[8] De An. III. 11. 434 a 19.   [9] Cf. Régis, op. cit. 134.
[10] Eth. Nic. XI. 10. 1180 b 13; cf. Eth. Nic. II. 5. 1106 b 5.

are concerned. And surely he who wants to make men, whether many or few, better, by his care must try to become capable of legislating, if it is through laws that we can become good. For to get any one whatever—any one who is put before us—into the right condition is not for the first chance comer; if any one can do it, it is the man who knows, just as in medicine and all other matters which give scope for care and prudence."

We can see from the above quotation that though knowledge is the cognition of the universal, it may also be applied to productive activities such as healing and gymnastics, as well as to practical activities such as politics and education. Although the things which can be otherwise than they are may be individuals, still it is possible to have universal cognition about the genus of such things, and such cognition is called either knowledge or opinion.

That the cognition of productive and practical affairs may be universal as well as individual, was already explained by Teichmüller's argument. Prudence is not a mere experience that meets individual circumstances, but also reaches a universal and master cognition;[1] a prudent man *par excellence* is the man who knows the essence of virtue and the highest end of life,[2] and lives a harmonious life.[3] A good disposition without practical wisdom, is merely a natural virtue and even not ethical.[4] Prudence, being the principle of ethical virtues, or that which gives λόγος to the irrational soul,[5] involves, of course, a universal cognition.[6] The Ethics and

[1] Eth. Nic. IV. 8. 1141 b 21-23; Met. I.2. 982 a 14 ff.; 30 ff.; Eth. Nic. VI. 12. 1143 b 4; cf. Teichmüller, Studien. etc. 224 f.; Pol. VI. 3. 1325 b 14; Newmann's Note on Arist. Pol. *ad loc.;* Plato, Pol. 259 C, E.

[2] Eth. Nic. VI. 13. 1144 a 31 ff.; VI. 5. 1140 b 16 ff.; a 25 ff.

[3] Eth. Nic. VI. 2. 1139 a 26 ff.; VI. 13. 1144 b 24, 31; Rhet. III. 16. 1417 a 26. X. 8. 1178 a 16 ff.; Trendelenburg, op. cit. II. 384; Hartenstein, Historisch-Philosophische Abhandlungen, 279.   [4] Eth. Nic. VI. 13. 1144 b 1 ff.

[5] Prudence is the right reason which makes desire moderate (Eth. Nic. VI. 13. 1144 b 28). It is a kind of intellectual virtue, which is in conformity with ethical virtues. Rhet. I. 9. 1366 b 29; 7. 1364 b 18; 1363 b 14; De Sensu 1. 437 a 1; Top. V. 7. 137 a 14; Eth. Nic. VI. 12. 1143 b 15; 5. 1140 b 26; 13. 1144 a 1; Top. V. 6. 136 b 11; VI. 6. 145 a 29. Namely, it is virtue in the secondary sense, that gives order to the desiring part, or to the irrational part in the secondary sense.

[6] Although Prudence is said to concern with particulars (Eth. Nic. VI. 12. 1143 a 34), it is also evident that it does not involve universal knowledge, for elsewhere it is said to concern itself not only with the universal but also with the particular (Eth. Nic. VI. 8. 1141 b 14).

Politics of Aristotle are nothing but the realization of this master prudence.[1] Similarly with art. It is generally the principle of production; and production, being concerned with what can be otherwise, yet contains various cognitions from the individual and immediate faculty of production to the most general knowledge of master (architectonic) art.[2] This, for its part, is considered to be essentially a universal cognition.[3]

But though there are universal knowledges about production and practice, they are restricted through being concerned with what can be otherwise. Compared with the practical wisdom of immediate action, they have of course much higher cognitive value, yet they are after all, inferior to such necessary knowledge of eternal beings as metaphysics.[4] Such a cognition might be called general opinion rather than knowledge. But the genus of what can be otherwise, is more constant than individual beings. It is just in this respect, that cognition of such genera is called knowledge in a derivative sense.

Nor should opinion and knowledge be distinguished as practical and theoretical. Opinion concerns what can be otherwise, which are also the affairs of practice, yet it does not follow from this, that opinion is practical cognition. For, such an inference would commit the fallacy of undistributed middle. What can be otherwise is not always practical; natural phenomena are surely what can be otherwise and not necessary, yet they are not the object of practice or production. Production and practice concern what are in our power, whereas in nature, the principle of movement and change is contained in things themselves.[5] And nature is the object of theoretical rather than of practical cognition.[6] For example, it is a general fact that the sum of the inner angles of a triangle is two right angles, and the cognition of it is universal and theoretical; while although the fact that the particular angle of this triangle is a right angle is an individual fact, its cognition is not practical, but theoretical, and this particular triangle is the object of theoretical knowledge. In the same way, rainfall is not eternal and constant, but temporary and what can be otherwise,

---

[1] Eth. Nic. I. 1. 1094 a 24-b 11.   [2] Eth. Nic. I. 1. 1094 a 6-15.
[3] Met. I. 1. 981 a 5-12; 981 a 12-17.
[4] Eth. Nic. I. 3. 1094 b 11-27; Eth. Nic. II. 2. 1103 b 34 ff.
[5] Eth. Nic. VI. 4. 1140 a 10-16; Met. VI. 1. 1025 b 18-24.
[6] Met. VI. 1. 1025 b 25-28; 1026 a 10-12.

nevertheless it is a matter of nature that it will rain tomorrow, because we cannot voluntarily make rainfall. Consequently cognition about rainfall is surely an opinion, yet theoretical rather than practical.

Aristotle really distinguishes προαίρεσις and δόξα in that whereas will is concerned with action, "opinion is thought to relate to all kinds of things, no less to eternal things and impossible things than to the things in our own power, and it is distinguished by its falsity or truth, not by its badness or goodness, while will is distinguished rather by the latter".[1] Here opinion is explained as if it were a kind of theoretical knowledge. It is not only once that we find it so explained: in making the distinction between the excellence of deliberation and that of opinion, he says, "The correctness of opinion is truth; and at the same time everything that is an object of opinion is already determined."[2] Now the first sentence involves more than what we need. It will be enough for our present purpose to look at the words "No less...... than to things in our own power". For it is enough to make evident that the object of opinion is not limited to practical affairs which are in our own power, but also the things beyond our power. We feel rather a little embarrassed when we find Aristotle referring to these objects as "eternal things and impossible things", for, if these words mean "what are necessary and cannot be otherwise", cognition about them should be knowledge rather than opinion. But what is here meant by "impossible things" seems to be rather what are beyond our power and cannot be realized by us, and what are paradoxical and cannot exist by their nature. These are nothing but the impossible things he speaks of when he says, "For will cannot relate to impossibles, ...but there may be a wish even for impossibles, i.e. for immortality".[3] Now if immortality as the object of wish be an example of the "impossible", the "eternal things" which were mentioned along with the impossibles, would be natural phenomena which appear independent of us, e.g. weather, or the angle of a particular triangle. We hear also Aristotle saying that the demonstration or knowledge about the eclipse of the moon is knowledge of the eternal, as far as it often happens, but of the particular, as far as it does not happen usually.[4] This

---

[1] Eth. Nic. III. 4. 1111 b 30.
[2] Eth. Nic. VI. 10. 1142 b 11; cf. 1142 b 34.
[3] Eth. Nic. III. 4. 1111 b 22.   [4] An. Post. I. 8. 75 b 33; cf. ibid. 21 ff.

might perhaps be regarded as an example of the eternal things to which theoretical opinion is related.

Though Aristotle often states opinion to be theoretical cognition, we cannot agree with Walter who wants to limit it to theoretical cognition.[1] For opinion is related to what can be otherwise, which however forms the region where practice has its being, and there is no ground for excluding practical affairs from the objects of opinion. Plato assumed the effect of opinion to be chiefly to lead practice where knowledge is lacking,[2] and Aristotle also describes opinion often as practical cognition.[3] As opinion is itself a cognition and is measured by truth and falsehood, not by goodness and badness, so sensation is itself a mere discrimination and not the immediate efficient cause of action.[4] We should not conclude from these facts that opinion and sensation are merely theoretical cognitions.

At any rate, opinion being the cognition that is concerned with what can be otherwise, its objects are restricted neither to individuals nor practical phenomena alone. It may be universal and theoretical as well. Shall we then infer that the intellect which is characterized by the adjective δοξαστικόν is not necessarily practical? Walter actually thought so. He refused any practical function whatever to the δοξαστικόν part, since he limited opinion to theoretical cognition alone. Hence Walter cannot follow the common view that identifies the δοξαστικόν part, to which Aristotle attributes prudence and cleverness, with the practical knowledge called deliberation. Therefore, according to the first classification above mentioned, which identifies the rational part in the secondary sense with the irrational part in the secondary sense, he takes the δοξαστικόν as the rational part in the primary sense, i.e., the rational part which involves both theoretical knowledge and practical knowledge.[5] But, in the first place, we should not restrict the concept of δόξα to theoretical cognition, and in the

---

[1] Walter, op. cit. 437 ff.   [2] Meno 99.

[3] Eth. Nic. VI. 11. 1143 a 12-15; Eth. Nic. VII. 5. 1147 a 25-28; 9. 1151 a 16 f.; 10. 1151 b 3 f.; Eth. Eud. II. 10. 1226 a 4-15; De An. III. 3. 427 b 21-24; Eth. Nic. III. 4. 1112 a 4; a 9-11; I. 12. 1101 a 24; 15. 1128 b 24; VI. 9. 1142 a 8.

[4] De An. III. 7. 431 a 8; 9. 432 a 15-17; cf. An. Post. II. 19. 99 b 35; Motu An. 6. 700 b 20.

[5] There are but few examples where the concept δοξαστικὸν μέρος seems to indicate practical intellect in the same way as βουλευτική or λογιστική. The remarkable example is found in the end of Eth. Nic. VI. 5, where making a

second place, even if it involves theoretical knowledge as well as practical cognition, we must investigate more carefully whether the word "δοξαστικόν" may not be the determinant of practical knowledge.

distinction between prudence and art, Aristotle says that "there is the virtue of art, but not of prudence, which is itself a kind of virtue", and further, Eth. Nic. VI. 5. 1140 b 25-30: δυοῖν δ' ὄντοιν μεροῖν τῆς ψυχῆς τῶν λόγον ἐχόντων, θατέρου ἂν εἴη ἀρετή, τοῦ δοξαστικοῦ· ἥ τε γὰρ δόξα περὶ τὸ ἐνδεχόμενον ἄλλως ἔχειν καὶ ἡ φρόνησις. ἀλλὰ μὴν οὐδ' ἕξις μετὰ λόγου μόνον· σημεῖον δ'ὅτι λήθη τῆς τοιαύτης ἕξεως ἐστι, φρονήσεως δ' οὐκ ἔστιν,

The δοξαστικόν is usually taken as the practical and calculative part which is opposed to the theoretical and scientific. This is reasonable in reference to the fact that the sixth book which treats of prudence, enumerates the five cardinal virtues of intellect, among which art and prudence are regarded as the representative of practical cognition. This is also congruent with the following statement in Eth. Nic. IV. 13. 1144 b 14-17: ὥστε καθάπερ ἐπὶ τοῦ δοξαστικοῦ δύο ἐστὶν εἴδη, δεινότης καὶ φρόνησις, οὕτω καὶ ἐπὶ τοῦ ἠθικοῦ δύο ἐστί, τὸ μὲν ἀρετὴ φυσικὴ τὸ δ' ἡ κυρία, καὶ τούτων ἡ κυρία οὐ γίνεται ἄνευ φρονήσεως. It seems that τὸ ἠθικόν means the irrational part in the secondary sense, or the desiring part, and τὸ δοξαστικόν means the rational part in the secondary sense, which is another side of the desiring part.

To Rassow and Walter, however, who attach importance to the determination of opinion as assertion rather than inquiry (cf. 1142 b 13), and take opinion as theoretical cognition, it appears to be contradictory to take the δοξαστικόν part as practical intellect. Therefore, they attempt to solve the difficulty either through making the statement in 1144 b 14 an interporation by a later hand (Rassow, Arist. Forsch. 43-45, 30 f.), or by taking the δοξαστικόν as the rational part in general (Walter, op. cit. 437-450). According to the latter, Aristotle did not identify opinion with prudence in saying they are both concerned with what can be otherwise. The "two kinds of the rational part of the soul" do not refer to the ἐπιστημονικόν and the λογιστικόν but to the ἠθικόν and the δοξαστικόν. And this δοξαστικόν is synonymous with the διανοητικόν.

Walter admits that intellect is divided in Eth. Nic. VI.20; into two parts. But assuming these parts to indicate the ἐπιστημονικόν and the λογιστικόν, he requires to distinguish this division of intellect from that duopartite division of the soul mentioned above. Walter continues arguing, what Aristotle in the argument about ethical virtues talks about is, in fact, the two parts of the soul (Eth. Nic. VI. 13. 1144 a 5). Thus the δοξαστικόν part would seem to mean the διανοητικόν part rather than the βουλευτικόν. The βουλευτικόν and the ἐπιστημονικόν are parts not of the soul, but of intellect. Whereas in determinating what prudence is (VI. 5. 1140 b 25), what is necessary is not to take it as the virtue of calculation, but as an intellectual virtue distinct from ethical virtues and other intellectual virtues. For, as the context shows, the distinction of art and prudence is presupposed, in that the former is ἕξις μετὰ λόγου ἀληθοῦς ποιητική, while the

§ 3. PRACTICAL AND THEORETICAL COGNITIONS

This investigation must be extended also to the relation between ἐπιστήμη and ἐπιστημονικόν, θεωρία and θεωρητικόν βούλευσις and βουλευτικόν, etc. What in the world do these adjectives derived from special cognitive faculties mean, when they are applied to the determination of intellect ? No doubt,

latter ἕξις ἀληθής μετὰ λόγου πρακτική, — the adjective "true" determining in the one case "reason", in the other directly "habit". A "true" habit means just that which involves a "true" end. Art does not necessarily involve such a good end, while a good end is necessary for prudence; hence it is said that there is the virtue of art, but not the virtue of prudence. And in reference to the fact that the object of investigation hitherto were restricted to the ethical virtues, Aristotle here calls prudence merely virtue, as being more similar to ethical virtue than to art, which is rather intellectual (VI. 5. 1140 b 24). But, then, prudence must be distinguished from ethical virtue being itself none the less an intellectual virtue. On account of this, prudence is assigned to the δοξαστικόν part. The δοξαστικόν part, therefore, is opposed to the ἠθικόν rather than to the ἐπιστημονικόν. It is intellectual and not practical. Prudence is an intellectual habit, but is indivisible from the ethical vitrues. Unless one considers the δοξαστικόν part — to which prudence belongs — to be the intellectual as opposed to the ethical part, the statement "It is not a mere habit which is accompanied by reason" (1140 b 26), would be reduced to nonsense. This may be proved also from the statement in chapter 13. In the preceding chapter, φρόνησις and σοφία are assigned to different parts of the soul, ethical virtue constituting the third part. In this chapter, the nutritive part is further counted as the fourth. This shows that in the consideration of prudence and ethical virtue, the opposition of theoretical and practical intellect is deemphasized, being replaced by that of the intelllectual and the ethical. Aristotle did not enumerate other intellectual virtues than δεινότης and φρόνησις as belonging to the δοξαστικόν part. This seems to be favourable to the opinion that takes the δοξαστικόν part as practical intellect. But, Walter avoids the difficulty by seeing this enumeration as an instance of analogical relation between the natural and the ethical virtues, instead of the complete enumeration of the intellectual virtues. As regards Rassow's supposition that the statement about the δοξαστικόν part is an interpolation, one must ask why Aristotle called it δοξαστικόν in spite of the usual usage of δόξα. This might be because δόξα is concerned with what can be otherwise, but this fact cannot be the ground for prudence being the virtue of the δοξατικόν part. Thus Walter, rejecting Rassow's opinion, restricts the interpolation to the sentence 1140 b 27: ἥ τε γὰρ δόξα περὶ τὸ ἐνδεχόμενον ἄλλως ἔχειν καὶ ἡ φρόνησις, and conjectures that this is a note of a later scholar who misunderstood the real meaning. Walter gives notice that he himself misunderstood the δοξαστικόν for βουλευτικόν in the first half of his work (cf. op. cit. 438 n. 2. & 174).

these adjective forms are not merely synonymous with the nouns. It may rather be supposed that they mean derivative mental functions which are characterized in one way or another through the basic ones—ἐπιστήμη, δόξα, etc.—or a group of similar functions founded upon them. But, while, e.g., ἐπιστήμη expresses in its widest sense cognition in general, and in its strict sense theoretical knowledge, especially the reasoning faculty, ἐπιστημονική does not necessarily mean "theoretical", because of its being founded upon such a cognition or derived from it. ἐπιστημονικὴ διάνοια can mean theoretical knowledge, because it aims at that kind of knowledge rather than because it consists of it. This is more evident from the fact, that θεωρητική which is derived from θεωρία gets the meaning of "theoretical". θεωρία, of course, means cognition in general, as opposed to production and conduct—although production and conduct, involving cognition in the form of practical wisdom or art, are by no means irrational action. Yet the πρακτική or the ποιητική intellect means the knowledge which serves for and aims at production or conduct. Likewise when θεωρητική, which is derived from θεωρία, is applied to cognition, the latter means the self-sufficient thinking which aims at itself.[1] θεωρία is not only limited to theoretical thinking. Needless to say, the cognition as the moment of production and conduct is not theoretical knowledge, but it by no means follows from this that it is not thinking or it does not involve thinking at all. In Aristotle, θεωρεῖν is an essential moment of art no less than τεχναζεῖν, and he does talk about practical θεωρία or productive θεωρία.[2] Thinking sometimes aims at something other than itself. When it aims at production, it is productive knowledge or art; when it aims at conduct, it is practical wisdom or prudence. Only thinking for thinking's sake, is pure contemplation or theoretical knowledge. Just as the ἐπιστημονική intellect is the intellect which aims at ἐπιστήμη as the knowledge of necessary objects, so θεωρητική knowledge is the knowledge which aims at θεωρία itself. While θεωρία or thinking signifies cognition in general which is co-ordinate to practice and production, ἐπιστήμη or knowledge more frequently means necessary cognition as op-

---

[1] De An. III. 9. 433 a 14 f.; Eth. Eud. I. 5. 1216 b 9-25; Eth. Nic. I. 1. 1905 a 5 f.; II. 2. 1103 b 26-30; X. 10. 1179 a 35-b 2.
[2] Eth. Nic. VI. 7. 1141 a 25 f.; IV. 4. 1122 a 34 f.; b 8-10; X. 10. 1181 b 6-9; VI. 2. 1139 a 6-12.

posed to opinion. In spite of such a difference, θεωρία relates to θεωρητική, just as ἐπιστήμη does to ἐπιστημονική. So that, though the concept, θεωρητική ἐπιστήμη is impossible gramatically,[1] because it is a case of qualification by a superordinate or coordinate concept, logically it involves no difficulty, as far as we take the meaning of qualification as above. Logically, we might also say ἐπιστημονική ἐπιστήμη or θεωρητική ἐπιστήμη, but διανοητική ἐπιστήμη[2] or θεωρητική ἐπιστήμη[3] would have been preferred, in order to avoid reduplication.

Knowledge may, in a sense, be concerned with what can be otherwise, but properly speaking, it is the universal cognition of necessary objects. On the other side, theoretical cognition is qualified by the adjective ἐπιστημονική, i.e. scientific, which is derived from ἐπιστήμη—the cognition of necessary and universal beings.[4] The same state of affairs is found also in βουλευτική διάνοια, λογιστική διάνοια, as well as δοξαστική διάνοια, of which we have studied above. Deliberation[5] and calculation[6] are reasoning about practical affairs, just as knowledge is about theoretical affairs. They are not the intuition of the universal or the individual, but the mediation of the two extremes. Being the most important functions of intellect in production and practice, their corresponding adjectival terms— βουλευτική, λογιστική— are used as names for practical knowledge in general. But the situation is a little different with regard to opinion. As aforesaid, it may be no less theoretical than practical; its object being properly what can be otherwise, and its modes particular, yet it may in its secondary usage mean universal knowledge about necessary beings. Strictly speaking, opinion is a subjective and dogmatic

---

[1] In Top. VI. 11. 149 a 17, θεωρητικόν is called a differentia and ἐπιστήμη a genus, but this is not inconsistent with our saying. For, though θεωρία is a genus, θεωρητική may be a differentia, in the sense that thinking is aimed at.

[2] Met. V. 1. 1025 b 5.

[3] Met. XI. 7. 1064 b 2; Top. VI. 6. 145 a 15; VIII. 1. 157 a 10; Top. I. 2. 101 a 27 f.

[4] An. Post. I. 31. 88 a 5-7.

[5] Eth. Nic. III. 5. 1112 b 21-23; VI. 10. 1142 a 31; De Memor. 2. 453 a 14; Eth. Nic. VI. 2. 1139 a 12 f. We shall study the syllogistic form in the next chapter.

[6] Calculation and deliberation are used almost in the same meaning. Cf. Eth. Nic. VI. 10. 1142 b 2, 15; VI. 2. 1139 a 12; 5. 1140 a 30, 26; Phys. II. 9. 200 a 23; Eth. Eud. II. 1. 1220 a 1; Met. V. 5. 1015 a 33.

judgement about what can be otherwise, and in this respect, it is opposed to knowledge or science. In its cognitive value, it is inferior to knowledge, but practically, it is equivalent. Our practice and production have their existence in just such a region of being which can be otherwise, concerning such problems which must be managed through more or less subjective judgements. Opinion as such has its greatest *raison d'être* in this practical region. Thus the δοξαστικόν part seems to be the practical intellect in general as well as the βουλευτικόν part or the λογιστικόν part. We do not, however, call practical knowledge δοξαστικόν for the same reason that we call it reasoning or deliberative. Plato's division of cognition into knowledge and opinion was inherited by Aristotle, only the Platonic distinction is not simply adopted by Aristotle; rather, he used it as the basis of his distinction between theoretical and practical knowledge, with much modification and through a complicated process.

In short, Aristotle divided the cognitive faculty at first into the theoretical and the practical, calling the one ἐπιστημονικὴ διάνοια, scientific intellect, or θεωρητικὴ ἐπιστήμη, theoretical knowledge, the other βουλευτή, λογιστική, or δοξαστικὴ διάνοια, i.e. deliberative, reasoning, or opinion-making intellect. This practical intellect is subdivided into the practical and the productive, which also seems to presuppose Plato's classification. Plato set knowledge in opposition to opinion, taking the former as the cognition of eternal, necessary, and universal truth, and the latter that of temporary, accidental, and particular facts.[1] But he tried another classification from another point of view; viz. in the *Statesman* 258, he divided knowledge into the ἐπιστημονική, i.e. the cognitive, and the πρακτιμή, i.e. the practical, and subdivided the former into the κριτική, the discriminating, and the ἐπιτακτική, the imperative. This appears at first sight, like the distinction between theoretical and practical knowledge. But, in fact, the ἐπιτακτική being synonymous with the so-called ἀρχιτεκτονική, i.e. master art, it means rather universal knowledge which comprises both practical cognition and theoretical, so that the πρακτικὴ ἐπιστήμη which is opposed to this has not so wide a meaning as common usage gives it, but is rather the habitual and empirical cognition which immediately guides individual acts. The ἐπιστημονική and the πρακτική are opposed to each other as the theoreti-

[1] Pol. 258 f., 267.

cal is to the practical, while the κριτική and the ἐπιτακτική being the species of the former, exhibit the opposition of the universal to the particular.

Thus, according to the classification in the *Statesman*, universal knowledge about practice appears to be a theoretical knowledge. This is correspondent to Aristotle's oscilation in calling this kind of cognition sometimes opinion, and sometimes knowledge. Nevertheless we would not assume the science about practical affairs to be theoretical in the strict sense. What we find here is rather the disharmony of thought brought about through the complexity of classification into practice and theory on the one hand, and universal and particular on the other. Aristotle seems to have inherited Plato's thought with some modification, when he divided knowledge into the theoretical and the practical, and subdivided the latter into the productive and the practical in the strict sense, so that he finally admitted theoretical, practical, and productive knowledges. In other words, he summed up Plato's imperative knowledge in practical knowledge, and set discriminating knowledge in opposition to them, calling the one the practical, the other the theoretical. Besides, Aristotle reduced knowledge about individual natural phenomena to theoretical knowledge,[1] whereas in Plato, there was ambiguity as to how this kind of knowledge should be characterized. When Aristotle states that opinion and sensation are discriminating, he seems to imply that, they may be at least in part, if not entirely, theoretical cognition.

We have stated in detail the growth and development of cognitive functions in Chapter II. To resume this briefly, the development of the functions of the soul is conditioned by the way of life of the organism, and the qualitative differences of these functions are founded upon the quantitative differences of the latter. The evolution of functions is proportionate to the complexity of animals, or, in other words, to the temporal and spacial expansion of the environment. The cognitive function itself is continuously developed from unconscious functions such as nutrition and generation, and there rules also the law of continuity and accumulation among the cognitive functions themselves. Thus, at first appear the sensations necessary for life, such as touch and taste, then higher sensations such as smell, hearing, and sight. And as abstraction and synthesis proceed, representation emerges, which is somewhat

[1] Cf. p. 210, n. 1; p. 223, n. 6.

independent of the outward world. This grows, combined with the consciousness of time, itself being a kind of representation, to representations of higher grade such as memory, remembrance, and expectation; and these are organized into experience. When this becomes conceptual through analysis and symbolization, and forms a more extensive and compact system, we possess art. Art, being generally a system of concepts organized through law, is further classified into master art and lower skill, the one tending to science, while the other is contingent with experience. Art already involves science in a sense, but science acquires its independence by degrees. When this independence becomes complete, we have science purely for the sake of congnition itself, apart from any practical interest. This is theoretical knowledge.[1] Even theoretical knowledge involves particular congnition, yet it is characterized through being the cognition of the universal, especially the cognition of the most universal and ultimate principles or causes. In this sense, the highest theoretical knowledge is σοφία as the knowledge of principles; more concretely speaking, it is metaphysics or theology. Thus, theoretical cognition is the last in the process of development, but in respect of value, it is the first.[2] Whereas practical and productive cognitions, being the necessary foundations of theoretical knowledge, are yet, in their value, inferior to this.

The virtues of the theoretical and practical intellects are enumerated: they are τέχνη, i.e. art, ἐπιστήμη, i.e. knowledge, φρόνησις, i.e. prudence, σοφία, i.e. wisdom, and νοῦς, i.e. reason. There is also a difficulty in calling them virtues. What Aristotle states in Eth. Nic. VI. 3,[3] is as follows: "Let it be assumed that the states by virtue of which the soul possesses truth by way of affirmation or denial are five in number, i.e. art, knowledge, prudence, wisdom, and reason; we do not include judgement and opinion, because in these we may be mistaken." Of these five concepts, Prantl[4] assumes only prudence and wisdom to be virtues, excluding the others as mere faculties, viz., knowledge and reason are the moments of theoretical intellect, the one being reasoning, and the other the intuition of principles; wisdom is the virtue of these theoretical

---

[1] An. Post. II. 19. 100 a 3; Met. I. 1. 980 a 28; 981 b 13; cf. p. 114, n. 1.
[2] Met .I. 1. 981 b 30-982 a 1; cf. An. Post. I. 31. 88 a 4.
[3] Eth. Nic. VI. 3. 1139 b 14.
[4] Prantl, Ueber die dianoetischen Tugenden der nikomachischen Ethik. (cf. Rassow, Forschungen. 124 n. Stewart's note on 1139 b 14.)

faculties. On the other hand, he denies art to be a virtue, and makes wisdom the virtue of it, because Aristotle says that there may be the virtue of art, but not that of prudence, and further omits only art where he is enumerating the forms of cognition of truth. So, according to Prantl, the only virtue of the practical intellect is prudence, and it involves εὐβουλία, σύνεσίς, γνώμη, δεινότης, etc. Zeller,[1] opposing Prantl, points out that the subject of the sixth volume is declared in the first chapter to be the intellectual virtues and that while virtues are regarded as excellent habits, knowledge, reason and art, which Prantl excluded from virtue, are all said to be habits. Though Zeller's grounds of argument are not sufficient, there is no doubt that Prantl's view is not right. In the first place, the text which precedes the quotation states thus: "The work of both the intellectual parts, then, is truth. Therefore the states that are most strictly those in respect of which each of these parts will reach the truth are the virtues of the two parts." In succession to this, the third chapter in question continues, "Let us begin, then, from the beginning, and discuss these states once more." From this context alone, it is quite natural to take the five states enumerated as intellectual virtues. Besides, the remark that "We do not include judgement and opinion because in these we may be mistaken", seems precisely to mean that, while judgement and opinion are mere faculties, the other five habits are virtues. For if three of the above enumerated habits were mere facultes without value, there is no reason why judgement and opinion should be particularly excluded from the virtues, since both judgement and opinion may be true as well as false. With regard to art, we may solve the difficulty by assuming two usages—the one as meaning a faculty, and the other as meaning a virtue. Aristotle really uses these concepts more frequently as virtues than as mere faculties. To see the virtue of art in wisdom is, without doubt, the worst solution;[2] for then the classification of intellect into the theoretical, the practical, and the productive, would be utterly overthrown. It might rather more suitably reduceed to prudence; but strictly speaking, art is after all an independent virtue. In short, we assume the above stated five concepts as the representative virtues of intellect. I say representative, because there are also other subordinate virtues. Among the cardi-

[1] Zeller, op. cit. II. 2. 649 n.2.
[2] In Eth. Nic. VI. 7. 1141 a 9, the excellence of art is called σοφία, but this is merely an example of vulgar usage.

nal virtues, reason, knowledge, and wisdom are the virtues of theoretical intellect, prudence that of practical intellect in the strict sense, and art is the virtue of practical intellect in a wider sense, i.e. of productive intellect. In as much as our chief interest is in the cognitive functions, and not in the virtues, the above arguments have no great importance. Moreover in order to solve the problems of practice, it is not necessary to go in detail through all of these virtues, but it will be enough, if we survey the theoretical intellect in such a degree that we may therewith understand the structure of the practical intellect.

We have seen above that the theoretical intellect is divided into reason, knowledge, and wisdom. Reason is the intuition of principles, and knowledge the reasoning about the universal and the particular, while wisdom, being the incorporation of the two, is regarded as the most complete actuality of the theoretical intellect. The chief moment of cognition is surely knowledge or science, its form being inference. But the highset major premise of inference cannot be proved through inference.[1] It cannot but be comprehended immediately. This intuition of universal principles is the faculty of reason or νοῦς.[2] It resembles sensitive perception as far as it is intuitive, but is opposed to it, as far as it is the cognition of the universal. Wisdom is the synthesis of reason and knowledge.[3] It realizes itself in philosophy, which is the most complete system of theoretical cognition.[4]

Knowledge is the mediation of the universal and the particular, of which there are two possible forms. The one is deductive inference, which descends, from the universal to the particular, and it is called ἀπόδειξις,[5] i.e. demonstration. The other, inductive

[1] Eth. Nic. VI. 3. 1139 b 29-31; cf. An. Post. I. 31. 72 b 6, 18; Met. IV. 4. 1006 a 10; III. 21. 997 a 7; An. Post. I. 19. 82 a 7; 84 a 31; Eth. Nic. VI. 6.

[2] An. Post. I. 23. 84 b 39-85 a 1; IV. 19. 100 b 8-12; Eth. Nic. VI. 6. 1141 a 7; 12. 1143 a 35 -b 1.

[3] Eth. Nic. VI. 7. 1141 a 18-20; Met. I.1. 981 b 21.

[4] We have stated at the beginning of this chapter that φιλοσοφία does not always mean philosophy in the strict sense.

[5] Not all inferences that come down from general principles to particulars are demonstration; there are also those which are διαλεκτική. Demonstration is the true cognition which starts from a necessary premiss, while dialectic starts from either one of two contradictory positions. An. Pr. I.1. 24 a 30, 20, 23; b 13; cf. An. Post. II. 2. 72 a 10; 6. 74 b 10; An. Post. II. 23. 68 b 10; Met. V.5. 1015 b 7; VI. 15. 1039 b 31; An. Post. I. 4. 73 a 24; Eth. Nic. VI. 5. 1140 a 34.

inference,[1] ascends from the particular to the universal. The universal principles which form the major premise of demonstration might be considered to be grasped intuitively through reason. But it is only a formal principle that may be thus grasped *a priori;* other principles must rather be induced by experience.[2] Though metaphysics and physics are counted in theoretical science along with mathematics, the cognitions of their principles are considered to be radically different. The objects of mathematics being purely abstract, their principles are able to be recognized *a priori*, whereas in metaphysics and physics, the principles require experience, therefore, a young man may master mathematics, yet he cannot be a physicist or a philosopher.[3]

Since the premises of deductive inference are recognized through induction, knowledge must require not only reason as the faculty of knowing universals, but also intuition into individuals. We have assumed opinion and sensation to be the cognition of individuals. But, opinion is not a mere perception of immediate data, but an estimation about future or past phenomena or remote objects, presupposing, moreover, an unconscious or subconscious inference behind it. Therefore, the starting point of induction must be sensation rather than opinion.[4] Sensation is naturally near and akin to practical cognition, and becomes the principle of volition when it is accompanied by pleasure and pain. But sometimes it is rather assumed to be the element of theoretical cognition. In such an immediate intuition, the distinction between practice and theory is not too clear, so that it may be as well an element of practical intellect as of theoretical intellect.

[1] An. Post. I. 13. 81 a 40-b 1; IV. 7. 92 a 35; Phys. VIII. 1. 252 a 24; Met. I. 9. 992 b 33; VI. 1. 1025 b 15; XI. 7. 1064 a 9; Top. I. 12. 105 a 11-14; An. Pr. I. 25. 42 a 3; An. Post. I. 1. 71 a 5; II. 7. 92 a 35; I. 31. 88 a 2.

[2] Eth. Nic. VI. 3. 1139 b 28 f.; cf. Eth. Nic. I. 7. 1098 b 3; Rhet. II. 20. 1393 a 27.

[3] Eth. Nic. VI. 8. 1142 a 11-20. Here the relation between knowledge and age is considered in three stages. In the first place, pure abstract theory such as mathmatics needs no experience and is comprehensible even to youths. In the second place, the principles of physics and metaphysics are induced from experience, but requiring no ethical virtue, are comprehensible even to youths. In the third place, ethics and politics presuppose ethical virtues, which are fostered through protracted habituation, so that they are incomprehensible until one grows to a mature age. Cf. Eth. Nic. I. 7. 1098 b 3.

[4] Eth. Nic. I. 7. 1098 a 33-b 4; An. Post. II. 19. 100 b 3-5; cf. ibid. 2. 90 a 28; I. 31. 88 a 3.

But sensation is not stated particularly to be a kind of theoretical cognition. This is natural enough, because knowledge aims at universal cognition rather than individual application. Sensation is the medium of theoretical knowledge; we must start from it, but it is the beginning, not the end.[1] We must perceive the universal along with the individual. The cognition of the individual is not highly appreciated in the theoretical area, because it is most remote from the end of cognition.

In regard to the present subject of consideration, practical intellect is divided into the practical in a narrower sense, and the productive; their virtues being represented by art and prudence. But "art" is sometimes used as almost synonymous with "knowledge",[2] and is in this sense appreciated more highly by Aristotle than experience, which is concerned with individuals. This presupposes Plato's thought which takes ἐπιστήμη as the knowledge of universals, and this sort of usage is naturally found more often in early parts of Aristotle's works. Restricting ἐπιστήμη to theoretical knowledge, art is opposed to it as a cognition related to another sort of object; namely, while theoretical knowledge properly concerns being which are necessary and cannot be otherwise, art is ralated rather to what can be otherwise.[3] Knowledge is the self-end, but art is the principle of production, and gives things that can be otherwise the form of man's own volition. Production, being the end of art, aims at something other than itself, and is concerned with the individuals. But the cognition which aims at individuals is not of necessity individual cognition. This is a matter of no little importance. Individuals are the end of the cognition, but are neither the objects nor the contents of it. In order to manage the individuals successfully, one must possess universal cognition. If we call universal cognition knowledge, art would presuppose this knowledge. Still it is not scientific in the sense of theoretical intellect. Productive knowledge also contains universal cognition, only differing from theoretical knowledge in that this universal cognition is not the end but the means. Con-

[1] An. Post. I. 31. 88 a 5; 2. 71 b 33-72 a 5.
[2] An. Pr. I. 30. 46 a 22; Met. I. 1. 981 a 3; b 8; XII. 8. 1074 b 11; Eth. Nic. I. 1. 1094 a 7, 18; Pol. III. 12. 1282 b 14; IV. 1. 1288 b 10; VII. 13. 1331 b 37; Rhet. II. 19. 1392 a 26; cf. Met. I. 1. 981 b 28; III. 2. 997 a 5; An. Post. I. 1. 71 a 4; Top. I. 9. 170 a 30; 11. 172 a 28.
[3] An. Post. II. 19. 100 a 8; Met. I. 1. 981 b 26; Eth. Nic. VI. 4. 1140 a 1; 12, 22; 5. 1140 b 2.

versely, theoretical knowledge also contains individual cognition, but its end is in any case the universal. The universal cognition in art is not theoretical knowledge, but the so-called ἀρχιτεκτονική or master art.[1] Being universal, it aims at the instruction about the means to manage individuals.

With respect to art, there is, as stated above, the question whether to regard it as a mere faculty or a virtue as well. One hypothesis takes it as a faculty[2] on the ground that Aristotle says "While there is such a thing as excellence in art, there is no such thing as excellence in prudence";[3] again, while prudence is defined as "a true practical habit with reason",[4] art is called "a productive habit with true reason".[5] This view assumes that art becomes virtue only when it serves for a good end, which in fact, seems to be endorsed by a statement in the *Magna Moralia*.[6] For all that, since virtue is not confined to ethical or moral virtues, but means the excellence of any kind of faculty,[7] and art is certainly a kind of cognitive faculty, so its virtue must also consist not in the good end, but in the rightness of that cognition. Consequently, even if the same concept is sometimes used in the sense of a mere faculty, it can by no means fail to be an intellectual virtue. In fact, we find that the concept ἀτεχνία[8] is used as the lack of this habit. Seeing that ἀτεχνία is called the habit of potential production with false reason, in opposition to τέχνη which is the habit of potential production with true reason, there cannot be any doubt that art is a kind of intellectual virtue.

Another kind of practical knowledge is prudence. According to Jaeger, φρόνησις in Plato is not restricted to practical wisdom, but means cognition in general and synonymous with ἐπιστήμη. The same usage is found also in Aristotle's early works, but later on, φρόνησις and ἐπιστήμη are distinguished as practical knowledge and theoretical knowledge. This change of terminology was regarded by Jaeger as the key to determining the period of the *Ethica Nicomachea*. But this argument is so well known and acknowledged that there is no need to state it in detail.[9] There

---

[1] Eth. Nic. I. 1. 1094 a 14;   Phys. II. 2. 194 b 1;   Met. V. 1. 1013 a 13.
[2] Walter, op. cit. 512; cf. 464 f.
[3] Eth. Nic. VI. 5. 1140 b 22.   [4] Eth. Nic. VI. 5. 1140 b 20.
[5] Ibid. 4. 1140 a 10, 21.   [6] Mag. Mor. I. 19. 1190 a 30.
[7] Met. V. 16. 1021 b 20- 23.   [8] Eth. Nic. VI. 4. 1140 a 21.
[9] Jaeger, Aristoteles. 241 ff.

is only one point to be noticed, namely that though Plato did not distinguish φρόνησις from ἐπιστήμη, it does not follow that he made no distinction between theoretical and practical intellect. This distinction may be found in the classification in the *Statesman* which we have already referred to. He also argued in his early works such as the *Meno*, that knowledge is instructible while virtue is not, and further that as far as virtue is useful and good for man what manages it must be in a sense knowledge — thus the leading cognition in practical affairs is true opinion or good opinion.[1] This is evidently the acknowledgement of the speciality of practical intellect and its limits of exactness. Consequently, it is not originality in Aristotle to use the concept φρόνησις especially as practical knowledge, but rather a progress of conceptual distinction.[2] As to its universality and speciality, we have already seen that it involves both moments. The same thing may also be applied to prudence or practical cognition: here also cognition aims at an act, which is however related to the individual; so that the end of practical intellect is individual affairs. Nevertheless it is more than a mere special knowledge, but includes also the cognition of universal laws, viz., here there is also required a kind of general knowledge of practical affairs. The most comprehensive of these practical knowledges is prudence. And prucence in the wider sense involves, as Teichmüller says, universal knowledge such as ethics and politics, as well as the most immediate and particular cognition of practical affairs.

Practical cognition is distinguished from theoretical knowledge in that it aims at an individual act; it is also distinguished from art in that it has no end other than act itself. It is none the less a mediated cognition of the universal and the individual. Now in theoretical knowledge, the individual is intuitively known by reason. How then is it with the act of practical intellect? On this point, Aristotle's statement is scanty, and there is no authoritative theory among interpreters. The representative virtue of practical intellect is φρόνησις. But as practical cognition involves many moments, prudence must bear a generic sense, and cannot be restricted to the intuition of principles or reasoning exclusively.

[1] Meno 98.
[2] Even in early works such as the Topica, we find the special usage of φρόνησις. Top. VII. 7. 137 a 12-14; IV. 21. 121 b 33.

The functions or virtues of practical intellect are $βούλευσις$,[1] $εὐβουλία$,[2] $σύνεσις$,[3] $δεινότης$,[4] $πανουργία$,[5] etc. Excepting $βούλευσις$, i.e. deliberation and $εὐβουλία$, i.e. good deliberation, they are all somewhat secondary habits, and fail to be the essential moments of $φρόνησις$, whereas deliberation is thought to be mediated or reasoned knowledge.[6] What is then the universal cognition of principles, and what is the intuition of individuals? It would seem most probable that they are the ethical virtues and the so-called practical reason. For Aristotle says that ethical virtues are the necessary condition of prudence, and that they form the premisses of practical syllogism[7] or set up the end which acts as the beginning of practical thinking.[8]

§ 4. PRACTICAL REASON

Remarkable as it is, we find at the "particular" limit of practical thinking the concept of the reason which knows individual facts intuitively. Putting off the problem about ethical virtues and prudence, let us study this interesting concept, $νοῦς\ πρακτικός$. We have hitherto recognized two meanings of reason. The one is intellect in general, which must be divided into the theoretical and the practical, the other, a kind of theoretical intellect which knows universal principles intuitively. Reason in the latter sense

---

[1] On deliberation, cf. ch. II. 2. We shall also deal with this subject in the next chapter. In short, it is concerned with what is in our power. It is the inference not of the end, but of the means to realize some end. Cf. Eth. Nic. III. 5. 1112 a 30; b 11; VI. 2. 1139 a 13; [Mag. Mor. I. 35. 1196 b 29;] Rhet. I. 2. 1357 a 4, 6; 1362 a 18; II. 5. 1383 a 7.

[2] Eth. Nic. VI. 10. 1142 b 22, 27.

[3] Eth. Nic. VI. 11. 1143 a 4-10; cf. Mag. Mor. I. 35. 1197 b 11; Pol. IV. 4. 1291 a 28.

[4] Eth. Nic. VI. 13. 1144 a 23-27; cf. 1144 b 2; VII. 11. 1152 a 11 ff.; [Mag. Mor. I. 35. 1197 b 17 ff.; II. 6. 1204 a 13 ff.;] Pol. V. 5. 1305 a 12; Eth. Nic. VIII. 7. 1158 a 32.

[5] Eth. Nic. VI. 13. 1144 a 27; cf. n. 4; Eth. Eud. II. 3. 1221 a 12.

[6] De Memor. 2. 453 a 14; Eth. Nic. VI. 2. 1139 a 12; 10. 1142 a 31; III. 5. 1112 b 22. cf. p. 237, n. 9.

[7] Eth. Nic. VI. 13. 1144 a 29-b 1; 1144 b 30.

[8] Eth. Nic. VI. 13. 1145 a 4-6. It is evident from the statement in this chapter that virtue sets up the end and is concerned with the means. This virtue, of course, means ethical virtue.

was one of the intellectual virtues above mentioned. Now we encounter a new concept, practical reason, which, being a kind of practical intellect, seems to constitute a moment of prudence. Since it is a kind of practical intellect, it must be different from practical reason in the generic sense. It is by no means an exaggeration to say that this is one of the most difficult concepts in Aristotle's philosophy, along with the active reason which we have already investigated.[1] Just as the concept of "active reason" appears only once in the *De Anima* amongst the whole works of Aristotle, and strictly speaking, there is no such word as νοῦς ποιητικός (although it is often discussed by commentators), the concept of "practical reason" in a specific sense also appears once only in the *Ethica Nicomachea*, and here again the word νοῦς πρακτικός as such does not appear. Consequently, just as the difficulty about the "active reason" was whether Aristotle really assumed a special reason, here also, the first question to be asked is whether it is Aristotle's real intention to admit such a special concept as "practical reason". The statement is as follows: Eth. Nic. VI. 12. 1143a35: καὶ ὁ νοῦς τῶν ἐσχάτων ἐπ' ἀμφότερα· καὶ γὰρ τῶν πρώτων ὅρων καὶ τῶν ἐσχάτων νοῦς ἐστὶ καὶ οὐ λόγος, καὶ ὁ μὲν κατὰ τὰς ἀποδείξεις τῶν ἀκινήτων ὅρων καὶ πρώτων, ὁ δ' ἐν ταῖς πρακτικαῖς τοῦ ἐσχάτου καὶ ἐνδεχομένου καὶ τῆς ἑτέρας προτάσεως· ἀρχαὶ γὰρ τοῦ οὗ ἕνεκα αὗται. ἐκ τῶν καθ' ἕκαστα γὰρ τὰ καθόλου· τούτων οὖν ἔχειν δεῖ αἴσθησιν, αὕτη δ' ἐστὶ νοῦς.

"And (intuitive) reason is concerned with the ultimates in both directions; for both the first terms and the last are objects of (intuitive) reason and not of argument, and the (intuitive) reason which is presupposed by demonstrations grasps the unchangeable and first terms, while the (intuitive) reason involved in practical reasonings grasps the last and variable fact, i.e. another premiss. For these variable facts are the starting points for the apprehension of the end, since the universal is reached from the particulars; of these therefore we must have perception, and this perception is (intuitive) reason."

There are three interpretations about the reason here mentioned. The first is that of Ritter[2] and Trendelenburg,[3] which takes the

[1] Cf. Robin, La pensée gréque. 365,   [2] Ritter, Gesch. d. Philos. III.
[3] Trendelenburg, Historische Beiträge zur Philosophie. III; Brandis, Handbuch der Geschichte der griechisch-römischen Philosophie. II. a. ii.; Zeller followed at first this theory, but afterwards turned to Walter's.

"reason in demonstration" as the intuition of universal principles in theoretical cognition, and the "reason in practical reasonings" as the intuition of special facts which forms the minor premiss of practical syllogism. The second is that of Teichmüller,[1] who takes "demonstrations" in the sense of practical syllogism, and makes what is here stated to be wholly about practical reason, so that the above statement would admit two kinds of practical intuition — both of the universal and of the particular limits of practical cognition. The third interpretation is that of Julius Walter,[2] who on the contrary, takes the reason as a kind of theoretical intellect in practical cognition as well as in demonstration, and admits no special faculty like "practical reason".

As far as "demonstration" and "the practical" are concerned, the first interpretation seems to be most plausible. What "demonstration" here means is that form of theoretical syllogism which starts from necessary principles, and the reason which is concerned with its first premiss is nothing but the reason which formed a moment of wisdom. Therefore, the reason, which, in contrast, is concerned with the other premiss is, no doubt, a kind of practical intellect. It is neither theoretical nor practical knowledge in the wider sense, but certainly a special function of practical and intuitive intellect. Why then are these cognitive faculties concerned with the opposite limits in the theoretical case on the one hand and in the practical case on the other—though they are similarly called reason? Is it not strange that admitting reason in the practical case, one does not regard it as a universal cognition of principles, but confines it to the cognition of individuals? Hartenstein would seem to have good reason to wonder at this.[3]

Among the three interpretations above mentioned, only that of Teichmüller is free from this difficulty. He maintains[4] that "demonstration" means practical syllogism, and that the reason here spoken of should be taken exclusively as the practical reason, which is quite different from theoretical reason. Further he assumes other instances wherein the word demonstration is used in

[1] Teichmüller, Neue Studien zur Geschichte der Begriffe, II.
[2] Walter, Die Lehre von der praktischen Vernunft in der griechischen Philosophie.
[3] Hartenstein, Ueber den wissenschaftliche Werth der Ethik des Aristoteles. The following quotations from this book are all through Walter, op. cit.
[4] Teichmüller, op. cit. 210.

this meaning, e.g., the "demonstration" in Eth. Nic. VII. 5,[1] where Aristotle speaks of those who under the influence of passions utter demonstration and the verses of Empedocles without really using practical wisdom; "demonstration" Teichmüller wishes to be taken not as theoretical but as practical syllogism. It follows that, according to him, Aristotle took practical reason as the intellectual intuition both of the highest major premiss and of the lowest minor one. This interpretation is fairly probable, because the statement in question is made in reference to the structure of practical intellect. Still to recite Empedocles's words and to make "demonstration" are not of necessity assumed to be identical. For even the man who is under the influence of passion may not be disturbed in his theoretical cognition.[2] Moreover, a demonstration is the mediation of the universal and the particular. Then, how can we say, as in the above statement, that in demonstration reason is concerned with the most universal, but in practice with the lowest particular? Naturally, Teichmüller restricts practice to a direct action. But, since he makes out both reason and demonstration to be practical, the statement that in demonstration the reason is concerned with the highest universal could scarcely have any significance other than that practical syllogism can exist only through the highest universal principle. Of course, theoretical syllogism also contains both universal and particular moments. Therefore, strictly speaking, it would be nonsense to say that in demonstration reason is concerned with the universal. Aristotle's statement would have some meaning only if we take "demonstration" as the theoretical cognition which aims at demonstration itself. The word demonstration appears to be applied to practical syllogism,[3] but in its strict sense, it is restricted to the syllogism

---

[1] Eth. Nic. VII. 5. 1147 a 19; VI. 5. 1140 b 14.
[2] Eth. Nic. VI. 5. 1140 b 11.
[3] Eth. Nic. VI. 12. 1143 b 11-13: ὥστε δεῖ προσέχειν τῶν ἐμπείρων καὶ πρεσβυτέρων ἢ φρονίμων ταῖς ἀναποδείκτοις φάσεσι καὶ δόξαις οὐχ ἧττον τῶν ἀποδείξεων. Part. An. I. 1. 640 a 1 f.: ἀλλ' ὁ τρόπος τῆς ἀποδείξεως καὶ τῆς ἀνάγκης ἕτερος ἐπί τε τῆς φυσικῆς καὶ τῶν θεωρητικῶν ἐπιστημῶν. From this statement alone, it might appear as if demonstration were concerned with natural sciences and theoretical sciences and not with practical intellect. But the physical demonstration which is mentioned in the following is nothing but a medical syllogism to realize health, this, however, is usually assumed to be an example of deliberation.

which has necessary premises. Aristotle denied any demonstration about variable facts decisively.[1] In order to keep a balance with theoretical reason, he should rather have admitted a universal cognition of principles to practical reason, than to have called sensation of individuals reason. Theoretical reason is not concerned with such individual matters. It would be more consistent to let practical reason concern the individual than to admit to practical reason the intuition of both extremities. For theoretical reason itself is related only with the universal extremity. We might rather more profitably ask why the universal principle of practice cannot be perceived by intuitive reason.

Walter's attempt[2] to deny the practical and intuitive intellect, restricting the word practical reason to the generic sense, is due to his assumption that the only function of the practical intellect is the cognition of means.

Our full criticism upon this point will be given when we inquire about deliberation. But Walter's is, no doubt, the most unsatisfactory interpretation of the sentence in question. It cannot avoid charge of abruptness for he presents pure theoretical cognition and assert that one part of it is the intuitive intellect concerned with the individual; and he does this in a context where practical intellect is referred to the individual. It is much the more constrained to assume a theoretical reason, where Aristotle speaks about the practical reason in opposition to the reason which, as a kind of theoretical intellect, grasps principles intuitively. Moreover, how in the world should this be taken—that this intuitive intellect of the individual is the beginning of the end, or that it is the principle of the end? Walter seems no ground for taking demonstration as theoretical, and "the practical" as practical reason. For, according to him,[3] σύνεσις, though taken by Aristotle to be the cognition of the individual, is none the less merely discriminating, while prudence is epitactic and practical; on the other hand, the reason which is concerned with the individual is not specifically said by Aristotle to be practical. Yet, what Aristotle really said is not that the reason which is concerned with the indivi-

---

[1] An. Post. I. 2. 71 b 18 f.; Eth. Nic. VI. 3. 1139 b 31 f.; 5. 1140 a 33-35; Met. V. 5. 1015 b 7; VII. 15. 1039 b 31; An. Post. I. 4. 73 a 24; Eth. Nic. VI. 5. 1140 a 34; An. Post. I. 8. 75 b 24.
[2] Walter, op. cit. 5-81.
[3] Ibid. 43.

dual is practical, but that in practical affairs reason is concerned with the individual. The practical character of this reason, therefore, cannot be denied by Walter's argument. In other words, Aristotle did not infer that the reason is practical when its object is individual, but rather recognized the object of reason which acts practically to be individual. Consequently, we cannot refuse practical reason, even though not all individual knowledges should be practical. Further, it is unreasonable for Walter, while dividing, on the one hand, the syllogism into the practical and the theoretical, to deny on the other hand, any practical character to the reason. Since he takes all universal knowledges as theoretical, the major premiss of both syllogisms should be, without boubt, taken as theoretical. But even the minor premiss of a practical syllogism is not practical; it differs from that of a theoretical syllogism only in being a perceptive judgement about the individual.[2] The practical syllogism is distinguished from the theoretical only in the point that the former reaches the individual, while the latter remains in the sphere of the universal; the difference is no more than a comparative difference between the universal and the particular. In spite of reducing the minor premiss of the practical syllogism to the function of reason, Walter refuses a practical character to reason, on the ground that it is not calculative but intuitive.[3] Why, then, is it necessary that reason should be calculative in order that it may be practical? Since practice is concerned with the individual, it would rather seem to be necessary that the premiss of this syllogism be practical. Walter failed to recognize this, because he was obsessed with Aristotle's classification of intellect into the scientific and the calculative or deliberative. But, if practical intellect could not do anything but to calculate, because of its being called calculative, for this same ground, theoretical knowledge or scientific intellect could not engage in anything but scientific cognition. Whereas $ἐπιστήμη$ or scientific knowledge *par excellence* is, as aforesaid, syllogistic knowledge, and cannot be the intuition of principles. We should not reject the intuition of individual knowledge, because of the practical knowledge being called calculative, just as we should not infer that theoretical knowledge cannot involve the intellectual intuition of principles as its moment, because of its being called scientific. Both knowledge and calculation must presuppose the intuition of principles,

[2] Ibid. 230, 242.   [3] Ibid. 32 f., 46, 60 f., 322.

as far as they are syllogistic cognition. Such an intuition may be involved in practical knowledge as well as in theoretical knowledge. It should neither be restricted to one of them alone, nor searched for outside of intellect. According to Walter, reason is strictly theoretical, and grasps both the universal and the particular extremities. Therefore reason is the intuition of individual facts, as well as that of universal principles, and the intuition of individuals is perception in the usual sense.[1] But how is it possible for theoretical reason to be concerned with the object of perception, which is what can be otherwise ?[2] If we take "reason" everywhere in the same sense, to admit that reason is concerned with what can be otherwise would directly contradict Aristotle's statement[3] that prudence is concerned with what can be otherwise, while reason is concerned with necessary beings. Walter's answer on this point grows more strange.[4] He says that calculation is the only intellectual act that may be concerned with the ἐνδεχόμενον,[5]

---

[1] Ibid. 314 f., 335.
[2] There is a question how we should take the last ἐνδεχόμενον in the statement Eth. Nic. VI. 12. 1143 b 3. Walter takes it rather to be the conclusion. According to Zeller (op. cit II. 2. 651 n. 2), the second premiss "This is sweet" is not enough to lead one to actual conduct. The immediate motive of an act is rather the conclusion, "This should be tasted". Zeller refers to Eth. Nic. VI. 8 and 9, where πρακτόν is shown as the last term. But, this is because Zeller takes the ἐνδεχόμενον as potential or future being. The same interpretation is also found in Walter, op. cit. 332. This is not unreasonable in reference to statements such as Eth. Nic. VI. 2. 1139 b 7-9: οὐδὲ γὰρ βουλεύεται περὶ τοῦ γεγονότος ἀλλὰ περὶ τοῦ ἐσομένου καὶ ἐνδεχομένου τὸ δὲ γεγονὸς οὐκ ἐνδέχεται μὴ γενέσθαι· or Motu An. 7. 701 a 23-25: αἱ δὲ προτάσεις αἱ ποιητικαὶ διὰ δύο εἰδῶν γίνονται, διά τε τοῦ ἀγαθοῦ καὶ διὰ τοῦ δυνατοῦ. And ἐνδεχόμενον means in fact logical potentiality or possibility, when it is used independently. But in the statement in question (1143 b 3), we should rather add καὶ ἄλλως ἔχειν and read as "may be otherwise": cf. Rassow, Forsch. 77: Stewart, note *ad loc*. Even without the addition, this would be the real meaning. For, the phrase in 1139 b 9: οὐκ ἐνδέχεται καὶ μὴ γενέσθαι means in reality, that it cannot be otherwise, so that its contrary would be "what can be otherwise" rather than "what is possible". If one should take it as do Walter and Zeller, it would mean that that theoretical reason is concerned with what is impossible, viz., a contradictory concept or a past event—which is surely unreasonable.
[3] Eth. Nic. VI. 6. 1141 a 4.   [4] Walter, op. cit. 319 ff.
[5] As mentioned above, Walter seems to have taken the ἐνδεχόμενον as a mere possible being or potentiality. Then μὴ ἐνδεχόμενον would mean what is impossible. Whereas in Eth. Nic. VI. 2. 1139 a 6, which he quotes in his work p. 322, there is: ὑποκείσθω δύο τὰ λόγον ἔχοντα, ἓν μὲν ᾧ θεωροῦμεν τὰ τοιαῦτα τῶν

while reason is not calculation, and the act of reason concerned with the ἐνδεχόμενον is not an intellectual act, but literal perception. Though perception sometimes appears in apposition to reason, there is a relation of development between them. Perception itself being potentially reason, it is said to be a reason, the first function of this reason in the wider sense is universal knowledge, and the second function of it, perception concerned with the ἐνδεχόμενον. According to Walter, when Aristotle says that prudence is concerned with the ἐνδεχόμενον, and reason with the μὴ ἐνδεχόμενον, he is speaking about the first function of reason, and this does not keep us from admitting that its second function is concerned with the ἐνδεχόμενον. The perception of individual things is called reason because it is the condition of all cognitions. Both prudence and reason are concerned with the ἐνδεχόμενον, only differing in that the one is concerned with remote existences, but the other with present beings. Reason is the moment of prudence as well as of wisdom. And since reason is a virtue of the theoretical intellect, prudence involves a virtue of the theoretical intellect, yet is itself another virtue of intellect.

In short, according ot Walter, both reason and perception are the essential moments common to all cognitions, so that both the opposition between the sensitive and the intelligible, and the clear distinction between theoretical and practical knowledge are given up. This is a creation of Walter's rather than an interpretation of Aristotle's thought. We shall take up only one difficulty in particular, viz., how is it possible for the prudence that involves theoretical reason or perception to become practical. For Walter, reason is always concerned with theoretical cognition, and knows intuitively both the universal and the particular extremities so that the only act reserved for other intellectual faculties is the reasoning which mediates between the universal and the individual. Now ἐπιστήμη or "knowledge" is the theoretical inference with regard to the universal and the particular, and calculation or deliberation is commonly assumed to be practical inference. Walter, however, who restricts the knowledge of both the univarsal and the particular extremities, of a syllogism to theoretical intellect, scarcely finds the room for

ὄντων ὅσων αἱ ἀρχαὶ μὴ ἐνδέχονται ἄλλως ἔχειν, ἓν δὲ ᾧ τὰ ἐνδεχόμενα κτλ.
Walter quotes Eth. Nic. VI. 6. 1141 a 1, omitting, either with or without intention, ἄλλως ἔχειν, which occurs in the text. This μὴ ἐνδεχόμενον would be nonsense without the addition of ἄλλως ἔχειν. Cf. p. 245, n. 1

practical intellect. Therefore, he narrowly manages an evasion in saying that the process of practical inference is not practical, but it is composed of theoretical knowledge through and through, only at last resulting in the conclusion as ἐπιτακτικόν.[1] But whence comes the imperative which appears so suddenly in this conclusion? It is not an intellectual function at all, but merely an immediate volition. There would thus for Walter be no real practical intellect, but reason or intellect, itself being theoretical, becomes only accidentally practical because of its accidental combination with a volition.[2] Thus the creative interpretation of Walter reduced all intellectual activities in the practical realm to mere accidentality. Hence it is evident that we must not take the reason in question, which recognizes the individual intuitively, as theoretical. What is then the individual intuition of practical reason? Let us return to the above-quoted text, and study the problem.

The individual cognition of the reason in question was said to be the ἀρχή of the end. ἀρχή means principle, cause, and beginning in general. What then does it mean to say that the individual intuition of practical reason is the ἀρχή of the end? There are many different interpretations. Trendelenburg takes it[3] as meaning that the essence of practical reason is the determination of the end. He tries to prove his supposition by the following statement in De An. III. 10, which, however, only puts the problem in confusion and fails to obtain the desired result, for there persists a radical difficulty about the essence of practical reason. The statement in question is as follows. De An. III. 10. 433 a 13: νοῦς δὲ ὁ ἕνεκά του λογιζόμενος καὶ ὁ πρακτικός· διαφέρει δὲ τοῦ θεωρητικοῦ τῷ τέλει. καὶ ἡ ὄρεξις, ἕνεκά του πᾶσα· οὗ γὰρ ἡ ὄρεξις, αὕτη ἀρχὴ τοῦ πρακτικοῦ νοῦ· τὸ δ' ἔσχατον ἀρχὴ τῆς πράξεως.

Trendelenburg seems to read it thus: "What I speak of is the reason that calculates about an end, namely, practical reason. It is different from the theoretical in its end. And desire is generally for the sake of an end. For what a desire is concerned with is the principle of practical reason, and the last is the principle of conduct." According to him, the object which is aimed at is the principle which moves practical reason, whereas in as much as every end leads to an act and every act is individual, the individual end which ought to be realized moves intellect without being itself moved—thus what is

[1] Walter, op. cit. 483, 499 f. [2] Cf. Teichmüller, op. cit. 42 ff.
[3] Trendelenburg, op. cit. II. 378; cf. Walter, op. cit. 44.

individual acts as the principle of practical reason. Walter criticizes this interpretation so severely as to call it an utter misunderstanding. But now that we know Walter's own theory, we cannot give hasty credit to his criticism, for it is quite doubtful which of the two opinions is utterly wrong. At any rate, Trendelenburg's interpretation has two main characteristics: the one is that he takes ἕνεκά του λογιζόμενος to mean "to calculate about the end", the other is that he takes ἔσχατον as "the ultimate", i.e. as "individual affairs". In fact, Hartenstein attacks these two points.[1] He points out that ἕνεκά του means not "about the end", but refers to the search for the means. Trendelenburg, considering on the one hand, that the essence of practical reason is the definition of the end, says on the other hand, that the end-object is the principle that moves practical reason. But Hartenstein points out that the first view is neither that of Aristotle, nor is it in accord with the second. In the first sentence, reason determines the end, while in the second, the former, on the contrary, is determined by the latter. In the first, the determination of the end depends upon reason, but in the second, the act of reason depends upon the end which is already determined. This criticism of Hartenstein's however, is due to a misunderstanding of Trendelenburg's real meaning. The first sentence in question really means that reason determines the image of an end, while the second means that the object which is aimed at acts upon the reason as efficient cause. There is no contradiction between them.[2] Reason determines the image of an end, in so far as the end-object moves reason. Reason is an efficient cause, and the object a final cause. The causality of an efficient cause involves that of the final cause. Walter is surely aware that Trendelenburg makes not the purpose but the object of the purpose the cause of reason. Even so, he does not really apprehend the meaning of this distinction, and asserts that it is merely in appearance that one may avoid contradiction by saying that the object of purpose moves.[3] This only betrays his ignorance about the distinction between efficient cause and final cause, as well as that between the image of an end and the end-object.

It is surely a confusion for Trendelenburg to identify the practical reason as an intuitive faculty which appears in Eth. Nic. VI.

---

[1] Hartenstein, op. cit. cf. Walter, op. cit. 45.
[2] Cf. Loening, Die Zurechnungslehre des Aristoteles, 30.
[3] Walter, op. cit. 52.

12, with the practical reason that calculates about the end, which is described in De An. III. 10. The practical reason in the *De Anima* is the generic concept, not the special moment of prudence. For Walter, who takes practical reason in the generic sense as deliberation about the means to an end, what occasions the beginning of thinking is an immediately given desire, and the end of thinking, i.e., the end of deliberation, is the starting point of conduct. ἕνεκα τοῦ λογιζόμενος is the cognition of the means, οὗ ἡ ὄρεξις is the ἀρχή of practical reason—indicating that desire forms the motive of searching for the means—and τὸ ἔσχατον is the end of deliberation which constitutes the beginning of the act. Thus, Trendelenburg would seem wrongly to have assumed τὸ ἔσχατον to be the individual which is a kind of τὰ ἔσχατα in the *Ethics*, viz., of the affairs of conduct.

In short, the opposition between these interpretations is due to a fundamental difference of opinion as to whether one may restrict the function of practical reason to the searching for a means, or recognize a practical reason which is concerned with an end. The decision between these views must as we have said, wait a study of deliberation. Now it is very probable that τὸ ἔσχατον means the last term of practical reason, yet even if we follow this assertion and reject Trendelenburg's theory on this point, it does not necessarily follow that the cognition of "the last" in the *Ethics* cannot be the principle of the end. The last term of practical reason in the generic sense is an individual fact, which is the first step of conduct and a concrete end determined somehow by reason. The practical reason in the special sense, which is found in the *Ethics*, may be a moment of this generic intellect. Even Walter admits that the practical reason in the generic sense is a mediated intellect. But, then, it would naturally involve many moments, among which we should also find the intuitive intellect which apprehends individuals. In a precisely similar way, the theoretical reason in a wider sense involves not only knowledge, but also reason in a narrower sense, viz. an intuitive intellect. We have previously assumed that the practical intellect in the *De Anima* determines the end.[1] From the grounds we then stated, we can by no means submit to the theory that restricts it to the cognition of the means. Moreover, it does not suit Aristotle's meaning to take, as Walter does, the sentence "οὗ ἡ ὄρεξις

[1] Ch. II. § 4.

is the ἀρχή of practical reason" only to mean that desire determines reason.

οὗ ἡ ὄρεξις is what a desire is concerned with, viz. an objective end, and not the idea of an end or a desire itself. That the end-object becomes the principle of practical reason must only mean that the object acts upon the desiring faculty through reason and results in a desire mediated by reason. Aristotle clearly divides desire into the rational and the irrational, and identifying the object of desire with that of reason, calls attention to the fact that a rational purpose is mediated by the estimation of an object and not the reverse. Of course, there is in practical reason the function of searching for a means, but there is also a practical reason that determines a desire itself for an end. The practical reason in the narrower sense may have such a faculty.

Since Walter confines practical reason to the cognition of means, the setting up of an end is assigned entirely to an immediate desire. The end is set up by the desire, and the practical reason contributes only to its realization. Combined with the desire, it produces a rational reaction towards what is originally desired.[1]—He does not, however, deny rationality altogether to the desire, but rather says: "*Dieses vermag sie aber nur durch Vernunftvorstellungen, die logisch vermittelt eine das Streben bestimmende Ueberzeugungskraft bestimmen. Zu diese Vorstellungen aber wird in erster Reihe der Zweck als Vernunftbegriff, der allgemeine Zweck gehören, ... Jenen allgemeine Zweck, z. B. der Mensch soll maashalten, kann die praktische Vernunft nicht aus sich schöpfen, ...sie muss ihn also anderwärts enthalten. Der allgemeine Zweck ist überhaupt nicht etwas Bestimmbares, sondern er steht ein für allemal fest und kann daher nur erkannt werden. Diese Erkenntniss aber ist wie alles Allgemeine Gegenstand wissenschaftlicher Einsicht, als dessen Prinzip Aristoteles eben den νοῦς oder Verstand einführte.*"[2]

But this argument is so confused that we can hardly understand his real meaning. If the function of practical reason is mere searching for the means, how can its determination of the end depend upon the rational image which determines the desire? How is it possible to say, "*Vernunftvorstellungen, die logisch vermittelt eine das Streben bestimmende Ueberzeugungskraft besitzen*", after saying "*der Zweck wird vom Streben gesetzt*" und "*Die praktische Vernunft kann hieran nichts ändern*"? Further it is no less

[1] Walter, op. cit. 207 ff. [2] Ibid. 53; cf. 208 ff.; 215 ff.; 230.

unintelligible to say that "*die Zweck als Vernunftbegriff, i.e. die Allgemeine Zweck*" belongs to those "*Vorstellungen*", since the end is said to be nothing but the object of desire. And further, the judgement that we should be moderate is said not to be the product of practical reason, but being itself a theoretical cognition, is borrowed from outside. Not only Teichmüller but anyone, would be astonished to hear that the fundamental judgement of prudence does not belong to practical intellect. All these absurdities follow from Walter's attempt to restrict the function of practical intellect to the searching for the means, excepting the determination of the end.

We have taken the practical reason in the *Ethics* as the intellectual intuition of the individual. What then does it mean to say that "from the individual comes the universal"? According to Hartenstein, the individual is the means, while the universal is the end.[1] Thus understood, the above statement would mean that the end comes from the means, or in other words, in the process of act, the first and highest end is realized through the nearest means. But even if ἕνεκά του λογιζόμενος may be the cognition of the means, ἀρχαὶ γὰρ τοῦ οὗ ἕνεκα αὗται cannot be translated as "it is the principle of the end". Consequently, the individual cannot be taken to be the means to an end. But we do not assert against Hartenstein that the universal is the means while the individual is an end. Rather we understand the meaning to be that the universal end comes from the individual one, that is to say, the universal end or the so-called moral intention which characterizes personality, is produced from individual ends and their realization.[2]

There remains lastly, the fact that this cognition of individuals is said to be a perception, and then this perception is identified with reason. No doubt, this reason must be taken to be practical from its context. What then does it mean to say that practical

[1] Ibid. 47 ff.

[2] Walter considers that both premisses of a practical syllogism are essentially theoretical, among them the minor premiss being a perception in the ordinary sense. So that for him the phrase in question would mean that general knowledge is induced from perception (op. cit. 324 f.). But, since he takes, on the other hand, deliberation as a cognition that searches for the means to a given end, it follows that this induction would proceed from the knowledge of a particular means to that of a universal end; thus the order of practical syllogism would be turned around which is surely unreasonable.

reason which intuitively knows the last minor premiss of practical cognition is a perception? Neither Walter nor Trendelenburg are successful in the interpretation of this point. Walter, who herein admits nothing but the theoretical reason, thinks that the perception of individuals here mentioned is perception in the literal sense, and it is called reason only because universal and theoretical knowledge is induced from perception of particular things.[1] We hardly find it necessary to disprove such a theory. Trendelenburg too, takes the designation of practical reason as perception to be a mere metaphor, employed on account of the intuitiveness common to them, while in reality, perception is concerned with present things, and the object of purpose, with future beings.[2] But there is no sufficient reason for taking it as a metaphor, and we can by no means recognize the essence of practical reason through such an interpretation. In this respect, the theory of Ritter is more preferable. According to him, that the practical reason as a moment of prudence is the perception of individuals, means that it is the *sensus communis*, which is the intellectual intuition discriminating between what is good and what is bad for oneself. This is probably founded upon the following statement in the *Ethics* which occurs a little before the statement in question—Eth. Nic. VI. 8. 1142 a 25: "It (prudence) is opposed, then, to reason, for reason is of the limiting premiss, for which no reason can be given, while prudence is concerned with the ultimate particular, which is the object not of scientific knowledge but of perception[3]—not the perception of qualities peculiar to one sense but a perception akin to that by which we perceive that the particular figure before us is a triangle;[4] for in that direction as well as in that of the major premiss there will be a limit."[5]

---

[1] Walter, op. cit. 323 ff.   [2] Trendelenburg, op. cit. II. 378.

[3] It is seldom that Aristotle calls moral valuation perception: e.g., Pol. I. 2. 1253 a 14 f.; Eth. Nic. II. 9. 1109 b 14-23.

[4] Eth. Nic. VI. 9. 1142 a 28 f.: ἀλλ' οἵᾳ αἰσθανόμεθα ὅτι τὸ (ἐν τοῖς μαθηματικοῖς) ἔσχατον τρίγωνον.—following Bywater and Ross. Michelet reads this as meaning the sensation that perceives that the last term of the mathematical analysis is the triangle, i. e., meaning that the triangle is the most simple figure. But as Stewart points out, then Aristotle should have presented as an example, the point rather than the triangle. Walter, who follows Michelet, cannot understand the reason why it is a common sensation. Cf. Walter, op. cit. 389 ff.

[5] Walter takes this στήσεται κα'κεῖ also as the end of pursuit and deliberation. But this only means the individual as the ultimate member of the conceptual series. Cf. Walter, op. cit. 392.

If we compare this with the first quotation from Eth. Nic. VI. 11. the correspondence is remarkable enough; hence there would scarcely be any doubt that the "reason in the practical", in the earlier quotation is the same as the prudence here mentioned.[1] It is evident enough from this alone that it should not be taken as theoretical reason. Walter's objections to this are not worthy of serious attention; e.g. that common sensation is not of necessity practical reason, or that it is a specially defined concept in the psychology and cannot be the same as this perception which is here identified with reason, or that this perception may teach us the good, yet does not teach us what is good for us, and the like. Though common sensation is not of necessity practical, it is not impossible for practical reason to be a function or a form of common sensation. And if one says that the common sensation in the *De Anima* is not the same as the perception here mentioned, one ought to state in detail the difference between them. Further, though common sensation is sometimes not followed by pleasure and pain, e.g. in the case of mathematical figures, it does not follow that it is always theoretical and does not teach us the good for us. Perception is naturally concerned with individuals, and makes one recognize the particular modes which appear to an individual subject.

[1] Trendelenburg's interpretation on this point is quite different from ours. According to him, the intuitive practical reason is different from prudence, the former bearing quite another resemblance to perception than the latter. Practical reason resembles perception in that they are both an immediate cognition; while prudence resembles perception in that they are concerned with the last term of research. Trendelenburg would seem to have arrived at this view because he also, like Walter, following the statement in Eth. Nic. III. 5. 1112 b 12, finds the function of prudence mainly in deliberation, and makes the essence of deliberation lie in the searching for the means. He finds an example in Motu An. 7. 701 a 20: πράττει δ' ἀπ' ἀρχῆς, εἰ ἱμάτιον ἔσται, ἀνάγκη τόδε πρῶτον, εἰ δὲ τόδε, τόδε· καὶ τοῦτο πράττει εὐθύς. Further, reading the text in 1142 a 28, like Walter, to mean "the perceptive judgement that assumes the triangle to be the ultimate element of geometrical analysis", he finds the ground for the function of ϱφϱόνησις being compared to the perception of the ultimate individual in geometry, in Eth. Nic. III. 5. 1112 b 20-24: ὁ γὰρ βουλευόμενος ἔοικε ζητεῖν καὶ ἀναλύειν τὸν εἰρημένον τρόπον ὥσπερ διάγραμμα ... καὶ τό ἔσχατον ἐν τῇ ἀναλύσει πρῶτον εἶναι ἐν γενέσει (cf. Trendelenburg, Beiträge etc. II. 381 ff.) But, it is surely a constrained solution, as Walter considers (op. cit. 377 f.). It is a bare contradiction to take on the one hand, the minor premiss of a practical syllogism for a perceptive judgement, and on the other hand, to assume the relation of practical reason and perception to be a mere metaphor. Besides, geometrical analysis is by no means the function of perception. What are

As a rule, it is followed by pleasure or pain, and teaches us the subjective and relative good rather than the objective.[1] There must certainly, be some restriction to a comparison of practical reason with common sensation; they are not identical through and through. For Aristotle says, after the above quotation, "But this is rather perception than prudence, while the former belongs to another form".[2] The interpretations of this last sentence are not in agreement, and even the text is not settled. It means presumably that the perception of individual figures in geometry is "perception rather than prudence", viz. it is sensation, while the practical reason as the limit of practical intellect should belong to "another form" than perception, i.e., to the form of prudence or of practical reason. Here the intuitive moment of prudence is assigned to common sensation. Yet some other concept is required on account of their essential difference—perhaps the difference that common sensation extends to such a theoretical idea as the figure of triangle, while practical reason is through and through an estimation. This indicates that even the generic concept of prudence did not satisfy Aristotle. Thus, we may comprehend Aristotle's state of mind when he used such an ambiguous and indefinite concept as "the reason in the practical". Also we may acknowledge the probability of Teichmüller's interpretation which denotes this special intuitive faculty as *"phronetische Wahrnehmung"*.[3]

Through the foregoing scrutiny of various interpretations, we have reached the conclusion that the intellectual intuition of the

perceived are only particular figures. Consequently, it cannot be right to compare prudence or deliberation to perception. Much the more unreasonable is it to ascribe the former to a geometrician, and the latter to a prudent man. This interpretation of Trendelenburg can hardly escape the charge of distortion.

[1] Cf. ch. II. § 2.

[2] Ross translates ἀλλ' αὕτη μᾶλλον αἴσθησις ἢ φρόνησις, ἐκείνης δ' ἄλλο εἶδος as "But this is rather perception than practical wisdom, though it is another kind of perception than that of the qualities peculiar to each sense". This would then speak only about the perception that perceives this figure to be a triangle, and would not touch prudence. But in reality, it means rather that prudence and *sensus communis* are not strictly identical. My view is nearer to Rolfes's translation: *Jenes Vermögen für die eigentümlichen Sinnesqualitäten ist mehr Sinn als Klugheit, das hier gemeint Varmögen aber ist von anderer Art.* On this point I cannot agree with Walter's opinion either.

[3] Teichmüller, Aristotelische Forschungen, I. 262; Neue Studien zur Geschichte der Begriffe, III. 297; cf. Walter, op. cit. 396, 383, 554.

minor premiss which is mentioned in Eth. Nic. VI. 13, is practical reason in a specific sense. It is a kind of practical intellect, which recognizes particular facts in a practical way and intuitively, and in this respect is assimilated to common sensation. This cognition of practical reason constitutes the minor premiss of practical inference, or the principle of the end, while a moral habit or character grows from the setting up of individual ends, and forms the major premiss of a practical syllogism.

Assuming such an interpretation, let us inquire into the problem we laid aside, viz., why the same word, reason, is applied both to theoretical and to practical cognition, indicating on the one hand the intuition of the universal principle, and on the other that of the particular limit. It is not easy to explain this successfully, but let us present a hypothesis.—It may be that the universal proposition of theoretical cognition is essentially different from that of practical cognition; the one being *a priori*, and the other *a posteriori*. For instance, the principle of identity or that of contradiction is universally applicable and *a priori*, while the general laws of morality and politics are probable and *a posteriori*. But the knowledge of principles which is said to be induced from individual perceptions is not limited to the practical. A naive rationalism that believes man is naturally endowed with the highest and most precious knowledge of universal principles, is not suitable to Aristotle's positivistic spirit. Many cognitions of universal principles grow *a posteriori* from sensation and experience. Still, from the essential or logical point of view, the universal knowledge of theoretical cognition precedes the sensation of individual facts. What is posterior for us is prior in itself. The principle of theoretical knowledge is in this sense *a priori*, and necessary. But it is otherwise with practical intellect. Moral principle is *a posteriori* and empirical, not only in the order of cognition, but also in itself. The universal principle of practical cognition has not such a necessity as that of theoretical cognition. Aristotle points out that it is here that we find the very characteristic of the method of practical philosophy. According to him, to require the same strictness

[1] Eth. Nic. II. 7. 1107 a 28-31; X. 10. 1179 a 35-b 10. Further, an incontinent character is assumed to be one which has only a general judgement and a good intention, yet is unable to practice it in a particular case, while on the contrary, continence can suppress an excessive disire, yet is lacking in perfect harmony. In this respect, it is inferior to temperance. Herein we may perceive the inferiority of general knowledge in practice; cf. ch. V.

in all departments of cognition is nothing more than a mark of ignorance about method or want of culture. Aristotle admits only *a posteriori* and probable morality. Nevertheless, in so far as there is a syllogism, the individual is founded upon the universal in practical cognition as well as in theoretical. Their universal principles grow from sensation and experience and are by no means intellectual intuitions *a priori*. But beyond this, once recognized through induction, they may be deduced from in each individual case. We may wonder how it is possible to distinguish the principles in practical from those of theoretical cognition through the mark of intuitiveness. Still, from the logical or essential point of view—by which the division between theory and practice is made—theoretical principles are self-evident, but practical laws are not. Consequently, the universal laws of practice cannot be the objects of intellectual intuition. On the other hand, the lowest limit of theoretical cognition is scarcely rational. It contains only the minimum potentiality of conceptual form in itself, which however, will be realized in a universal knowledge. The end of theoretical cognition is not the individual but the universal. On the contrary, the individual, in the realm of practice, is the end, wherein practical rationality will be realized. The universal knowledge of practice is nothing more than the *résumé* or the regulative principle of practical experience.[1] In theoretical knowledge, the universal is more precious, while in practical cognition, the individual is more important.[2] Hence Aristotle would have said that reason in the theoretical realm is concerned with the universal limit, while in the practical, it is rather concerned with the individual limit. It seems to be a proof of this supposition that the practical reason is also replaced by the generic concept, prudence.

§ 5. PRUDENCE

Practical reason or prudence is not quite identical with common sensation, only resembling it in function. But the resemblance gets too close to kinship to be merely metaphorical. Common sensation is a function of imagination based on the heart,[3] and practical reason or prudence is the principle which regulates desire,

[1] Eth. Nic. I. 2. 1095 a 30-b 7; cf. Stewart's and Grant's note *ad loc.*; Eth. Nic. VI. 12. 1143 b 4; I. 7. 1098 b 3 f.
[2] Eth. Nic. VI. 8. 1141 b 14-22.   [3] Cf. p. 121 f.

or in other words, the actual form of moderation.[1] Whereas imagination and desire are, so to say, two aspects of the same activity, differing only in that the one is static and cognitive, and the other dynamic and active.[2] Hence prudence or practical reason is said to be in a sense, common sensation, only differing in that the former is practical while the latter extends to the theoretical as well. Thus, practical reason or prudence is also considered to be founded upon the body, especially upon the heart, as the organ of common senastion.[3] It can manage and control a desire, which is derived from the body, by being itself a form of this body. We may rather say, that the primary form of the body being desire, the secondary form, i.e. the complete actuality of a moderate desire, is prudence or practical reason. Hence practical wisdom cannot be taught, but rather must be habituated.[1] As far as it is a kind of reason, it does not, of course, remain a mere function of the body, but must possess some transcendent character, otherwise it will not be able to constitute the rational part of the soul along with theoretical intellect. This transcendent aspect of practical intellect may be recognized in the objective mind in such forms as politics or education. We have interpreted the active reason in general as the objective mind. This kind of activity is found in practical intellect as well. Whether theoretical or practical, human thinking is not sufficiently accounted for by either the active or the passive reason alone; theoretical cognition requires none the less the medium of imagination and a bodily foundation. Theoretical cognition is different from practical cognition only in that the former aims at thinking itself, while the other aims at practice. In theoretical cognition, actual reason predominates, but in practical cognition, imagination, desire, and conduct, which are combined with passive reason, are rather predominant. Acive reason and passive reason are different from each other as being respectively the form and the matter of

[1] Cf. p. 138.   [2] Cf. p. 128 f.
[3] Cf. Teichmüller, op. cit. 138 ff. Prudence is not directly assigned to the heart, but is assumed as the highest principle of the ethical virtues. Now ethical virtue depends upon our body (Eth. Nic. X. 8. 1178 a 15), being excellence of character with regard to pleasure and pain (Phys. VII. 3. 247 a 7, 24; Eth. Nic. II. 2. 1104 b 9; VII. 12. 1152 b 9). Whereas pleasure and pain depend upon the heart (Part. An. III. 4. 666 a 11), or in other words, the physiological condition of the heart determines the character (ibid. 667 a 11). Hence we may conclude that prudence depends upon the physiological condition of the heart.
[1] Eth. Nic. X. 10. 1179 b 21; Pol. VIII. 3. 1338 b 4.

cognition. This does not entirely cover the distinction between theoretical intellect and practical intellect, or theoretical reason and practical reason—for this is rather a distinction based upon the objects or the ends of thinking. Whether theoretical or practical, thinking always requires active and passive principles, or formal and material elements, so that both the active and the passive reason are equally necessary to practical cognition as well as to theoretical. If there should none the less be any affinity between active reason and theoretical intellect on the one hand, and passive reason and practical intellect on the other, it would be no more than a peculiarity of predominant moments. In theoretical cognition, passive reason is necessary but not the end; its end is rather a system of universal and eternal truths. Human thinking is finite as far as it is bound to the body through passive reason, but the ideal of theoretical intellect is to remove such a limitation. One might follow Socrates in saying that man can only reach the ideal end through death. The thinking of a living man is inevitably limited and cannot be free from accidental influences. The ideal of theoretical knowledge is pure spiritual activity, independent of the body.[1] Quite otherwise is it with practical intellect. Its end is on the contrary to answer the problem of the individual subject in a particular state. Active reason is here a mere *conditio sine qua non* of cognition, the end is rather found in conduct, so that passive reason and its subject, body, are herein predominant. Just on this account, practical reason or prudence is especially intimate with imagination and the body.

Now since the subject of prudence is desire, and desire depends upon the heart, prudence is founded, though indirectly, upon the heart. The heart is the factory and the depository of the blood,[2] and the nature of the blood determines not only the desire, but also the intelligence,[3] of an animal. Generally speaking, an animal of cold and thin blood is more intelligent than one of warm and dense blood. The heart is also the central organ of sensation, and its physiological changes are experienced as pleasure and pain,[4] while its expansion and contraction cause the reaction of the limbs. It is not that conduct comes from the mind which is independent of physiological changes in the body, but rather that psychological phenomena such as feeling, image, or desire are always accompanied

---

[1] Cf. ch. II. § 4. [2] Part. An. III. 4. 666 a 7.
[3] Ibid, II. 2. 648 a 3-12; II. 4. 650 b 18-26.   [4] Ibid. III. 4. 666 a 11.

by physiological phenomena, especially those of the heart.[1] As prudence or practical reason is after all the principle which is due to the natural care to regulate desires and allow their finality to be realized,[2] it is potentially contained in the physiological structure and function of the heart, and is influenced by it. Consequently, the complete actuality of prudence is indeed proper to man, but all animals are considered to possess the function or virtue of prudence in some degree.[3] All living beings want to preserve themselves, and as prudence is the function of conscious self-preservation, the principle which dominates all behavior such as generation, nutrition, love, or intercourse among the same species, is prudence in its extended meaning.[4]

That prudence is founded upon the heart, implies the domination of nature over the ethical virtues. A physiological phenomenon is potentially regulated by prudence in so far as it is mediated by desire, but if prudence itself depends upon the physiological conditions of the heart, it will follow that the ultimate principle of the ethical virtues is what is natural and physiological. Now as action is free in so far as it is dominated by reason, it is a serious matter for prudence, through which the ethical virtues are based upon freedom, to be fundamentally determined of necessity. Is it still possible to admit freedom even if prudence depends upon natural and physiological phenomena? Does it not follow that neither is virtue a merit, nor vice a sin, if our moral character is necessarily determined through the natural constitution of our heart?[5]

To answer this suspicion, let us inquire about Aristotle's theroy of freedom. In Aristotle, and generally in all ancient philosophers, there was no problem of freedom in the sense of *liberum arbitrium*. The only concept of freedom is ἑκούσια, which means the voluntarity of an act, viz., that an act is the realization of one's own desire. προαίρεσις or will is something more than a desire, to be sure, but the only superiority of this is that it is mediated through deliberation about means. Will is considered to be the principle through which we distinguish the moral character of a man, because it shows voluntarity in a higher degree.

The origin of this desire or will was irrelevant to the question

---

[1] Ibid. III. 4. 666 a 31, b 13.
[2] Ch. II. § 2.   [3] Eth. Nic. VI. 7. 1141 a 25 f.
[4] Gen. An. III. 2. 753 a 7-11; Eth. Nic. VI. 7. 1141 a 26-28.
[5] Eth. Nic. III. 7. 1114 a 31-b 8.

of freedom.[1] The so-called *liberum arbitrium indifferentium* in later ages, which seems to indicate an accidental decision of a will without any sufficient cause or reason in nature or in spirit, is by no means the principle of responsibility of a person. We are responsible only for the willing which we do by ourselves through our own characters. That character is conditioned and determined by disposition or circumstances does not discharge us from our responsibility, but rather is ita *sine qua non*. We presuppose a metaphysical dogma which regards personality as a transcendent substance independent of society and of nature, if we consider that this makes responsibility impossible. Such might be the notion of personality in Christianity or in Buddhism, but there is no place for such a mysterious substance in the realistic mind of Aristotle. Personality is impossible without the influence of heredity and circumstances, and there is no place for the operation of heredity and circumstances apart from this specially determined personality. Personality can be the subject of responsibility, just because it is the place where such powers are unified. Freedom for Aristotle belongs to a concrete individual with natural and social determinations, who is rational as well as sensitive, mental as well as corporeal.

Thus understood, human freedom is by no means denied by the fact that the ethical virtues are founded upon prudence, which in its turn depends upon physiological conditions of the body. Prudence may be the principle of morality, without being quite independent of nature.[2] Even if prudence depends upon nature, it neither follows of necessity that there is only nature and no prudence, nor that the morality based upon prudence is a false appearance. Prudence is a reality, even though it depends upon the body, and nature is not a mysterious substance either. That prudence depends upon nature, just means that nature ensures the existence of prudence. It is a false inference to think that nature alone exists without prudence, because prudence depends upon nature. Rather, prudence exists of necessity, because it depends upon nature, viz., the necessity of nature is transferred to the existence of prudence.[3]

Further, because prudence exists of necessity, its functions,

---

[1] Eth. Nic. III. 7. 1114 b 12 ff.; III. 3. 1111 a 29. ff.; III. 1. 1110 b 9 ff.; Eth. Eud. II. 7. 1223 a 21 ff.; cf. ch. II. § 4.
[2] Cf. Phys. VIII. 21. 253 a 8 ff.
[3] Cf. Phys. II. 8. 199 a 5 ff.; cf. p. 184, n. 2, 3.

advice and prohibition, are also necessary for us. In other words, nature controls us through prudence. We should not confuse nature without prudence with nature through prudence; the former is the mode through which nature commands the animal and the plant, while the latter is that through which it commands human beings. Nature makes itself appear in various modes: there is no nature itself which is independent of phenomena. If there should be such a nature, it would be quite inactive, and an inactive nature is mere nonsense. Nature does appear. Once nature is admitted, we ought to admit the reality of its appearance, too. Similarly with free will. The motives which determine the will do not make the freedom of personality impossible, but rather constitute its substance. We often confuse nature as the ground of will and prudence with the natural phenomena which appear both in living and non-living beings, thus assuming personal freedom to be a false appearance. The nature which was regarded as the ground was what may appear in various modes, but now we take one of its forms to be nature itself, so that we cannot but deny human freedom. But nature which was found to lie behind freedom rather makes the existence of freedom necessary. There must be freedom, because human will or conduct has sufficient causes. If on the contrary, these be quite accidental, freedom would become nonsense and man would become quite irresponsible for his acts. There would no longer be independence of personality, and we would fall into complete nihility.

While prudence is the principle and form of the ethical virtues, the physiological construction and function of the heart is their subject. Nevertheless prudence is not a mere corporeal function, but the principle and actuality of ethical virtues. Though desire is under the influence of bodily conditions, a good disposition is not an ethical virtue in actuality, but merely a natural virtue, and an ethical virtue in potentialty.[1] Consequently, Aristotle does not admit that every man is equally virtuous. Men's characters are differentiated through their natural disposition, but a man is not yet actually good or wise, in so far as his (good) disposition remains merely as a disposition. And, when this disposition becomes quite actual, his desires are dominated by prudence. Prudence is also due to a natural disposition, but its development requires other conditions as well, viz. education.[2] And this education is

---

[1] Eth. Nic. VI. 13. 1144 b 1-17.
[2] Eth. Nic. X.10. 1179 b 31-1180 a 12; Pol. III. 4. 1277 a 14.

carried out methodically by a wise man who has perfected his personality.[1] Nature aims at intellect, which in its turn, acts upon nature. Intellect grows and sows its seeds in the good soil—the good soil being a young man of good disposition, and the seeds being the virtues. Thus in theory as well as in practice, intellect maintains its immortality through being revived in new generation and new personality.[2]

What, then, does it mean to say that prudence is the complete actuality of the natural virtues? Natural virtue is different from ethical virtue in that the one is sectional and lacks unity while the other is entire and co-ordinated.[3] For instance, courage is surely founded upon a natural disposition, but that alone is not sufficient to make one behave well, in such a way that he does not fear death in circumstances in which he should not. Natural virtue alone is apt to be rash and unjust. Natural virtue is a receptive disposition to obey the command of prudence. It is the most primitive virtue of the irrational soul in the secondary sense—the minimum of ethical virtue. But on the other side, prudence is acquired *a posteriori*. It is the complete actuality of that natural disposition which is cultivated by education. Therefore, prudence is the gift of seniors as well as the development of natural virtue. In prudence, what is interior is inseparably united with what is exterior, the rational with the irrational, the passive with the active. Natural virtue realizes its end completely when it has developed itself into prudence.

Moreover, natural virtue is one-sided. For instance, one may have a courageous dispostion, but not the dispostion of temperance, whereas prudence does not allow such a separation of virtues. A prudent man is considered to be always consistent with reason. This is because natural virtue is a mere fact, while the virtue of prudence is the ideal. A complete prudence is the very ideal of humanity. It produces a complete harmony among the virtues. Through such a principle of harmony, man can adapt himself to his circumstances—this adaptation is of course natural as well as spiritual—successfully, and preserve his body and soul. In this sense prudence is the perfection of the ethical virtues. Striking its root deep into the earth, it rises high up in the spiritual world. Originating in the same source as the animal and the plant, yet it makes the human

[1] Eth. Nic. X. 10. 1180 b 25-28; 10. 1180 a 14-22; 1180 a 32 ff.
[2] Eth. Nic. X. 10. 1179 b 23 ff.
[3] Eth. Nic. VI. 13. 1144 b 34-1145 a 2.

mind participate in divine thinking. Prudence itself is just a kind of human intellect, and is concerned with human affairs, but man ought to maintain harmony of body and calmness of mind in order to communicate with eternal spirits and to partake in the divine activity through the theoretical cognition of the world. Just as a state ought to be well governed and to be rich in order to be prosperous in its culture and civilization, so it is with the individual man. (One might oppose the objection that some cultures are prosperous rather in ages of political confusion, but this is similar to the fact that grass decays after flower and fruit, or the fact that an insect dies after its egg-laying. The mother, culture, finishes her life on account of her overripeness. It is not culture itself which produces the decadence of life. A mere material prosperity which begets no culture is like a strong body without virtue, which would only degrade the man to the status of a lower animal.) Prudence is necessary for the actualization of thoretical cognition which is *per se* the most valuable of all things. It is as much the medium of the eternal intelligible world and the human beings, as the process from the irrational soul to the theoretical intellect.[1]

Prudence is based upon the heart and is interdependent with ethical virtue, which originates in natural virtue. Consequently, though in its strict sense, it is proper to man, in its wider sense it may be found in animals as well. Here is a continuity among reason, sensibility, and the body. Human virtue is associated with the virtues of animals. Man and animal were strictly separated by Christianity, and the modern view of humanity has long been under the yoke of this prejudice. Even after the moderns discovered society, it has been regarded as a spiritual world and compared to the state of God, so that morality was quite alien to life. One might suspect that Aristotle's theory of ethics is biological and not social. But it would be rather strange, if the Greek who found the essence of man in political activity, should have neglected the social character of morality. It does not follow that human virtue is unsocial even if it is continuous with the self-preservation of animals. Moarlity is not a mere spiritual affair, nor is society a mere spiritual community. Though the idea of society may be spiritual, there lurks in its depth the immediate demand for the preservation and development of mankind. Human virtue must in this respect, be connected with animal instinct. Needless to say,

[1] Eth. Nic. VI. 13. 1145 a 6-11; cf. ibid. 7. 1141 a 20; Pol. VII. 15. 1334 a14-20.

Aristotle's concept of justice or freindship is by no means merely individualistic. Even temperance is more than a means of clever enjoyment, but presupposes social norms. Being thus founded upon the demand to preserve and promote life, it is rather the end of living creatures in general, than an individual end. Thus, social virtue is connected with natural fitness. This is indeed a merit, rather than a fault, of Aristotle's ethical theory.

Thus far, we have studied the prudence which is conceived in the same sense as practical reason or the intellectual intuition of practical affairs. But prudence is not limited to such a narrower sense. It was said that in practical affairs, reason is concerned not with the general but with the individual. Since there is a universal cognition of practical affairs, we must investigate what it is. We can find in Aristotle no special concept that signifies such a faculty. δεινότης is concerned with the individual rather than with the universal. According to our previous consideration, δεινότης and πανουργία could not be concerned with the universal, just because intuition was impossible with regard to the practical universal. On the other side, however, Walter's attempt to borrow the highest principle of practical cognition from theoretical intellect is not successful. For theoretical reason cannot conceive the practical principle, while knowledge is the function of theoretical inference and not the intuition of principles. The object of Aristotle's theoretical intellect is through and through an eternal and necessary being which is beyond human interest. If it were the major premiss of practical inference, it would aim at individual affairs or utility and lose its qualification as theoretical. For Aristotle, a theoretical knowledge about a practical object would be a mere *contradictio in adjecto*. Then, is practical thinking lacking in the highest kind of universal cognition? Aristotle repeatedly says that a strict and necessary cognition is impossible in practical affairs and there is at best only a probable and statistic knowledge. Not that it is quite impossible to have universal knowledge, e.g., the knowledge which constitutes the contents of ethics or politics—that contemplation is the highest happiness, or that the essence of ethical virtue is the mean, or that justice lies in proportional distribution, etc. The faculty of such cognitions is nothing other than prudence or master prudence. As aforesaid, prudence is sometimes called an intuition of individual affairs which is like common sensation, and is sometimes considered to be the cognition of universal laws of prcatcice.

The end of practical cognition is an individual act, yet we need a universal knowledge to act rightly in a particular case. A man of practice is not yet a prudent man or a wise man, unless he has also a general cognition about the essence of practice. Not even moral conduct is possible if one have only particular cognitions. If it were possible, it would only be by much good fortune. Real morality depends upon such a master prudence as ethics and politics. A wise man or a man of prudence is he who has a universal knowledge about practice. Moral cognition and conduct are accompanied by each other. In order to be really moral in individual cases, it is not sufficient for one to possess experience; one is required to know the moral principles as well. And in order to possess a universal knowledge about moral affairs, one is required to have a constant devotion to and investigation about practice, for the cognition of moral principles presupposes experience. Hence children are able neither to have moral cognition nor to act morally. Now these two kinds of prudence, i.e. the universal and the particular, are mediated with each other and form a kind of inference similar to scientific knowledge. This is the so-called practical syllogism; and as we have said before, deliberation, cleverness, and the like, seem to be appearances of this practical syllogism.

CHAPTER V

THE PRACTICAL SYLLOGISM

§ 1. DELIBERATION

THE end of practical cognition may be a particular act, yet its directing principle must be something universal. Therefore, prudence in a wider sense contains both universal and particular cognitions, and takes a syllogistic form. As an example of such a syllogism, we find first of all βούλευσις or deliberation. We said something about this previously,[1] but we must now again study the essence of this main concept of practical cognition. According to the *Ethica Nicomachea*,[2] the objects of deliberation are neither eternal things, such as heavenly bodies or geometrical figures, nor natural phenomena which always happen in the same way, such as the solstices or the rising of the stars. Nor are they the things which happen now in one way, now in another, e.g. draughts or rains; nor chance events like the finding of treasures. They are rather human affairs and what are in our power. We deliberate about what may be done by us, and not always in the same way, e.g. the healing of sickness or the accumulating of wealth, and especially what involves indefiniteness. Besides, we deliberate not about ends but about means. For a physician does not deliberate whether he shall heal, nor an orator whether he shall persuade, nor a statesman whether he shall produce law and order, nor does anyone else deliberate about his end. They assume the end and consider how and by what means it is to be attained; and if it seems to be produced by several means, they consider by what it is most easily and best produced, while if it is achieved by one only, they consider how it will be achieved by this and by what means this will be achieved, till they come to the first cause, which in the order of discovery is the last. And if we come on an impossibility, we give up the search. Thus deliberation is the search for the series of possible means within our power. Just by this special character, is deliberation distinguished from wish. In summarizing the above statements, Aristotle says: "It seems, then, as has been said, that man is a moving principle of actions; now deliberation is about the things to be done by the agent

---

[1] Ch. II. § 2.   [2] Eth. Nic. III. 5. 1112 a 18–1113 a 2.

himself, and actions are for the sake of things other than themselves. For the end cannot be a subject of deliberation, but only the means; nor indeed can the particular facts be a subject of it, ... If we are to be always deliberating, we shall have to go on to infinity." This object of deliberation is also the object of προαίρεσις, only differing in that the object of will is determined but the object of deliberation is not. "Since the object of will is one of the things in our own power which is desired after deliberation, will must be deliberate desire of things in our own power; for when we have decided as a result of deliberation, we desire in accordance with our deliberation."[1] The end is said to be what we wish for, and the means what we deliberate about and will.[2]

Thus Aristotle repeats that the object of deliberation and will is not the end, but the means.[3] Therefore, in order that deliberation may begin to act, a desire must precede it as its motive.[4] The search for the means to realize this original desire being deliberation, this deliberation must be subordinate to that desire. But the deliberation allows us to have a concrete desire or a will, which may be regarded as the determination of that primary desire. Will is a desire determined through deliberation as to the means.[5] But, as said before, deliberation may be the efficient cause of desire as well, and the desire which presupposes such deliberation was called not a προαίρεσις but a βούλησις i.e. a wish. This wish, being a calculated desire, was more highly estimated than ἐπιθυμία or θύμος. Deliberation as the moment of will was the cognition of means. But deliberation as the moment of desire, was according to our interpretation, the estimative calculation of ends.[6]

Thus the concept of deliberation is divided into two kinds, the one being the estimation of ends, and the other the calculation of means. Though Aristotle does not mention the matter explicitly, these two kinds of deliberation would have presumably some reference to the distinction between practice and production. Production was assumed to be the realization of a real form, and practice that of a moral value. Production realizes the form in a process, while practice realizes it at once.[7] May we not then presume that the βουλευ-

[1] Eth. Nic. III. 5. 1113 a 2-14.   [2] Eth. Nic. III. 7. 1113 b 3.
[3] Eth. Nic. III. 4 1111 b 26; 5. 1112 b 32; VI. 2. 1139 a13; Eth. Eud. II. 10. 1226 b 10; [Mag. Mor. I. 35. 1196 b 29;] Rhet. I. 2. 1357 a 4; 6. 1362 a 18; III. 5. 1383 a 7;   cf. Eth. Eud. II. 11. 1227 b 20 ff.
[4] Eth. Eud. II. 10. 1226 b 16-20.
[5] Eth. Eud. II. 10. 1226 b 29 f.   [6] Ch. II. § 2.   [7] Ch. III. § 3.

σις which is here qualified as estimative calculation, is practical cognition or φρόνησις, while the βούλευσις which was qualified as the searching for means is productive cognition or τέχνη. In fact, the object of βούλευσις are what can be otherwise—not natural phenomena of which the determinative principles exist in the phenomena themselves, but what are in our power, and can be brought about by our efforts. But conduct is either practice or production, so that deliberation is not only the cognition of practice, but also the principle of production.[1] If it be admitted that deliberation is the cognition that guides conduct in general, including both practice and production, there should be, corresponding to the difference between practice and production, in deliberation itself the distinction between practical deliberation and productive. The one forms the moment of prudence, and the other that of art.

But, the distinction between practice and production was not maintained explicitly enough by Aristotle, and a mere actualization of a real form was often presented as an instance of practice. As a moment of prudence, deliberation surely contains practical intellect, but it is in most cases explained as being an technical intellect—just as in the above quotation, where it is illustrated by healing, oration, or administration, and in other places, by navigation, gymnastics, and accumulation of wealth.[2] They are all productions, so that deliberation about them would be technical. But according to our interpretation of practice and production, deliberation as the moment of practice and prudence should not be a searching for the means to realize a state of affairs, but an estimative calculation to actualize a moral value.

Deliberation is generally said to be a searching for the means, whereas the end of production lies in the result, and that of prac-

---

[1] Eth. Nic. III. 5. 1112 b 6 - 8. But, Phys. II. 8. 199 b 28: καίτοι καὶ ἡ τέχνη οὐ βουλεύεται seems to suggest that deliberation does involve art. According to Teichmüller, it means that art is concerned with the universal, whereas deliberation applies it to the particular (Arist.Forsch. II. 398). According to Zeller, this is a statement about an expert. Ross, quoting Eth. Nic. III. 5. 1112 a 34, interpretes it to mean that strict and self-sufficient knowledge involves no deliberation. These are all probable interpretations, but what is stated in the text is the analogy between nature and art, so that this should be rather taken as "In the minimum consciousness of art, there is only minimum deliberation". This means certainly that deliberation is the essential element of production, but becomes weak, as art approaches either to science or to nature.

[2] Eth. Nic. III. 5. 1112 b 4 f.

tice in the act itself.¹ Therefore, deliberation in production is the thinking of the process which will lead to the end, i.e., the thinking of the means *par excellence*. But practice is not a movement that realizes its real end gradually, but an actuality without process, its end being equally actual throughout the act. Consequently, the consideration of the means to reach a practical end is not a thinking about cause and effect, but a thinking about the subordination or subsumption of eternal meanings or values. It refers not to cause and effect, but to the universal and the particular. But is it true that Aristotle really assumed deliberation to be such an estimation of moral values? To answer this question, let us study his statements about the virtue of deliberation.

The concept which indicates the virtue of deliberation most literally is εὐβουλία. According to Aristotle, excellence in deliberation is a certian correctness of deliberation, but there being more than one kind of correctness, excellence in deliberation plainly is not any and every kind; for an incontinent man or a bad man, if he is clever, will reach as a result of his calculation what he sets before himself, so that he will have deliberated correctly, but will get for himself a great evil.² Consequently, not every correctness is a good thing. Now excellence of deliberation is thought to be a good thing. In what sense, then, is it correct?

Since it is a good thing, and brings about happiness, it must be the correctness of deliberation which tends to attain what is good,³ for however correctly the means to a bad end may be deliberated, it will only lead to an evil. When the value of an end is left out of account, and the deliberation concentrates itself upon the means, excellence in it is called δεινότης, i.e. cleverness. When it subordinates itself to a good end, it may be prudence, but if, on the contrary, to a bad end, it will be πανουργία or craftiness.⁴

If we should distinguish excellence of deliberation from craftiness by attributing the goodness of the end to the former, excellence of deliberation would not only be the virtue of cognition about the means, but also the virtue of desire, which, in its turn, depends on deliberation about the means. Now deliberation was assumed to be thinking about the means. Besides, there is the concept pru-

---

[1] Eth. Nic. VI. 2. 1139 b 5; 5. 1140 b 6 f.
[2] Eth. Nic. VI. 10. 1142 b 16-20.   [3] Eth. Nic. VI. 10. 1142 b 20 ff.
[4] Eth. Nic. VI. 13. 1144 a 23 - 28.

dence which is the virtue both of desire and of thinking. How, then, does εὐβουλία refer to φρόνησις? Talking only of prudence, Aristotle makes it contain both the good end and the excellence of deliberation.[1] In comparison with the ethical virtues, he talks about prudence as if it were concerned with the means.[2] But when distinguishing it from εὐβουλία, he says that prudence is the grasping of a good end and treats it as the intuition of the end.

Surely, it is a one-sided view to take prudence as the mere holding of a good end.[3] For to establish an immediate purpose is the function of desire rather than that of intellect. And the virtue of desire is an ethical virtue, while prudence is regarded as a kind of intellectual virtue.[4] Of course, desire is not irrelevant to prudence: ethical virtue is another side of prudence, being only different from it as the potential is from the actual. Prudence as an intellectual virtue is the formal principle of the ethical virtues or their complete actuality. Hence it must have sufficient grounds and must be verified as to the rightness of its end, even though it presupposes desire through which one holds the good end. Prudence is neither the setting up of a particular end, nor the understanding of a universal law, but the mediation of the universal and the particular.[5] It must be in its concreteness a syllogism. But, if on the other hand, εὐβουλία be a syllogistic cognition which inquires about the means of a good end, prudence will hardly be different from the excellence of deliberation. The only possible difference would be whether the emphasis is laid on the end or on the means.

For all that, we must not forget that εὐβουλία does not mean the general excellence of deliberation, but is confined to a particular one. It is the excellence of deliberation in so far as it is the moment of prudence,[6] and deliberation may have other excellences than this. Here is found the distinction between practical and productive deliberation, which we have postulated before. In order to elucidate the essence of prudence, Aristotle asks what is a prudent man:—"Now it is thought to be the mark of a prudent man to be able to deliberate well about what is good and expedient

[1] Eth. Nic. VI. 5. 1140 a 29.
[2] Eth. Nic. VI. 13. 1144 a 8 f.; 1145 a 4 - 6.
[3] Eth. Nic. VI. 10. 1142 b 31-33.
[4] Eth. Nic. I. 13. 1102 b 28-1103 a 10; VI. 5. 1140 b 26; 13. 1144 b 14.
[5] Eth. Nic. VI. 8. 1141 b 14 f.; ibid. 21-23.
[6] Eth. Nic. VI. 8. 1141 b 8-10.

for himself, not in some particular respect, e.g., about what sorts of thing conduce to health or to strength, but about what sorts of thing conduce to the good life in general."[1] "The man who is without qualification good at deliberating is the man who is capable of aiming in accordance with calculation at the best for man of things attainable by action."[2] Hence deliberation as the moment of prudence is generally the consideration of what is good and bad or expedient and inexpedient, and it is implied that there may yet be other realms of activity for deliberation or calculation.

εὐβουλία is not merely the virtue of deliberation in general, but particularly that which serves for a good end. But if it is nothing more than deliberation of the means to realize the end, the good and bad of the end would be merely accidental to deliberation in itself. As far as it is the excellence of deliberation, there should be no essential difference, whether it may subserve a good end or a bad. There would be the one virtue of deliberation, only differing in its value accidentally in accordance with what end its value might serve. In fact, Aristotle presents us a pure pragmatic intellect, viz. δεινότης or cleverness. "This is such as to be able to do the things that tend towards the mark we have set before ourselves, and to hit it. Now if the mark be noble, the cleverness is laudable, but if the mark be bad, the cleverness is mere smartness; hence we call even men of practical wisdom clever or smart. Prudence is not this faculty, but it does not exist without this faculty." It is compared to the soul's eye, and is said to require ethical virtue in order to become prudence.[3] Further, both cleverness and prudence belong to the opinion-making part, and they are related to each other just as natural virtue is to ethical virtue. Cleverness and natural virtue are both natural dispositions without any moral value in the strict sense. A mere natural virtue is possible even to children and animals, and is not under the control of reason. "But without reason these are evidently hurtful. Yet, ...while one may be led astray by them, as a strong body which moves without sight may stumble badly because of its lack of sight, still, if a man once acquires reason, that makes a difference in action; and his state, while still like what it was, will then be virtue in the strict sense. ... This is why some say that all the virtues

[1] Eth. Nic. VI. 5. 1140 a 24-28; cf. Mag. Mor. II. 3. 1199 a 4 ff.
[2] Eth. Nic. VI. 8. 1141 b 13 f.; cf. ibid.10. 1142 b 29.
[3] Eth. Nic. V. 13. 1144 a 28.

are forms of prudence, and why Socrates in one respect was on the right track while in another he went astray; in thinking that all the virtues were forms of prudence he was wrong, but in saying they implied prudence he was right. This is confirmed by the fact that even now all men, when they define virtue, after naming the state of character and its objects, add 'that (state) which is in accordance with the right rule'; now the right rule is that which is in accordance with prudence. All men, then, seem somehow to divine that this kind of state is virtue, viz. that which is in accordance with prudence. But we must go a little further. For it is not merely the state in accordance with the right rule, but the state that implies the presence of the right rule, that is virtue; and prudence is a right rule about such matters.... It is clear, then, from what has been said, that it is not possible to be good in the strict sense without prudence, nor prudent without ethical virtue."[1]

Thus considered, it is evident that cleverness and natural virtues are the foundations of prudence and ethical virtues, but we cannot say that cleverness accompanied by natural virtue is prudence or an ethical virtue. Ethical virtue, which is essentially a habitual character, cannot result from the mere addition of two kinds of natural disposition. Though cleverness is necessary for prudence, we cannot reason that cleverness is the intellectual element of prudence, and when it is removed from prudence, there will remain only natural virtue. Similarly, cleverness is not the residue of natural virtue from ethical virtue. Much less can we get ethical virtue by abstracting cleverness from prudence, or prudence by abstracting natural virtue from ethical virtue. Cleverness and natural virtue are not the elements of prudence or ethical virtue. In conforming to reason, natural virtue ceases to be natural and becomes ethical virtue. When cleverness subserves ethical virtue, it is no longer natural sagaciousness, but has altered its quality. Such is what is really meant by saying that it is "a moment". Cleverness as the moment of prudence is changed into ἐυβουλία. And this excellence of deliberation is no longer the searching for the means to a real end. It is not sufficient to be a moment of prudence, if it be unchanged in its intellectual activity and only subserve accidentally both good ends and bad. Being the moment of prudence, ἐυβουλία must be ethical in its intellectual activity. It is not the excellence of deliberation in general, but

[1] Eth. Nic. VI. 13. 1144 b 9-32; X. 8. 1178 a 16-19.

that of judgement or inference about the value of conduct, viz. the excellence of practical deliberation.

It was said, on the other hand, that ethical virtue presupposes prudence. Now, if prudence is a mere searching for the real means, we cannot understand the reason why it is necessary for ethical virtue. That prudence presupposes ethical virtue, would in this case contribute nothing to prudence in its reference to ethical virtue; if we suppose otherwise, we will only be lead into a circle. But when we abstract ethical virtue from prudence, there remains only practical intellect. If this practical intellect is the cognition of a mere fact, ethical virtue might well have found in it a useful instrument, yet by no means would have become really ethical through it. In order to be qualified in such a manner, ethical virtue must owe to it something more important. The ὀρθὸς λόγος which accompanies ethical virtue, should be not the cognition of the means to realize a state of affairs, but the estimation of what is good and what is bad, or of what is the mean between too much and too little.[1] It must be practical rather than productive deliberation. Otherwise it would not be possible to say, "with the presence of the one quality, prudence, will be given all the virtues".[1] If the intellectual moment in prudence is merely

---

[1] Eth. Nic. VI. 5. 1140 b 8-10; 1140 a 25; II. 6. 1106 b 36-1107 a 2: ἔστιν ἄρα ἡ ἀρετὴ ἕξις προαιρετική, ἐν μεσότητι οὖσα τῇ πρὸς ἡμᾶς, ὡρισμένη λόγῳ καὶ ᾧ ἂν ὁ φρόνιμος ὁρίσειεν. This ὀρθὸς λόγος which is the measure of moderation, is precisely the intellectual moment of φρόνησις. It is not a mere cognition of causality, which helps us to realize any end whatever efficiently, but rather the faculty of discriminating about passion and conduct, about what is suitable in respect of time, matter, person, and other situations. Also calculation as the moment of continence, is not the cognition of how to attain execssive enjoyment, but the estimating of what is suitable enjoyment. Cf. Eth. Nic. VII. 2. 1145 b 10; Eth. Nic. V. 2. 1139 a 21-31: ἔστι δ' ὅπερ ἐν διανοίᾳ κατάφασις καὶ ἀπόφασις, τοῦτ' ἐν ὀρέξει δίωξις καὶ φυγή· ὥστ' ἐπειδὴ ἡ ἠθικὴ ἀρετὴ ἕξις προαιρετική, ἡ δὲ προαίρεσις ὄρεξις βουλευτική, δεῖ διὰ ταῦτα μὲν τόν τε λόγον ἀληθῆ εἶναι καὶ τὴν ὄρεξιν ὀρθήν, εἴπερ ἡ προαίρεσις σπουδαία, καὶ τὰ αὐτὰ τὸν μὲν φάναι τὴν δὲ διώκειν. αὕτη μὲν οὖν ἡ διάνοια καὶ ἡ ἀλήθεια πρακτική· τῆς δὲ θεωρητικῆς διανοίας καὶ μὴ πρακτικῆς μηδὲ ποιητικῆς, τὸ εὖ καὶ κακῶς τἀληθές ἐστι καὶ ψεῦδος. τοῦτο γάρ ἐστι παντὸς διανοητικοῦ ἔργον· τοῦ δὲ πρακτικοῦ καὶ διανοητικοῦ ἀλήθεια ὁμολόγως ἔχουσα τῇ ὀρέξει τῇ ὀρθῇ. How is it possible to take such an intellect as the cognition of means employed by a good desire? Eth. Nic. VI. 5. 1140 b 20 - 24: ὥστ' ἀνάγκη τὴν φρόνησιν ἕξιν εἶναι μετὰ λόγου ἀληθῆ περὶ τὰ ἀνθρώπινα ἀγαθὰ πρακτικήν. ἀλλὰ μὲν τέχνης μὲν ἔστιν ἀρετή, φρονήσεως δ' οὐκ ἔστιν· καὶ ἐν μὲν τέχνῃ ὁ ἑκὼν ἁμαρτάνων αἱρετώτερος, περὶ δὲ φρόνησιν ἧττον, ὥσπερ καὶ περὶ τὰς ἀρετάς.

the cognition of causality, this intellect would require all the ethical virtues, each independently, in order to acquire moral value. It is just because the cognition in prudence is essentially ethical that one may say, "with the presence of prudence, will be given all the virtues".

Thus, deliberation must contain a moral estimation of passion and conduct besides pure technical cognition such as cleverness or the deliberation which is used by an incontinent man.

§ 2. PRACTICAL AND PRODUCTIVE SYLLOGISMS

So far we have assumed that deliberation as the chief moment of prudence should be divided into what is concerned with practice or moral value, and what is concerned with production of mere fact. This may be proved through the study of the practical syllogism as the form of deliberation. Deliberation is the main function of practical intellect, just as knowledge is of theoretical intellect. Just as knowledge, being the association of the universal and the particular in the theoretical area, forms a syllogism, deliberation, being the association of the universal and the particular in the practical area, realizes itself in the so-called practical syllogism. But the concept "practical syllogism" does not appear in Aristotle's works except in the incomplete expression in Eth. Nic. VI. 13. 1144 a 31. This is a strange fact for a philosopher who analysed the forms of the syllogism in his logical works so minutely. It might be supposed that Aristotle assumed the syllogism in general to be theoretical and only applicable accidentally to practice. On the other hand, however, in the *Analytica* and the *Topica*, the syllogism is divided into the demonstrative and the dialectic. This presumably suggests the distinction between the theoretical and the practical syllogisms. According to the statement in the *Topica*, the demonstrative syllogism starts from

---

This is because art is concerned merely with the means, while prudence is concerned with the value of ends. By the virtue of art, Walter understands, presumably not rightly, the art which serves for a good end. The foregoing passage would rather seem to mean that art may sometimes signify a mere faculty. Virtue is not confined to the ethical; the virtue of art is certainly an intellectual virtue. Eth. Nic. X. 8. 1178 a 16.

[1] Eth. Nic. VI. 13. 1145 a 2.

asserting one of the contradictory opposites, whereas the dialectic depends upon the adversary's choice between two contradictories which are both probable.[1] Also, according to the *Topica*, the one starts from a true and fundamental principle, while the other starts from a general opinion.[2] Now the principle of the demonstrative syllogism is evidently the object of theoretical reason, but the so-called general opinion which is considered to be the principle of the dialectic syllogism, is according to the explanation in the *Topica*, "the opinions which are accepted by every one or by the majority, or by philosophers—i.e. by all, or by the majority, or by the most notable and illustrious of them".[3] Now, theoretical knowledge was the theory concerning the kind of being which is necessary and cannot be otherwise, and practical cognition was the probable knowledge of that kind of being which is accidental and may be otherwise than it is. Further the principle of the former is grasped *a priori*, without experience or skill, while that of the latter presupposes the ethical virtues which are acquired through habituation. Taking this into account, we cannot deny an afinity between the demonstrative syllogism and the theoretical syllogism on the one hand, and between the dialectic syllogism and the practical syllogism on the other. It is true that the distinction between demonstration and dialectics is essentially a difference of form of thinking and of intention rather than that of objects.[4] The one aims at the truth, while the other aims at persuasion. But the form and certainty of a cognition is different in accordance with its object, and the certainty which is possible with regard to eternal and necessary being, is not looked for in the area of changeable and accidental appearances. It is no less a methodical fallacy to demand a demonstration in the area of practice than to argue dialectically in the area of theoretical knowledge.[5] Plato was lacking in this reflection on methodology, and even Aristotle was not sure enough about the correspondence of method and object in his early age as represented by the *Organon*. But we may regard this distinction between demonstration and dialectics to be equivalent to Aristotle's later distinction between theoretical

[1] An. Pr. I. 1. 24 a 22-26; ibid. a 30-b12; An. Post. I. 2. 72 a 8.
[2] Top. I. 1. 100 a 27 ff. Here Aristotle enumerates ἐριστικὸς συλλογισμός and παραλογισμός.
[3] Top. I. 1. 100 b 21. [4] Met. IV. 2. 1004 b 22 - 26.
[5] Eth. Nic. I. 1. 1094 b 19-27; Eth. Nic. II. 2. 1103 b 34 ff.

knowledge and practical knowledge. In reality, practical affairs were especially a hot bed for the quibbles of the Sophists, and both Socrates and Plato devoted themselves to establishing a science about these matters. Whereas the merits of Aristotle lie, in his early age, in the organization of logical formulae as the weapon of this science, and, in his later age, in the recognition of the peculiarity of practical cognition. The principle of the dialectic syllogism, which remained indefinite *a priori*, is now determined through a habitual character or a desire. This is a practical determination through the ethical virtues. Without such virtues, a theory would result in nothing.[1] In spite of this remarkable resemblance between the dialectic syllogism and the practical syllogism, a detailed treatment of the practical syllogism is found only in the later works.

The most fundamental mark of the practical syllogism is that the conclusion forms the principle of practice directly. The distinction between theoretical and practical cognitions was not, as aforesaid, that the one is concerned with the universal and the other only with the particular, but in whether the cognition is self-sufficient or subserves practice. Therefore, the theoretical syllogism should be distinguished from the practical in respect to the end, viz. the former results in nothing but knowledge, while the latter produces conduct. It is said in Eth. Nic. VII. 4. 1147 a 25: "The one opinion is universal, and the other is concerned with the particular facts, and here we come to something within the sphere of perception; when a single opinion results from the two, the soul must in one type of case affirm the conclusion, while in the case of opinions concerned with production, it must immediately act."[2] Similarly in the *De Motu Animalium,* following the statement that the animal acts through imagination, sensation, or reason, it is argued: "But how is it that reason (viz. sense, imagination, and reason proper) is sometimes followed by action, sometimes not; sometimes by movement, sometimes not ? What happens seems parallel to the case of thinking and inferring about the immovable objects of science. There the end is the truth seen.. but here the two premisses result in a conclusion which is an action...."[3] But whence comes this practical conclusion ? If the principle of practice comes from outside of the inference,

---

[1] Eth. Nic. I.1. 1095 a 2; 2. 1095 b 4; II. 3. 1105 b 11; VI. 12. 1143 b 6; VII. 5. 1147 a 10.   [2] Eth. Nic. VII. 5. 1147 a 25.
[3] Motu An. 7. 701 a 7 - 13.

the inference itself can no longer be essentially practical, but at most only accidentally so. That a cognition itself may be essentially practical, the inference itself must involve a practical element. Now the inference consists of two elements, viz. the major premiss and the minor. Therefore in order that the practical syllogism may be essentially practical, either both or at least one of these premisses must be in some sense or other practical.[2] A practical judgement must be an expression of some volition. And the object of volition is generally a value or a valuable being, so the judgement which expresses a volition concerns itself with a value. There are two possible ways of such concernment. The one orders one to pursue a general value, and the other recognizes a particular object as bearing the value in question. In a wider sense, both may be called estimation, but estimation in the strict sense is confined to the second kind of judgement which recognizes a particular thing to be valuable. If the practical syllogism consists of these two sorts of estimation, the major premiss should be the former, and the minor the latter. Now, there are various kinds of value, and Aristotle divides them into three, viz. virtue, pleasure, and utility.[3] The former two are themselves valuable, while the third is valuable only as a means to an end.[4] Consequently, we will expect estimation and syllogism to be divided into three kinds. The one is that which involves the recognition of virtue and the ordering of its pursuit, the second involves the desire for pleasure, and the third the pursuit of utility. Virtue and pleasure are themselves valuable and the imperative that orders us to pursue them is without qualification, but the advice of utility presupposes a volition towards an ultimate value. The one is the so-called categorical imperative, and the other the hypo-

---

[2] Cf. Teichmüller, Neue Studien etc. III. 42 ff.

[3] Eth. Nic. VIII. 2. 1155 b 18 - 21. A similar division of values is also given corresponding to the three modes of life; e.g. Eth. Nic. I. 3. 1095 b 14-19; ibid. 1096 a 5 - 7. Also in Eth. Eud. I. 1. 1214 a 32, and 4. 1215 a 32, virtue, prudence, and pleasure are enumerated as the contents of the good or of happiness. Since this φρόνησις or θεωρία is a kind of intellectial virtue, what is above called merely virtue, is ethical virtue that is essential to political life. Therefore, the second and the third kind of virtue in the division following the forms of life correspond to the first kind of φιλητόν and the money-making life is a part of the third life which pursues utility. A more detailed enumeration of value is found in Rhet. I. 6.

[4] Cf. Pol. VII. 13. 1332 a 7.

thetical. As for the infinite pursuit of wealth, Aristotle takes it as the pursuit of the means to satisfying bodily pleasure.[1] But it might rather be more suitably regarded as pleasure in the acquisition of wealth. At any rate, if the syllogism is thus divided according to three corresponding kinds of value, the practical intellect also should be divided into three; viz., prudence which determines the moral value of a practice, cleverness which advises for the enjoyment of pleasure, and technical calculation about the means which leads to virtue or pleasure. But the second, which is concerned with enjoyment, has no importance with regard to the practical syllogism. For a mere pursuit of pleasure scarcely takes a syllogistic form, but it is by nature impulsive and irrational.[2] Only when an appetite asserts itself against the moral wish under the cloak of rationality, does it appear in the form of the sophistic syllogism.[3] We must suppose that the practical syllogism in the strict sense to be the form of the second and the third. Thus according to our investigation, the practical syllogism consists of the major premiss which orders one to purpose a value in general, and the minor premiss, which recognizes the presence of a value in a particular case. This value is sometimes the virtue *per se* valuable, sometimes a utility for an end. Accordingly, the practical syllogism would be divided into that which infers about the moral value of a practice and that which does about the real means for an end. We must investigate whether our supposition be confirmed by the statements of Aristotle himself.

To begin with, let us examine the *Organon*. For, logic being the science of the formulae of thinking, it precedes the distinction between theoretical and practical thinking. Judgement as the element of inference, is here divided in modality, as well as both in quality and quantity. Aristotle's "modality" is not the same as that of Kant, viz., the degree of certainty, but is rather the ontological relation between a subject and a predicate. A mere difference of certainty is a psychological distinction and lacks in logical objectivity. Even for Kant, modality was a secondary distinction and was only arbitrarily ranked with other categories. Much less for Aristotle's ontological logics should there be room for a non-

---

[1] Pol. I. 9. 1258 a 4; cf. ibid. 1257 a 1-1258 a 19; 10. 1258 a 38 ff.; Eth. Nic. I. 3. 1096 a 5.

[2] Eth. Nic. VII. 7. 1149 a 34; Eth. Eud. II. 8. 1224 b 2.

[3] Eth. Nic. VII. 5. 1147 a 24; cf. Teichmüller, Neue Studien etc. III. 43 f.

objective distinction. In his system, modality must be an attribute of being rather than of thought.

Possible judgement, pure judgement, and necessary judgement are the judgements in which the predicate is attributed to the subject either possibly, purely, or necessarily. Now, there is a certain correspondence between modality of the premisses and that of the conclusion. Generally speaking, a pure conclusion is inferred only from pure premisses, and if at least one premiss is possible or necessary, the conclusion must also be possible or necessary. In other words, to get a possible or a necessary judgement, at least one of the premisses must be possible or necessary.[1]

Now practical affairs are able to be otherwise, viz., are "possible", and practice realizes a moral value in such a realm. An experience of desire is simply expressed by the subject in a pure assertion, but the end-object of a certain desire is *necessary* for this particular subject, whereas the means to realize this end-object is only *potentially* an object of the desire. Thus, if we let "A" represent the desiring subject, "C" the desired end-object, and "B" the means to the end, the relation between the subject and its end will be expressed as "A *necessarily* seeks C", e.g., "I *must* be healthy". The relation between means and end-object, on the other hand, will be formulated as "B *potentially* leads to C", e.g., "The meat of birds, if eaten, *potentially* (under the right conditions) leads to health"; therefore, "The meat of birds is *potentially* what I seek in order to be healthy"; and so we have "A *potentially* (or *possibly*) seeks B" (this is only *possible*, i.e., it could be otherwise: the meat of birds is not dictated by my desire *necessarily* as my end in the way health is). When certain conditions are fulfilled, the possible judgement may be transformed into the hypothetical judgement, "If A seeks C, A will seek B", e.g., "If one wishes health, one will wish the meat of birds". Of course, even if practical judgement is either possible or necessary, possible or necessary judgement is not always practical. There may be some possible or necessary judgements which are not practical. Therefore, we cannot afford to infer the axiological character of practical syllogism from the formal law of modality. We must content ourselves if we can be certain that the law which holds among the elements of the practical syllogism is consistent with the formal law of inference.

Now, the principle that the inference which leads to a possible

[1] An. Pr. I. 12. 32 a 6 - 12.

or necessary conclusion must have possible or necessary premises is homologous with the principle that the judgement which gives a practical conclusion must be practical. For, supposing that the element of the practical syllogism may be a mere theoretical assertion of a fact, an inference which consists of pure judgements may also lead to a necessary or to a possible conclusion. This, however, is, as aforesaid, incompatible with the statement in the *Analytica*. — What we can deduce from the argument concerning the forms of thinking in the *Organon* is only such a negative proof. Among the statements about the practical syllogism, the most complete description of its form is that in De An. III. 11.[1] Its major premiss is "Such and such a man should do such and such a thing", and its minor premiss: "I am such and such a man", and "This is such and such a thing." Form these two premisses, we conclude: "I should do this." And this conclusion is immediately the principle of conduct. Now, this is a combination of two inferences, about the subject and the object. It will be analysed into one pair of syllogisms: "Such and such a man should do such and such a thing." "I am such and such a man." Therefore, "I should do such and such a thing". These judgements form the first group; and making this conclusion of the first inference the major premiss, we add a minor premiss: "This is such and such a thing" and get the second conclusion: "So I should do this". From this formula, we may see that the major premiss of the practical syllogism expresses that a certain act is practically necessary to a certain subject, or in other words, that a certain value demands to be realized through a certain subject.[2] Whereas, the two minor premisses express that a certain subject (or rather an act) satisfies the requirement. Hence it is inferred that a certain act is practically necessary for a certain subject. But from such a mere formal determination, we cannot recognize what value these acts or beings have, or what kind of practical necessity there be. The middle term of the major premiss, "such and such a thing" expresses a certain value for a subject. But, is it self-value or utility ? And what is the ground of the practical

[1] De An. III. 11. 434 a 16.

[2] Cf. Teichmüller, op. cit. 43. In Eth. Nic. VI. 12. 1144 a 31 ff. the major premiss of practcal syllogism is given as: ἐπειδὴ τοιόνδε τὸ τέλος καὶ τὸ ἄριστον, and there is no particular determination such as δεῖ. It would seem to be because, as Teichmüller conjectures, such a concept as τέλος or ἄριστον implies in itself oughtness or value.

necessity to realize the value? If it be virtue as self-value, the demand would be without qualification. But if it be utility, the ground would be a volition to some particular self-value, and it is only valuable as a mere means. To explain the point, we must study the contents of the practical syllogism.

Regrettable as it is, of the practical syllogism, there are but few examples. The most remarkable is the statement in Eth. Nic. VII. 3.[1] Its major premiss being "Dry food is useful for every man", the minor premisses are of two kinds, one dealing with the subject, the other with the object, viz. "I am a man" and "This is a dry food". Thence we conclude, "This is useful for me". It is obvious from the fact that the predicate of this major premiss is "useful", that this premiss is not the necessary judgement which immediately commands the pursuit of a moral value, but only advises the adoption of a means for an end. The taking of dry food is necessary for a man only hypothetically. This usefulness is, of course, usefulness for health. It is only necessary for a man to take dry food, in so far as he wants health: the necessity cannot be applied to a man who prefers pleasure to health.

Health is surely *per se* valuable, but its value demands further ground. It may be useful either for pleasure, or virtuous conduct, or for scientific and philosophic contemplation. Its necessity must be proved by another inference. Therefore, this major premiss is no more than a hypothetical imperative, or an advice such as "If one desires health, he should take dry food", or "If one ought to be healthy, he should take dry food". Further, the minor premisses of these examples are not estimations, but mere judgement of facts. Not only that I am a man, but also that this is dry food, is a recognition of fact. Consequently, the minor premiss of this practical syllogism is not concerned with a special value. Everything that is useful is not *per se* valuable, it is valuable only indirectly through being the means to an end which is *per se* valuable. Since the predicate of this major premiss is utility, it is natural enough that the particular object which bears this utility should be *per se* a mere fact without value. The dry food as a mere fact becomes valuable only through the causality which was stated in the major premiss. It seems to be natural from the above distinction of practice and production, that this kind of inference should be called ποιητικὸς συλλογισ-

[1] Eth. Nic. VII. 5. 1147 a 5.

μός, i.e. the productive syllogism. It cannot be subsumed to practical intellect or prudence in the strict sense,[1] since it is concerned not with the moral value of an act, but with the cognition of particular means to a subjective end. This inference is essentially the same as the considering of means, which is usually called deliberation and assumed to be a moment of will. The deliberation of means is the tracing back of causal relation; it traces the series of means from a given end to the matter

[1] Teichmüller further discusses the essence of practical syllogism considering the following statement in Eth. Nic. VI. 8. 1141 b 18-21: εἰ γὰρ εἰδείη ὅτι τὰ κοῦφα εὔπεπτα κρέα καὶ ὑγιεινά, ποῖα δὲ κοῦφα ἀγνοοῖ, οὐ ποιήσει ὑγίειαν, ἀλλ' ὁ εἰδὼς ὅτι τὰ ὀρνίθεια κοῦφα καὶ ὑγιεινὰ ποιήσει μᾶλλον.

This is the explanation that particular knowledge is more useful to practice than universal knowledge. Teichmüller says that if we arrange this as a theoretical syllogism, the minor concept would be the meat of birds, the middle concept, light, and the major concepts, both digestable and healthy, whereas it is theoretically unexplainable that there should be found another factor or major concept, "healthy", besides the middle concept, "light". Teichmüller interpreted the statement as follows:

Major premiss: "Light meat is digestable and healthy."
Minor premiss: "The meat of birds is light and healthy."

He also noticed that Aristotle admitted the knowledge of the minor premiss to be more efficient for conduct than that of the major. Thus the conclusion would be:

"I want the meat of birds." or
"Choose the meat of birds."

Such a conclusion could not be derived from purely theoretical premisses, because the premisses do not involve words such as "'I want" or "Choose". Now Teichmüller believes that this difficulty might be solved if we took the statement as a practical syllogism, which recognizes the object in reference to our volition. In this example, the concept, "healthy", implies already a human volition. And Aristotle omits the determination of the subject in the premiss, "Such a man should do such and such a thing", and the determination in the premiss, "I am such a man, viz., weak in digestion". Thus, according to Teichmüller, the above inference would be arranged as follows:

(1) "I want health." or "Man ought to desire health."
(2) "Digestable food is good for health."
(3) "Light meat is digestable."
(4) "The meat of birds is light."
(5) "So, I want the meat of birds." or "You ought to desire the meat of birds."

Instead of acknowledging this reference Aristotle only assumed that the minor premiss orders one to do, from experience, what the major premiss implies, so that the minor premiss must involve the reference to the desirable, i. e. health. Therefore, Trendelenburg would seem to have overlooked the essence of the

immediately at hand. Thus, e.g. Met. VII. 7. 1032 b 6: "Since this is health, if the subject is to be healthy, this must first be present, e.g. a uniform state of body, and if this is to be present, there must be heat, and the physician goes on thinking thus until he reduces the matter to something final which he himself can produce. Then the process from this point onward, i.e. the process towards health, is called a production."[1] The means to produce heat is elsewhere[2] stated to be rubbing, which is the first step of healing.

Thus technical thinking as the principle of production or making, viz. prodctive deliberation in my terminology, would be as follows: If health is to exist, there must be a uniform condition of the body, and if the uniform condition of the body is to exist, there must be heat, and if heat, then rubbing. Therefore, if health is to exist, there must be rubbing.[3] Compared

practical syllogism when he struck out the "light" from the proposition, "The meat of birds is light and healthy", and made it "The meat of birds is healthy". In truth, the minor premiss must involve both the middle and the major concept (cf. Teichmüller, op. cit. 226-229).
    The statement in question may be rather more naturally interpreted as follows:
Major premiss: "Light meat is digestable and healthy."
Minor premiss: "The meat of birds is light."
Conclusion: "The meat of birds is healthy."
Even if one knows the major premiss, he cannot get the conclusion and consequently cannot act, unless he knows the minor premiss. But even if he should not know the major premiss, it will be more efficient for conduct if he knows through experience both the minor premiss and the conclusion—if "light" be preserved, or only the conclusion—if "light" be struck out. Needless to say, the major premiss of this formula is an epicheirema concluded from the second and the third proposition of Teichmüller's scheme described above.
    Teichmüller held that the concept, healthy, implies volition or order. But, in truth, it does not follow of necessity, from its merely being healthy, that one really desires that food or that he ought to take it. We can expect being "healthy" here to imply only potential volition or potential order. That is to say, the inference in question is not theoretical, to be sure, but is it not a practical inference in the strict sense, which orders an act without qualification, but a productive inference, or in Kant's terminology, the advice of cleverness that gives us a hypothetical imperative.

[1] Met. VII. 7. 1032 b 6.   [2] Met. VII. 7. 1032 b 15-26.
[3] Walter makes a strange interpretation about the scheme of the practical syllogism. He distinguishes end and end-concept, and makes the former the transcendent and individual end, which precedes deliberation, and the latter the universal end which is immanent in deliberation. The individual end is, e.g., "This should be cured", the universal end-concept is, e.g., "Health is so and

with the foregoing syllogism about food, wherein the two minor premisses were co-ordinate to the same major premiss, stating the real qualities of an object, in this all premisses are hypothetical judgements, and form a sorites. This is, however, not an essential difference, but only a difference of degree between two homogeneous instances of thinking. Productive deliberation is not different from the productive syllogism, and the two examples differ only in that the one expresses the whole process of productive deliberation, while the other expresses only the last stage of it. If one object that there is wanting the affirmation of a fact in the last stage of deliberation about healing, we may easily add the most immediate technical knowledge, "This is rubbing". And if one require us to distinguish deliberation from syllogism, we shall say that deliberation is the searching for the means, while syllogism is the justification of it. The order of thinking is reversed. We might also say that deliberation is constructive, while syllogism is reflective.

§ 3. PRACTICAL COGNITION OF ENDS

Admitting that the above-mentioned forms of the practical syllogism be after all productive, we must further inquire if there be a practical syllogism with more independent values. The productive syllogism presupposes a certain end and estimates some fact in so far as it serves for the realization of the end, so that its conclusion is after all a hypothetical imperative or

so". Deliberation is the application of knowledge to the individual, and the knowledge comes either from mathematics or from perception, its origin being a matter of no importance. The most important moment of deliberation is the end-concept, which determines the whole process of deliberation (cf. op. cit. 208 ff.). We can by no means agree with this theory. The essential element of this practical syllogism is not the analysis of a concept, but the causal reference. Not what health is, but how we should produce it, is in question. The πρότασις of the practical syllogism is not "Health is so and so", but rather "This should be cured". That the Eudemian Ethics is essentially different from the Nicomachean Ethics on this point, is evident from the following statement, which Walter assumes to be peculiar to the Nicomachean Ethics.—Eth. Eud. I. 8. 1218 b 16-20: ὅτι δ' αἴτιον τὸ τέλος τῶν ὑφ' αὑτό, δηλοῖ ἡ διδασκαλία. ὁρισάμενοι γὰρ τὸ τέλος τἆλλα δεικνύουσιν, ὅτι ἕκαστον αὐτῶν ἀγαθόν. αἴτιον γὰρ τὸ οὗ ἕνεκα. οἷον ἐπειδὴ τὸ ὑγιαίνειν τοδί, ἀνάγκη τόδε εἶναι τὸ συμφέρον πρὸς αὐτήν·

an instance of what Kant calls the advice of cleverness.[1] Both the means of healing and the taking of dry food are necessary only as the means, which one should adopt if he wants health. But there is no command that one should be healthy. Practical intellect, however, should not be confined to the cognition of means, but rather should be employed in the estimation of the end itself. The most important function of prudence is the moral estimation of conduct rather than a technical consideration, its fundamental proposition being the universal imperative of morality. This imperative will be specialized through virtues, and it commands the performance of good acts. When it commands a particular act, there must be of necessity the moral estimation of that particular act. The major premiss demands that a certain moral value should be realized, while the minor premiss assumes that a certain act bears that value, and thus a particular act is ordered to be realized as morally valuable. If there be such a form of practical syllogism, this is precisely the practical syllogism in the strict sense which we are now looking for.

The productive syllogism formulates, as aforesaid, hypothetical necessity as distinguished from absolute necessity.[2] Hypothetical necessity is causality among things which are ontologically accidental and can be otherwise, viz., if A should exist, B must exist, and if B then C, and so on. This is the same pattern which the productive syllogism or deliberation follows to realize the end. The example given is also a medical deliberation for realizing health. On such a hypothetical necessity, the fundamental premiss itself is not grounded. For instance, it is left to one's choice whether he aims at health or not: the inference does not refer to it. Production is determined by the "desire or will" which is mentioned in the *Metaphysica*[2] as the determinative principle of rational potency. Generally speaking, desire may be either direct or indirect[3] it may be either instinctive appetite or rational wish. What employs the productive syllogism is in many cases[4] a wish, which demands a higher cognition or the practical syllogism.

[1] Kant, K. d. p. V. I.I.1. 8. Lehrs. IV. Anm. 2. WW. Cass. V. 42.

[2] Part. An. I. 1. 639 b 23-640 a 2; Part. An. I. 1. 642 a 1 ff.; 32 ff.; Phys. II. 9. 199 b 34; Met. V. 5. 1015 a 20 ff.

[3] Met. IX. 5. 1048 a 8; 8. 1050 b 30.

[4] Walter, op. cit. 214. It is far from our real intention to confuse the rationality of desire with that of will. We only consider the former to be the condition of the latter; rational desire especially demands the cognition of the means.

But this is not yet the cognition of absolute necessity. For absolute necessity is found only in eternal being, e.g. mathematical images or logical concepts. Consequently, hypothetical necessity comprises not only technical, but also practical connection, and what is more conspicuous, natural causality.[1] For a natural phenomenon also happens in time and suffers alteration, so that it belongs to what can be otherwise, and in this respect, resembles technical production: the only difference is in whether the definitive principle exists in things or in the human mind, and nature is a teleological system ruled by cosmic reason.[2] This is quite reasonable from the fact that human intellect is a function of life and constitutes part of the force of nature. Conduct is after all a form of nature.[3]

In short, practice like production and nature lies in the hypothetical area and is lacking in categorical necessity. For the highest major premiss of the practical syllogism depends upon one's character which varies in accordance with one's way of life. Speaking more precisely, however, man's character is somewhat fixed. This particular character gives a determinate direction to the so-called productive syllogism. Character determines a desire, which in its turn, employs a productive deliberation as an instrument. But the major premiss of the practical syllogism is not left to one's choice like that of the productive syllogism. In the beginning of its formation, character is comparatively indefinite and free, but in an adult individual, it becomes an established fact.[4] So that the wish which results from a character determines the hypothetical syllogism as categorical. What the major premiss of such a practical syllogism is may be found in the following proposition: Eth. Nic. VI. 13. 1144 a 31:[5] "For the syllogisms which deal with acts to be done are things which involve a starting-point, viz. (it will begin,) 'since the end, i.e. what is best, is of such and such a nature', ... and this is not evident except to the good man; for wickedness perverts us and causes us to be deceived about the starting-points of action. Therefore it is evident that it is

[1] Part. An. I. 1. 640 a 2. It seems to reflect Aristotle's early thought which opposes changeable phenomena to the unchangeable essence, that he here opposes physics to the theoretical scinces and reduces it to the same genus as practical intellect. This suggests the period of this work.
[2] Cf. p. 184, n. 2, 3.
[3] Cf. ch. IV. § 4. ch. II. § 4; Phys. VIII. 2. 253 a 8 ff.
[4] Eth. Nic. III. 7. 1114 a 12-21.
[5] Cf. Eth. Nic. VI. 5. 1140 b 16-20.

impossible to be prudent without being good." No doubt, this is the remark about the major premiss of the practical syllogism, and we find here the standard of moral value as the highest major premiss of the practical syllogism. This standard is just the same as the standard of rational or calculative imagination which Aristotle discusses in the *De Anima*.[1]

Practical estimation also must form itself as a syllogism. For even though one knows the highest good and the ultimate end of life, his practical intellect does not yet discharge its functions unless he knows the particular conduct which represents this universal value. Such a particular cognition should be distinguished from the knowledge of real causality. We may find a more specific example of moral estimation in the following case. To make the context distinct, let us venture a somewhat longer quotation.

Eth. Nic. VI. 5. 1140 b 7-20: "It is for this reason that we think Pericles and men like him have practical wisdom, viz. because they can see what is good for themselves and what is good for men in general; we consider that those can do this who are good at managing households or states;—this is why we call temperance (σωφροσύνη) by this name, we imply that it preserves one's practical wisdom (σῴζουσα τὴν φρόνησιν). Now what it preserves is a judgement of the kind we have described. For it is not any and every judgement that pleasant and painful objects destroy and pervert, e.g. the judgement that the triangle has or has not its angles equal to two right angles, but only judgements about what is to be done. For the originating causes of the things that are done consists in the end at which they are aimed; but the man who has been ruined by pleasure or pain forthwith fails to see any such originating cause—to see that for the sake of this or because of this he ought to choose and do whatever he chooses and does; for vice is destructive of the originating cause of action."

The concepts here used such as θεωρεῖν, ὑπόληψις, and φαίνεται imply moral estimations, especially φαίνεται is the appearance of φαντασία λογιστική.[2] We may quote a similar statement from Eth. Nic. III. 6. 1113 a 30: "....since the good man judges each class of things rightly, and in each the truth appears to

---

[1] De An. III. 11. 434 a 8 f.
[2] De An. III. 10. 433 b 29; 11. 434 a 5; cf. ch. II. § 3.

him. For each state of character has its own ideas of the noble and the pleasant, and perhaps the good man differs from others most by seeing the truth in each class of things, being as it were the norm and measure of them. In most things error seems to be due to pleasure; for it appears a good when it is not. We therefore take the pleasant as a good, and avoid pain as an evil." In this quotation also the moral estimation of practice is expressed by κρίνειν, φαίνεται, or ὁρᾶν, just in the same way as in the previous quotation. The cognition of what is good for oneself in which one is apt to be misled by pleasure and pain, is neither theoretical nor the searching for the means. For such cognitions are never misled by pleasure and pain. So Teichmüller was right in spite of Walter's opposition when he recognized a *phronetische Wahrnehmung* in the first quotation.[1]

The premisses of the practical syllogism, the universal as well as the particular, are the expression of ethical virtue. The cognition of the ultimate end or the highest good which presupposes ethical virtue, is evidently most universal and forms the highest major premiss of the practical syllogism. But since conduct really is concerned with the particular, it requires not only a universal, but also a particular cognition, viz. the individual judgement as to what is good. Yet this individual judgement requires in its turn ethical virtues and appears as an intuitive reason in the strict sense or as a perceptive prudence. The foregoing two quotations would seem also to imply such a particular practical cognition or something like it. Such an expression as "seeing the truth in each class of things" can not be taken otherwise than as an individual cognition. Therefore that ethical virtue is the necessary cognition of practical intellect, does not mean, as Walter interprets, that the function of practical intellect or the practical syllogism is merely the searching for the means, the end itself being left to the immediate desire. The statement "virtue makes us aim at the right mark, and prudence makes us take the right means",[2] etc., might seem to prove this interpretation. But on the other hand, ethical virtue is said to presuppose prudence,[3] and wish, being rational desire, is founded upon calculation.[4] Further every desire follows imagination, and in the case of rational desire,

---

[1] Teichmüller, Arist. Forsch. II; Neue Stud. III. 294 f.; Walter, op. cit. 382 f.
[2] Cf. p. 267, n. 1, 2.   [3] p. 272, n. 1
[4] Rhet. I. 10. 1369 a 1; Eth. Eud. VII. 2. 1235 b 22;

imagination itself is deliberative or calculative.[1] "But desire is consequent on opinion rather than opinion on deisre."[2] From what has been said, it seems to be undeniable that Aristotle assumed some intellect which determines desire itself.[3]

We cannot keep ourselves from associating again the reason which determines desire with the practical reason of Kant. The fundamental proposition of Kant's ethics is that the reason becomes by itself practical. Wherefore if we admit such a reason in Aristotle, it would seem that it cannot be ascribed to Kant's originality. Indeed this, (along with the problem of active reason,) is the most important and difficult problem in Aristotle's philosophy.[4] We have previously postulated the reason which determines desire

---

[1] De An. III. 11. 434 a 5; cf. p. 130, n. 2.
[2] Met. XII. 7. 1072 a 29.
[3] Eth. Nic. VII. 7. 1149 a 25-b 3: ἔοικε γὰρ ὁ θυμὸς ἀκούειν μέν τι τοῦ λόγου, παρακούειν δέ,...... οὕτως ὁ θυμὸς διὰ θερμότητα καὶ ταχυτῆτα τῆς φύσεως ἀκούσας μέν, οὐκ ἐπίταγμα δ' ἀκούσας, ὁρμᾷ πρὸς τὴν τιμωρίαν. ὁ μὲν γὰρ λόγος ἢ ἡ φαντασία ὅτι ὕβρις ἢ ὀλιγωρία ἐδήλωσεν, ὁ δ' ὥσπερ συλλογισάμενος ὅτι δεῖ τῷ τοιούτῳ πολεμεῖν χαλεπαίνει δὴ εὐθύς· ἡ δ' ἐπιθυμία, ἐὰν μόνον εἴπῃ ὅτι ἡδὺ ὁ λόγος ἢ ἡ αἴσθησις, ὁρμᾷ πρὸς τὴν ἀπόλαυσιν. ὥσθ' ὁ μὲν θυμὸς ἀκολουθεῖ τῷ λόγῳ πως, ἡ δ' ἐπιθυμία οὔ. αἰσχίων οὖν. ὁ μὲν γὰρ τοῦ θυμοῦ ἀκρατὴς τοῦ λόγου πως ἡττᾶται, ὁ δὲ τῆς ἐπιθυμίας καὶ οὐ τοῦ λόγου. The reason which temper obeys, is no doubt practical deliberation instead of the cognition of means. Similarly with calculation (λογισμός) in De An. III. 10. 433 b 6, and a 25, in contradication to which appetites are said to become the principle of conduct. This becomes more evident, when we compare the statement about appetites in Eth. Nic. VII. 7. 1149 b 13-20: ἔτι ἀδικώτεροι οἱ ἐπιβουλόμεροι. ὁ μὲν οὖν θυμώδης οὐκ ἐπίβουλος, οὐδ' ὁ θυμός, ἀλλὰ φανερός· ἡ δ' ἐπιθυμία, καθάπερ τὴν Ἀφροδίτην φασίν "δολοπλόκου γὰρ κυπρογενοῦς" καὶ τὸν κεστὸν ἱμάντα Ὅμηρος· "πάρφασις, ἥ τ' ἔκλεψε νόον πύκα περ φρονέοντος." ὥστ' εἴπερ ἀδικωτέρα καὶ αἰσχίων ἡ ἀκρασία αὕτη τῆς περὶ τὸν θυμόν ἐστι, καὶ ἁπλῶς ἀκρασία καὶ κακία πως. The incontinent man is previously said not to listen to reason, but temper does in a certain sense, whereas here on the contrary, the former is said to be plotting and the latter not. We may avoid the contradiction by taking the λόγος in the first statement for valuation, and the ἐπιβουλή in the second statement for the searching for the means. ἐπιβουλή being a kind of βούλευσις, acts in this case as productive deliberation; cf. ibid. 1150 a 4 f.: ἀσινεστέρα γὰρ ἡ φαυλότης ἀεὶ ἡ τοῦ μὴ ἔχοντος ἀρχήν, ὁ δὲ νοῦς ἀρχή. This νοῦς is also productive deliberation instead of practical. The vicious man may have productive deliberation, but not practical.

[4] Walter, op. cit. 31 ff.; cf. Trendelenburg, Hist. Beiträge. III. Herbarts praktische Philosophie und die Ethik der Athen, VI; Der Widerstreit zwischen Kant und Aristoteles in der Ethik.

itself in opposition to Walter who restricts the function of practical reason to the searching for the means. We must confront our arguments with Walter's in more detail.

According to Walter, the function of practical reason is deliberation, and its ideal is the so-called ὀρθὸς λόγος. Therefore, the essence of deliberation ought to be explained through the investigation of ὀρθὸς λόγος. This does not mean a right concept as Brandis supposed,[1] but a right reason, which is the principle of moderation and that which constitutes a virtue as such. But, strictly speaking, right reason is not sufficient for ethical virtue, and moderation is confined to the area of practice and production, so Walter argues.[2] But to make right reason the principle of ethical virtue runs counter to Walter's previous interpretation of practical reason. If practical reason be restricted to the deliberation about means, how may its equivalent ὀρθὸς λόγος be the principle of moderation? If virtue consists of good desire and deliberation, the rational moment of good desire should not be the searching for the means, but the calculation to estimate the end.

Walter, who misunderstood the rationality of the end, is led to neglect the practical character of reason itself. He says that the reason of Kant may become practical by itself, whereas that of Aristotle requires will in addition,[3] in order to be practical. Seeing that will or προαίρεσις is defined as deliberated desire, it is not only superfluous but also unreasonable to say that practical reason requires will besides, and Walter mentions no valid proof of this assertion. What is more strange is that he infers in continuation that Aristotle's classification of reason is not that of cognitions but of faculties. According to him, in the division of reason into the theoretical and the practical, Aristotle does not

---

[1] Brandis, Handbuch etc. II. 2. ii. 1441; Walter, op. cit. 65. The text in question is as follows: Eth. Nic. VI. 2. 1139 a 21-31: ἔστι δ' ὅπερ ἐν διανοίᾳ κατάφασις καὶ ἀπόφασις, τοῦτ' ἐν ὀρέξει δίωξις καὶ φυγή· ὥστ' ἐπειδὴ ἡ ἠθικὴ ἀρετὴ ἕξις προαιρετική,[1] ἡ δὲ προαίρεσις ὄρεξις βουλευτική, δεῖ διὰ ταῦτα μὲν τόν τε λόγον[2] ἀληθῆ εἶναι καὶ τὴν ὄρεξιν ὀρθήν, εἴπερ ἡ προαίρεσις σπουδαία, καὶ τὰ αὐτὰ τὸν μὲν φάναι[3] τὴν δὲ διώκειν. αὕτη μὲν οὖν ἡ διάνοια καὶ ἡ ἀλήθεια πρακτική· τῆς δὲ θεωρητικῆς διανοίας καὶ μὴ πρακτικῆς μηδὲ ποιητικῆς τὸ εὖ καὶ κακῶς τἀληθές ἐστι καὶ ψεῦδος. τοῦτο γάρ ἐστι παντὸς διανοητικοῦ ἔργον· τοῦ δὲ πρακτικοῦ καὶ διανοητικοῦ ἡ ἀλήθεια ὁμολόγως ἔχουσα τῇ ὀρέξει τῇ ὀρθῇ. Brandis translates 1) ἕξις προαιρετική as Fertigkeit des Vorsatzes, 2) λόγος as Begriff, and 3) φάναι as bestimmt.

[2] Walter, op. cit. 232 ff.   [3] Walter, op. cit. 242 f.

imply a distinction between the science of variable phenomena (presumably ethics, politics, etc.) and necessary sciences, e.g. theology or mathematics, but rather a distinction between acts and cognition, because reason is concerned with the possible and the necessary, whereas the possible cannot be the object of knowledge.[1] This explanation of Walter's is also extremely unsatisfactory. It is a sheer contradiction to say on the one hand that reason cannot be practical by itself but requires will, and on the other hand that Aristotle's classification of reason is that of faculties of reason and not of cognitions.[2]

A reason which does not recognize is surely a paradoxical concept, but if practical reason were such a faculty, isn't it just the reason *per se* practical that he himself is longing for? Whether it may be called reason or not, at least, it is from his theory necessary that it is practical. What else would he call such a reason but practical reason? Assuming, as he did, that reason requires will in order to be practical, should this "reason" of his be called will? Then it is either necessary that will be itself reason or that at least there be practical reason which determines will. To our surprise, he says that practical reason is only deliberation or the searching for the means. Assuming, on the one hand, that deliberation forms the practical syllogism, he asserts, on the other hand, that its premisses are both theoretical cognitions. It would be therefore the function of theoretical reason. Where is then the practical reason? A practical conclusion must result from theoretical premisses. The practical character of the conclusion would result from outside of the inference, i.e. from a desire or a will. The process of inference may be rational but never practical, and

---

[1] Ibid. Walter, saying "*Das Zukünftige ist aber überhaupt nicht Gegenstand der Erkenntnis. Die Vernunfttätigkeit deren Object das Mögliche als Zukünftiges ist, kann keine erkennende sondern muss eine bestimmende, eine beratschlagende Thätigkeit sein*" quotes Eth. Nic. VI. 3. 1139 b 7. But, thus he confused ἐνδεχόμενον ἄλλως ἔχειν with mere ἐνδεχόμενον and misunderstood the well-known proposition of Aristotle, that ἐνδεχόμενον ἄλλως ἔχειν is not the proper object of ἐπιστήμη, for the potential or future being cannot be recognized. There are plenty of such mistakes in this author, and Teichmüller's ridicule is not without reason.

[2] Eth. Nic. VI. 2. 1139 b 12 f.; Eth. Nic. VI. 2. 1139 a 29-31; Met. IX. 2. 1046 b 2-4. This last quotation shows that art is both knowledge and power to act. It is not Aristotle's way of thinking to consider that cognition is not practical at all.

will may be practical but never rational. Practical reason would thus become nonsense.[1]

On Walter's interpretation, it would turn out that practical reason is either not practical or not reason. He maintains moreover that Aristotle divided reason into the calculative and the scientific, not meaning that reason by itself performs these two functions, but that it makes cognition to be combined with desire.[2] It will follow then, that neither is the former theoretical reason, nor the latter practical reason. Rather a single reason becomes sometimes theoretical and sometimes practical only incidentally. So that reason itself would neither recognize nor act.

Deliberation was conceived to be the searching for the means, and the major premiss of the practical syllogism is theoretical knowledge, while the minor premiss is perceptive judgement, which is the function not of practical reason, but of perceptive reason. Thus, it seems as if there be no practical moment. But none the less, he rejects Prantl's theory which takes deliberation for theoretical cognition.[3] Walter considered therefore that deliberation is neither theoretical nor practical but merely cognition in general. But Aristotle really admits practical cognition or practical truth, as is evident from the statement to which Walter himself refers a little later.[4] The only difference between the theoretical and productive reasons is, according to Walter, not in the contents, but in the forms of cognition. He says that productive cognition is a kind of practical one, and is in its contents near to that of theoretical cognition.[5] But is it not an obvious distinction of contents, that practical intellect is concerned with what can be otherwise, and theoretical intellect with necessary being? On what ground does Walter neglect this manifest distinction of contents? By the difference of forms, he might imply that theoretical intellect has by itself no practical power. Aristotle states about the efficient cause of conduct, that "no animal which is not either seeking or avoiding something, moves except under compulsion".[6] "Similarly, it is not the sensitive faculty."[7] "Nor, again, is it the reasoning faculty or what is called intellect that is the

[1] Teichmüller, Neue Studien. III. 42 ff. cf. ch. IV. § 4.
[2] Walter, op. cit. 245.
[3] Ibid. 249; cf. Prantl, Ueber die dianoetischen Tugenden nach Aristoteles, 11.
[4] Walter, op. cit. 252; Eth. Nic. VI. 2. 1139 a 30.
[5] Walter, op. cit. 255.
[6] De An. III. 9. 432 b 16.   [7] ibid. 19.

cause of motion."¹ "For the theoretical intellect thinks nothing practical and makes no assertion about what is to be avoided or pursued,....But, even if the mind has something of the kind before it, it does not forthwith prompt avoidance or pursuit. For example, it often thinks of something alarming or pleasant without prompting to fear; the only effect is the beating of the heart, or when the thought is pleasant, some other bodily movement."²

Walter's peculiarity lies in taking the reason which fails to determinate desires, as theoretical instead of practical. He considers that if it were practical reason, as generally admitted, there would be the practical reason which is indifferent to practice, and the theoretical reason would be incapable of thinking of any matter which may arouse emotion. Further, practical reason would be distinguished from theoretical reason through the object, whereas in reality, the difference is that the one is cognition while the other is determination. Such a mistaken distinction, he says, would result in the misinterpretation to assume practical reason to be referring to moral concepts.[3] In short, Walter asserts that the difference of theoretical and practical reasons is a formal one—it lies in whether the reason has practical potency or not.

Let us admit, without qualification, that theoretical reason lacks practical potency while practical reason has it. But, this does not conform to Walter's foregoing theory. For he said that the only function of practical reason is deliberation which is nothing but the searching for the means. Therefore, it must follow of necessity that what has really practical ability is not practical reason—which is considered by Walter as practical only accidentally —but volition. As for practical knowledge which does not command, there is no need to repeat our foregoing statement.

On the other hand, as to the commanding reason, Walter refers to the following statement in Aristotle De An. III. 10. 433 a 9:[4] "The motive causes are apparently at any rate, these two, either appetency or intelligence, ...Both these, then, are causes of locomotion, intelligence and appetency. By intelligence we mean that which calculates the means to an end, that is the practical intellect, which differs from the speculative intellect in the end at which it aims. Appetency, too is directed to some end in every case; for that which is the end of desire is the starting point of the practical

[1] ibid. 26   [2] De An. III. 9. 432 b 27; cf. ch. II. § 2.
[3] Walter, op. cit. 256 f.   [4] Walter, op. cit. 260

intellect, and the last stage in this process of thought is the starting point of action." But Walter is not right when he translated νοῦς δὲ ὁ ἕνεκά του λογιζόμενος καὶ πρακτικός, as *die eines Zweckes Willen betrachtende oder praktische Vernunft*, i.e. "the reason which deliberates for an end, or practical reason". By Trendelenburg,[1] to whom Walter is opposed, this was taken rather to be the reason which determines the end. If it were nothing more than the consideration of the means, as Walter considered, how is it possible for it to be commanding reason or to bring about harmony with desire ?[2] We should rather say that reason obeys desire than that it orders desire. Nevertheless, what requires the command must be just the desiring faculty. If what is commanded were a mere body, it would not matter for the value of conduct, whether it obeyed the command of reason or the command of desire. Here we may see one difficulty of Walter's view, which identifies practical reason with the cognition of means. And Walter himself repeats the statement of Aristotle which undeniably implies the function of reason that determines the desire, a little later on.[3] Namely, the primary movent is the object of desire, which is aimed at both by desire and thinking. It is the object of desire, in so far as it is desired, but it is also the object of thinking as far as it is an end-concept. It moves other things, itself being unmoved. But we desire what we think to be good, rather than thinking to be good what we desire. And a good will is said to be the will which desires a thing on account of its goodness. This means evidently that the desire for an end presupposes the estimation of that end, and that the reason determines the desire. The ultimate determinant is the end itself and not the end-concept, to be sure.[4] But we can by no means deny

[1] Trendelenburg, Hist. Beitr. etc. II. 378; Walter, op. cit. 44.
[2] Cf. Walter, op. cit. 495 f. Walter as well as Hartenstein (Hist. Phil. Abhandl.) denounces Aristotle as entirely failing to supply any ground for harmony between will and reason. This only betrays their false interpretation of these concepts. Such a difficulty is never found in Aristotle. As we have seen in the second and fourth chapters of our enquiry, Aristotle's concept of will, desire, and practical wisdom, have their sufficient foundation in his physiological and psychological thought. This difficulty of harmony should rather be pointed out in Kant's theory. For Kant himself recognized that the fact that reason itself becomes practical was inexplainable. This is a difficulty of Kant's ethics along with the posutlate of the accompaniment of happiness and good conduct. Cf. Trendelenburg, Hist. Beitr. etc. III. 189 ff.; 195 ff.; 209 ff.
[3] Walter, op. cit. 264 f.; Part. An. 6. 700 b 28; 701 b 1; Met. XII. 7. 1072 a 30.
[4] Walter, op. cit. 265.

that there is admitted some reason which precedes and determines the desire. It is different from the deliberation which presupposes desire and subserves it.

Walter, never admitting any specific differentia of practical reason, identifies it with deliberation, which however, presupposes some desire. Thus, the end, being the unmovable movent, moves at first desire, which in its turn, moves practical reason. Practical reason presupposes an end as the direct object of desire, yet takes the latter in itself and forms an end-concept. This accepted end-concept constitutes the major premiss, and in combination with a particular judgement as a minor premiss forms the practical syllogism, which is the function of deliberation or practical reason. Desire mediates the object of desire (as the end) with conduct, and reason mediates the end-concept with conduct. From the combination of reason and desire grows will, which consists of ὄρεξις and λόγος ὁ ἕνεκα τινός. The latter is deliberation instead of an end-concept; it is concerned with the means, not with the end.[1]

In short, practical reason is concerned only with practice and does not enter into a scientific cognition. A man of practice is concerned with practice, but a philosopher is concerned with ethics. Their tasks are assumed to be quite different. Walter nevertheless admits that Aristotle was an ideal Greek[2] in attributing truth to art and morality, even though making a division of practical and theoretical reason similar to that of Kant. But once we admit that Aristotle really attributed truth to art and morality, we can by no means assume that he denied cognition to practical reason. Besides, if practical reason is related only to practice, it is rather a matter of course that it should be practical. Whereas Walter in fact allowed to it only the cognition of cause and effect, and he regarded their premisses to be purely theoretical. This is nothing but a sheer contadiction.

In admitting practical cognition or the practical syllogism about the end, the most embarrassing point is the following statement in Eth. Eud. II. 11. 1227 b 23:[3] "Does then virtue make the aim, or the means to that aim ? We say the aim, because this is not attained by inference or reasoning. Let us assume this as a starting point. For the doctor does not ask whether one ought to be in health or not, but whether one ought to walk or not; nor does

---

[1] Ibid, 265 ff.   [2] Ibid. 269 f.
[3] Cf. Eth. Eud. II. 10. 1227 a 5-15; VI. 14. 1248 a 18-21.

the trainer ask whether one ought to be in good condition or not, but whether one should wrestle or not. And similarly no art asks questions about the end; for as in theoretical sciences the assumption are our starting points, so in the productive the end is starting point and assumed. E. g., we reason that since this body is to be made healthy, therefore so and so must be found in it if health is to be had—just as in geometry we argue, if the angles of the triangle are equal to two right angles, then so and so must be the case. The end aimed at is, then, the starting point of our thought and the end of our thought the starting point of action." The opinion that there is neither syllogism nor argument about the end, which is rather set up directly by ethical virtue, and forms the supposition or starting-point of practical intellect as the searching for the means to realize the end, seems here so manifestly maintained, that there would appear to be no room to admit a practical syllogism which determines the end itself. The same opinion is also found in Eth. Nic. VII. 9. 1151 a 17: "For virtue and vice respectively preserve and destroy the first principle, and in actions the final cause is the first principle, as the hypothesis is in mathematics; neither is it in that case argument that teaches the first principles, nor is it so here—virtue either natural or produced by habituation is what teaches right opinion about the first principle." So, we are prohibited from dismissing this as an immature idea of Aristotle's in his early years. As for this statement alone, deliberation or syllogism seems to be mainly limited to the productive, the end which makes the starting point of this cognition being set up by ethical or natural virtue.

Indeed, technical deliberation is not a thinking about the end itself. But, is it true that Aristotle thought it quite impossible to deliberate about the end itself? Is it really possible for the author of the *Nicomachean Ethics* and the *Eudemian Ethics* to have repudiated the practical thinking which is realized in his lectures? This is a supposition absolutely beyond our consent. Of course it is not the art that makes the end right. We have also no objection to the view that it is founded upon a good habit which is acquired through ethical virtue.[1] Still, Aristlote asserts that ethical virtue is also impossible without prudence. What makes an end good, is its rationality. The end which is set up by ethical virtue is also founded upon estimation. Ethical virtue, being the

---

[1] Eth. Nic. VI. 13. 1144 a 8, 21; 1145 a 5.

principle of estimation, realizes itself in this estimation. The essence of ethical virtue is moderation, which is right reason or prudence. Consequently, rational desire arising from virtue, viz. wish, must be in accordance with, and accompamied by, prudence. In other words, it must pursue the object of intellect, and this object becomes the object of desire through being thought of. Wish gains its rationality only through this mediation by intellect. Aristotle admits these points one by one. So that, what he wishes to say is not that all desires are irrational and immediate, or that practical cognition is purely technical and aims at utility, but that end grows rather from character than from technical deliberation. To emphasize this point, Aristotle characterized art as concerning the means and indifferent to the end. None the less, this does not make it impossible for ethical virtue to appear in intellectual form, and even in the form of a syllogism. It is merely that this matter is dealt with by Aristotle elsewhere.

It seems, at a glance, to be contradictory to say on the one hand that deliberation and the practical syllogism do not determine the end but search for the means, and on the other hand that rational desire or wish presupposes deliberative or calculative imagination, or to demand a reason which regulates desire by saying that moderation as the essence of ethical virtue consists in right reason which is nothing else than prudence. This difficulty, however, may be solved by investigating the notions of end and means. The means is the method and the starting point of the end, whereas the end is either the result or the act itself.[1] Therefore the means also either serves the result or the act itself. In the former case, the means is concerned with a mere fact, and its form is quite different from that of the result, while in the latter case, it is concerned with a value realized in its process the form of the end. In modern usage "means" is mainly restricted to the former sense. But this is not the case with Aristotle. The means in modern usage is only an efficient cause, but, as is well known, Aristotle assumed besides this the formal cause, the final cause, and the material cause.[2]

[1] Eth. Nic. VI. 2. 1139 b 1; 5. 1140 b 6; X. 6. 1176 b 6; [Mag. Mor. I. 36. 1197 a 11;]
[2] Phys. II. 3. 194 b 23 ff.; 7. 198 a 16; III. 7. 207 b 34; IV. 1. 209 a 20; De Somno 2. 455 b 14; Gen. An. I. 1. 715 a 4; V. 1. 778 b 8; An. Post. II. 11. 94 a 21; Met. I. 3. 983 a 26; V.1. 1013 a 16; 2. 1013 a 24 ff.; 1013 b 16; VIII. 4. 1044 a 33 ff.; XII. 4. 1070 a 26.

Therefore, besides the means that produces a fact, there is another means which realizes a certain value. In this latter case, the cause should be taken as a formal or a final cause. An act which is performed to realize a moral value, is the means for that end. In this case, the means is the result rather than the cause.

Thus, there is besides the searching for the means as an efficient cause, that for the means as a formal cause. The former may be seen in productive deliberation, the latter in practical deliberation.[1] In practical deliberation, what is searched for is the particular practice which represents a general value. The end thus attained, is not yet really actual, but needs to be realized through productive operations. Starting from this point, art continues to search for the real means to realize this particular value. What we have previously recognized as the practical cognition which determines the end itself, is just this thinking. In this kind of thinking too, the highest universal end is immediate and cannot be inferred. That the practical intellect does not infer this highest universal end is one thing; that it does not determine a particular end is another. The highest universal end is set up immediately by ethical virtue.[2] Only it is quite indefinite in its contents; for instance, a wish for a good and beautiful life or a pleasant life is of this sort. No doubt, this universal intention is an important moment of conduct, but, since an act must be individual, a mere universal end is not sufficient for actual conduct. A particular end which represents the universal value, must be set up. Here is the necessity of the so-called practical syllogism or practical deliberation which deals with the subsumption of values. It is different from the productive syllogism which deals with the causal relation of facts. The practical syllogism does not create the end, but only determines and specialize it.[3]

The productive syllogism which is concerned with causal references, forms a hypothetical syllogism, while the practical syllogism which is concerned with the subsumption of values, forms a categorical syllogism. The conclusion of the latter determines the former

[1] Eth. Eud, I. 8. 1218 b 20-22; An. Post. I. 24. 85 b 23-27.

[2] This highest universal end too, might be given to an individual through his character. Yet, this character itself is formed through the habit which is nurtured by parents, teachers, and statesmen, so that from the generic point of view, it does presuppose deliberation and calculation. This deliberation and calculation should be the substance of politics and ethics.

[3] Cf. Loening, Die Zurechungslehre des Aristoteles, 29.

and makes it categorical. The practical syllogism which has categorical form is analogical to subsumptive inference. This is evident from An. Post. I. 24. 85 b 23: "Demonstration is the syllogism that proves the cause, i.e. the reasoned fact, and it is rather the commensurate universal than the particular which is causative (as may be shown thus: that which possesses an attribute through its own essential nature is itself the cause of the inherence, and the commensurate universal is primary; hence the commensurately universal is the cause). Consequently, commensurately universal demonstration is superior as more especially proving the cause, that is, the reasoned fact." Thus the cause is found in the universal. This is explained in the following examples. Ibid. 27: "Our search for the reason ceases, and we think that we know, when the coming to be or existence of the fact before us is not due to the coming to be or existence of some other fact, for the last step of a search thus conducted is *eo ipso* the end and limit of the problem. Thus: 'Why did he come? To get the money—wherewith to pay a debt, —that he might thereby do what was right.' When in this regress we can no longer find an efficient or final cause, we regard the last step of it as the end of the coming—or being or coming to be—and we regard ourselves as then only having full knowledge of the reason why he came. If, then, all causes and reasons are alike in this respect, and if this is the means to full knowledge in the case of final causes such as we have exemplified, it follows that in the case of the other causes also full knowledge is attained when an attribute no longer inheres because of something else. Thus, when we learn that exterior angles are equal to four right angles because they are the exterior angles of an isosceles, there still remains the question 'Why has isosceles this attribute?' and its answer 'Because it is a triangle, and a triangle has it because a triangle is a rectilinear figure.' If rectilinear figure possesses the property for no further reason, at this point we have full knowledge—but at this point our knowledge has become commensurately universal, and so we conclude that commensurately universal demonstration is superior."

As is evident from the above statement, inference, being the searching for the means in Aristotle's usage, may vary corresponding to the variety of causes. The "cause" in modern usage is confined to efficient cause. The geometric demonstration in the second example essentially has the same construction as this kind of thinking, only differing in that its cause is the formal.[2] That deliberation or the practical syllogism is not concerned with the end would mean that it does not set up the final end. The starting point of production is the final end of practical deliberation. This is an indeterminate term, yet surely an end for production. In the above quotation, to return the money is the end for which one came there and gained the money, yet it is the means for taking care lest one commit an unjustness. Whereas it is not a mere production to return money lest one commit an unjustness. Rather, returning the money has itself the moral value of justice. Though the end to do justice and not to commit a fault is not the result of inference but the realization of ethical value, deliberation about moral value is needed in order to realize that end. The theoretical syllogism about a triangle is categorical, and is ruled by eternal or absolute necessity, but a productive syllogism is ruled by hypothetical necessity, viz., "If one is to return the money, he must gain it. And if one is to gain the money, he must come here. So that, if one is to return the money, he must come here." What makes this hypothetical syllogism categorical, is the judgement that one should return the money, or the wish to return it. This wish further presupposes the inference: One should not commit an injustice. It is an injustice not to return the money. So he must return the money. This is what we call practical syllogism. It is a categorical syllogism. Thus, a complete practical cognition should be a mixed hypothetical syllogism, which consists of the conclusion of a pure hypothetical syllogism and the conclusion of a categorical syllogism.

§ 4. CONTINENCE AND TEMPERANCE

Regrettable as it is, there is no complete example to explain the form of the practical syllogism as opposed to the productive. But it is not so difficult to point out examples which are essentially of this sort. The statement in Eth. Nic. III. 7, might be summerized as follows:

Major premiss: The man is brave who fears the right things and from the right motive, in the right way and at the right time, and who feels confidence under the corresponding conditions.

[1] Met. XII. 7. 1063 b 36-1064 a 1; XIII. 4. 1078 b 23-25.

Minor premiss: This is the right thing, the right motive, the right way, and the right time one should fear.

Conclusion: He is brave, who fears this thing, for this motive, in this way, and at this time.

This conclusion directly determines our conduct and feeling. It presupposes moreover the highest universal practical knowledge, and without it one would fall into vice. What is then the character which lacks the particular cognition? Teichmüller overlooked the characteristic of this syllogism which he himself pointed out as an example of the practical syllogism, for he says that the ignorance of this minor premiss is the cause of involuntariness, which is repented of by the doer and forgiven by the criticizer.[1] But the judgement, "This is the thing that should be feared", is not a mere judgement of facts, but a moral estimation.[2] Just for this, it was assumed to be particularly difficult, whereas Aristotle found the cognition of individual facts not so difficult.[3] He is a complete fool who cannot judge whether this is bread or water, whether he is a king or a slave. On the contrary, the estimation[4] of individual affairs being dependent upon character or desire, a good character is required to be right in this judgement.[5] It is not so easy as the perception of a mere fact. Strange as it is, Teichmüller took rather the ignorance of the minor premiss of the aforesaid inference which advises the taking of dry food to be the cause of incontinence. He considers namely, that the ignorance that this is dry food, is the cause of incontinence which leads one to take some food harmful to health.[6] The truth is just the contrary; the ignorance of the minor premiss is the cause of involuntarity rather than of incontinence. Teichmüller committed a fault on account of his misunderstanding about the essential difference between the foregoing examples. He did not notice the difference between the ignorance which results in incontinence and that which results in involuntariness.

It is rather a strange fact, that almost all scholars, including of course Teichmüller, did not notice that there is a difference be-

[1] Teichmüller, op. cit. 76 f.; Eth. Nic. III. 7. 1115 b 17 ff.
[2] Teichmüller, op. cit. 78.
[3] Eth. Nic. V. 13. 1137 a 9-17; Eth. Nic. IV. 11. 1126 a 32-b 4.
[4] Met. I. 2. 982 a 11 f.
[5] Eth. Nic. I. 2. 1095 b 4.
[6] Teichmüller, op. cit. 75.

tween the ignorance in incontinence and that in involuntariness. But we regard the difference quite essential, being, so to say, the mark of distinguishing practical thinking from productive.

Ignorance about individual facts is certainly enumerated as a cause of involuntariness. But the examples of it all concern a lack or error of the judgement about the fact, as in the case when one kills an enemy being ignorant of the fact that he is one's son, and when one poisons somebody mistaking a poison for a remedy.[1] The minor premiss of the first example, "This is dry food," belongs to this class. The lack of this knowledge is not the cause of incontinence as Teichmüller mistakenly supposed, but rather the cause of involuntariness. Whereas the minor premiss of the second example is a kind of estimation about individual affairs. It is not involuntariness wrongly to fear or not to fear something because one does not know whether it should be feared or not. Let us focus the problem on temperance, since incontinence is not found in regard to fearing. Now he who does wrong being ignorant of the proper quantity of wine that one may drink, is not so involuntary in his act as one who drinks spirits being ignorant of whether it is wine or water. The former kind of ignorance should be censured as incontinence, but in the case of the latter the doer is not responsible. For, man is ignorant of the proper quantity of wine, because he is tempted by the appetite of drinking, or ignorant of the wickedness of having intercourse with another man's wife, because of his attachment.[2] When the ignorance becomes complete, it is indulgence rather than mere incontinence.[3]

We may thus explain the essence of the practical syllogism through the investigation of cahracters resembling each other, viz. continence and temperance, or their opposites, incontinence and indulgence. Here is found a cognition of moral value, which is

---

[1] Eth. Nic. III. 2.

[2] Eth. Nic. VI. 5. 1140 b 11-16; VII. 2. 1145 b 10-14; VII. 8. 1150 b 20 f.; V. 10. 1134 a 20 f.; καὶ γὰρ ἂν συγγένοιτο γυναικὶ εἰδὼς τὸ ᾗ, ἀλλ' οὐ διὰ προαιρέσεως ἀρχὴν ἀλλὰ διὰ πάθος. This is a statement which distinguishes incontinence from indulgence, but we may also find in it the distinction between the knowledge of facts and that of values. If one had intercourse with a woman being ignorant who she was, this ignorance is concerned with the fact, and it is the cause of involuntariness, whereas in the above example, though there is the cognition of facts, the valuation is not real enough (not wanting altogether, for if so, the act will be voluntary and indulgent), so that one is incontinent.

[3] Eth. Nic. VII. 9. 1150 b 36; 1151 a 11; III. 2. 1110 b 31-1111a 1.

beyond productive deliberation. It is especially in setting incontinence against indulgence and involuntarity that we may distinguish the forms of practical cognition.

Incontinence is a character intermediate between virtue and vice. In its strict sense, it is confined to the appetites of eating and sex, but in its wider sense, it is also found in other desires.[1] Now a man is incontinent, if he is not quite ignorant of what moderation is, but knowing it in a sense, yet carries its enjoyment to excess owing to a disharmony of desire and intellect. A continent man, on the contrary, dominates his desire by intellect and keeps moderation, yet the harmony is not so complete as in temperance, and desire is enforced by intellect. Thus the fault of incontinence consists in the disharmony of desire and intellect together with the weakness of the power of intellect. What is then the weakness of the practical intellect ? If the function of intellect is confined to judgement and inference, intellect would be neither strong nor weak, but only right or wrong. Now since intellect may be weak though it is right, it must be a source of power, and its act must be the origin of conduct. When it acts as an inference, its conclusion must possess practical power. The practical syllogism was surely considered to produce such a power. If the power of conduct thus belongs to the essence of the practical syllogism, the corresponding impotency must also originated in the act of intellect itself. The impotency of intellect which is the cause of incontinence must arise from the fault of intellectual action itself. Otherwise, the practical power would be something exterior and accidental to the inference, so that it would result in the negation of practical intellect in the strict sense.

Now the incontinent man commits a fault in one sense knowing, and in another sense not knowing. For, "to know" has two senses: it is either to have the ἕξις of knowledge, or to know actually. Though it is strange to act against knowledge while one is exercising this knowledge, it is not strange if one has the knowledge only as a habit.[2] Is it then in this manner, that the incontinent man

[1] Rhet. I. 12. 1372 b 12 f.
[2] Eth. Nic. VII. 5. 1146 b 31; cf. Cat. 8. 8 b 29; Pol. IV. 1. 1288 b 17; Eth. Nic. VI. 3. 1139 b 31; p. 6, n. 6. Similar notions about the use of knowledge are found in Plato's Theaetet. 197. Namely, knowledge is either in the state of ἕξις or of κτῆσις. The one case is like the wearing of a garment, and the other its possession. In another metaphor, the one is like using a dove one has caught, but the other like possessing it in an aviary. Now, one who has an opinion, is

commits a fault though he knows it to be bad ? Then, what does it mean to have the habit of knowledge and not to excercise it ? If practical cognition forms a syllogism, a habitual cognition without actuality would be a state, in which all or part of the elements of cognition are present, except that they are not yet being mediated. The syllogism consists of major and minor premisses, and it combines the universal and the particular with the intermediate term. Therefore, in an incomplete inference, at least one of the two premisses would remain a mere potentiality. Let Aristotle himself speak. Eth. Nic. VII. 3. 1147 a 1: "Further, since there are two kinds of premisses, there is nothing to prevent a man's having both premisses and acting against his knowledge, provided that he is using only the universal premiss and not the particular; for it is particular acts that have to be done. And there are also two kinds of universal term, one is predicable of the agent, the other of the object; for example, 'dry food is good for every man', and 'I am a man', or 'such and such food is dry'; but whether this food is such and such', of this the incontinent man either has not or is not excercising the knowledge. There will, then, be, firstly, an enormous difference between these manners of knowing, so that to know in one way when we act incontinently would not seem anything strange, while to know in the other way would be extraordinary."[1]

Thus the incontinent man has the universal knowledge but cannot apply it to the particular, so that his cognition does not realize itself in an actual syllogism. But, Aristotle, continuing the statement, pointed out that there is another way of possessing knowledge, as in the case of a man who is asleep, mad, or drunk. Such a man may utter the words that follows from knowledge, but this is no more than an utterance by actors on the stage. The knowledge of the man who is under the influence of passion, as is the case with an incontinent man, is such an inertial one.[2] We must appreciate the significance of the fact that Aristotle mentioned the somnambulistic states of mind along with the ignorance of individual facts

possessed of knowledge, as far as he has memory, but not always using it, and there is the possibility of it being a wrong opinion. This opposition of ἕξις and κτῆσις corresponds to Aristotle's opposition of χρῆσις and κτῆσις. This ἕξις in Plato, corresponds to Aristotle's ἐνέργεια, but according to Aristotle's usage, ἕξις is a habitual state and remains a kind of potential being or the potency which is most active. The ἕξις of knowledge in Aristotle, would mean, to use the above metaphor, no more than the possessing of a dove in the aviary.

[1] Eth. Nic. VII. 5. 1147 a 1 ff.   [2] Ibid. 10 ff.

about food. For, Aristotle would have admitted the latter to be a more suitable example to explain the state of incontinence, because the former is rather the cause of involuntarity than that of incontinence. Incontinence and involuntarity should be distinguished not through the degree of ignorance, but in the respect whether this ignorance is concerned with facts or with values. And estimation or the judgement of value is disturbed not by accidents, but by emotion. For the state in which the disturbance of knowledge in incontinence becomes extreme, is, as aforesaid, not involuntarity but indulgence. Aristotle explains this more in detail as follows. Eth. Nic. VII. 4. 1147 a 25: "Again, we may also view the cause as follows with reference to the facts of human nature. The one opinion is universal, the other is concerned with the particular facts, and here we come to something within the sphere of perception; when a single opinion results from the two, the soul must in one case affirm the conclusion, while in the case of opinions concerned with production, it must immediately act (e.g. if 'everything sweet ought ot be tasted", and 'this is sweet', in the sense of being one of the particular sweet things, the man who can act and is not prevented must at the same time actually act accordingly). When, then, the universal opinion is present in us forbidding us to taste, and there is also the opinion that 'everything sweet is pleasant', and that 'this is sweet', (now this is the opinion that is active,) and when appetite happens to be present in us, the one opinion bids us avoid the object, but appetite leads us towards it."[1]

This statement implies that the conduct of an incontinent man is determined by the maxim of enjoyment, which dominates individual cognition against the advice of prudence. The cause of incontinence is that the particular knowledge of practice is not made actually practical in a particular case. Hence Aristotle concludes: "Now, the last premiss both being an opinion about a perceptible object, and being what determines our actions, this a man either has not when he is in the state of passion, or has it in the sense in which having knowledge did not mean knowing but only talking, as a drunken man may utter the verses of Empedocles."[2] The opinion about a perceptible object here means, no

---

[1] Eth. Nic. VII. 5. 1147 a 25 ff.
[2] Ibid. 9 ff. According to Teichmüller (op. cit. 46 f.), the knowledge which Walter assumes to be deliberation, viz., which consists of theoretical premisses

doubt, the practical reason which perceives individual affairs. Therefore, the above statement would imply that the defect of intuitive reason about the moral value of an individual act, results in the state of incontinence.

The impotency of rational desire, which results in incontinence, is founded upon a defect in practical syllogism. This kind of syllogism is practical and not productive. For, it is said, "Nothing prevents a clever man from being incontinent".[1] But, since an incontinent man is not unable to distinguish between good and bad, but only unable to realize the good which he wishes, it may appear as if he were lacking in productive or technical knowledge. Yet, ignorance of causality is the cause of involuntarity rather than that of incontinence. The want of such a productive deliberation is also a kind of vice, but not incontinence. An incontinent man harms his health not because of his ignorance of medical art, but because of his ignorance of practical wisdom that he is indulging in an excessive enjoyment, though he knows generally that excessive enjoyment is hurtful. We have already mentioned that what disturbs this particular estimation is an irrational desire or an appetite. What then is the practical intellect in a continent man ? Seeing that continence is the contrary of incontinence, and incontinence results from the lack of actual particular estimation, a continent man ought to be regarded as performing a complete practical deliberation. But then, we shall feel a difficulty in distinguishing an continent man from a temperate one. Complete practical deliberation is complete prudence, and complete prudence is the complete domination of intellect over desires, the appearance of this dominence in appetites being temperance. Compared with temperance, continence is somewhat an incomplete virtue, or a character intermediate between virtue and vice. A difference of degree similar to that which is found between the practical cognitions of a continent man and of an incontinent man, is also found between the cognitions of a temperate man and a continent one. Since the cause of practical weakness of an incontinent man is the lack of actuality in his estimating a minor premiss, we may suppose that a continent man is strong through the actuality in his estimating of this same premiss. Whereas a continent man is different

and results in a conclusion which is a categorical imperative, is rather a sophistic syllogism of an incontinent man, instead of prudence and a practical syllogism.

[1] Eth. Nic. VII. 11. 1152 a 10.

from a temperate man in being obliged to suppress and manage appetites through intellect, because he is not blessed with a complete harmony of desire and intellect, that is to say, the intellect is not practical enough, and is always threatened with falling into incontinence.

So, a continent man and a temperate one have the same kind of practical cognition, the former only being inferior to the latter in that its syllogism is not practical enough on account of poor experience and lack of training. The practical cognition of an incontinent man as well as of a continent one is not heterogeneous with that of a temperate man; it is the same prudence, only differing in its practical power. The essence of prudence may surely be explained through the character of a prudent man. Yet this requires some precaution.[1] The complete actuality is certainly found only in a wise man. But a wise man is the ideal of prudence and its incarnation. So that in reality, prudence is somewhat incomplete, and there is no real complete prudence. We may admit an incomplete prudence as well as a complete one. Such an incomplete prudence is precisely the intellect of a continent man and also, in the lowest degree, that of an incontinent man. φρόνησις is related to φρόνιμος just as ἐπιστήμη is to ἐπιστημονικός or θεωρία to θεωρητικός. Knowledge or thinking is not always scientific or theoretical intellect, but may be a moment of practical intellect, the corresponding adjective form (ἐπιστημονικός or θεωρητικός) expressing the special intellectual attitude that aims at knowledge or thinking itself as the final end and the ideal; just so, prudence also is not confined to the ideal wise man, but may be acting in a lower character in some degree. Temperance is the most complete actuality of prudence concerning eating and sexual appetites, but a continent man and even an incontinent man somehow partake in it, and may advance to temperance through effort. A character which has no possibility of improvement is indulgence, which has lost not only the minor premiss but also the major premiss of the practical syllogism.[2] Such a character, performs no practical syllogism in the strict sense. Yet there is a kind of practical deliberation, which is just what we called productive syllogism. A man with such a character does not know whether what he wishes to do is good or bad. His desires are not regulated

[1] Walter, op. cit. 492; Eth. Nic. VII. 11. 1152 a 6.
[2] Eth. Nic. VII. 9. 1151 a 20-27; 11. 1152 a 4-6.

by intellect at all. Nevertheless he knows the means to realize his desire, and is intellectual as far as he acts according to such a technical deliberation. He is a clever man, only his cleverness brings him a great evil.[1]

As aforesaid, temperance and indulgence, as well as continence and incontinence are confined in the strict sense, to eating and sexual appetites, but speaking more generally, one who lacks in the universal knowledge of moral estimation, or who has a bad intention, is an evil man or a vicious one. What is called ignorance in will or ignorance of the advantages of life, is such a character. Such a man may be clever, and knows well in what way he can satisfy his vicious desires. Such a knowledge is surely a kind of practical syllogism, of deliberation, or of calculation. Therefore, a vicious man is in a sense possessed of practical knowledge. Only he is either quite ignorant of moral value[2] or is confident of false cognition.[3] Whereas an incontinent man has, though incompletely, the right estimation of moral values, and is better than an indulgent and vicious man. His practical syllogism is incomplete in the minor premiss that denotes the particular estimation, though it contains the major premiss or the universal estimation. He retains a knowledge of the obligation or "oughtness" to realize virtue in general.[4] Universal oughtness is derived not from the subject, but from outside. It is, e.g. an ideal, which is imposed upon him as the advice of his predecessors. Man ought to regulate his individual conduct through such a universal precept.[5] The precepts and commands that were at first external become internal by degrees, till at last they become the expression of a man's own character, and a complete ethical virtue will then be realized. The completion of ethical virtue is at the same time the accomplishment of prudence, i.e. the complete harmony of passion and intellect. The lowest stage of this moral progress is incontinence, next comes continence, and it reaches at last to temperance. Thus the highest universal principle of practical cognition is derived from outside and becomes immanent. This is related to the state of affairs that we have observed concerning active reason. According to our interpretation, active reason was

---

[1] Eth. Nic. VI. 10. 1142 b 20; VII. 11. 1152 a 10.
[2] Eth. Nic. III. 2. 1110 b 28-1111 a 1; cf. Loening, op. cit. 177, 179, 115.
[3] Eth. Nic. VII. 4. 1146 b 22; 11. 1152 a 5.
[4] Ibid. 9. 1151 a 20 ff.   [5] Cf. ch. IV. § 4, 5.

an objective mind or culture, which gives forms to passive reason and actualizes a real cognition. This is equally applicable both to theoretical and to practical intellect. The moral cultivation of man is a formation taking place gradually upon the basis of natural disposition, by the implanting of principles which were designed by wise men. The principle of this formation is λόγος, reason, morality, and universal practical knowledge, and this cultivation is performed through natural feelings of pleasure and pain, viz., starting from the good for each man gradually makes one feel what is good without qualification for everybody.[1] Moral cultivation lies not in the categorical imperative of reason, but in the harmonization of feeling and reason.[2]

Principle is important both for practical and theoretical reasons, and if it once be destroyed, the whole of thinking would be done away with. Therefore, an indulgent man or a vicious man who is deprived of the highest principle of practical cognition, is the worst.[5] Next, incontinence is divided into προπέτεια, i.e. impetuosity and ἀσθένεια, i.e. weakness. The first is the failure after deliberation to stand by the conclusion of one's deliberation owing to his emotion, the other consists in being led by emotion because one has not deliberated.[3] In the former case virtue is defeated by violence, in the latter by the quickness of passion. Of these two characters, weakness is said to be inferior to impetuosity, because it involves the weakness of reason. One might suppose the contrary, as there is no room for intellect in impetuosity, but Aristotle rather considered that such a man potentially has intellect and would be able to control his emotion if he recovers his composure, while weakness is beyond remedy.[4] This is the same thought that appears when Aristotle depreciates the indulgence and vice which are corrupted in the intellectual principle, rather than brutishness which entirely lacks in intelligence.[5] It is the necessary condition of moral improvement, that we preserve the universal knowledge of practice. This is respect for the reason and law, the good will and steadfastness. Man is reclaimable as long as he has not lost this principle.[6]

[1] Met. VII. 3. 1029 b 5-7; Eth. Nic. V. 2. 1129 b 5.
[2] Cf. Trendelenburg, Beiträge. etc. III. 209 ff.; Eth. Nic. VI. 3. 1139 a 26 ff.; cf. ch. III. § 2.
[3] Eth. Nic. VII. 9. 1151 a 15, 26.   [4] Eth. Nic. VII. 8. 1150 b 19 ff.
[5] Eth. Nic. VII. 9. 1151 a 1-5.
[6] Eth. Nic. VII. 7. 1150 a 1-8. The end-congruent functions are unconscious in

In short, incontinence, indulgence, or vice is a condition in which either the minor or the major premiss of the practical syllogism is lacking. We may find in the foregoing inquiry of these types of character a key for discriminating the two forms of the practical syllogism, viz. the productive and the practical *par excellence*.

§ 5. THE RELATION OF PRACTICAL AND PRODUCTIVE SYLLOGISMS

We have previously distinguished the practical syllogism from the productive syllogism. The one tracing the causal series, searches for the means for a given end. This is the function of deliberation that forms an element of προαίρεσις or will. Whereas the practical syllogism is the thinking which makes desire rational from its ground, the desire thus made rational being βούλησις or wish. This kind of syllogism is concerned with the end rather than the means. It considers about the moral significance of conduct, and estimates an individual act, measuring it according to moral laws. The productive syllogism consists of hypothetical judgements or sometimes with one perceptive judgement as the last minor premiss, and concludes that a particular act should be performed to realize a given end. While in the practical syllogism, the major premiss orders moral conduct in general or a somewhat definite kind of virtuous conduct, the minor premiss perceives that a particular act bears this moral value; this is the so-called *phronetische Anschauung* or moral perception—and hence it is concluded that a particular act ought to be done. The productive deliberation or syllogism is hypothetical and presupposes some end, which is given either through an irrational desire or through a wish, which is a desire rationalized by the practical syllogism. This has some reference to the theory of two-sided rational potency, which we have studied previously. The potentiality was then divided into the rational and the irrational, the one, being one-sided, either realizes itself or not, the other, being

plants, they are subconscious or at least not reflective in animals, but reflective-conscious in man. So that a man who loses this directing principle, is unable to perform these functions, which are possible for plants and animals. Hence the perversion of reason becomes a positive vice. cf. ch. II. § 4.

5 Eth. Nic. VII. 8. 1150 a 19-22; 9. 1150 b 29-35; 1151 a 11-16.

two-sided, may produce contrary results. What decides this two-sidedness and resolves it into one, was προαίρεσις or ὄρεξις, i.e. will or desire.[1] We also considered that δύναμις was properly speaking, one-sided power, which inclines so as to break the equilibrium of the opposites. This analysis is applied both to rational and irrational potencies. It was also maintained that the original dynamism of potency in Aristotle's thought faded away,[2] when Aristotle found the determinative moment of rational potency outside it, and the dynamic moment passed gradually into the concept of ἕξις or habit. But, considering more fundamentally, just as matter is correlative with form, and what is form to one thing may be matter to another, so there might be a difference of degree in the one-sidedness of potency or potentiality. What is active in one stage might be passive in another. Thus, rational potency would be active and one-sided as far as it is potent, passive and indefinite as far as it is rational. In fact, art is sometimes treated as a mere potency, sometimes as a habit.[3] Habit is one-sided. Being a habit, art is inclined to one side. Therefore, even rational potency is not indifferent to opposite actualities, but refers to one *per se* or naturally, to another accidentally, e.g. medical art refers to health naturally and to illness accidentally;[4] grammar is naturally the principle

[1] Met. IX. 2. 1046 b 15-24; 5. 1048 a 10 f.; 8. 1050 b 30.
[2] Cf. p. 6, n. 6.
[3] Met. IX. 2. 1046 b 2-4; 3. 1046 b 34-36; cf. ibid. 2. 1046 b 4-24; 8. 1050 b 31; Eth. Nic. V. 1. 1129 a 12. What is implied in these places under rational potency, is, no doubt, art. Also art is treated as somewhat similar to potency in Met. VII. 8. 1033 b 8; VI. 1. 1025 b 22; Eth. Nic. VII. 13. 1153 a 25; Pol. II. 8. 1268 b 36; VIII. 1. 1337 a 19; Rhet. I. 2. 1358 a 6; Top. IX. 9. 170 a 36 etc. On the other hand, art is as aforsaid, defned as a productive habit accompanied by true reason. Cf. Eth. Nic. VI. 4. 1140 a 7, 10, 22. [Mag. Mor. I. 35. 1197 b 22.] Similarly with knowledge. ἕξις is not much different from active potency, but both of them are intermediate between possibility and actuality. To develop in art and knowledge, means to acquire a habitual potency through the repetition of acts. A mere possibility becomes through this process an acquired habit. Thus, habit mediates potentiality and reality, and act mediates potentiality and habit. They develop through this reciprocal mediation.
[4] Eth. Eud. II. 11. 1227 a 25-28; Pol. I. 2. 1253 a 31-37: ὥσπερ γὰρ καὶ τελεωθὲν βέλτιστον τῶν ζῴων ἄνθρωπός ἐστιν, οὕτω καὶ χωρισθὲν νόμου καὶ δίκης χείριστον πάντων. χαλεπωτάτη γὰρ ἀδικία ἔχουσα ὅπλα· ὁ δ' ἄνθρωπος ὅπλα ἔχων φύεται φρονήσει καὶ ἀρετῇ, οἷος ἐπὶ τἀναντία ἔστι χρῆθαι μάλιστα. διὸ ἀνοσιώτατον καὶ ἐδωδὴν χείριστον. There is some difficulty with 1. 34: ὅπλα ἔχων φύεται φρονήσει καὶ ἀρετῇ. We read, following Newmann, "Man is furnished from birth with arms for prudence and virtue, for to make prudence or virtue the arms would

of right speaking, only accidentally that of wrong speaking; this much more evident with the arts of navigation and building. Yet art cannot act alone but needs some principle that moves it. It is only an instrument of volition. Hence it is said that medical art is the potency which may both heal and make illness, and it depends upon will or desire to decide which direction it takes. Now, will, being a deliberated desire, consists of deliberation and desire, so that, what determines rational potency in one direction must be either deliberation or desire. And if deliberation be the searching for the end, that is determined by art, this would lead to a *regressus ad infinitum*. Consequently, either this deliberation must be different from art, or else desire, as another moment of will, must be the determinative principle. The deliberation which is other than art, being, as aforesaid, the estimative calculation of moral values, which is after all, the immanent moment of wish, this determinative principle must be, in either case, a kind of desire. Thus rational potency implies an art, and this is determined by a desire. Art, being hypothetical, presupposes a desire outside itself. What makes the productive syllogism categorical is desire. Therefore desire as an expression of habit and character determines the direction of art. Art is, as it were, the passive and material principle, and desire, the active and formal principle of a will. And thus determined, will forms the principle of production. Art is active and formal as against the material of production, but it is passive and material in relation to a concrete act. It commands only a hypothetical form, and requires desire outside itself. The productive syllogism becomes categorical through the determination of desire. What makes an end good, is desire rather than art. Now desire may be either rational or irrational. Rational desire, or wish, seeks the good and avoids the evil, and irrational desire, or appetite, seeks pleasure and avoids pain. Art is in any case a formal principle of production, but in relation to volition, it is merely matter. There is the practical cognition of a higher grade, which conditions this dominating desire. This intellect determines the desire for happiness into the wish for virtuous conduct. This is, of course, not art, but prudence; it is not the productive, but the practical *par excellence*.

be an incomprehensible statement, and virtue is not used in such a sense in the next line. Newmann is presumably right in taking these arms as passion and anger; while Barker takes them, for instance, as language. Art is, of course, not a natural ability, but as it is potentially innate in human nature, we might treat it as analogous to natural disposition, as the arms here suggest.

It deliberates not about the means for an end, but about the value of a concrete end. Though deliberation or calculation is more frequently used in the productive meaning, it is sometimes applied also to the estimating inference of practice, and what determines the direction of rational potency will then be the wish which is mediated by practical cognition. The desire that determines art is not of necessity rational as well, but may be irrational, i.e. an appetite. Art is employed either by a virtuous or a vicious man. When employed by a good man, it promotes goodness, but employed by a bad man, it aggravates evil. We may at all events perceive here a relation between productive and practical cognition.

Conduct is the realization of desire, which may appear either as instinctive appetite or as wish founded upon deliberation. The former is determined by pleasure and pain which follow sensitive imagination, the latter by moral estimatin. This moral estimation, however, forms a kind of practical syllogism. This syllogism is practical in the strict sense, and forms the rational principle of desire itself instead of presupposing a direct desire. Its major premiss is the master-prudence of a wise man which orders virtuous conduct, and the minor premiss is the practical intuition that a particular act bears this moral value. Moral estimation is an expression of character, and in order to grasp the objective value, we need an education through master-prudence. On the other hand, virtuous acts which are guided by such an excellent education, gradually foster master-prudence in everybody. The complete harmony of emotion and intellect is just the moral ideal.

Now the realization of desire requires a right art. Both rational and irrational desire require the deliberation of real means. Here is the necessity of the productive syllogism. The productive syllogism requires an aim, while the practical syllogism requires an instrument. Complete conduct is accomplished only through the cooperation of both cognitions. We read as follows in Eth. Nic. VI. 2. 1139 a 35: "Intellect itself, however, moves nothing, but only the intellect which aims at an end and is practical; for this rules the productive intellect as well, since every one who makes makes for an end, and that which is made is not an end in the unqualified sense (but only an end in a particular operation)—only that which is done is that; for good action is an end, and desire aims at this."

The first expression of ethical virtue was, as aforesaid, a universal practical judgement, 'The highest good and the ultimate end of human life is happiness'. This is a categorical judgement founded upon ethical virtue, its minor premiss being, e.g. 'Health is happiness', and the conclusion, 'Health is the end'; or in other words, 'You should heal'. This practical syllogism gives an end to medical deliberation and through its conclusion the doctor undertakes healing. What makes his act a production is productive deliberation or the practical syllogism in the secondary sense, while what makes the same act a practice must be rather practical deliberation or the practical syllogism in the primary sense. Let us give another example.

Happiness is the highest good.[1]
Virtuous conduct is happiness.[2]
Justice is a virtue.
One ought to do justice.
Justice is the right distribution of wealth, more to a wise man, less to a slave.[3]
A is a wise man, and B is a slave.
One ought to give more wealth to A, and less to B.[4]

This is a practical syllogism in the form of a sorites. In order, then, to make such a distribution without struggle, we should act e.g. through law and authority instead of private discretion,[5] and the ways are such and such.[6] This is the productive syllogism that realizes the conclusion of the practical syllogism. Generally speaking, the main contents of ethics are practical syllogisms, and those of politics productive syllogisms. Since ethics is part of politics in a wider sense, and forms apparently an independent work, they seem to relate to each other just as elemental theory does to methodology. Thus, the practical syllogism produces a wish, which is realized in the will through the productive syllogism. Will is the principle of conduct as well as of other immediate desires.

[1] Eth. Nic. I. 2. 1095 a 16; 9. 1099 a 24; X. 6. 1176 a 31; b 31; Eth. Eud. I. 1. 1214 a 7; 1217 a 40; II. 1. 1219 a 28; Pol. VII. 8. 1328 a 37; 13. 1331 b 39; Rhet. I. 6. 1362 b 10.
[2] Eth. Nic. I. 6. 1098 a 16; X. 6. 1177 a 10; Eth. Eud. II. 1. 1219 a 39, 35; [Mag. Mor. II. 7. 1204 a 28;] Pol. VII. 1. 1323 b 21; 8. 1328 a 37; 13. 1332 a 9; Poet. 6. 1450 a 18; Phys. II. 6. 197 b 4. [3] Eth. Nic. V. 1. 1129 a 6.
[4] Eth. Nic. V. 5. 1130 b 30 ff.; 9. 1134 a 1 ff.
[5] Pol. III. 15. 1286 a 9; 16. 1287 a 19, 29; IV. 4. 1292 a 2, 4, 32; 5. 1292 b 6; 6. 1293 a 16, 32; cf. Eth. Nic. V. 10. 1134 b 1; X. 10. 1180 a 21; Pol. III. 16. 1287 a 32; 15. 1286 a 19. [6] Cf. Pol. III. 9.

Every instance of conduct which grows from a desire and is followed by the consciousness of individual circumstances is voluntary, but will requires moreover the productive syllogism. Without such a deliberation and the will, we cannot perform an effective act. Every realization of the will may be said to be a production, but it is a practice as far as it is mediated by a practical syllogism. In complete intellectual conduct, the practical syllogism is followed by the productive syllogism, and the conclusion of the latter passes into conduct. A mere practical syllogism does not guarantee the possibility of conduct. Not every good thing is realized; even if a man has a good will, he is not always able to realize it. For such a man, after all, might be a phantastic idealist. If we may say, following Kant, "You can do because you ought to do", it is only when we restrict the meaning of "can do" or "ought to do" in a special sense. In their usual meaning, possibility and oughtness do not refer to each other in this way. The circumstance is similar to that of Socrates and his theory that identified knowledge with virtue. Just as he can duly assert the identity of knowledge and virtue, as far as he has secretly brought virtue into knowledge, and knowledge into virtue, so we may assert the identity of possibility and oughtness only when we use the words in a particularly modified sense.

It would be needless to say, that the productive syllogism alone cannot be sufficient to produce conduct. For art is nothing but an instrument of human volition, and by no means independent. The so-called domination of the machine is, in fact, the domination of brutality in human nature over art. The imperative of an art is merely hypothetical, and what makes it categorical, or its active and formal principle, is desire. And the rationality which rules desire was the deliberation of moral values. These series of mental activities should have their own virtues. The virtue of the practical syllogism is prudence, and that of good wish is the ethical virtues. Similarly, there are two kinds of defect with regard to the practical syllogism; that of the major premiss is indulgence or more generally, vice, and that of the minor premiss incontinence or the want of virtue. On the other hand, the virtue of the productive syllogism is cleverness or art (art being a virtue as well as a faculty). The defect of the major premiss is $ἀτεχνία$[1] or the want of art, and that of the last minor premiss is involuntarity, which is outside of human resposibility. The lack of mere perception is a natural fault and

[1] Eth. Nic. VII. 4. 1140 a 21.

does not constitute responsibilty for a moral subject, if it be not reduced indirectly to a careless way of living. The subject of responsibility should be a constant and universal principle.

The combination of the virtues of productive and practical deliberation is φρόνησις in the strict sense, he who is possessed of this virtue is a φρονιμός or a wise man. His wish is good, and his art is right; he can do a great good. Pericles[1] would be an approximate example of this type. Of course, this is not the highest character, for practice is not the highest of human activities. What is highest is the philosophical character, e.g. that of Anaxagoras or Thales.[2] The combination of the virtue of productive deliberation and the vice of the practical syllogism is the worst. From the intellectual side, it is πανουργία, and from the emotional side, μοχθηρία;[3] Arcibiades might be an example of it. He who lacks in both virtues is brutal, Palalis[4] being an example, but this is frequent rather in a savage race.[5] It is surely the lowest character, from an objective point of view, but it is less dangerous for social life.[6] There is no name for the character which is the possession of the virtue of practical deliberation combined with a lack in productive deliberation. Such a one is a gentle ordinary person, who has good will and good judgement, but lacks in the ability for great conduct.[7] From the active side, he is a man of good understanding, from the negative side, an incompetent fellow.[8]

§ 6. COMPARISON WITH KANT

Let this suffice for a construction of Aristotle's idea of practice and of practical intellect. Yet to divide thus the practical syllogism from productive, making the one categorical, and the

---

[1] Eth. Nic. VII. 5. 1140 b 8.
[2] Eth. Nic. VII. 7. 1141 b 7. He makes no distinction between φρονιμός and σοφός, and takes as an example of the godlike man, Hector. Cf. Eth. Nic. VII. 1. 1145 a 20.   [3] Eth. Nic. VII. 1. 1145 a 30.
[4] Eth. Nic. VII. 6. 1149 a 14.
[5] Eth. Nic. VII. 6. 1149 a 11; 1. 1145 a 31.
[6] Eth. Nic. VII. 7. 1150 a 1-8.
[7] Eth. Nic. VI. 11. 1143 a 11.
[8] The ἀτεχνία in Eth. Nic. VI. 4. 1140 a 21, or ὀκνηρός in Eth. Nic. IV. 9. 1125 a 24, excepting the feeling of self-depreciation, would appear to be akin to the character in question.

other hypothetical, might remind one of Kant's theory of practical reason. Therefore, it will be by no means pointless for us to attempt to compare the two theories. It is well known that Kant divided generally the use of reason into the theoretical and the practical; in the one use it is concerned only with the object of cognition, and in the other it is the determinative principle of will.[1] It is further said that practical reason orders an act as the means for an end which is aimed at, and practical rules either determine the causal conditions of rational being as an efficient cause, but only in so far as these conditions produce a result, or they determine only the will without regarding whether it is sufficient for the result or not. The one is a hypothetical imperative and an advice consisting of mere skill, the other a categorical imperative, and only this latter is a practical law.[2] A hypothetical imperative is necessary only in order to realize a certain desire, but a categorical imperative commands one to will something without presupposing any arbitrary desire. Every practical principle which is determined by the object of desire, being empirical and relative, has no necessity; a universal and necessary law is given only when reason directly gives the law itself, the determinative principle of which is not the object of desire but a pure form.[3]

It is evident that the hypothetical imperative corresponds to productive deliberation, and the categorical imperative to practical deliberation. Productive deliberation is applied only by presup-

[1] Kant, K. d. p. V. Einl. WW. Cass. V. 16.
[2] Ibid. I. 1. i. 1. Erk. Anm. WW. V. 22.
[3] Ibid. I. 1. i. Kap. 3. Lehrs. 2. Anm. II. WW. V. 29. Kant assumes the productive syllogism in the form of the hypothetical imperative, to be theoretical. "*Prinzipien der Selbstliebe können zwar allgemeine Regeln der Geschicklichkeit (Mittel zu Absichten anzufinden) enthalten, alsdann sind es aber bloss theoretische Prinzipien (z.B. wie derjenige, der gerne Brot essen möchte, sich eine Mühle auszudenken habe).*" He explains the theoretical principle as follows: "*Sätze, welche in der Mathematik oder Naturlehre praktisch genannt werden, sollten eigentlich technisch heissen. Denn um die Willensbestimmung ist es diesen Lehren gar nicht zu tun; sie zeigen nur das Mannigfaltige der möglichen Handlung an, welches eine gewisse Wirkung hervorzubringen hinreichend ist, und sind also ebenso theoretisch als alle Sätze, welche die Verknüpfung der Ursache mit einer Wirkung aussagen. Wenn nun die letztere beliebt, der muss auch gefallen lassen, die erstere zu sein.*" Walter's misinterpretation about the practical syllogism—viz., that the premisses being purely theoretical, only the conclusion is made categorical through the will or desire that comes from outside the syllogism—would be due to Kant's thought as we see it here.

posing a desire, while practical deliberation sets up a desire itself. But what is the real meaning of saying that reason gives laws by itself? Is it that the law-giving practical reason orders a particular act without syllogistic deliberation? And does this agree with the view of Aristotle that makes reason an intellectual intuition? By no means; what Kant's remark really implies is that practical reason commands one to have a desire directly without the supposition of another desire. It never prohibits the reason to take a syllogistic form. Kant implied that practical reason forms a syllogism, when he required us in the case of individual resolution to ask whether the contents of the will may be regarded as a universal law. He admitted the practical syllogism, the major premiss of which being moral principle, the minor premiss the subsumption of a particular act under the moral principle, and the conclusion the determination of a subjective will.[1]

With regard to the theory that reason produces a desire without presupposing any other desire, its real meaning is that reason sometimes determines a will by itself, this being distinguished from the case when the rule of reason is employed by a sensitive desire. In Aristotle similarly, productive deliberation searches for the means to realize a given desire, so that the application of its advice depends upon that desire, which is not of necessity rational. Besides that, Aristotle admitted the case in which desire itself is fundamentally dominated by reason. Wish presupposes a deliberation, which calculates the values of wishes. This is what we called practical deliberation. A wish, which is thus dependent upon deliberation or syllogism, is neither an accidental sensitive desire, nor a purpose that depends upon such a desire. This desire is *eo ipso* rational, or in other words, it is produced by reason itself. According to Kant, such a reason is by no means empirical or material, but entirely formal and generally applicable; whereas Aristotle considered it to be derived from a character which is after all fostered through experience.[2] There is, however, not as much of a decisive divergence between the two philosophers as Kant considered. That practical reason determines a will merely through the form of law-giving, means in plain words, that one wills something not because it is pleasant to him, but only because it is a good thing or a duty. Kant maintains that good and bad

---

[1] Kant, K. d. p. V. I. 1. iii. Kritische Beleuchtung d. An. d. p. V. WW. V. 99.   [2] Cf. p. 197, n. 2.

do not precede the consciousness of duty, but are only another expression of the fact that a certain thing is suited to the laws and is a duty. But as we have considered, the consciousness of duty is a mere secondary and subjective appearance of the good. For Aristotle, for a thing to be good is not different from its being an object of desire. The highest good is the object of desire for every one or for an ideal person; man desires it because it is good, and there is no existence of goodness apart from being the object of desire. Though the good is prior to duty, it is nonsense to ask which is prior, good or desire.[1] Yet while taking notice of this point, we must not forget that the fundamental principle of practical reason is in Aristotle none the less ordered by reason of its goodness. To wish something on account of its goodness, is after all, the same as having a fundamental desire for it. And the satisfaction of a desire is happiness in a wider sense. Subjectively, one desires something not for the sake of satisfaction or pleasure, but for the sake of its realization. Since however, pleasure is the necessary concomitant of satisfaction,[2] every desire may objectively be said to aim at pleasure.[3] Of course, in this case, the end is not taken as a purpose, but as an objective form.

As regards the sense of duty, it is the consciousness which accompanies an immoral desire, but is not essential to the moral law. An ideal character, Aristotle supposes, would rather feel pleasure in the realization of a rational wish. Such an ideal character is not produced directly from mere reason, but is fostered somewhat in an irrational way. The training of character must be guided by a rational design. It is not accomplished at once through mere persuasion, rather it must be fostered gradually, and becomes a semi-instinctive habit.[4] That the moral imperative

[1] Eth. Nic. I . 1. 1094 a 2 f.; 5. 1097 a 18, 20: V. 6. 1131 b 23; [Mag. Mor. II.7. 1205 b 35;] Eth. Eud. I. 8. 1218 b 6; Rhet. I. 6. 1362 a 22; 1363 a 9; 7. 1363 b 13; 1364 b 17, 25; Pol. I. 2. 1252 b 34; II. 8. 1269 a 4; III. 12. 1282 b 15; Met. I. 3. 983 a 32; 7. 988 b 9; III. 2. 996 a 24; XI. 1. 1050 a 36; XII. 10. 1075 a 37; Top. III. 1. 116 a 19; De An. III. 10. 433 a 27-29; Pol. I. 1. 1252 a 3; Eth. Eud. VII. 2. 1235 b 26; Met. V. 2. 1031 b 26.

[2] Eth. Nic. VII. 13. 1153 a 14; 14. 1153 b 9 ff.; X. 5. 1175 b 27; 1175 a 19.

[3] Eth. Nic. VII. 14. 1153 b 31 f.; Rhet. I. 6. 1362 b 6; 7. 1364 b 23; Eth. Nic. X. 1. 1172 a 20. [Mag. Mor. II. 7. 1205 b 36.]

[4] Eth. . ic. I. 2. 1095 b 4; X. 10. 1179 b 24; cf. Rhet. II. 12. 1389 a 36; 13. 1.90 a 18.

is an imperative only through being a law, not through the pleasure which accidentally follows from the special quality of an object, does not prevent the realization of such a moral law from demanding an acquired character which feels satisfaction in the attainment of moral conduct.

Further, to Kant, the essence of moral law is universal applicability, of which the archytype is the natural law. To Aristotle on the contrary, moral principles are rather essentially particular. For neither may everyone act in the same manner, nor ought he to act in the same way, but the right conduct is variously different in everybody. A lord has his own morality, and a slave another.[1] The moral law is not so universal and necessary as the natural law, but rather relative and probable. One ought not to act as though his own maxim were the universal law; he should rather make it the ideal to know himself and act in his proper manner. There is actually a difference of value among these moralities. The ideal of human conduct is certainly that of a wise man or a godlike man. Man should endeavour for the harmonious progress of intellect and sensibility aiming at this ideal state.[2] Nevertheless, it would contribute nothing to moral improvement to neglect the fundamental excercise of sensibility and give a mere formal law as duty. In order to accept the order of reason and obey it with pleasure, one must have endeavoured in the excercise of sensibility. The command of reason itself is the expression of the character which is acquired in such a way, or the manifestation of the will towards the harmonious accomplishment of his moral character.

But how far may we see in Aristotle the correspondence of the practical syllogism and with the categorical imperative on the one hand, and the productive syllogism with the hypothetical imperative on the other? To Kant, the categorical imperative was a pure duty free from all attachments, a pure formal law-giving without material determination. To Aristotle on the contrary, the ground of morality was the universal desire for happiness, i.e. the tendency of self-love. Thus, though it be admitted that the practical syllogism be categorical, would it not finally be reduced to a hypothetical imperative as far as every man desires happiness? Indeed, as far as the desire for happiness is the universal fact

[1] Pol. I. 13. 1259 b 21; 1260 a 15, 31, 33; cf. Pol. I. 13. 1259 b 33; 1260 a 3; III. 4. 1277 b 19, 27.
[2] Cf. p. 309, n. 1, 2.

of human nature, this hypothetical imperative is supported by a categorical imperative. And since happiness itself is merely an object of desire and it is not ordered that we pursue it, the moral imperative would seem to be after all a mere hypothetical imperative. Besides, happiness is, as Aristotle assumed, nothing more than a formal term, which is infinitely various in its contents, and it is left to individual character to determine in what thing he will find his own happiness. Consequently, it might appear as if the moral imperative of which the highest principle lies in the desire for happiness, had no more significance than being an advice of the means which serves for various attachments or desires. It is true that Aristotle considered the desire for happiness to be the fundamental fact of morality and the contents of happiness to be infinitely various. But it does not follow of necessity that the moral imperative is merely the advice of a means or of utility. Practice is good because it gives satisfaction to human feelings, but this does not amount to saying that such practice is nothing more than a means to happiness or self-contentment. Means has in itself no value, it is valuable only through the result which it produces. Whereas virtuous conduct is happiness *eo ipso* apart from the result. If one realizes an interest through just conduct, justice would be a mere means to interest. But the happiness which accompanies just conduct, is the essential attribute of just conduct rather than its result. Here is found the essential difference between practice and production, and consequently that between practical deliberation and productive deliberation. Happiness is not the result of movement, but the essence of action.[1]

On the contrary, if we deny, like Kant, any connection between moral law and attachment, we will not be able to understand how morality may be realized. Man naturally wishes happiness, and without this nature, human conduct would be impossible. If moral law contains nothing more than the negation of attachment, how is it possible that he obeys such an unpleasant thing? How is it possible that the moral law becomes a motive of will, and practical reason practical? There is nothing for it but to admit it as an inexplicable fact. The fact that the moral law arouses not only a negative and unpleasant feeling, but also an active feeling or at least a feeling which involves some positive character, viz. respect, cannot but make us admit that moral conduct produces a kind of

[1] Cf. ch. III. § 3.

happiness.[1] It was Kant's fundamental mistake that he assumed all material objects of desire to be sensible. We must recognize something spiritual and rational in material desire.[2] And here is really found the condition of moral realization. Just as in the theoretical area we should proceed from what is knowable for us to what is knowable by itself, so in the practical area, we must start from what is good for us and proceed to what is good by itself. This is Aristotle's way of moral elevation.[3] Neither to reject nature, nor to fall into it, but to follow and to accomplish it—to found culture and virtue upon nature, it was just this that was the method of Aristotle.

[1] Kant, K. d. p. V. I. 2. 2. WW. V. 128.
[2] Cf. Scherer, Formalismus etc. 56; Hartmann, Ethik, 88 ff.
[3] Met. VII. 3. 1029 b 2; Eth. Nic. V. 2. 1129 b 5.

GENERAL INDEX

Absolute
  being, 79.
  form, intelligence, thought, 29.
  cf. active reason, God.
Abstraction, 25, 26, 116.
Accidental, 61, 121, 176.
Act, 127, 137, 266.
Action (ἔργον), 14f. cf. affection.
Activity, 20.
  productive, 222.
  rational, 113, 176.
  practical, 222.
Actuality (ἐντελέχεια, ἐνέργεια), actualization, 6ff., 20, 29, 185f.
Adjective, 227f. 307.
Administration, 268.
Advice of cleverness, 285.
Affection, (πάθη) 14f. 68. cf. action.
Affirmation and negation, 218.
Agent, 32f. 53.
ἀγνοῦντες, in ignorance; δι' ἄγνοια, through ignorance, 169.
Air, 70, 105, 110.
αἴσθησις, v. sensation, 115, 175, 186, 217.
αἴσθημα, 118 v. sense impression.
αἰσθητικόν, 93.
Alexander of Aphrodisias, 20, 29.
Ambition, 141.
ἀμιγής, 37f. v. unmixed.
Analytica 30, 274, 280.
An. Post. 299.
ἀνάμνησις-theory, 219.
Anaxagoras, 30, 38, 72, 208, 316.
Anderssein, 79.
Anger, 14, 15, 141, 170.
Animal, 6, 100, 108, 109, 125f. 167, 220, 271.
  moved movent, 164.
  an organism, 160.
  relation to circumstance, 136.
  a. soul, 175.
Anthropomorphism, 184.
ἀπαθές, 37f. v. impassive.
ἀπόδειξις, 234, v. demonstration.
Aporematic, 98.

ἀπορία, 17, 98
Appetite, appetitive, ἐπιθυμία, 12, 90, 99, 126, 134, 139f. 143, 159, 161, 175, 303.
  a. with reason, ἐπιθυμία μετὰ λόγου, 141.
ἀρχή of the end, 247f. v. Starting point.
ἀρχιτικτονική, architectonic, 223, 230, 237 v. Master-art.
Archer, 212.
Arcibiades, 316.
Aristotelianism, a short history of. 1.
Aristotle, 2, 183.
  metaphysical principle (teleology), 11, 105, 107, 183.
  method of his philosophy, 98, 99, 275, 322.
  a moralist, 11, 153, 263f.
  an opponent of Plato, 11, 78, 99.
  a positivist, scientist, 2, 9, 10, 84, 183; 11, 153.
  a successor of Plato, 2, 11, 99.
  terminology of. 177, 179.
  transition of his thought. 98.
Arnim, 12.
Art, 73, 114, 130, 182, 184, 211f. 223, 228, 233, 236f. 311f. v. technical
  realization of a., 203.
  essence of a. 118.
  a virtue, 233, 237.
Artist, 215.
Asceticism, 143.
ἀσθένεια, weakness, 309.
ἀτεχνία, 237, 315. v. want of art.
Atheniensium Respublica, 1.
Attribute,
  accidental, 61, 121.
  essential, 109, 121.
Automatic
  subject, 186.
Averroes, 22.
Averroism, 30.
Avicenna, 21f. 29.
Awaking, 7, 168.
Axe, 8f.
Bacon, 3.

323

GENERAL INDEX

Bad. v. Good.
Beautiful, 161.
Bed, 182.
Behavior, 90, 203.
Being, 217.
    cognition of. 218.
(Belief) πίστις, 218.
Bergson, 108, 115f. 118.
Biology, biological, 2, 17, 142.
    division, 13. 96.
    evolution, 107, 108.
    teleological, of Aristotle, 108.
Bliss, 151
Blood, 103f. 258.
Bodily element, 218.
Body, 3, 5, 176, 257. v. Soul.
    the central organ of. heart, 103f.
    & desire. 160f.
    form of. 6, 33, 94, 102, 257.
    natural body, 5
    the substratum of soul, 105.
    the tool (ὄργανα) of soul, 9.
βούλευσις, 180, 208, 239, 266ff. v. deliberation.
βουλευτική, 209, 227.
    β. διάνοια, 229.
    β. ὄρεξις, 132, 180.
βούλησις, 267, v. wish.
Boy, 68, 213.
Brain, 22, 56.
Brandis, 28, 290.
Bravery, 189, 301.
Brentano, 13, 20, 26, 28, 29, 30, 31ff., 62, 65, 89, 90, 100.
Brutality, 315, 316.
Brutishness, 309.
Buddhism, 260.
Building, 372.
Calculation, λογισμός, 132, 244f. 267, 308.
    of virtue, 200.
    moral c., 309.
    technical 278.
Calmness, 263.
Category, 80, 178.
    categorical imperative, 277, 319, 317, 320. of substance, 5.
Causality, 285
    cognition of. 274.
    causal relation, 282.
    natural c., 286.

Cause, 32f. 53, 64f. 248, 297ff. cf. End, Form.
    four causes, 64; material cause, *causa materialis;* efficient cause, *causa efficiens,* 64 69f. 126, 175, 248, 297, 299; formal cause, *causa formalis,* 69f. 297; final cause, *causa finalis,* 64, 77, 159, 296, cf. Divine Reason.
    the modern usage of c., 297, 299.
    Plato's concept of c., 77f.
    secondary cause, 25.
    c. in the universal, 299.
Certainty, 278.
Chance events, 266.
Change, 64.
    changeable phenomena, 217, v. Otherwise.
Character, 130, 144, 145, 174, 286, 301.
    formation of, 202, cf. education.
    habitual ch., 276.
    ideal, 319.
    rearing of. 149.
Charity, 192.
Child, 22, 167, 265, 271.
Christianity, 57, 75, 194, 260, 263.
χωριστός, 37f. cf. Separate, Soul.
Circumstance, 164, 166.
Citizen, 215.
Cleverness, δεινότης, 225, 269, 271f. 278, 306, 308.
Clothes, 182.
Cognition, 22, 62, 81, 113, 116f. 218, 220.
    actual c., 23, 27.
    habitual c., 304.
    intellectual c., 111.
    particular (practical) c., 301.
    practical c., 176, 238, 255, 257, 267ff., 295, 300, 303. cf. Prudence
    Productive c., 268. v. Art.
    Productive c. conj. practical c., 313.
    pure c., 139.
    spiritual c., 22f.
    theoretical c., 176, 257.
    universal c., 222f.
    universal c. of practical affairs, 264.
Cognitive faculties of soul, 57, 87, 109, 217, 231.
Colour, 20, 25, 34, 65, 69.

GENERAL INDEX

Common sensation, 46. v. Sensus communis.
Compulsion, 164, 165.
Concept, 62, 71, 119.
Conclusion, 279.
Concrete.
   c. cognition, 116.
   c. obiects, 58.
Conduct, 3, 149, 174, 175f. 181, 188f. 257, 313. cf. Moral; Value.
   efficient cause of. 157.
   essence of. 154.
   moral c. 192f.
   originative power of. 120.
   a part of nature, 286.
   principle of. 159.
   rational c. 176.
   sine qua non of. 157.
   social utility of. 195.
   value of. 273, 274.
   virtuous, just, temperate c., 189.
Conscious, Consciousness, 10, 118, 127, 183f. 199f. 259.
Consideration 212.
Constitution, 1, 212.
Contemplation, 53, 114, 177, 186, 204ff. 264. cf. Reason, God.
   absolutely free c., 113.
   an action, 149, 177.
   active principle of. 53.
   habitual, 70.
   knowledge and c., 6, 40.
   a pleasure, 147f.
   concerning with practice or production, 228f.
Continence, Continent, 139, 201. 213, 302f. 213, opp. Incontinence. cf. Temperance.
   Aristotle and Kant, 194f.
   c. and temperance, 307.
Continuous series of life, etc. 104f.
Contradiction, 11, 204.
Conventional, 213.
Conviction, 220f.
Corporal object, 5.
Correctness, 269.
Courage, 14, 15, 134, 141f. 198, 213, 262.
Cowardice, 189.
Creation, Creative, Creator, 29, 76ff., 108. cf. Platonic myth.

Creature, 73.
Culture, 83, 176, 187, 309.
   and civilization, 263.
   want of. 102. 256.
Dancing, 187, 188.
De Anima, 12, 14, 17, 18, 19ff. 30, 36, 55, 82, 85, 87, 91, 92, 93, 221, 249, 253, 280, 287.
   Active Reason ($νοῦς\ ποιητικός$) 19ff.
   Platonism. 17f.
Death, 168.
   in War, 141.
Decay, 168.
Decision, 212.
Deductive, 234f.
Defect, 301, 305.
Definition, 6.
$δεινότης$, Cleverness, 233, 239, 264, 269, 271f.
Deliberation, Deliberative, $βούλευσις$, 131f., 134, 171ff., 214, 225, 266f. 308, 316, 317.
   technical or productive d., 296. 298, 308, 317.
   chief moment of prudence, 274f.
   practical d., 273, 283, 298.
   dist. Syllogism, 284.
   virtue of. 269f.
De Motu Animalium, 159, 168, 276.
Democritus, 183.
Demonstration, demonstrative, 241ff, 274f.
Descartes, 2, 105, 184.
Desire, $ὄρεξις$. 14, 15, 90, 99, 100, 104, 120, 126, 128ff., 133f., 137ff., 143, 159, 175, 297, 303, 311f.
   conj. body, 160f.
   complication of the object of desire and wish, 143.
   conscious, 154.
   control of, 138.
   efficient cause of motion, 162, 175.
   formal aspect of, 154ff.
   $ἕξις$, 162, 276.
   the matter, 143f.
   the motive of deliberation, 257.
   a moved movent, 162.
   natural, 143.
   object of. 158f.
   rational, 176.
   rational principle of, 313.

conj. sensation (esp. pleasure and pain), 126.
Desiring part of soul, 18, 89, 90,160.
Development
  of Aristotle's thought, 12f., 17,
  of psychical function, 106, 107,110.
Diagonal, 220.
διανοητικόν, 93.
  διανοητικαὶ ἀρεταί, 208.
  διανοητικὴ ἐπιστήμη, 229.
διάνοια, 208, 216, 218, v. Intellect.
Discontent, 146.
Discrimination discriminative, 109, 112.
Disharmony, 303.
Disposition, 261.
Distance of space, 111.
Distribution, 264, 314.
Division, 13 (of Soul), 216 (of Intellect)
Divine, 149, 208 cf. Reason.
  d. reason, 16, 20, 27, 28, 32, 41f.,
  56f., 62f., 69f., 75, 208.
Doctor, Physical, 215, 216, 221, 266,
  283, 295.
Dog, 136.
Dogmatic conclusion, 221.
Domination of the machine, 315.
Door, 182.
δόξα, opinion, 217ff, 224. v. Opinion.
  Plato's concept, 217ff.
  Aristotle's concept, 220.
δοξαστική 216, 217.
  δ. διάνοια 229.
  δ -part, 225, 230.
Draughts, 266.
Dreaming, 121.
Drunkness, 170, 302, 304.
Dry food, 281, 301, 304.
Dualism, 9, cf. 105.
  d. of value and fact, 189.
  contradiction of Aristotle's d., 204.
δύναμις, 96, 239. v. Potentiality.
Dynamism of potentiality, 311.
Duopartite Theory (on Soul), 12, 18.
  cf. Soul.
Durandus, 26.
Duty, 151, 191, 319. cf. Kant.
  consciousness of. 192f., 196.
Earth, 105.
Earthworm, 85.
Eating and drinking, 88.

Education, educated, 67ff., 149,199, 202,
  222, 257, 261, 313.
Effect, 172.
Efficient cause, v. Cause.
Egoism, 191; 153 (spiritual).
Einbildungskraft (of Kant), 122ff. 218.
Element, 105
Emanation, 21
Emotion, 141, 175.
Empirical, 2.
  Empiricist, 113.
Empedocles, 242, 305.
End, opp. Means, cf. Purpose, ἕνεκα,
  Final Cause. 135, 153, 172, 176,
  182ff., 212, 247ff., 266f., 295f.,
  297f.,
  actual e., 185.
  concept of e. (a fundamental idea
    of Aristotle's metaphysics), 183ff.
  e. in contemplation, practice and
    production, 204f.
  estimation of, 285.
  Kant's theory of, 191f.
  objective e., 184, 188.
  e. of practical cognition, 265.
  practical cognition of e., 284.
  principle of, 255.
  subjective e. 191.
  ultimate e. of conduct, 153.
End-object, 279.
ἐνδεχόμενον, 66, 163, 246.
ἐνέργεια, 94. v. Activity.
Enforcement, 165f.
Engels, 72.
Enjoyment, 278, 306.
ἐντελέχεια, 6, 93. v. Actuality.
Epicurus, 183.
Epicurianism, 151, 153.
ἐπιστήμη, 6, 208, 217f., 232ff., 244.
  v. Knowledge.
  classification, 216.
  and ἐπιστημονικόν 227ff.
  generic concept, 209f.
  ἐ. θεωρτική πρακτική, ποιητική,
    209f.
ἐπιστημονικὴ διάνοια, 228.
Epitactic rational part, 95, cf. Soul.
ἐπιτακτική 230, 247.
ἐπιθυμία, 266. v. Appetite.
  ἐ. μετὰ λόγου, 141, v. Appetite
    with Reason.

GENERAL INDEX

Error, 158, 288, 302.
Escaping, 189
ἔσχατον, 248f.
Essence, Essencial, 220.
Estimation, 277, 297, 306, cf. Value.
   moral e., 163, 173, 285, 313.
   practical e., 287.
Eternal, Eternity, cf. God, Active Reason.
   e. and necessary beings (=object of contemplation), 176, 210, 266.
   e. of creatures, 142.
   e. forms, 176.
   e. intelligible world, 263.
   of soul, 32, 41.
   spiritual beings, 23, 70, 263.
Ethica Eudemia, 93, 94, 96, 145, 163, 295, 304.
Ethica Nicomachea, 13, 91, 93, 99 f., 132, 145, 163, 164, 165, 167, 188, 190, 197, 209, 214, 221, 232f., 237, 249, 252, 266, 274, 276, 281, 286, 287, 300, 304, 305, 313.
Ethics, Ethical, 2, 92, 101, 137f., 143f., 156f., 162, 187, 210ff., 239, 272, 288, 296f., 398, 313f. cf. Virtue, Value.
   e. of Aristotle, 222f.
   e. conj. psychology in Aristotle, 2, 138.
   contents of e. 213.
   essentially ethical, 274.
   practical utility of e. 156.
ἔθος, 162.
ἦθος, habitual character, 196.
ἠθική, (ἀρετή) 208, 213, 216.
εὐβουλία, 233, 239, 269, 270, 272, v. good deliberation.
Eudaemonism, 149, 153.
εὐπραξία, 177, 186.
εὐζῆν, living well, 189.
Evil, 308, cf. Good.
   great e. 269.
Exactness, 213.
Excess and Defect, 139f. cf. Mean.
Experience, 14, 114, 130, 213, 222, 235, 307.
External force, 165, 169.
Extremity, 243, 246f.
Eye, 8, 65, 67, 271.

Fact
   realization of f. 190.
   fact-form, 195, 203, cf. 190.
Faculty
   of soul, 85ff.
   of cognition, 216.
False, Falsehood, Falsity, 218, 219, 220, 224.
Fantacy, 121
Father, 57, 99, 101, 137.
Fear, 14, 301f.
   of death, 142.
Feeling, 14, 104, 127, 161 (good & bad, beautiful & ugly) v. Pleasure and pain, natural f. 309.
Fighting, 189.
Figure, 122, 253, 254.
Final cause, v. cause, ἕνεκα
Fire, 69, 105, 186.
The first actuality, 8.
The first impulse, 29.
The first mover, 29.
The first universal thought, 30.
Food, 100, 111, 118, 140.
Foreknowledge, 111.
Form, 2, 5, 20, 59, 117, 176, 215.
   absolute, 29.
   actual, 57, 185.
   conceptual, 62, 78.
   essential, 60, 184.
   form of forms (concept)=rational form= active principle of thinking, 21, 31, 58f., 61f, 62, 63, 64, 66, 69, 75, 78.
   imaginable form, 61.
   f. of intention, 275.
   material (ized) f., 61, 62..
   mathematical, 59.
   f. and matter, 5, 33, 61f., 195, 311.
   conj. matter, 105f., 107.
   objective, 78, 185.
   place of., 58.
   potential, 29, 57.
   a pure form, 59, 62.
   realization of f., 185.
   soul, as the form of the body, 6.
   special form, 61.
   subordinate f., 115.
   f. of (sensible) things, 24, 58, 61.
   of thinking, 275, 280.

universal form, 61, 62.
Formal principle, 5, 108.
   f. element, 6.
   f. and generally applicable, 318.
Formation (of character), 202.
Fortune, 200, 265.
Free
   f. citizen, 73.
   f. will, 261, cf. ἐκουσία, προαίρεσις
   Freedom of an act, 163,
   Freedom of personality, 261.
Friendship, 264.
Function of soul, v. soul.
Future, 129.
General, special, individual, 120.
Generality, 157, 318.
Generation, 65, 108, 110.
   Cognition of. 218.
Gentle ordinary person, 316.
Genus, 120.
Geometry, Geometric figures, 215, 254, 266.
Giving, 189.
γνώμη 155, 156, 233. v. judgement.
God, 21, 28, 29, 73, 105f., 150, 157, 176, 177.
   Actual reason, 40, 42f. 70.
   Aristotle's, (=Unmoved mover, pure actuality), 71, 77, 183.
   a created g., 76.
   direct interference of, 29.
   Godlike (=Reason), 27.
   g. and idea, 79f.
   John's Gospel, 74f.
   conj. man, 57.
   personal g., 108, 184.
   Plato's, 76. 78,
Good, 143f, 152, 158, 213, 216, 253, 316.
   Good and bad, 29, 143, 252, 307, 319.
   Good and evil, 212, 224, 273.
   apparent g., 158.
   Good act, practical good, good of human conduct, 158f. 212, 285.
   g. end, 269f. 296f.
   external g., 142.
   a feeling, 161.
   g. for us and by itself, 322.
   highest g. 150f. 156.
   Idea of the Good, 76f., 80f., 201.
   Good for individual cases, 212.
   g. life, 161
   g. man, 144, 201, 286, 287.
   man of good understanding, 316
   Plato's, 76, cf. the Idea of the Good,
   something good, 143
   good temper, 141, 144
   good will, 191, 198, 309, 315.
Grammer, 311
Greek ideal, 73
Gymnastics, 221, 222, 268
Habit, ἕξις, habitus, 7. 8. 20, 22, 53, 69, 96, 162, 197, 203, 233, 296, 303
Habituation, 275
ἁπλῶς, 167
Happiness, 102, 151, 200f. 205, 212, 269, 314, 319, 320f.
   Aristotle's, 150, 205
   the essence of action, 321.
   Highest h., 24, 102, 151, 205.
   Kant's, 150
   a moment of morality, 150
   end morality, 153f.
   h. of nation (or state), 212.
   h. and virtue, 150f.
Hard, 122
Harm, 213
Harmony, 114, 200, 262, 307, 320
Harp, 187, 188
Hartenstein, 241, 248, 251
Hartman, Nicolai, 197.
Healing, 188, 222, 266. cf. Doctor.
Health, 279, 282, 306, 314
Hearing, 90, 110, 111f. 139
Heart, 56, 103, 109, 155, 160f. 256f.
   an organ of intellect, or thought, 56,
   an organ of sensation, 121, 122, 160, 162.
Heavenly body, 106, 186, 266
Hedonism, 151, 153
Hegel, 2, 185, 192
ἐκουσία, 259. cf. Voluntarity
ἕνεκα, 247f.
Heraclitus, 81
Hesiod, 76
ἕξις 7, 8, 20 etc. v. Habit.
Hicks, 12, 15, 54
Highest principle of practical cognition, 308
   h. Good, v. Good.
   h. Happiness, v. Happiness.

GENERAL INDEX

Homo 72f.
    (h. faber; h. religiosus; h. sapiens;)
Honour, 141, 143.
ὁρᾶν, 288.
Horse itself, 79.
Household management, 214.
Human part of soul = Reasoning Part, 88ff.
Humanity, modern view of. 263.
Humirity, Humble, 141.
Hurtful, 271.
Huzii, Yosio.
    Eth. N. is earlier than De An., 93f., 101.
    Against this theory, 94f.
ὑπόληψις, 287, judgement.
Hypothetical, Hypothesis, 219, 277, 284f., 298f., 317f.
Ideas (Platonic), 26, 29, 76ff. v. Idea of the Good.
    the model, 76, 78f.
Ideal, 191.
    i. character, 319.
Ignorance, 167ff, 172, 301f., 304.
    cf. Involuntarity.
Illumination, 22, 25
Image, φάντασμα, 22ff., 25, 26, 31, 59, 60, 119f., 127.
    deliberative im. 130.
    subjective im. 78.
Imagination, φαντασία, 14, 15, 18, 21, 22, 23, 45f. 49ff, 58f, 89, 99f, 104, 128f, 137, 159, 175, 256ff.
    dis. sensation, 119ff, 125f.
    i. and *sensus communis*, 122ff.
Immanence, 56f. (cf. Reason); 59 (cf. Universal).
Immaterial (Reason), 20, 25; (on image and sensation) 59, 60.
Immediate purpose, 270
Immortal, Immortality, 20, 23, 32, 41, 45, 66, 71, 83f., 149, 150, 224, 262. cf. Soul, Reason
Impassive, 17, 20, 37, 43f. v. Active. Reason,
Imperative
    categorical im., 277, 309, 317.
    hypothetical im., 284, 317, 320.
    im. will, 285.
Impinging of bodily element, 218
Impossible things, v. Eternal.

Impotency of rational desire, 306.
Impression, 25·
    Elementary im. 122.
Impulsive, 278.
Inclination, 150, 153.
Incompetence, i, fellow 309, 316
Incontinence, 139, 170, 269, 301, 302ff.
    cf. Continence.
Individual, 59, 119, 121, 172, 212, 236, 256.
    i. act, 214.
    a concrete i., 70.
    i. fact, 172, 173.
    i. intuition of practical reason, 247.
    i. limit, 256.
Individualism, Aristotle's. 263f.
Induction, inductive inference, 235.
Indulgence 139f. 170, 213, 302ff, 309.
    opp. Temperance.
Information, 110.
Inference, 220f. 233f.
    deductive i. 234f.
    practical i., 212, 221, 255. v. practical Syllogism.
Innate Cognition, 22, 23.
Insect, 125.
Inseparability of soul, v. Soul.
Insight, 155, 201, 213.
Instrument, 72, 112, 181.
    i. of life, 120.
    i. of practice, 182.
    i. of volition, 312.
Instinct, 22, 56.
    organ of, 56.
Intention, 129, 184, 193, 216, 251.
Intellect, 3f., 78, 89, 114, 158, 159, 193, 218, 297, 303, 307, 313.
    classification, 217, 233, 278
    construction of practical i., 316f.
    conj. imagination, 119.
    origin of. 109, 114.
    practical i. 101, 114, 137, 138, 174, 175, 212, 239, 240ff., 249, 255, 256.
    technical, 268
    theoretical i. 101, 129, 174, 175, 234.
    weakness of practical i. 303.
Intellectus materialis, νοῦς δυνάμει 21ff. v. Reason, Averroes, Avicenna.

GENERAL INDEX

Intellectus passibilis, νοῦς παθητικός, 22ff. 30. v. Passive Reason.
Intellectus possibilis (=What becomes all things), 25, 29.
Intellectus agens, νοῦς ποιητικός, (=What makes all things), Active Reason, 18, 20, 239.
Intelligence, absolute. 29.
Intelligentia agens, v. Active Reason.
Intelligenzia, 73
Intelligible form, 23ff.
Intelligible principles, 29.
Intuition, νόησις,
    into individual, 235, 251, 254f.
    intellectual i., 254f.
    in (νοῦς) reason, 234.
    practical i., 313
Involuntarity, 165f. 301, 302, 306.
Irrational part of soul, 91f. 95, 99f. 175. v. Soul.
Irascibility, 141.
Jaeger, 17, 93, 237.
Jesus, 75.
John the Baptist, 75.
St. John's Gospel, 74f.
Joy, 14, 151.
Judgment, 22, 155, 220f, 232f. 287.
    categorical j. 314.
    in general, 218.
    hypothetical j. 279, 284.
    indirect j. 155.
    individual j. 221, 288.
    a lack or error of j. 302.
    practical j. 277.
    in syllogism, 278ff.
Judicial, v. Law.
Justice, 141, 142, 264, 314.
Kallias, 60, 61, 79.
Kant, 122f. 150f., 153, 189, 191ff., 194. 278, 285, 315, 320ff.
    practical reason, 289ff., 315ff.
    κατὰ λόγον & μετὰ λόγου (in accordance with reason & accompanied by reason), 196f.
κίνησις, 185 v. Movement.
Knowledge, Scientific knowledge, Science, ἐπιστήμη, 67ff., 70, 222, 234ff., 307.
    actual, 20, 40ff.
    classification of, 210ff., 231.

for us, & by itself, 322.
    grades of, 130
    habitual knowledge, 23, 40, 303
    highest universal practical knowledge, 301, 308
    inert 155f.
    object of, 210
    origin of, 25, 29, 57
    potential 20, 40ff.
    practical, 156
    principle of. 27
    syllogistic, 244.
    productive kn. 228, v. Art.
    theoretical kn. 130, 156f.
    theoretical kn. about practice, 156.
κρίνειν, 288
κριτική, 230
Law, (legal law), 170, 214; 309, 314.
Law-giver, 318.
Laws, 81
Layman, 6.
Learning, 22, 185
Lebensphilosophie, 116
Legality (Kant), 193
Legislation, legislative, 212, 214
Leibniz, 105
Leisure, 130, 204
Machine, 316
Mad, 304
Magna Moralia, 12, 187, 189, 237
Magnificience, 141
Magnitude (extension), 122
Man, 22, 75, 127, 137, 176
    and animal, 263
    Aristotle's ideal of, 114, 194.
    differentia, 22
    virtue of. 137
Master-arts, ἀρχιτεκτονική 216 230, 237
Master prudence, 223, 264f. 313.
Material, 23
    m. cause, v. Cause
    m. objects of desire, 322.
Materiality, 62
Mathematics, matematical, μαθηματική 59, 157, 211, 213, 216, 235, 285
Matter, 5, 20, 32f., 117. cf. Form, Prima Materia.
    Exclusion of. 115.
Maxim (of enjoyment), 305, 320
The Mean, 264
Meaning, 62, 66, 71, 78

GENERAL INDEX

eternal, 269.
Meanness, 141.
Means, 135, 266ff, 278, 279, 282f. 297f.
   cf. End; Purpose.
Means-value, 205.
Measure, 288.
Meat, 279.
Mechanical action of elements, 108.
Medium, Mediated, 2, 65, 110, 176, 237f. 257.
   Mediation, 121, 233.
Medical science, 215. cf. doctor.
   m. art, 311.
Mediocrity, 212.
Meekness, 141.
μὴ ἐνδεχόμενον καὶ ἄλλως ἔχειν, 176.
   (a necessary being which cannot be otherwise)
Memory, 20, 23, 43-48 (Memory and Reason), 114, 121, 125.
Meno, 68, 218, 219, 238.
Mental experience, 14.
   m. enforcement, 165f.
μετὰ λόγου v. κατὰ λόγον
Metaphysica, 96, 112, 115, 209, 283, 285.
Metaphysics, Metaphysical, 11, 105, 107, 157, 183, 210, 211, 235.
Mildness, 15.
Mind, 117.
Minor premiss, v. Syllogism.
οὐ μνημονεύομεν δέ 'We do not remember.' 47ff. cf. Memory.
Modality, 278f.
Mode
   of being. (πάθη), 14.
Model (Idea), 76.
Moderation, 139, 144, 257, 290, 297, 301
Moment, 272.
Monadology, 105, 107.
Money, 300.
Money-making, 180, 188.
Monism, 9.
Monologue, 218.
Moral
   accomplishment, 201.
   assurance, 213.
   goodness, 173, 198.
   ideal, 150.
   law, 213, 320.
   philosopher, 93.
   principle, 255.

significance, 189.
   stage of m. progress, 308.
Moralität, 193
Morality, 3, 151, 153, 193, 199, 213, 309.
Mortal
   of soul, 20. cf. Soul.
   of passive reason, 52.
Movement, 64, 99, 105, 186, 266.
   dist. Actuality, 185f.
   aspects of m. 178.
   Moving faculty, 85.
   natural m. 186.
   process of m. 159f.
   conj. Production, 186.
   in respect of place, 154.
   Unmoved Mover, Moved Movent, The Moved, 29, 159f.
Multiplicity, 79. cf. Soul.
Murder, 188.
Must, 289.
National life, 142.
Natural, 213.
   n. body, being, 5, 7, 20.
   n. endowments, 215.
   n. fault, 315.
   n. law, 320.
   n. phenomenon, 165, 168, 223, 266, 286.
Nature, 5, 105, 107, 157, 183, 184, 211, 260, 286, 322.
   Mode of. 261.
   force of. 286.
Navigation, 268, 312.
Necessary, Necessariness, 157, 279, 285.
   n. being (which cannot be otherwise) 176, 211.
   n. judgement, 279.
Necessity, 157, 213, 285f.
   Absolute n. 285
   n. of life. 109f.
Neo-Kantian, 189
Nietzsche, 73
Niggardliness, 141, 189.
Noematic object, 78.
νόησις, 218.
νόησις νοήσεως, (thinking of thinking) 71.
Norm, 199, 288.
   general norm of practice, 170.
Not-voluntarity, 167f.
Nourishing part of soul, 13. v. Soul.

v. Reason.
v. δυνάμει, 21f. 31. v. Intellectus materialis.
v. παθητικός, 22, 31. v. Intellectus passibilis, Passive Reason.
v. ποιητικός, 18, 21, 240. v. Intellectus agens, Active Reason.
v. πρακτικός, 238. v. Practical Reason
v. ὑλικός, 21.
Number, 122, 186.
Nutrition, nutritive, 18, 58, 85, 89, 95, 99, 104.
   mode of n. 198f.
   n. part of soul. v. Soul.
   conj. sensation, 198ff., 115.
to Obey, 101.
Object, 57, 220.
   o. of desire, 158.
   form of o. 58.
   o. of knowledge, 210.
   matter of o., 58.
   o. of opinion, 217, 219ff., 224.
   sensible o. 57.
   o. of thought, 57.
Objective, 78f.
   o. mind, 176, 309.
   o. spirit, 103.
Obligation, 150.
οἰκονομική, house-management, 216.
Opinion, 131, 144, 217ff, 232f., 235.
Orator, 266.
to Order, 101.
ὄρεξις, 132, v. Desire.
ὄργανα, 9, Tool.
Organism, 8f.
Organon, 275, 278.
Orphics, 81.
ὀρθός λόγος, 273, 290, v. Right Reason.
Otherwise
   What can be otherwise, 163, 176, 220, 222f. 236. cf. Potentiality.
   What cannot be otherwise, 176, 186, 286. cf. Necessity.
Ox, 181.
παιδεία 102, v. Culture.
Pain, 120, 146, 165, 169 cf. Pleasure.
Palalis, 316.
πανουργία, 239, 264, 269, 316. v. Craftiness.
Particular, 255, 298, 301, 306. cf.

Universal, Practice.
Parva Naturalia, 17.
πάσχειν 78 .v. to Suffer.
Passion (θυμός), 73, 134, 136, 143, 159, 175, 200.
Passive, 14, 174, 178.
   p. reason, v. Reason.
Passivity, 6, 14, 25.
πάθη, of the Soul, 14f. 81. cf. affection
πάθημα, v. affection.
Patriotism 191.
Perception, Perceptive, 90, 124, 175, 246.
   concrete p., 122, 175.
   a metaphor, 252 (rel. practical reason)
   moral p., 310.
   conj. Prudence, 288.
Perfection, 184.
Pericles, 287, 316.
Personality, 260.
   accomplishment of p., 202.
Phaedo, 81, 217, 219, 220.
'φαίνεται', 287, 288.
φαντασία λογιστική, 21, 22, 297.
φάντασμα, 21, 23, 32, 115, 119.
   v. Imagination.
Phantastic idealist, 315.
Pharisaism, 192.
Philo, 74.
Philological method, 18, 98.
Philosopher-king, 206.
Philosophy, φιλοσοφία 211, 234.
   concerning human affairs, 211.
   political ph., 211.
   practical ph., 222.
   theoretical ph., 210.
   philosophical character, 317.
φρόνησις, 94, 138, 156, 209, 213, 216, 232f., 268, 307, 316. v. Prudence.
phronestische Anschauung, 310.
   phr. Wahrnehmung, 254, 288.
φρόνιμος, 212, 307.
Physician, v. Doctor.
Physics, 157, 211, 235.
φυσική, 216.
φύσις, 5, v. Nature.
Physiological, 3, 168.
Piety, 114.
   29, 208, 209, 216, 232ff.

πίστις, 218.
Pity, 14, 15.
Place. v. Locomotion, Space.
Plant, 88, 108, 136.
Plato, 2, 98, 183, 215.
    Cognition, 81, 230, 256, 238.
    Creation story (on the generation of the world and the formation of knowledge), 76ff.
    δόξα (opinion), 217ff, 225.
    Form, 77f.
    Idea, 78f.
    The Idea of the Good, 76, 80.
    Image, 26.
    Methodical fallacy 275.
    φρόνησις (Prudence), 237.
    practical knowledge, 276.
    Reason, 82.
    Sensation and Intellect, 112.
    Soul, 11f., 36, 66, 80ff, 86, 88, 94, 140.
    Virtue, 139.
Platonic myths, 76ff., 183.
Platonism, 11, 17, 84, 85, 93.
Play, 140.
Pleasure, 15, 120, 146f., 165, 278.
    Aristotle's concept, 146.
    appearance of, 288.
    p. and pain, 126ff, 146f, 175, 213, 253f., 309.
    bodily, natural and necessary, motion or generation, action, par excellence, essence, spiritual, 147.
    p. of cognitive action, degree and value of p., 148.
    conj. desire, 148, 161.
    p. of contemplation, of moral conduct, suitable to man relation to character, 149.
    a value, 277.
Plotinus, 75, 183.
Poetics, 210, 211.
ποιεῖν, concept of. 178f.
ποίησις, 174, 176. v. Production.
ποιητική 216.
    Π. διάνοια, 228.
ποιητικὸς συλλογισμός, 281f.
πόλις, 73.
πολιτική, 213, 214, 216.
Politics, 2, 114, 157, 187, 202, 210, 211ff., 222, 223, 257, 314.
Political
    affairs, 149.
    animal, 203.
    wisdom, 214.
Portrait, 121.
Positivist, 2. 9 183.
Possibility, possible, 6, 279.
Potency, 67, 69.
    Active, 162.
    Actual, 6.
Potentiality, Potential, δύναμις, 6, 20, 33, 66, 106, 279, 310f. cf. Form, ἐνδεχόμενον
    conj. Activity, 107.
    of being otherwise, 163.
    degree of. 311f.
    of form, 6.
    meanings of. 6f.
    in practical syllogism, 304.
    rational, 311.
    second p., 8.
Power, 143.
Practical
    essentially pr., 277.
    pr. subject, 176.
Practice, 4, 174, 176, 179ff., 187, 207. 267.
    an actuality, 186f.
    concepts of. 177f.
    conj. contemplation, 204.
    the end of, 176f.
    essence of, 188.
    general norm of, 170.
    hierarchy of, 181.
    to movement (practice, production, and actuality), 185.
    dist. production, 181, 187f. 202f.
    dist. sensation, 180.
πρακτική 216.
    Πρ. διάνοια 228.
    ἐπιστήμη 230.
Pragmatist, pragmatism, 108, 109.
Praisable, 152.
Prantl, 232f. 292.
Preestablished harmony (Leibniz), 107,
Premiss, v. Syllogism.
Present, 129.
Pride, 114, 141.
Prima materia, 105.

Primitive man, 73.
Primitive universality, 116.
Principle, 29, 309. cf. Idea.
  pr. of division, 13, 98.
  pr. of Form and Matter; Soul and Body, 105.
Prior by itself, posterior for us, 255, 322.
Private person, 215.
Probability, 213, 264.
Prodigarity, 141.
Production, Productive, 4, 65, 117, 174, 176f., 179ff., 203f., 207, 222 267f. cf. Practice, Art, Technical.
  conj. contemplation, 204f.
  conj. intellect, 73.
  movement, 187.
  dist. practice, 180ff., 187f.
  principle of. 223.
  pure, 203.
τῇ προαιρέσει ἄγνοια, 170 ignorance in the will.
προαίρεσις 180, 201, 224, 259, 267. v. Will.
Property, 141, 143, 166.
προπέτεια (impetuousity), 309.
Prosperity, 263.
πρώτη φιλοσοφία, 216.
Providence, 107, 150, 183.
Prudence, Prudent, 56, 104, 114, 130, 138, 196, 211ff, 222f., 225, 237f., 253f, 256ff., 266ff., 270, 274, 278, 297, 307. cf. Practical Reason, Practice.
  architectonic, 156.
  constant state of, 212.
  homogeneity of practical philosophy and pr. 212ff.
Psychical function of soul, 96, 107. v. Soul.
Psychology, psychological, 215, 2, 3, 17, 101f.
Punishment, 195.
Pupil (of the eye), 9, 24, 65, 176.
Pure self-sufficient thinking, pure theoretical knowledge, 204, 208. v. Contemplation.
Quality, 278.
Quantity, 278.
Rain-fall, 186, 223, 266.
Rational, rationalize, 2, 23, 173.

absolutely r., 15.
r. animal; being, 72f.
r. part of soul, v. Soul. 4, 92, 100ff., 138, 176, 209.
rationalist, 113.
Ravaisson, 29.
Reaction, 127ff., 175.
Reality, 9, 29.
Reason, νοῦς Intellectus, 16ff., 26ff., 53ff., 159, 199f., 234f..
natural being, 34.
a part of soul, 12, 16, 18, 20, 34.
a faculty of soul, 25.
material part of r., 20,
  = Potential, 31f.,
  = Passive,
νοῦς παθητικός, Intellectus passibilis 23.
  = passive, 19ff., 29, 32, 48ff., 52f, 56, 64, 75, 257. cf. Active Reason.
  = receptive r., 49ff, 53.
  = mortal, 20, 52.
  = what becomes all things, 19, 21, 28, 29, 33, 34, 39f.
  = inseparable (from the body), 20.
  formal part of r., 20.
  = Actual, 28, 53, 257.
  = Active, νοῦς ποιητικός Intellectus agens, (De An. III. v. 430a 10ff.) 19-85, 19ff, 80, 160, 176, 240, 257, 278, 289, 308.
  Trendelenburg, 27f, 54.
  Brandis, 28.
  Brentano, 26, 28ff..
  Theophrastus, 20, 29.
  Alexander of Aphrodisias, 20, 29.
  Avicenna, 21, 29.
  Averroes, 22ff, 29.
  St. Thomas, 25.
  Durandus, 26.
  Suarez, 26.
  Ravaisson, 29.
  Renan, 30.
  Zeller, 30.
  Hicks, 54.
  essence and function of, 57ff.
  divine, 20, 62f.
  causes, 64f.
  the nature of (Culture), 83.
  system of knowledge, 81, 83.
  a pure, spiritual, rational substance, 20.

GENERAL INDEX

Reason (cont'd)
= immortal (Active Reason), 70, 20, 53. v. Immortality
= eternal action, 20, 32, 41, 53
= What makes all things, 19, 21, 33, 34, 39f.
= cause of thinking, active principle of thought, 34
= separable, 18ff, 34, 41.
= Active Reason. 53.
= transcendent, 53, 56f., 64f.
= immanent, 41, 56f., 64f.
= before birth and after death, 43, 45, 54.
= Divine Reason, 16, 20, 27, 28, 32, 41f., 56., 62f., 69f., 75, 208.
= impassiveness, 16, 36, 37.
  r. dist. Sensation, 29.
  r. dist. Imagination, 16, 19.
  r. conj. Desire, 99, 137, 295.
  agreement of r. and passion, 196.
  Human Reason, 54, 56f., 74, 176.
  Theoretical r. = Contemplative r., 28, 74, 77, 129.
  Intuitive r., 234, 306.
  r. in Demonstration, 241ff.
  Practical character of r. 290.
  object of r., 159.
  r. concerned with the individual, 243f.
  r. in practical reasoning, 241.
  Practical Reason, 128, 138, 159, 239-323, 239, 258 cf. Prudence.
  Practical Reason, specific sense, a kind of practical intellect (Eth. Nic. VI, 12. 1143a35) 240.
  Practical Reason, generic sense, 249, 256.
  Practical Reason, its weakness, 303
  r. and Prudence, 245.
  conj. an End, 247ff.
  conj. Perception (=Practical Reason), 251ff.
  Right r. 143f, 289, 296.
  the law-giver, 318.
  command of r. 99, 320.
  Platonic view of r., 17, 76.
Reasoning, λογισμός, Calculation. 132. 158.
  r. part of soul, 12, 13, 88ff.

Rectilinear figure, 299.
Red, 122.
Reflection, reflective, 70, 71ff., 210.
Reflex, 128. v. Reaction.
Reine Anschauung (of Kant), 73.
Relative and probable, 320.
Religion, Religious, 9, 73.
  r. and Intellect, 73.
  r. consolation, 150.
Remember
  'We do not remember', 43ff. v. Memory.
Renan, 30.
Repentance, 167, 169.
Reproduction, 89, 143.
  a function of soul, 99.
Republic, 217, 218, 219.
Resolution, 213.
Respect (for the Reason and Law), 309.
Respectable (Happiness), 152.
Respiration 168.
Responsibility, 163, 260, 315.f.
Resting, 122.
Résumé of practical experience, 256.
Result, 172, 268, 297.
Rhetorics, ῥητορική 210, 216.
Richness, 213.
Right
  r. art, 313.
  r. opinion, 218.
  r. reason, 144f., 290, 297.
Righteousness, 200.
Rigorism (of Kant), 149, 191f.
Rising of the stars, 266.
Ritter, 240, 252.
Rule, right, 262.
Rule, right. 272.
Saint, 206.
Satisfaction, 146, 151.
Savage race, 316.
Scheler, Max., 192.
Science, scientific, 2, 70, 149, 176, 210, v. Knowledge
  practical sc., 157, 213, 215.
Scientific-self-sufficient rational part of Soul, 92, 95, v. Soul.
Sculptor, 205.
Secondary principle, 29.
  s. cause (=the matter of cause), 25
Seed, 184, 185.
Seeing, 185.

GENERAL INDEX

Self-preservation, 153.
Self-sufficient, 206, 276.
Self-value, 205.
Seniors, gift of. (=Prudence), 212.
Sensation, αἴσθησις 18, 25, 57ff., 59f (cf. Imagination), 87ff, 91f., 99f., 104, 109ff., 130, 159, 175, 217f., 235.
    as cognition, 109.
    conj, Desire, 126ff., 137.
    as efficient cause of desire and conduct, 127f.
    elementary s., 175.
    first s., 30.
    higher sensation, 110f.
    conj. Intellect, 111f.
    interrelation of s., 110.
    lower sensation, 108, 110.
    conj. nutrition, 109f. 115ff.
    origin of s., 109.
    as passivity, 116.
Sensation in general, 14, 15. cf. πάθη
Sense, 57, 110.
    central organ of. 121, 122.
Sense impression, αἴσθημα, 119f.
Sensible.
    s. object, 57, 60f.
    s. part of soul, 13, 18, 95, 99. v. Soul.
Sensitive
    s. faculty, 85.
    s. part of soul, 95. v. Soul.
    s. principle, 29.
Sensus Communis, Common Sensation, 46, 118, 121, 122f., 160, 175, 252f., 256.
Separability of Soul, v. Soul.
Separateness, χωριστός 37.
Sequence of phenomena, 159.
Sermon on the Mount, 189, 202.
Servant
    s. of God, 73.
    hasty s., 136.
Sexual activity, 140, 190.
Ship, 165.
Sight, 9, 10, 110, 111f., 139, 271.
Simplicity, 79.
Simplicius, 54.
Sittlichkeit, 193.
Slave, 73, 182, 314..
    as means of life, 182.

Sleeping, 7, 168, 304.
Small, 122.
Smell, 110, 139, 140.
Snake, 57.
Social,
    s. character of morality, 263.
    s. life, 316.
    s. norm, 264.
    s. utility of conduct, 195.
Society, 215, 263.
Socrates, 2, 68, 81, 196, 215, 217, 258, 272, 276, 315.
    ὁ Σώκρατης, 61, 79.
Soldier, 191.
Solon, 200.
Solstices, 266.
Somnambulistic state of mind, 304.
Son of God, 74.
σοφία, 209, 216, 232ff. v. Wisdom
Sophist, 218, 219, 276.
σοφίστης, 73.
σωφροσύνη, 195, 213, 287. v. Temperance
Sorites, 284.
Soul, 3, 5f., 20, 102f., 175f.
    Aristotle's definition, 6, 33, 94, 102, 104.
    Plato's, 10, 86, 76ff, 183 (Cosmological s.).
    Aristotle's definition (form of the body), 6, 94, 102, 104.
    Form of the body, 6, 33.
    = the first incomplete actuality of the body, 6ff. 86, 104.
    = the second potentiality (ἕξις) of b. 7f.
    = λόγος, the concept, the essence of b. 8f.
    = the second actuality, 8f.
    = Active power, activity of b., 9, 94, 102.
    = cause, principle of life, unification, 6, 86.
    Separability, inseparability, 9, 11, 14, 20, 37ff., 81f., 176, cf. Active Reason.
    transmigration, 10, 81.
    Division, 13, 86f., 95ff., 98, 136.
    logical-psychological division, 90ff., 96f.
    biological, 13, 91ff, 96f.

GENERAL INDEX 337

metaphysical-physical, 90ff., 97ff.
ethical, 92ff., 97ff.
Function, 3, 10, 14, 87ff., 90, 137
  Vegetative, animalistic, pure human *or* superbiological f.'s. 137.
Parts of soul, 10, 20, 85ff., 99, 175f., 208.
Duopartite theory, 12, 86f, 88, 91, 93ff., 96, 133.
Tripartite theory, 11f., 86f., 88, 133, 140. cf. Plato.
Multipartite theory, 133.
Origin of Parts of soul, 115.
Irrational parts of soul, 4, 92f., 96, 100f., 138, 176.
Vegetable soul = Physiological, Unconscious, 99f. 139, 175.
  Nutrition, Growth, Reproduction,
Animal soul = Sensitive, 16, 100, 175.
  Sensation, Imagination, Desire, Movement.
Pure human soul = thinking part =
Rational part, 4, 92, 100ff., 138, 176, 209,
  Theoretical Intellect = scientific part = absolutely rational, 95 101, 129, 174, 175, 234.
  Reason, Knowledge, Wisdom.
  Practical Intellect = reasoning part = ethical, epitactic-rational, 94, 101, 114, 137, 138, 174, 175, 212, 239, 257.
  Practical - Prudence; Productive - Art.
Human soul, 137, 175, 208.
Specific difference of soul, 85.
conj. Body, 3, 9, 81, 86, 102f.
independence of its parts, 13, 83, 99.
Immortal, 6, 20, 81, 83. cf. Reason
Space, 111.
Special, 119.
  special sense impression, 122.
Species, 120.
Speculative
  method, 19.
  thinking, 29.

Spengler, 72.
Spherical, 122.
Spinoza, 105.
Spirit, spiritual, 26.
  area of s., 24.
  embodiment of, 162.
  universal, 30.
  s. cognition, 22, 23, 25.
  s. substance, 24.
  spiritualization of the body, 162.
Starting point (ἀρχή), 247f., 286, 296, 300.
  the state (city), 142.
Statesman, 230, 231, 238, 266.
Statesman, 76, 205, 215. v. Politics.
Steadfastness, 309.
Steward, 204.
Stimulus, 127, 175.
Stoics, 151.
Strategy, 181.
Strictness, 256, 264.
Suarez, 26.
Subject and predicate in judgement, 278ff.
Subjective, 78f.
Substance,
  meanings of. 5.
  a pure spiritual substance, 2, 21, 22, 25.
Suffer, 14, 78.
Sweet, 122, 221, 305.
Syllogism, 131f., 216, 266, 274ff.
  categorical, 297.
  Classification of, 274f.
  Conclusion, 278f.
  dialectic, 274.
  hypothetical, 298, 300.
  Practical Syllogism, 131f., 216, 239, 241f., 265, 266ff., 274f., 295f., 298, 300, 308, 310ff., 313f., 318.
  formula, 280.
  fundamental mark, 276.
  essence, 312f.
  the highest major premiss, (standard of moral value), 287.
  major premiss, 212, 221, 235, 252, 286f. 300, 307ff., cf. Indulgence.
  minor premiss, 213, 221, 301ff.

cf. Involuntarity.
Conclusion, 301.
Premisses, 244. 278f.
Productive. 281f.. 298, 310.
Sophistic, 278.
Symposium, 219.
σύνησις, 155, 156, 233, 243, 264, v.
Insight, Intuition.
Synthetic, 98, 99, 122, 202.
Systematic, 2, 99, 234.
Tabula rasa, 25, 49.
Taking, 189.
Taste, 89, 109f., 139.
    209, 216, 232, 268, v. Art.
τεχναζεῖν, 228.
Technical v. Art. production, 2, 268, 182, 186, 274, 278, 283, 284, 285, 286, 308,
Teichmüller, 132, 134, 182, 202, 204, 212ff., 222, 238, 241f., 251. 254, 288, 301
Teleology, 108, 183ff., 191, 286.
τέλος, 183.
Tendency of self-love, 320,
Temperance, 139f, 142, 144, 194, 264, 287, 302f., 307.
Terminology, 214.
    Aristotle's, 177, 179, 208, 221.
Thales, 208, 316.
Theaetetus, 218, 219, 220.
Themistius, 24f.
Theophrastus, 20, 24, 26, 29.
Theoretical
    th. intellect, 101, 129, 174, 175, 234, v. Intellect.
    th. reason, 28, 74, 77, 129.
    v. Reason.
θεωρία 186, v. Contemplation.
    ἐπιστήμη, and, 6.
    practical, and productive th., 228
    th. and θεωρητικόν, 227, 229.
θεωρεῖν, 287.
θεωρητική, 209.
θεωρητικὴ ἐπιστήμη 209, 211, 229.
Thinking, 14, 20, 57, 66f., 74, 83, 120, 176, 185, 258.
    active principle of, 26, 31, 34, 78.
    th. and active reason and passive reason, 54.
    constitution of, 57f. (cf. Form)

Eternal th., 54, 74.
faculty, 119.
th. in general, 211.
human thinking 54, 78.
th. and imagination, 14f.
material and physiological substratum of, 56.
practical, 296.
technical 283.
th. and sensation, 58f.
thinking of thinking, 79.
Thought, 25, 29, 58f.
    absolute thought, 29.
    bodily organ of, 56.
θρεπτικόν 93.
θυμικόν the passionate part of soul, 12.
θυμός 136, 267, v. passion.
Timaeus, 76.
    difficulties in the creation-story, 76f,
    division of soul, 82.
Time, 101, 111, 122.
    mode of, 121.
    perception, 125.
    time and space, 123 cf. Kant.
Topica, 12, 274, 275.
Touch, 89, 109f., 139.
Trainer, 296 v. gymnastics
Transcendentale Einbildungskraft, 122f.
Transmigration theory, 10.
Transparent (Medium), 110.
Treasure, 266.
Tree, 184, 185.
Trendelenburg,
    Active Reason, 27f., 30, 53, 80,
    Practical Reason, 151, 240, 247f. 252, 294.
Triangle, 60, 61, 121, 220, 223, 224, 252, 287, 299.
Tripartite Theory, 11ff., 18.
True
    true or false, 218, 224.
    true opinion, 218, 220.
Truth, 68.
    t. in art and morality, 295.
    a witness of, 27.
Tyrant, 206.
Ugly, 161.
Ultimate end of life, 287, 314.
Unambitiousness, 141.
Unconscious, 90, 118, 175.
Uninterested cognition, 130.

GENERAL INDEX

Unity, 122.
   u. of a person, 7.
Universal, 119, 210.
   u. applicability, 320.
   u. concept, 27.
   u. imperative, 285.
   u. and individual, 59f., 236, 251.
   intuition of universal principle, 234.
   u. knowledge, 22, 212.
   u. oughtness, 308.
   u. and particular, 234, 266, 269, 276.
   u. practical knowledge, 309.
   u. principle, 176.
   u. spirit, 30.
Universe, 76, 105f.
Unmixedness (Soul), 20, 32, 34, 37.
Unmoved mover, 77, 159.
Unskillful tragedy, 98.
Utility, 141, 277.
Value, 141, 269, 278, 298.
   apprehension of, 199f.
   classification of, 277.
   ethical, 92, 137f., 143., 162.
   expression of, 190.
   v. and fact, 189.
   hierarchy of values, 205f.
   highest v., 205.
   material v., 139, 141.
   moral v., 154, 173f., 191, 194, 198ff., 278, 301.
      most universal v., 205.
   practical v., 96.
   rank of moral v., 200.
   rational v., 143.
   spiritual v., 139, 141.
   ultimate v., 277.
   vital v., 139, 141.
Value-form, 195. cf. 190.
Vanity, 141.
Vegetable soul, Vegetative (part of) soul, 91, 99, 139, 175. cf. 88.
Vice, 139, 287, 296, 301, 303, 316.
Vicious, 144, 308, 309.
Virtue, 29, 101, 137f., 141ff., 196f., 212, 213, 277, 296, 303, 316.
   Aristotle's, 195.
   essence, of ethical virtue, 374.
   ethical, 239, 272, 288, 296f., 308, 313.
   human v; v. of man, 137, 156.
   intellectual, 95.
   v. of intellect, 232ff.
   irrational, 138.
   moral, 216.
   natural, 222, 262, 281f.
   practical, 174.
   primitive, 262.
   principle of ethical virtue, 222.
   v. and prudence, 271f.
   rational, 137.
   v. of soul, 92.
   virtuous action, 190.
virtus aestimativa naturalis, 22 (natural instinct)
Voice, 112.
Volition, 142, 176, 277.
   blind v., 142.
   volitional attitude, 194.
Voluntarity, 3, 162ff., 166f., 259f.
   cf. Involuntarity, Not-voluntarity, ἑκουσία.
   causality of desire, 154.
   essence, 163f.
   intellectual moment, 167, 191.
   potentiality (conj. will), 173.
Vulgarity, 141.
Walking, 185.
Walter, Julius., 132, 133, 134, 156, 211, 214, 225, 241, 245ff., 248, 250, 252, 253, 264, 288, 290ff.
Want, 146.
War, 142, 181, 191.
Washing of clothes, 182.
Water, 105, 110.
Wax, 9.
Weakness, 303, 306, 309.
Wealth, riches, 182, 213, 266, 268, 278.
Weather, 224.
Wickedness, 296.
Will, προαίρεσις, 29, 117, 132, 134f., 170, 173ff.
   holy, 194.
   rational, 198.
Wine, 140, 302.
Wisdom σοφία 232ff., 234.
   Divine, 29.
   gift of god. 57.
   as to snake, 57.
   practical, 215, 257, 287. v. Prudence
Wise man, 200, 202, 213, 216, 265, 307 309, 316.
Wish, βούλησις 12, 132ff., 143, 159,

161, 175, 297.
Word, 74.
World,
   corporal, 24.
   spiritual, 73.
   teleological, 183, 286.
   World of generation, 217.
   World-spirit, 28, cf. Cosmic Reason
the Worst, 316.

Worth in general of life, 212.
Young man, 213, 235.
You can do because you ought to do, 315.
Zabarella, 54.
Zarathustra, 73.
Zeller, 30, 54, 77, 156, 210, 233.
ζῷον λόγον ἔχων a rational animal, 72.
Zweck, 250f.

INDEX OF REFERENCES*

Ando, T.,
   Aristoteles no Sonzairon (Aristotle's Ontology), Tokyo, 1958.
      6, 96, 119, 157.
Arnim, H. v.,
   Das Ethische im Aristotelischen Topik. Vienna, 1927.
      12.
Baeumker, C.,
   Das Problem der Materie in der griechischen Philosophie. Münster, 1890.
      9, 78, 117.
Bergson, H.,
   L'évolution créatrice. Paris, 1926.
      80, 109, 199.
   Matière et mémoire. Paris, 1929.
      115, 118, 119.
Biehl, G.,
   Aristoteles, De Anima. Leipzig, 1884.
      48.
Bonitz, H.,
   Index Aristotelicus. Berlin, 1870.
      210.
Brandis, C.,
   Die Entwicklung der griechischen Philosophie und ihrer Nachwirkungen in römischen Reiche. Berlin, 1862.
      28.
   Handbuch der Geschichte der griechisch-römischen Philosophie. Berlin, 1857.
      12, 28, 240, 290.
Brentano, F,.
   Aristoteles Lehre vom Ursprung des menschlichen Geistes. Leipzig, 1911.
      9. 39, 55, 64, 67, 70, 71, 72, 84.
   Die Psychologie des Aristotels insbesondere seine Lehre vom Nous Poietikos. Mayens, 1867.
      10, 13, 20, 22, 24, 27, 28, 31, 32, 35, 36, 37, 41, 45, 50, 52, 54, 66, 70, 71, 89, 91, 100, 106, 108, 184.

* This index is confined to the references in foot notes; as regards references in the text, see general index. The numbers indicate the pages of this book, not of the books referred to.

Burnet, J.,
Greek Philosophy: Thales to Plato. London, 1914.
217.
Bywater, J.,
Aristotelis Ethica Nicomachea, Oxford, 1890.
252.
Cornford, F.M.,
Plato's Cosmology. London, 1937.
76.
Corte, M. de.,
La doctrine de l'intelligence chez Aristote. Paris., 1934.
41, 42, 66.
Coulange, F. de.
La cité antique. Paris, 1890.
81.
Dilthey, W.,
Beiträge zur Lösung der Frage vom Ursprung unseres Glaubens an der Realität der Aussenwelt. (Gesamm. Schr. V)
117.
Grant, A.,
The Ethics of Aristotle. 4 ed. London, 1885.
256.
Grote, G.,
Plato and the other Companions of Socrates. 2 ed. London, 1885.
81, 82.
Häcker, F.,
Das Eintheilungs-und Anordnungsprinzip der moralischen Tugendlehre in der nikomachischen Ethik. Berlin, 1863.
142.
Hartenstein, G.,
Historisch-philosophische Abhandlungen. Leipzig, 1879.
222, 294.
Über den wissenschaftlichen Wert der aristotelischen Ethik. Berlin. Abh. d. Kgl. Sachs. Ges. d. Wiss. Leipzig. 1859.
241. 248.
Hartmann, N.,
Ethik. Berlin, 1935.
142, 192, 194, 198, 199, 201, 322.,
Hicks, R. D.,
Aristotle, De Anima. Cambridge, 1907.
36, 40, 43, 54, 113, 125, 160.
Hildenbrandt, K.,
Geschichte und System der Recht und Staatsphilosophie. Leipzing 1860.
167.
Huzii, Y.,
Aristoteles Kenkyu. (A Study of Aristotle), Tokyo, 1940.
93.
Ide, T.,
Aristoteles no Rekonron to Nodo Rise. (Aristotle's Theory of the Soul and the Active Reason)—Tetugakuzassi, No. 622.
65, 66.

Jaeger, W.,
Aristoteles, Grundlegung einer Geschichte seiner Entwicklung. Berlin, 1923.
5, 17, 93, 101, 237.
Studien zur Entstehungsgeschichte des Aristotelischen Metaphysik. Berlin, 1912.
63.
Joivet, R.,
Essai sur les rapport entre la pensée grecque et la pensée chrétienne. Paris, 1931.
77.
Kampe, F.,
Erkenntnistheorie des Aristotels. Leipzig, 1870.
43, 56.
Kant, I.,
Grundlegung zur Metaphysik der Sitten. (Werke, Hrsg. v. E. Cassirer. IV)
191, 192, 195.
Religion innerhalb der Gnenzen der blossen Vernunft. (WW. VI)
191.
Metaphysik der Sitten. (WW. VII)
191.
Kritik der reinen Vernunft. (WW. III)
123. 124.
Kritik der praktischen Vernunft. (WW.IV)
150, 151, 152, 191, 192, 193, 194, 285, 317, 318, 322.
Kritik der Urteilskraft. (WW. V)
151, 191.
Kastil,
Zur Lehre von der Willensfreiheit in der nikomachischen Ethik. Prag, 1901.
167.
Loening, R.,
Die Zurechnungslehre des Aristoteles. Jena, 1903.
158 167, 181. 248, 298, 308.
Michelet, C.,
Aristoteles, Ethica Nicomachea. Berlin, 1829-48.
252.
Miki, K.,
Gizyutu no Tetugaku. (Philosophy of Art), Tokyo.
186.
Newmann, W. L.,
The Politics of Aristotle. Oxford, 1887-1902.
222.
Nisitani, K.,
Aristoteles Ronko (A Study of Aristotle), Tokyo, 1948.
124, 131.
Aristoteles no Kosoron (Aristotle's Theory of Imagination) — Tetugakukenkyu, 1935.
130.
Nuyens, F.,
L'évolution de la psychologie d'Aristote. Louvain, 1948.
5, 9, 10, 11, 38, 41, 42, 77, 82, 94, 103, 177.
Ontwickelings momenten in de zielkunde van Aristoteles, 1939.
18.